INSTRUCTOR'S RESOURCE MANUAL WITH CHAPTER TESTS

RICHARD N. AUFMANN

VERNON C. BARKER

JOANNE S. LOCKWOOD

MARIA H. ANDERSEN

BASIC COLLEGE MATHEMATICS: AN APPLIED APPROACH

SEVENTH EDITION

Richard N. Aufmann
Palomar College

Vernon C. Barker
Palomar College

Joanne S. Lockwood
Plymouth State College

HOUGHTON MIFFLIN COMPANY   BOSTON NEW YORK

Senior Sponsoring Editor: Lynn Cox
Senior Development Editor: Dawn Nuttall
Editorial Assistant: Melissa Parkin
Senior Manufacturing Coordinator: Florence Cadran
Marketing Manager: Ben Rivera

Printed in the U.S.A

ISBN: 0-618-20288-9

1 2 3 4 5 6 7 8 9 – POO – 06 05 04 03 02

A LABORATORY GUIDE TO THE NATURAL WORLD

Dennis J. Richardson and Kristen E. Richardson

Prentice Hall

Upper Saddle River, NJ 07458

Editor-in-Chief: Sheri Snavely
Project Manager: Karen Horton
Executive Managing Editor: Kathleen Schiaparelli
Assistant Managing Editor: Dinah Thong
Production Editors: Megan L. Williams and Debra A. Wechsler
Supplement Cover Management/ Design: Paul Gourhan
Manufacturing Buyer: Ilene Kahn
Electronic Composition and Formatting: Clara Bartunek
Artworks:
   Productions Manager: Ronda Whitson
   Manager, Prodution Technologies: Matt Haas
   Project Coordinator: Jessica Einsig
   Illustrators: Jacqueline Ambrosius, Kathryn Anderson, Brandon Gilbert, Mark Landis
   Art Quality Assurance: Timothy Nguyen, Stacy Smith, Pamela Taylor
   Cover Photo Credit: Gary Irving/Getty Images, Inc./PhotoDisc, Inc.

© 2003 by Pearson Education, Inc.
Pearson Education, Inc.
Upper Saddle River, NJ 07458

The author and publisher of this book have used their best efforts in preparing this book. These efforts include the development, research, and testing of the theories and programs to determine their effectiveness. The author and publisher make no warranty of any kind, expressed or implied, with regard to these programs or the documentation contained in this book. The author and publisher shall not be liable in any event for incidental or consequential damages in connection with, or arising out of, the furnishing, performance, or use of these programs.

Printed in the United States of America

10 9 8 7 6 5 4 3 2 1

ISBN 0-13-092242-0

Pearson Education Ltd., *London*
Pearson Education Australia Pty. Ltd., *Sydney*
Pearson Education Singapore, Pte. Ltd.
Pearson Education North Asia Ltd., *Hong Kong*
Pearson Education Canada, Inc., *Toronto*
Pearson Educación de Mexico, S.A. de C.V.
Pearson Education—Japan, *Tokyo*
Pearson Education Malaysia, Pte. Ltd.
Pearson Education, *Upper Saddle River, New Jersey*

PREFACE

The Instructor's Resource Manual for Aufmann/Barker/Lockwood's Basic College Mathematics: An Applied Approach contains suggested Course Sequences, Chapter Tests, Answers to the Chapter Tests, AIM For Success Slide Show printouts, and Transparency Masters.

The Chapter Tests contain four multiple-choice and four free-response tests per chapter as well as assorted cumulative tests. These ready-to-use tests may be photocopied and are designed to take one hour. Answers are provided in a separate section.

A PowerPoint® Slide Show, which presents a lesson plan for the AIM for Success student preface in the text, is available on the instructor's Class Prep CD as well as the text website. Full printouts of the ten slides (which may be used as transparency masters) as well as a smaller printout of each slide with its accompanying instructor notes are provided in this resource manual.

Blackline transparency masters of many of the tables and graphs in the text are provided at the end of this manual. Each master contains figures that are identified by a T icon in the Instructor's Annotated Edition. You may photocopy any of these masters onto clear transparencies to be used on an overhead projector. This will significantly ease class discussions of the data presented in the tables and graphs. It will also make it easier to manipulate the data.

Contents

COURSE SEQUENCES

Basic Course Sequence

Week	Suggested Assignment
1	Sections 1.1, 1.2, 1.3, and 1.4
2	Sections 1.5, 1.6, and 1.7
3	Test, Chapter 1 Sections 2.1, 2.2, and 2.3
4	Sections 2.4, 2.5, and 2.6
5	Sections 2.7 and 2.8 Test, Chapter 2
6	Sections 3.1, 3.2, 3.3, and 3.4
7	Sections 3.5 and 3.6 Test, Chapter 3
8	Sections 4.1, 4.2, and 4.3
9	Test, Chapter 4 Sections 5.1, 5.2, 5.3, and 5.4
10	Test, Chapter 5 Sections 6.1 and 6.2
11	Sections 6.3, 6.4, 6.5, and 6.6
12	Section 6.7 Test, Chapter 6 Sections 7.1 and 7.2
13	Sections 7.3 and 7.4 Test, Chapter 7
14	Sections 8.1, 8.2, and 8.3 Test, Chapter 8
15	Sections 9.1, 9.2, and 9.3 Test, Chapter 9
16	Sections 10.1, 10.2, 10.3, and 10.4 Test, Chapter 10

Average Course Sequence

Week	Suggested Assignment
1	Sections 1.1, 1.2, 1.3, 1.4, and 1.5
2	Sections 1.6 and 1.7 Sections 2.1 and 2.2
3	Sections 2.3, 2.4, 2.5, and 2.6
4	Sections 2.7 and 2.8 Test, Chapters 1–2
5	Sections 3.1, 3.2, 3.3, and 3.4
6	Sections 3.5 and 3.6 Sections 4.1 and 4.2
7	Section 4.3 Test, Chapters 3–4 Sections 5.1 and 5.2
8	Sections 5.3 and 5.4 Sections 6.1 and 6.2
9	Sections 6.3, 6.4, 6.5, and 6.6 Test, Chapters 5–6
10	Sections 7.1, 7.2, 7.3, and 7.4
11	Sections 8.1, 8.2, and 8.3 Test, Chapters 7–8
12	Sections 9.1, 9.2, 9.3, and 9.4
13	Sections 10.1, 10.2, and 10.3
14	Sections 10.4 and 10.5 Test, Chapters 9–10 Section 11.1
15	Sections 11.2, 11.3, and 11.4
16	Sections 11.5 and 11.6 Test, Chapter 11

Comprehensive Course Sequence

Week	Suggested Assignment
1	Sections 1.1, 1.2, 1.3, 1.4, and 1.5
2	Sections 1.6 and 1.7 Sections 2.1, 2.2, and 2.3
3	Sections 2.4, 2.5, 2.6, 2.7, and 2.8
4	Test, Chapters 1–2 Sections 3.1, 3.2, 3.3, and 3.4
5	Sections 3.5 and 3.6 Sections 4.1, 4.2, and 4.3
6	Test, Chapters 3–4 Sections 5.1, 5.2, 5.3, and 5.4
7	Sections 6.1, 6.2, 6.3, and 6.4
8	Section 6.5 Test, Chapters 5-6 Sections 7.1, 7.2, and 7.3
9	Sections 7.4 and 7.5 Sections 8.1 and 8.2
10	Section 8.3 Test, Chapters 7–8 Sections 9.1, 9.2, and 9.3
11	Section 9.4 Sections 10.1, 10.2, and 10.3
12	Sections 10.4 and 10.5 Test, Chapters 9–10 Section 11.1
13	Sections 11.2, 11.3, and 11.4
14	Sections 11.5 and 11.6 Section 12.1
15	Sections 12.2, 12.3, and 12.4
16	Sections 12.5 and 12.6 Test, Chapters 11–12

CHAPTER TESTS

Form A Tests

Free Response

Chapter 1 Test Form A

Name: _____

Date: _____

1. Place the correct symbol, < or >, between the two numbers:

   72   27

2. Write 57,003 in words.

3. Write four million seven thousand eighty-five in standard form.

4. Write 307,420 in expanded form.

5. Round 47,928 to the nearest ten.

6. Add: 63,091
        + 21,904

7. Find the sum of 2047, 9351, and 886.

8. Susan had $429 in her checking account before making deposits of $104, $79, and $247. Find the amount in the checking account after making the deposits.

9. Subtract: 1289
            − 146

10. Find the difference between 46,492 and 27,504.

11. Pedro's total wages are $823. Deductions of $119 for taxes, $21 for insurance, and $45 for savings are taken from his pay. Find Pedro's take-home pay.

12. Find the product of 26,431 and 8.

13. Multiply: $\begin{array}{r} 2076 \\ \times\, 608 \\ \hline \end{array}$

14. A computer programmer has a car payment of $323 each month. What is the total amount paid over a 36-month period?

15. Divide: $8\overline{)4824}$

16. Divide: $7\overline{)12,347}$

17. Divide: $67\overline{)10,293}$

18. A Ford Escort is driven 319 miles on 11 gallons of gas. How many miles did this car travel on 1 gallon of gas?

19. Write $3 \cdot 3 \cdot 5 \cdot 5 \cdot 5$ in exponential notation.

20. Simplify: $2^4 \cdot 3^3$

21. Simplify: $3 \cdot 4 \cdot (6-1) - 20$

22. Simplify: $3^2 + 2(5-1) - 6$

23. Find all the factors of 55.

24. Find the prime factorization of 48.

25. Find the prime factorization of 110.

1. Find the LCM of 8 and 20.

2. Find the GCF of 15 and 35.

3. Express the shaded portion of the circles as an improper fraction.

4. Write $\dfrac{10}{3}$ as a mixed number.

5. Write $4\dfrac{7}{12}$ as an improper fraction.

6. What number must be placed in the numerator so that the following fractions are equivalent?

$$\dfrac{7}{8} = \dfrac{}{24}$$

7. Write $\dfrac{12}{80}$ in simplest form.

8. Add: $\dfrac{5}{8} + \dfrac{7}{8}$

9. Add: $\dfrac{7}{12}$
   $+\dfrac{5}{16}$

10. Add: $2\dfrac{1}{4}$
    $+5\dfrac{2}{5}$

11. A carpenter built a header by nailing a $1\dfrac{7}{8}$-inch board to a $4\dfrac{1}{2}$-inch beam. Find the total thickness of the header.

12. Subtract: $\dfrac{9}{10} - \dfrac{3}{10}$

13. What is $\dfrac{9}{16}$ minus $\dfrac{5}{24}$?

14. Subtract: $5\dfrac{3}{8}$
    $-2\dfrac{11}{12}$

15. A mechanic cuts lengths of $5\frac{1}{4}$ inches and $3\frac{2}{3}$ inches of radiator hose from a roll containing 36 inches. Find the amount of radiator hose remaining on the roll.

16. Multiply: $\frac{3}{14} \times \frac{7}{12}$

17. What is $3\frac{3}{7}$ multiplied by $2\frac{5}{8}$?

18. A plumber earns $154 for each day worked. What are the plumber's earnings for working $3\frac{1}{2}$ days?

19. Divide: $\frac{7}{9} \div \frac{14}{27}$

20. Find the quotient of $3\frac{5}{12}$ and $2\frac{1}{4}$.

21. A package contains 18 ounces of granola. How many $1\frac{1}{2}$-ounce portions can be served from this package?

22. Place the correct symbol, < or >, between the two numbers: $\frac{3}{4}$ $\frac{13}{14}$

23. Simplify: $\left(\frac{5}{7}\right)^5 \left(\frac{49}{25}\right)^2$

24. Simplify: $\left(\frac{2}{3}\right)^2 \div \left(\frac{1}{2} + \frac{2}{3}\right)$

25. Simplify: $\frac{1}{6} + \left(\frac{1}{3} - \frac{3}{10}\right) \div \frac{7}{15}$

Chapter 3 Test Form A

Name: _____
Date: _____

1. Write 42,085 in words.

2. Write in standard form: four hundred nine and sixteen thousandths.

3. Round 15.15043 to the nearest thousandth.

4. Round 24.1796 to the nearest hundredth.

5. What is the total of 67.5012, 89.06, and 153.567?

6. Add:
$$6.327$$
$$18.1$$
$$206.51$$
$$+\,4319.99$$

7. A broker received a salary of $638.50, a commission of $845.29, and a bonus of $186.49. Find his total income.

8. Subtract:
$$0.78964$$
$$-\,0.039944$$

9. Find 3.9276 less than 18.04.

10. A machine lathe takes 0.036 inch from a bushing that is 1.421 inches thick. Find the resulting thickness of the bushing.

11. Multiply:
$$9.075$$
$$\times\ \ 2.9$$

12. Find the product of 1.29 and 45.6.

13. A motorist uses 32.5 gallons of gasoline on a short trip. How much does the gasoline for the trip cost at 124.9 cents per gallon? Round your answer to the nearest cent.

14. Divide: $0.26\overline{)1.534}$

15. Divide. Round to the nearest tenth.

$$0.081\overline{)523.21}$$

16. A Ford Ranger with a sticker price of $14,824.84 can be bought for a down payment of $2965 and 48 equal monthly payments. Find the amount of each monthly payment.

17. Convert 7.24 to a fraction.

18. Convert $\dfrac{9}{11}$ to a decimal. Round to the nearest thousandth.

19. Place the correct symbol, < or >, between the two numbers: 3.02 3.2

20. Place the correct symbol, < or >, between the two numbers: 0.78 $\dfrac{7}{9}$

Chapters 1-3 Cumulative Test A

Name: _____
Date: _____

1. Divide. Express your answer in remainder form.

$$18\overline{)5574}$$

2. Simplify: $3^4 \cdot 5^2$

3. Simplify: $16 - 8 \div (9 - 7)$

4. Find the LCM of 20 and 24.

5. Write $\dfrac{27}{13}$ as a mixed number.

6. Write $4\dfrac{7}{9}$ as an improper fraction.

7. Find the numerator for an equivalent fraction with the given denominator: $\dfrac{5}{12} = \dfrac{}{48}$

8. Add: $\dfrac{2}{5} + \dfrac{5}{9} + \dfrac{4}{15}$

9. What is $2\dfrac{5}{7}$ increased by $4\dfrac{3}{5}$?

10. Subtract: $5\dfrac{1}{3} - 2\dfrac{4}{5}$

11. Multiply: $\dfrac{11}{12} \times \dfrac{30}{37}$

12. Find the product of $2\dfrac{3}{5}$ and $6\dfrac{1}{2}$.

13. Divide: $\dfrac{8}{9} \div \dfrac{4}{27}$

14. What is $4\dfrac{1}{4}$ divided by $3\dfrac{1}{6}$?

15. Simplify: $\left(\dfrac{2}{3}\right)^3 \left(\dfrac{3}{8}\right)^2$

16. Simplify: $\left(\dfrac{3}{4}\right)^2 - \dfrac{1}{2} \cdot \left(\dfrac{3}{8} - \dfrac{1}{4}\right)$

17. Write 22.037 in words.

18. Add:

$$\begin{array}{r} 285.06 \\ 3.759 \\ + 1428.9 \\ \hline \end{array}$$

19. What is 1.862 less than 49.05 ?

20. Multiply: 7.029
                    × 3.04

21. Divide. Round to the nearest thousandth.

$$0.024\overline{)0.3614}$$

22. Convert $\dfrac{7}{24}$ to a decimal.
Round to the nearest thousandth.

23. Convert 0.74 to a fraction.

24. Place the correct symbol, < or >, between the two numbers: $\dfrac{4}{11}$ 0.364

25. A health spa instructor exercised $1\dfrac{1}{4}$ hours, $2\dfrac{1}{3}$ hours, 2 hours, $2\dfrac{1}{4}$ hours, and $1\dfrac{1}{2}$ hours last week. Find the total number of hours the instructor exercised last week.

26. A flight from Boston to San Francisco takes $5\dfrac{3}{4}$ hours. After the plane is in the air for $3\dfrac{1}{2}$ hours, how much time remains before it lands?

27. During a 650-mile trip, you drove $\dfrac{3}{5}$ of the distance on the first day. How many miles were left to travel?

28. On a shopping trip, Keri spent $42.99 for shoes, $120.75 for a coat, and $24.98 for a scarf. Find the total amount spent.

29. Gabriel bought a used car for $2500 down and payments of $209.98 per month for 24 months. Find the total cost of the car.

30. You bought small bolts for $0.13 each and paid $3.51 for them. How many bolts did you buy?

1. Write the comparison 7 minutes to 14 minutes as a ratio in simplest form using a fraction, a colon (:), and the word TO.

2. Write the comparison 15 cars to 20 cars as a ratio in simplest form using a fraction, a colon (:), and the word TO.

3. Write the comparison $39 to $13 as a ratio in simplest form using a fraction, a colon (:), and the word TO.

4. Write the comparison 24 minutes to 36 minutes as a ratio in simplest form using a fraction, a colon (:), and the word TO.

5. The college bookstore sold 2025 books on Monday and 2475 books on Tuesday. Find the ratio, as a fraction in simplest form, of the number of books sold on Monday to the number of books sold on Tuesday.

6. In 1 month, the Simpson family's income was $3640 and they spent $520 for food. Find the ratio, as a fraction in simplest form, of the amount spent for food to the total income.

7. Write "40 miles in 12 hours" as a rate in simplest form.

8. Write "$15 for 6 boards" as a rate in simplest form.

9. Write "$117.75 earned in 15 hours" as a unit rate.

10. Write "$2.52 for 4.2 pounds" as a unit rate.

11. A clerk earns $348.80 for working a 40-hour week. Find the clerk's hourly wage.

12. A Geo Prism traveled 180.6 miles in 3.5 hours. Find the car's speed in miles per hour.

13. Determine if the proportion is true or not true.
$$\frac{3}{7} = \frac{81}{189}$$

14. Determine if the proportion is true or not true.
$$\frac{4}{9} = \frac{52}{108}$$

15. Solve the proportion: $\dfrac{n}{20} = \dfrac{3}{8}$

16. Solve the proportion: $\dfrac{5}{12} = \dfrac{n}{80}$
Round to the nearest hundredth.

17. The sales tax on a $420 purchase is $24. Find the sales tax on a $490 purchase.

18. Pittsburgh Paints suggests using 1 gallon of paint for every 350 square feet of wall. At this rate, how many gallons of paint would be required for a room that has 1330 square feet of wall?

19. Defects were found in 12 out of 600 compact discs. At this rate, how many defects would be found in 1500 discs?

20. Life insurance costs $2.34 for every $1000 of insurance. What is the cost of $50,000 of insurance?

Chapter 5 Test Form A

Name: _____
Date: _____

1. Write $2\frac{3}{4}$ as a percent.

2. Write $45\frac{1}{3}\%$ as a fraction.

3. Write 5.9 as a percent.

4. Write 0.0087 as a percent.

5. Write $\frac{3}{16}$ as a percent.

6. Write 3.8% as a decimal.

7. What is 16% of 90?

8. 9.34% of 125 is what number?

9. Which is larger: 85% of 15 or 10% of 120?

10. Which is smaller: 1.2% of 60 or 0.3% of 90?

11. Sales tax is 5.5% of the cost of an item. What is the tax on a stereo system costing $896?

12. An office manager's hourly wage is $15.60 before a 7.5% raise. What is the new hourly wage?

13. What percent of 220 is 28?
    Round to the nearest hundredth.

14. 42 is what percent of 17?
    Round to the nearest hundredth.

15. A company pays a dividend of $3.78 per share on stock that is selling at $75.60 per share. What percent of the stock is the dividend?

16. The Republican candidate received 430,500 of the 750,000 ballots cast in an election. What percent of the vote did this candidate receive?

17. 20.8 is 32% of what number?

18. 19.8 is 22% of what number?

19. Steven missed 6 questions on an exam. This was 12% of the questions on the exam. How many questions were on the exam?

20. A person receives a salary of $2052 per month. This is 108% of last year's salary. Find last year's salary per month.

21. 15.96 is 38% of what number?

22. What percent of 90 is 18?

23. A Chevrolet dealership requires a 10.5% down payment on new cars. What down payment must be made on a car costing $22,500?

24. One month after graduation, 592 students out of a class of 640 had found jobs. What percent of the students were still unemployed?

25. A salesperson makes a commission of 3% of each sale. How much, in dollars, must the salesperson sell in order to make a commission of $225?

Name: _____
Date: _____

1. An 18-ounce jar of peanut butter costs $2.16. Find the unit cost.

2. Find the most economical purchase: 16 grams for $.64, 28 grams for $1.04, 30 grams for $1.05, or 42 grams for $1.52.

3. Lean ground beef costs $2.79 per pound. Find the total cost of 12 pounds. Round to the nearest cent.

4. A messenger was making $9.75 an hour before a 7% increase in pay. What was the messenger's new hourly wage? Round to the nearest cent.

5. The value of a $4500 investment increased to $4815 in 1 year. What percent increase does this represent?

6. A department store uses a markup rate of 30% on all office supplies. What is the selling price of a ream of paper that cost the store $2.90?

7. An appliance store uses a markup rate of 35%. What is the markup on a refrigerator that cost the store $550?

8. The price of gasoline dropped from $1.42 per gallon to $0.97 per gallon over a 6-month period. What was the percent decrease in price? Round to the nearest percent.

9. A video store's income in March was $69,700. In April the income decreased by 11%. What was the income for April?

10. A la-Z-Boy that regularly sells for $449 is on sale for 35% off the regular price. What is the sale price?

11. A formal dress that usually sells for $109 is on sale for 20% off the regular price. What is the discount?

12. A home is purchased with a mortgage of $92,900. The buyer pays a loan origination fee of 2 percent of the loan (points). How much is the loan origination fee?

13. An employee invests $6000 in a corporate retirement account that pays 9% annual interest compounded monthly. Find the value of the investment after 10 years. Use the Compound Interest Table. Round to the nearest cent.

14. A motor home is purchased, and a $32,000 loan is obtained for 4 years at a simple interest rate of 11%. Find the simple interest due on the loan.

15. A home has a mortgage of $64,000 for 30 years at an annual interest rate of 11%. Find the monthly mortgage payment. Use the Monthly Payment Table. Round to the nearest cent.

16. A pharmacist purchases a diamond ring for $16,500 and pays sales tax that is 4.5% of the purchase price. How much is the sales tax?

17. A used Ford Bronco was purchased for $7800 with a down payment of $1500. The balance is financed for 3 years at an annual interest rate of 13%. Find the monthly car payment. Use the Monthly Payment Table. Round to the nearest cent.

Chapter 6 Test Form A (*continued*)

18. A plumber's hourly wage is $22.60. The plumber earns time and a half for working on Saturday. How much does the plumber earn for working 6 hours on Saturday?

19. Marissa had a checking account balance of $154.69. She deposited checks of $413.62 and $119.15 and wrote checks of $287.29 and $89.13. Find her new checking account balance.

20. Balance the checkbook shown.

		RECORD ALL CHARGES OR CREDITS THAT AFFECT YOUR ACCOUNT								
NUMBER	DATE	DESCRIPTION OF TRANSACTION	PAYMENT/DEBIT (-)		√ T	FEE (IF ANY) (-)	DEPOSIT/CREDIT (+)		BALANCE 374	43
	1/2	House Payment	252	79					121	64
	1/7	Magazines	17	42					104	22
	1/9	Deposit					152	68	256	90
	1/10	Deposit					312	42	569	32
	1/12	Credit Card	116	90					452	42
	1/15	Cash	20	00					432	42
	1/12	Groceries	83	50					348	92
	1/15	Stationery	12	96					335	96
		REMEMBER TO RECORD AUTOMATIC PAYMENTS/DEPOSITS ON DATE AUTHORIZED								

CHECKING ACCOUNT Monthly Statement		Account Number : 924-297-8	
DATE	Transaction	Amount	Balance
1/2	OPENING BALANCE		374.43
1/5	CHECK	252.79	121.64
1/9	CHECK	17.42	104.22
1/11	DEPOSIT	312.42	416.64
1/15	CHECK	116.90	299.74
1/16	INTEREST	3.69	303.43
1/20	CHECK	83.50	219.93
1/31	SERVICE CHARGE	10.50	209.43
1/31	CLOSING BALANCE		209.43

Do the bank statement and the checkbook balance?

Chapters 4-6 Cumulative Test A

Name: _____

Date: _____

1. Write the comparison 56 miles to 14 miles as a ratio in simplest form using a fraction, a colon (:), and the word TO.

2. The original value for a Honda Civic was $12,600. One year later, the car had a value of $9450. What is the ratio of the decrease in value to the original value?

3. Write "2639 words on 13 pages" as a unit rate.

4. Mark can type 360 words in 5 minutes. What is his typing speed per minute?

5. Solve the proportion: $\dfrac{21}{50} = \dfrac{n}{20}$

6. A sales manager estimated that 3 out of 5 employees would attend a company-sponsored seminar. At this rate, how many employees would attend the seminar if the company employs 455 people?

7. Write 9% as a decimal.

8. Write 62% as a fraction.

9. Write 0.042 as a percent.

10. Write $\dfrac{11}{25}$ as a percent.

11. 28% of 86 is what number?

12. Your department has a budget of $6500 and allots 12% of the budget for office supplies. What amount is allotted for office supplies?

13. What percent of 48 is 60?

14. In a new housing development, 63 of the 72 homes have already been sold. What percent of homes in the development have been sold?

15. 12 is 8% of what number?

16. At a major intersection, 17 car accidents occurred last year. This was 25% of the accidents that occurred in the entire city during the year. How many accidents were there in the city that year?

17. Red potatoes cost $2.45 for a 5-pound bag. Find the cost per pound.

18. APM AUTO SUPPLY CO. uses a markup rate of 32%. What is the markup on a replacement headlight that cost the company $4?

19. J & M Sports Company is selling tents for 15% off the regular price. What is the discount on a tent that has a regular selling price of $120?

20. Bell Electronic borrows $12,500 for 8 months at an annual rate of 12%. What is the simple interest due on the loan?

The pictograph shows sales at a bookstore over a 4-month period. Each book represents 100 books sold.

1. How many books were sold during April?

2. Find the ratio of the number of books sold in April to the number of books sold in June.

3. What percent of the total sales over the 4 months is the number of sales in June? Round to the nearest tenth of a percent.

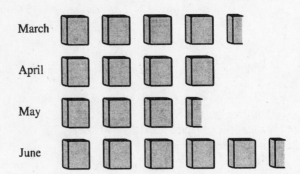

The circle graph shows the annual expenses of owning and operating a car.

4. Find the ratio of the annual fuel cost to the total annual car payments.

5. Find the ratio of the cost of maintenance to the total annual car payments.

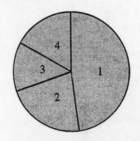

ANNUAL CAR EXPENSES
1: $2160 - Car Payments
2: $ 960 - Fuel
3: $ 600 - Insurance
4: $ 750 - Maintenance

The double-bar graph shows the number of books (in hundreds) sold in the book department of a store during the first 4 months of 2000 and 2001.

6. What is the difference between the February sales for 2000 and 2001?

7. How many books were sold in January of 2001?

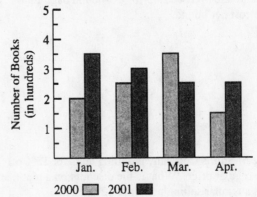

8. The passengers on a train were asked to rate the food. The responses were: 54, excellent; 67, very good; 78, good; 92, poor. What was the modal response?

9. The selling prices of eight homes listed by a real estate agent are: $156,000, $175,000; $172,000; $189,000; $158,000, $184,000, $210,000; and $182,000. Find the median price of these six homes.

The double-line graph shows the quarterly income (in millions of dollars) for a company during 2000 and 2001.

10. Find the difference between the company's fourth quarter incomes for 2000 and 2001.

11. During which quarters did 2000 sales exceed 2001 sales?

12. How much greater than the fourth quarter 2001 sales were the third quarter 2000 sales?

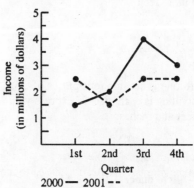
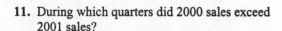

The histogram shows the fuel usage of 125 cars.

13. Find the ratio of the number of cars that had a fuel usage of 15–18 mpg to the number of cars with a fuel usage of 24–27 mpg.

14. How many cars had a fuel usage of less than 21 mpg?

15. What percent of the cars had a fuel usage of more than 24 mpg?

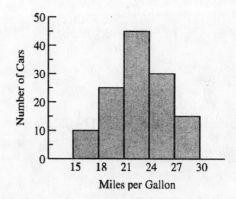

The frequency polygon shows the monthly salaries of a computer company's 29 employees.

16. Find the ratio of the number of employees whose salary is between $25,000 and $45,000 to the total number of employees.

17. How many employees have salaries of less than $25,000?

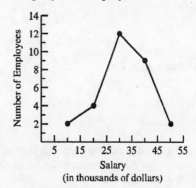

18. A coin is tossed three times. What is the probability that the outcomes of the tosses are exactly in the order HTH?

19. The average time, in minutes, it takes for a factory worker to assemble 14 different toys is given in the table. Determine the first quartile of the data.

10.5	21.0	17.3	11.2	9.3	6.5	8.6
9.8	20.3	19.6	9.8	10.5	11.9	18.5

20. The box-and-whiskers plot represents data taken from the SAT scores of high school seniors. Determine the third quartile for these scores.

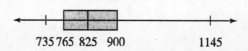

Name: _____
Date: _____

1. Convert 46 in. to feet.

2. Subtract: 12 ft 5 in. – 7 ft 9 in.

3. A board 7 ft long is cut into four pieces of equal length. How long is each piece? Express your answer in feet and inches.

4. Convert: 9000 lb = _____ tons _____ lb

5. Convert $3\frac{1}{4}$ lb to ounces.

6. Twenty-three yards of fabric were used for making a slipcover for a couch. How many feet of fabric were used?

7. Find the sum of 5 lb 8 oz and 9 lb 6 oz.

8. Divide: $(5\text{ lb }8\text{ oz})\div 2$

9. A case of canned peas weighs $11\frac{1}{4}$ lb. Find the weight of a stack of 12 cases.

10. A package weighing 3 lb 9 oz is mailed at the rate of $.16 per ounce. What is the cost of postage?

11. Convert 36 fl oz to cups.

12. Convert 1 pint to cups.

13. Add: 3 gal 2 qt + 4 gal 3 qt

14. Multiply:
$$\begin{array}{r} 2\text{ gal }3\text{ qt} \\ \times\ \ \ \ \ \ \ 3 \\ \hline \end{array}$$

15. If one serving of fruit punch contains 12 fl oz of pineapple juice, how many servings can be made from 3 qt pineapple juice?

16. Small cans of tomato paste contain 6 oz. How many quarts of tomato paste are in a case of 48 cans?

17. Find the power in foot-pounds per second needed to raise 200 lb a distance of 60 ft in 20 s.

18. Three tons are lifted 22 ft. Find the energy required in foot-pounds.

19. Convert $1925\dfrac{\text{ft}\cdot\text{lb}}{\text{s}}$ to horsepower.
$$\left(1\text{ hp}=550\dfrac{\text{ft}\cdot\text{lb}}{\text{s}}\right)$$

20. How much energy is required to lift a 5000-lb elevator a distance of 60 ft?

Chapter 9 Test Form A

Name: _____

Date: _____

1. Convert 0.73 m to centimeters.

2. Convert 3427 cm to meters.

3. Convert 8.4 km to centimeters.

4. Convert 26 cm 4 mm to centimeters.

5. Two pieces of ribbon are cut from a spool containing 3 m of ribbon. The two pieces are 112 cm and 62 cm. How much ribbon (in meters) remains on the roll?

6. A carpenter is installing four shelves, each 324 cm long. Find the total length of material (in meters) needed to build the shelves.

7. Convert 0.47 kg to grams.

8. Convert 0.8 g to centigrams.

9. Convert 390 g to kilograms.

10. Convert 2 g 372 mg to milligrams.

11. Find the cost of a piece of cheddar cheese weighing 1200 g if the price per kilogram is $5.24. Round to the nearest cent.

12. A baby weighs 4100 g at birth and 1 month later weighs 5080 g. Find the baby's weight gain (in kilograms).

13. Convert 62 ml to liters.

14. Convert 9.51 L to milliliters.

15. Convert 280 cm^3 to milliliters.

16. Convert 6 kl 48 L to kiloliters.

17. One hundred sixty students are enrolled in a chemistry laboratory at Western County Community College. During one experiment each student is required to use 60 ml of an acid. How many liters of the acid are required for the experiment?

18. Swimming requires 450 calories per hour. How many calories do you lose by swimming $\frac{3}{4}$ h per day for 15 days?

19. For football tryouts, Scott had to run the 50-yard dash. How many meters did he run? Round to the nearest tenth. (0.91 m = 1 yd)

20. Convert a 1000-meter run to feet. (1 m = 3.28 ft)

The circle graph shows the annual expenses for a student at a university.

1. Find the ratio of the annual tuition to the student's total expenses.

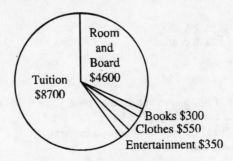

2. What percent of the student's total budget is spent on entertainment? Round to the nearest percent.

Tuition $8700

Room and Board $4600

Books $300
Clothes $550
Entertainment $350

Annual Student Expenses

The double-bar graph shows the number, in hundreds, of video recorders sold during the first 3 months of 2000 and 2001.

3. Find the difference between the 2000 and 2001 sales for February.

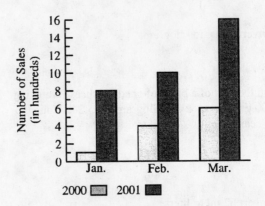

4. Find the ratio of February 2001 sales to March 2001 sales.

2000 ☐ 2001 ■

5. On five biology exams, Theresa's scores were 76, 92, 84, 88, and 95. Find the mean score of Theresa's exams.

6. A city's high temperature readings over 7 days were 67°, 75°, 68°, 69°, 72°, 70°, and 66°. Find the median high temperature over the 7 days.

7. Convert 90 in. to yards.

8. Subtract: 10 yd 1 ft
            − 2 yd 2 ft

9. Convert $5\frac{1}{2}$ lb to ounces.

10. Find the product of $6\frac{1}{2}$ oz and 8.

11. Convert 7 gal to pints.

12. A recipe calls for 12 oz of tomato sauce. How many cups of tomato sauce will be needed if the recipe is doubled?

13. Enrique carried three boxes weighing 7 lb 3 oz, 8 lb 14 oz, and 10 lb 5 oz into his new apartment. What was the total weight of the three boxes?

14. Convert 67 cm to kilometers.

15. Convert 71 mg to grams.

16. Convert 9 L 269 ml to liters.

17. Find the number of quarts in 8 liters. (1 L = 1.06 qt)

18. Express 176 km/h in miles per hour. Round to the nearest tenth. (1 mi = 1.61 km)

19. Three pieces of wire are cut from a 60-meter roll. The lengths of the pieces are 1230 cm, 795 cm, and 455 cm. How many meters of wire are left on the roll?

20. A wheelbarrow contains 30 bricks, each weighing 890 g. What is the total weight, in kilograms, of the bricks?

Chapter 10 Test Form A

Name: _____
Date: _____

1. Place the correct symbol, < or >, between the two numbers:
$$-2.3 \qquad -3.2$$

2. Place the correct symbol, < or >, between the two numbers:
$$1 \qquad -6.5$$

3. Evaluate $-|-36|$.

4. Find the sum of -12 and 7.

5. Add: $-20 + 43 + (-12) + (-4)$

6. Subtract: $-3 - (-7)$

7. Subtract: $16 - (-1)$

8. Find the product of -6 and 11.

9. Divide: $-24 \div 6$

10. Find the temperature after a rise of 20°C from −4°C.

11. The daily low temperature readings for a 3-day period in Minneapolis were as follows: $-10°$, $-2°$, and $9°$. Find the average low temperature for the 3-day period.

12. Add: $\dfrac{1}{4} + \left(-\dfrac{1}{2}\right)$

13. Find the sum of $-\dfrac{1}{6}$, $\dfrac{2}{3}$, and $-\dfrac{1}{2}$.

14. Subtract: $-\dfrac{2}{7} - \dfrac{2}{3}$

15. Subtract: $\dfrac{3}{4} - \left(-\dfrac{2}{3}\right)$

16. Multiply: $\dfrac{2}{7} \times \left(-\dfrac{1}{4}\right)$

17. Find the quotient of -8 and $-\dfrac{4}{5}$.

18. What is -1.003 decreased by 2.1?

19. Subtract: $-31.9 - 12.2$

20. Find the product of 0.012 and -1.6.

21. Divide: $8 \div (-0.4)$

22. Simplify: $12 - (-3)^2 \div (7 - 4)$

23. Simplify: $12 - 9 \div 3 + 3$

24. Write $1,020,000$ in scientific notation.

25. The boiling point of fluorine is $-188.14°C$. The melting point of fluorine is $-219.62°C$. Find the difference between the boiling point and the melting point of fluorine.

Chapter 11 Test Form A

Name: _____
Date: _____

1. Evaluate $a - (a^2 - b) + c$ when $a = -2$, $b = 3$, and $c = 1$.

2. Evaluate $b^2 - 4ac$ when $a = 3$, $b = -1$, and $c = 4$.

3. Simplify: $5x - 6y - 2x - y$

4. Simplify: $2x - 4(3 - 2x)$

5. Is 1 a solution of $x^2 - 7x - 8 = 0$?

6. Solve: $y + 9 = -8$

7. Solve: $-4x = 36$

8. Solve: $-\dfrac{3}{4}b = 9$

9. Solve: $2x - 4 = -14$

10. Solve: $\dfrac{2}{3}x - 8 = -12$

11. A clothing store's regular price for a suit is $225. During a storewide sale, the suits were priced at $160. Use the formula $S = R - D$, where S is the sale price, R is the regular price, and D is the discount, to find the discount.

12. Find the cost per unit during a week when the total cost was $68,000, the number of units produced was 500, and the fixed costs were $8000. Use the formula $T = U \cdot N + F$, where T is the total cost, U is the cost per unit, N is the number of units made, and F is the fixed costs.

13. Solve: $10 = 2 - 6y$

14. Solve: $2x - 5 = 4 - 3x$

15. Solve: $5 - 4(x - 2) = 3$

16. Translate "the sum of five times the square of y and the square of x" into a mathematical expression.

17. Translate "the sum of twice a number and 5" into a mathematical expression.

18. Translate "the quotient of a number and seven is two" into an equation and solve.

19. The sum of three-fourths of a number and two is eight. Find the number.

20. A grocery store is selling hamburger for $1.89 per pound. This is $.28 less than the price at a competitor's store. Find the price at the competitor's store.

Name: _____

Date: _____

1. Find the complement of a 63° angle.

2. Two angles of a triangle are 82° and 19°. Find the measure of the third angle of the triangle.

3. In the figure, $L_1 \| L_2$. $\angle x = 110°$. Find $\angle y$.

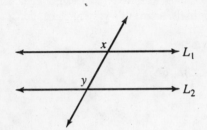

4. In the figure $L_1 \| L_2$. $\angle x = 130°$. Find $\angle a + \angle b$.

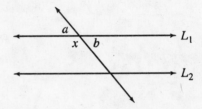

5. Find the diameter of a circle with a radius of 35 in.

6. Find the perimeter of the composite figure. Use 3.14 for π.

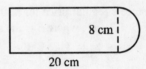

7. A playground 80 ft by 100 ft is enclosed with a chain link fence that costs $10.25 per foot. How much did it cost to fence the playground?

8. Find the area of a right triangle with a base of 2.6 m and a height of 3.5 m.

9. Find the area of the composite figure.

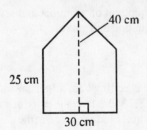

10. Find the area of the composite figure. The distance between the parallel lines is 6 cm. Use 3.14 for π.

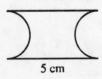

11. An irrigation system waters a circular field that has a 50-foot radius. Find the area watered by the irrigation system. Use 3.14 for π.

12. Find the volume of a cube with a side of 9 cm.

13. Find the volume of the solid in the figure.

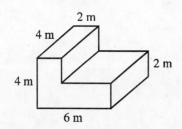

14. Find the volume, in cubic feet, of a concrete footing that is 30 ft long, 9 in. wide, and 12 in. high. The footing is in the shape of a rectangular solid.

15. Find the square root of 160. Round to the nearest thousandth.

16. Find the unknown side of the triangle.

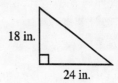

17. A 25-ft cable holds a telephone pole in place. The cable is attached to the telephone pole 20 ft above the ground. Find the distance along the ground from the base of the pole to the cable.

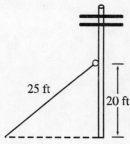

18. Triangle *ABC* and *DEF* are similar. Find side *DF*.

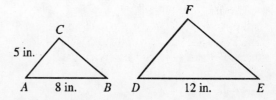

19. A flagpole 12 ft high casts a shadow of 8 ft. How high is a flagpole that casts a shadow of 20 ft?

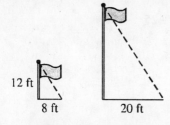

20. In the figure, triangles *ABC* and *DEF* are congruent. Find the length of *DE*.

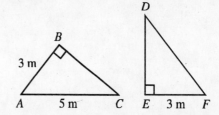

Chapters 10-12 Cumulative Test A

1. Find the sum of -9, 5, and -20.

2. Add: $-\dfrac{3}{4} + \left(-\dfrac{1}{6}\right)$

3. Subtract: $32 - (-14)$

4. What is 9.21 decreased by -1.09?

5. Find the product of -7 and 15.

6. Multiply: $-\dfrac{4}{9} \times \left(-\dfrac{3}{8}\right)$

7. Find the quotient of -2.5 and 10.

8. Write 5.3×10^4 in decimal notation.

9. Simplify: $-4 - (-2)^2 + 4 \cdot 6$

10. Evaluate $3ab - c^2$ when $a = 2$, $b = 3$, and $c = 4$..

11. Simplify: $-ab - 5ab - 8ab$

12. Solve: $m - 7 = -12$

13. Solve: $\dfrac{x}{7} = 3$

14. Solve: $3x - 25 = -1$

15. Solve: $7 - (x + 2) = 2(x + 4)$

16. Translate "the sum of a number and six is fifteen" into an equation and solve.

17. A bookstore manager paid $1940 in state income tax this year. This is $80 more than last year. Find the amount paid in state income tax last year.

18. Using the formula $C = \frac{5}{9}(F - 32)$, where C is Celsius temperature and F is Fahrenheit temperature, find the Fahrenheit temperature when the Celsius temperature is $35°$.

19. In the figure, $L_1 \parallel L_2$. $\angle x = 42°$. Find $\angle y$.

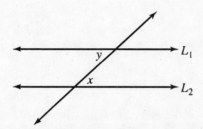

20. Two angles of a triangle measure $35°$ and $47°$. Find the measure of the third angle.

21. Find the circumference of a circle with diameter of 40 cm. Use 3.14 for π.

22. Find the volume of a cylinder with a height of 4 cm and a radius of 14 cm. Use $\frac{22}{7}$ for π.

23. Find the area of the figure. Use 3.14 for π.

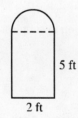

5 ft

2 ft

24. Find the unknown leg of the right triangle. Round to the nearest tenth.

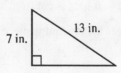

7 in.   13 in.

25. In the figure, triangles ABC and DEF are similar. Find EF.

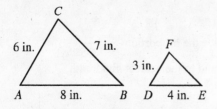

1. Subtract: $4096 - 827$

2. Find 20,794 divided by 562.

3. Divide: $\dfrac{5}{12} \div 3\dfrac{1}{3}$

4. Renee had a bank balance of $1627 before writing checks for $85, $327, and $64. What is her new account balance?

5. Add: $2\dfrac{1}{3} + 4\dfrac{3}{4}$

6. What is $2\dfrac{5}{8}$ less than $5\dfrac{1}{2}$?

7. Find the product of $\dfrac{4}{9}$ and $1\dfrac{1}{8}$.

8. Simplify: $5 + 3 \times 7 - 4^2$

9. Simplify: $\dfrac{1}{2} + \dfrac{1}{3} \times \dfrac{5}{6} - \left(\dfrac{1}{2}\right)^2$

10. Divide: $60 \div 0.04$

11. Find 6 decreased by 0.327.

12. Multiply: 0.9×1.82

13. A piece of wood $1\dfrac{1}{2}$ ft long is cut from a board $8\dfrac{1}{4}$ ft long. How long is the remaining piece of board?

14. Convert 0.95 to a fraction in simplest terms.

15. Convert to a decimal: $\dfrac{7}{9}$
    Round to the nearest thousandth.

16. Write the comparison "$20 to $45" as a ratio in simplest form using a fraction.

17. Write "$1.25 for 25 nails" as a unit rate.

18. Solve the proportion: $\dfrac{8}{n} = \dfrac{12}{35}$
    Round to the nearest hundredth.

19. A stock investment of 75 shares paid a dividend of $225. At this rate, what dividend would be paid for 325 shares of stock?

20. Write $\frac{5}{16}$ as a percent.

21. What is 42% of 568?

22. 65 is what percent of 250?

23. 42 is 28% of what number?

24. Five of a baseball team's 80 games were rained out. What percent of the games were rained out?

25. Find the unit cost of 10 pens for $2.90.

26. A hardware store uses a 40% markup rate. Find the selling price of a hammer that was purchased by the store for $8.

27. The price of CompTech stock dropped from $48 per share to $30 per share. What percent decrease does this represent?

28. A software sales executive earns a salary of $26,000 per year plus a 3% commission on sales. During the year, the executive's sales were $280,000. Find the executive's total income for the year.

29. The circle graph shows how a family's monthly income of $2600 is budgeted. How much of the family's income is budgeted for food?

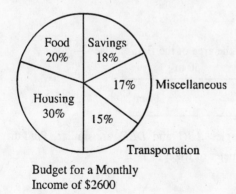

Budget for a Monthly
Income of $2600

30. The double-line graph compares two employees' quarterly sales for 2000. What is the difference between their third quarter sales?

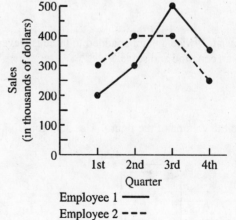

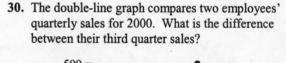

31. Convert $4\frac{1}{6}$ ft to inches.

32. Convert $2\frac{3}{8}$ lb to ounces.

33. A board 2 ft 8 in. long is cut from a board 10 ft 6 in. long. Find the length of the remaining piece of board.

34. How many 10-oz mugs can be filled with coffee from a $1\frac{7}{8}$ qt thermos?

35. Convert 2.91 kg to grams.

36. Convert 4.6 mm to centimeters.

37. The Gift Emporium is mailing two packages weighing 4375 g and 5225 g. What is the combined weight, in kilograms, of the packages?

38. Place the correct symbol, < or >, between the two numbers.
$$-19 \quad -32$$

39. Add: $-12+(-34)$

40. Find the difference between 3.1 and -0.9.

41. Find the product of $\frac{5}{8}$ and $-\frac{8}{11}$.

42. Simplify: $(-4)^2 + 3 \cdot (-1) - (-6)$

43. Evaluate $a^2 - b$ when $a = -2$ and $b = 1$.

44. Solve: $x - 8 = -7$

45. Solve: $3y - 5 = -8$

46. Solve: $-2x + 3(x+4) = 1$

47. Translate "twice a number added to three is eleven" into an equation and solve.

48. Find the area of the figure. Use $\frac{22}{7}$ for π.

50 m

14 m

49. Find the volume of the figure. Use 3.14 for π.

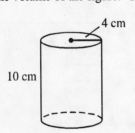

4 cm

10 cm

50. Triangles *ABC* and *DEF* are similar. Find the perimeter of triangle *DEF*.

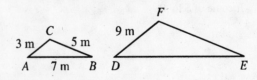

Form B Tests

Free Response

Name: _____

Date: _____

1. Write seven hundred eight thousand twenty in standard form.

2. Write 3,007,609 in words.

3. Place the correct symbol, < or >, between the two numbers:

   19   21

4. Write 609,005 in expanded form.

5. Round 29,673 to the nearest ten.

6. Add: 923,411
         + 21,327

7. Find the sum of 314,829 , 77,413 , and 109,842 .

8. An insurance executive receives commissions of $1483, $972, $806, and $1055 during a 4-week period. Find the total income from the commissions for the 4 weeks.

9. Find 2347 minus 312 .

10. Subtract: 8207
              − 2705

11. The down payment on a computer system costing $2249 was $449. Find the amount that remains to be paid.

12. Find the product of 43,072 and 6.

13. Multiply: 1403
             × 902

14. The Environmental Protection Agency (EPA) estimates that a compact car travels 38 miles on 1 gallon of gas. How many miles could such a car travel on 15 gallons of gas?

15. Find the quotient of 609 and 7 .

16. Divide: $6\overline{)21,368}$

17. Divide: $34\overline{)27,745}$

18. The total cost of a Dodge truck, including finance charges, is $12,744. This amount is to be repaid in 24 equal payments. What is the amount of each payment?

19. Write $3 \cdot 3 \cdot 3 \cdot 5 \cdot 5 \cdot 5 \cdot 5$ in exponential notation.

20. Simplify: $2^3 \cdot 5^2 \cdot 7$

21. Simplify: $5 - 2 \cdot (7 - 3) \div 4$

22. Simplify: $4 + 3 \cdot (8 - 2) - 12$

23. Find all the factors of 28 .

24. Find the prime factorization of 20 .

25. Find the prime factorization of 150 .

1. Find the LCM of 40 and 60.

2. Find the GCF of 36 and 63.

3. Express the shaded portion of the circles as a mixed fraction.

4. Write $\dfrac{24}{5}$ as a mixed number.

5. Write $3\dfrac{5}{9}$ as an improper fraction.

6. What number must be placed in the numerator so that the following fractions are equivalent?

$$\dfrac{5}{12} = \dfrac{}{72}$$

7. Write $\dfrac{24}{46}$ in simplest form.

8. Add: $\dfrac{3}{7} + \dfrac{4}{7}$

9. Add: $\begin{array}{r} \dfrac{5}{8} \\[2mm] +\dfrac{7}{12} \\ \hline \end{array}$

10. What is $2\dfrac{5}{7}$ more than $3\dfrac{3}{5}$?

11. Omar bought stock in an energy company for $\$42\dfrac{5}{8}$. The price of the stock gained $\$5\dfrac{3}{4}$ during a 6-month period. Find the price of the stock at the end of the 6 months.

12. Subtract: $\dfrac{31}{38} - \dfrac{11}{38}$

13. What is $\dfrac{11}{12}$ minus $\dfrac{3}{8}$?

14. Subtract: $\begin{array}{r} 16\dfrac{5}{12} \\[2mm] -8\dfrac{11}{18} \\ \hline \end{array}$

15. A salesperson cuts $2\frac{5}{8}$ yards of material from a roll containing $12\frac{1}{3}$ yards. Find the amount of material remaining on the roll.

16. Multiply: $\frac{7}{8} \times \frac{24}{63}$

17. What is $4\frac{3}{8}$ multiplied by $6\frac{2}{5}$?

18. A person can walk $3\frac{2}{3}$ miles in 1 hour. How many miles can the person walk in $1\frac{1}{2}$ hours?

19. Divide: $\frac{12}{13} \div \frac{5}{26}$

20. Divide: $18 \div 3\frac{1}{5}$

21. Toy Medeiros bought $5\frac{1}{3}$ acres of land for $26,000. What was the cost of each acre?

22. Place the correct symbol, $<$ or $>$, between the two numbers: $\frac{5}{21}$ $\frac{3}{14}$

23. Simplify: $6 \cdot \left(\frac{2}{3}\right)^3 \left(\frac{1}{2}\right)^2$

24. Simplify: $\frac{1}{6} \div \left(\frac{1}{3}\right)^2 - \frac{1}{2}$

25. Simplify: $\left(\frac{1}{2}\right)^2 + \left(\frac{3}{5} - \frac{1}{2}\right) \div \frac{4}{15}$

Name: _____
Date: _____

1. Write 84.13 in words.

2. Write in standard form: eighty-four and thirteen hundredths.

3. Round 534.018 to the nearest tenth.

4. Round 37.09734 to the nearest thousandth.

5. Add: 316.90734
          19.397
       + 1463.4975

6. Find the sum of 31.8, 5.27, 214.031, and 12.004.

7. On a weekend trip you spent $13.18, $9.54, and $11.81 for gasoline. The motel bills were $42.63 and $51.24. Find the total amount spent for gasoline and motel rooms.

8. Subtract: $241.09 - 63.578$

9. What is 4.3728 less than 6.051?

10. The down payment on a Chevrolet Cavalier costing $13,961.32 is $2929.95. Find the amount that remains to be paid.

11. Multiply: 63.025
           $\times$ 3.7

12. Find the product of 84.7 and 6.03.

13. A student works 19 hours per week at an hourly rate of $6.35. Find the student's weekly income.

14. Find the quotient of 3.875 and 0.062.

15. Divide. Round to the nearest tenth.

    $0.048\overline{)207.32}$

16. Rebecca bought 4.5 pounds of chicken for $12.87. Find the cost for one pound of chicken.

17. Convert $2\frac{5}{9}$ to a decimal.
    Round to the nearest thousandth.

18. Convert 0.625 to a fraction.

19. Place the correct symbol, < or >, between the two numbers: 4.1109   4.109

20. Place the correct symbol, < or >, between the two numbers: $\frac{3}{5}$ 0.66

Name: _____

Date: _____

1. Divide. Express your answer in remainder form.

    $14\overline{)8449}$

2. Simplify: $3^3 \cdot 4^2$

3. Simplify: $(9 \times 8) - 3^2 \cdot (7 - 4)$

4. Find the LCM of 10, 24, and 60.

5. Write $\dfrac{45}{7}$ as a mixed number.

6. Write $6\dfrac{3}{8}$ as an improper fraction.

7. Find the numerator for an equivalent fraction with the given denominator: $\dfrac{2}{17} = \dfrac{}{85}$

8. Add: $\dfrac{3}{5} + \dfrac{1}{3} + \dfrac{11}{12}$

9. What is $15\dfrac{3}{5}$ increased by $3\dfrac{2}{3}$?

10. Subtract: $7\dfrac{1}{3} - 2\dfrac{1}{2}$

11. Multiply: $\dfrac{2}{9} \times \dfrac{15}{28}$

12. Find the product of $2\dfrac{4}{5}$ and $1\dfrac{3}{7}$.

13. Divide: $\dfrac{8}{27} \div \dfrac{4}{9}$

14. What is $3\dfrac{3}{4}$ divided by 8?

15. Simplify: $\left(\dfrac{2}{3}\right)^3 \cdot \left(\dfrac{6}{7}\right)^2$

16. Simplify: $\left(\dfrac{1}{2} + \dfrac{2}{5}\right) - \dfrac{2}{3} \cdot \dfrac{3}{5}$

17. Write 19.0501 in words.

18. Add: 37.093
                2.3591
           + 584.6
           _____

19. What is 201.93 decreased by 97.488 ?

20. Multiply: 12.06
                    × 0.024

21. Divide. Round to the nearest thousandth.

$2.37\overline{)0.619}$

22. Convert $\frac{2}{9}$ to a decimal.

Round to the nearest thousandth.

23. Convert 72.3 to a fraction.

24. Place the correct symbol, < or >, between the two numbers: $\frac{7}{15}$ 0.47

25. Last winter, there was $3\frac{5}{8}$ inches of snow in November, $12\frac{3}{4}$ inches of snow in December, and $16\frac{1}{8}$ inches of snow in January. How much snow fell in those 3 months?

26. A dollmaker uses $1\frac{2}{3}$ yards of fabric to make a doll. How many dolls can be made with $8\frac{1}{3}$ yards of fabric?

27. Shaquille had a balance of $1231.50 in his checking account. He then wrote checks for $159.60, $32.95, and $211.80. Find the new balance in the checking account.

28. A songwriter received a total of $9735.04 for the use of an advertising jingle. If the jingle was used 32 times, how much did the songwriter receive each time the jingle was used?

29. On a trip to the supermarket, you bought 3.25 pounds of bananas, 1.4 pounds of mangoes, and 4.75 pounds of apples. How many pounds of fruit did you buy in all?

30. A used car can be bought for $1500 down and $298.90 each month for 24 months. Find the total cost of the car.

1. Write the comparison 60 seconds to 15 seconds as a ratio in simplest form using a fraction, a colon (:), and the word TO.

2. Write the comparison $16 to $6 as a ratio in simplest form using a fraction, a colon (:), and the word TO.

3. Write the comparison 3 quarts to 7 quarts as a ratio in simplest form using a fraction, a colon (:), and the word TO.

4. Write the comparison 20 feet to 65 feet as a ratio in simplest form using a fraction, a colon (:), and the word TO.

5. A service station sold 180 tires in March and 135 tires in April. Find the ratio, as a fraction in simplest form, of the number of tires sold in March to the number of tires sold in April.

6. A car was bought for $12,200 5 years ago and is now being sold for $8000. Find the ratio, as a fraction in simplest form, of the decrease in price to the price 5 years ago.

7. Write "$27 for 9 pounds" as a rate in simplest form.

8. Write "8 pounds of fertilizer for 10 trees" as a rate in simplest form.

9. Write "1210 miles in 5 days" as a unit rate.

10. Write "$14.57 for 6.2 pounds" as a unit rate.

11. A costume designer earns $742.40 for working a 40-hour week. Find the costume designer's hourly wage.

12. A truck traveled 165 miles in 2.5 hours. Find the truck's speed in miles per hour.

13. Determine if the proportion is true or not true.
$$\frac{4}{9} = \frac{19}{42}$$

14. Determine if the proportion is true or not true.
$$\frac{4}{3} = \frac{48}{36}$$

15. Solve the proportion: $\dfrac{10}{25} = \dfrac{n}{35}$

16. Solve the proportion: $\dfrac{n}{15} = \dfrac{9}{32}$
Round to the nearest hundredth.

17. A manufacturer expects 2 out of every 300 circuit boards to be defective. How many circuit boards out of a batch of 1800 would be expected to be defective?

18. A cookie recipe calls for $1\frac{1}{2}$ teaspoons of baking soda for each 2 cups of flour. How many teaspoons would be required for 7 cups of flour?

19. The real estate tax rate is $10.45 for each $1000 of house value. What is the real estate tax on a home valued at $125,000?

20. An opinion poll showed that 3 out of every 7 voters was opposed to a particular candidate. At this rate, how many voters out of 8680 would be opposed to the candidate?

Name: _____

Date: _____

1. Write 3.9 as a percent.

2. Write 3.2% as a fraction.

3. Write 0.876 as a percent.

4. Write 641% as a decimal.

5. Write $\frac{3}{10}$ as a percent.

6. Write $\frac{1}{80}$ as a percent.

7. What is 15% of 36?

8. 0.064% of 2500 is what number?

9. Which is larger: 90% of 25,000 or 115% of 19,000?

10. Which is smaller: 1.8% of 6 or 0.3% of 12?

11. A company spends 8% of its budget on building maintenance. If its yearly budget is $200,000, how much is spent on maintenance?

12. Sales tax is 5.5% of cost. What is the sales tax on a washing machine costing $470? Round to the nearest cent.

13. What percent of 9 is 14.4?

14. 12 is what percent of 96?

15. A family whose monthly income is $2240 spent $336 last month on groceries. What percent of their monthly income was spent on groceries?

16. In a survey of 520 people, 234 people favored a particular candidate on the ballot. What percent of the people favored this candidate?

17. 37.5 is 60% of what number?

18. 154 is 175% of what number?

19. In a city, 59,760 people are registered to vote. This is 83% of the population of the city. What is the city's population?

20. Vanessa has read 36 pages, which is 75% of the assignment. How many pages were assigned to be read?

21. 584 is 36.5% of what number?

22. What percent of 150 is 24.6?

23. In a shipment of 1250 auto parts, 5 parts were found to be defective. What percent of the shipment was defective?

24. Darrell is aiming for a grade of 85% on a test. If the test contains 160 questions, how many questions does he need to answer correctly?

25. Thirty-five students completed a British literature course. This was 87.5% of the original enrollment. How many students were originally enrolled in the course?

Name: _____

Date: _____

1. Three pounds of gourmet coffee cost $20.55. Find the unit cost.

2. Find the most economical purchase: 5 quarts for $6.20, 12 quarts for $12.96, 24 quarts for $27.60, or 48 quarts for $52.80.

3. Vermont Cheddar Cheese costs $2.89 per pound. Find the total cost of 2.25 pounds. Round to the nearest cent.

4. The price of a gallon of gasoline rose from $1.02 to $1.42 in 1 year. What percent increase does this represent? Round to the nearest percent.

5. During 1 week of a keyboarding course, Derek increased his typing speed by 20%. If Derek's original speed was 40 words per minute, what was his speed at the end of the week?

6. Bates Sporting Goods uses a markup rate of 45% on all exercise equipment. What is the markup on a treadmill that cost the store $490?

7. A garden supply center uses a markup rate of 48% on all tools and equipment. What is the selling price of a mulcher that cost the store $82?

8. It is estimated that the value of a certain car model decreases 22% in the first year. If that model car is currently selling for $13,400, how much will it be worth next year?

9. Muskegon Community College bookstore sold 768 math books during the fall semester. During the spring semester, the store sold 704 math books. What percent decrease does this represent? Round to the nearest percent.

10. A motorcycle that regularly sells for $4600 is on sale for 15% off the regular price. What is the discount?

11. A Gap sweater than regularly sells for $78 is on sale for 20% off the regular price. What is the sale price?

12. A doctor makes a down payment of 25% of the $145,000 purchase price of an office building. How much is the down payment?

13. A money market fund pays 10% annual interest compounded daily. What is the value after 20 years of $5000 invested in this money market fund? Use the Compound Interest Table.

14. An ice cream shop needs to purchase new freezers. The shop borrows $25,000 at a simple interest rate of 12% for 18 months to buy the new freezers. Find the simple interest due on the loan.

15. An office building is purchased for $225,000. A down payment of $22,500 is required, and a 25-year mortgage at an annual interest rate of 10% is obtained. Find the monthly mortgage payment. Use the Monthly Payment Table. Round to the nearest cent.

16. Rodney buys a computer system for $3740 and makes a down payment of 15% of the purchase price. Find the amount financed.

17. A Dodge Caravan is purchased for $13,500 with a down payment of $2075. The balance is financed for 4 years at an annual interest rate of 12%. Find the monthly payment. Use the Monthly Payment Table. Round to the nearest cent.

18. A real estate broker receives a commission of 3% of the selling price of a house. Find the commission received by the broker for selling a house for $79,500.

19. An accountant had a checking account balance of $2321.02 before making a deposit of $3192.50. The accountant then wrote checks for $1160.40 and $522.03. Find the current checkbook balance.

20. Balance the checkbook shown.

RECORD ALL CHARGES OR CREDITS THAT AFFECT YOUR ACCOUNT

NUMBER	DATE	DESCRIPTION OF TRANSACTION	PAYMENT/DEBIT (-)	√ T	FEE (IF ANY) (-)	DEPOSIT/CREDIT (+)	BALANCE
							$ 496 12
	2/1	Mortgage	$ 289 76	s	s	s	206 36
	2/2	Electric bill	117 30				89 06
	2/6	Drugstore	13 50				75 56
	2/7	Deposit				416 32	491 88
	2/9	Plane tickets	375 00				116 88
	2/10	Deposit				27 54	144 42
	2/15	Deposit				117 90	262 32
	2/16	Dentist	45 00				217 32

REMEMBER TO RECORD AUTOMATIC PAYMENTS/DEPOSITS ON DATE AUTHORIZED

CHECKING ACCOUNT Monthly Statement		Account Number : 924-297-8	
DATE	Transaction	Amount	Balance
	OPENING BALANCE		496.12
2/2	CHECK	289.76	206.36
2/4	CHECK	117.30	89.06
2/8	DEPOSIT	416.32	505.38
2/11	DEPOSIT	27.54	532.92
2/17	CHECK	45.00	487.92
2/17	INTEREST	5.75	493.67
2/28	CLOSING BALANCE		493.67

Do the bank statement and the checkbook balance?

1. Write the comparison 5 days to 30 days as a ratio in simplest form using a fraction, a colon (:), and the word TO.

2. One bottle of detergent contains 22 ounces while a larger bottle contains 36 ounces. Find the ratio of the amount of detergent in the smaller bottle to the amount in the larger bottle.

3. Write "$175.68 for 18 pounds" as a unit rate.

4. A bicyclist travels 39 miles in 4 hours. Find the bicyclist's speed in miles per hour.

5. Solve the proportion: $\dfrac{n}{8} = \dfrac{14}{56}$

6. For every 150 seeds you sow, 97 germinate. At this rate, how many seeds will germinate if you sow 2550 seeds?

7. Write 59% as a decimal.

8. Write 8% as a fraction.

9. Write 9.36 as a percent.

10. Write $\dfrac{7}{8}$ as a percent.

11. 21% of 73 is what number?

12. During its first year, Brinks Alarm Company had sales of $124,300. During the second year, sales increased by 17%. What were the company's sales during the second year?

13. What percent of 48 is 60?

14. Circuit City sold 45 of the 55 television sets that it had in stock. What percent of the television sets in stock was sold? Round to the nearest tenth of a percent.

15. 100 is 40% of what number?

16. A major city reported 210 crimes this month. This was 125% of the crimes reported last month. How many crimes were reported last month?

17. Spaghetti costs 99¢ for an 8-ounce box. Find the cost per ounce. Round to the nearest tenth of a cent.

18. The Computer Source uses a markup rate of 40%. What is the markup on a box of disks that cost the store $3.25?

19. Abe's Hardware is having a "25% off" sale. What is the sale price of a set of wrenches that regularly sells for $32?

20. A restaurant owner borrowed $92,000 to renovate his kitchen. The money was borrowed for 10 months at an annual interest rate of 12%. What is the simple interest due on the loan?

The pictograph shows the amount of money a family spends on certain expenses every month.

1. What are the total monthly expenditures for the three items?

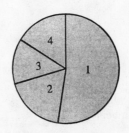

2. What is the ratio of the amount of the monthly telephone bill to the amount of the monthly heating oil bill?

The circle graph shows the annual expenses of owning a home.

3. Find the ratio of the annual cost of utilities to the annual interest expenses.

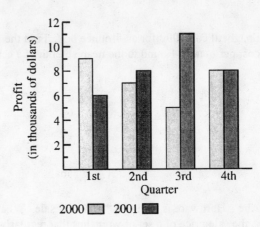

4. Find the ratio of the annual interest expenses to the upkeep expenses.

ANNUAL HOME-OWNER EXPENSES
1: $7200 - Interest
2: $1500 - Upkeep
3: $1800 - Utilities
4: $2200 - Principal

The double-bar graph shows quarterly profits (in thousands of dollars) for a company for the years 2000 and 2001.

5. Find the difference between the company's third-quarter profits for 2000 and 2001.

6. In which quarter did the 2000 profits exceed the 2001 profits?

7. What are the total profits for 2000?

8. The bowling scores for eight people were 138, 125, 162, 144, 129, 168, 184, and 173. What was the mean score for these eight people?

9. The numbers of compact discs sold by a record store for eight consecutive days were 90, 134, 119, 183, 200, 148, 130, and 175. Find the median number of compact discs sold per day.

The double-line graph shows the number of cars (in thousands) sold by an automobile manufacturer during the first five months of 2000 and 2001.

10. In which month in 2000 did the manufacturer have the most sales?

11. Find the difference between the April 2000 sales and April 2001 sales.

12. What were the manufacturer's total sales during 2001?

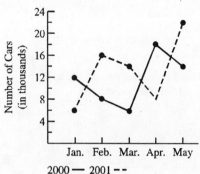

2000 —— 2001 ----

The histogram shows the hourly wages of the 32 employees of a pool service company.

13. Find the number of employees whose hourly wage is between $8 and $12.

14. What percent of the employees make between $6 and $12 an hour? Round to the nearest tenth of a percent.

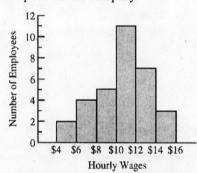

The frequency polygon shows the energy bills received by 37 customers.

15. How many customers received bills between $40 and $80?

16. What percent of the customers have bills of more than $80? Round to the nearest percent.

17. What is the ratio of the number of customers who received bills of between $60 and $80 to the total number of customers?

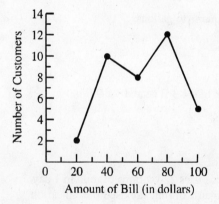

18. Two dice are rolled. What is the probability that the sum of the dots on the upward faces is three?

19. The scores of 14 second-grade students on a modified IQ test are given in the table below. Determine the third quartile of the IQ scores.

103	98	110	124	92	96	102
100	128	116	90	105	106	98

20. The box-and-whiskers plot represents data for the average annual income, in thousands of dollars, for each state in the United States. Determine the first quartile of this data.

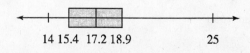

14 15.4 17.2 18.9   25

Name: _____

Date: _____

1. Convert 63 ft to yards.

2. Subtract: $4\dfrac{2}{5}$ mi $- 3\dfrac{7}{10}$ mi

3. How long must a board be if four pieces, each 2 ft 5 in. long, are to be cut from the board?

4. Pots of geraniums are to be spaced every 10 in. between two fence posts. How many pots of geraniums can be planted along a fence that is 5 ft long?

5. Convert: 50 oz = _____ lb _____ oz

6. Convert 7600 lb to tons.

7. Subtract: 7 lb 2 oz
             -2 lb 5 oz

8. Multiply: 3 lb 5 oz
             $\times$ 9

9. A large piece of beef weighing 12 lb 3 oz is cut into five equal pieces. How much does each piece weigh?

10. A baby weighed 5 lb 6 oz at birth. Two months later, the baby weighed 9 lb 2 oz. What was the baby's weight gain over the 2 months?

11. Convert 22 quarts to gallons.

12. Convert $2\dfrac{1}{2}$ qt to pints.

13. Find the sum of 9 c 3 fl oz and 3 c 9 fl oz.

14. Subtract: 8 c 3 fl oz
             $-$ 2 c 6 fl oz

15. A food service uses 220 cartons of milk in 1 day. How many quarts of milk are used if each carton contains 1 cup?

16. If 45 people are expected to attend a party, how many quarts of punch should be prepared if each person is expected to drink 3 c?

17. A crane lifts a 1500-pound concrete slab to the top of a construction site 30 ft high. Find the amount of energy required by the crane.

18. A 2-ton truck is being lifted 20 ft onto a loading dock. How much energy is required?

19. Convert 4.5 hp to foot-pounds per second.
$$\left(1\ hp = 550\ \frac{ft \cdot lb}{s}\right)$$

20. Find the power in foot-pounds per second needed to raise 1 ton a distance of 30 ft in 15 s.

Chapter 9 Test Form B

Name: _____

Date: _____

1. Convert 56 cm to millimeters.

2. Convert 76.5 km to meters.

3. Convert 3 m 5 cm to centimeters.

4. Convert 18 km 25 m to kilometers.

5. A piece of wood 510 cm long is cut from a board 8 m long. Find the length (in meters) of the remaining piece.

6. A hiker can walk 7750 m in 1 hour. How far can the hiker walk (in kilometers) in 3 hours?

7. Convert 0.023 g to milligrams.

8. Convert 3716 g to kilograms.

9. Convert 7 g 83 mg to grams.

10. Convert 5 kg 760 g to kilograms.

11. A wrestler loses 1150 g one week and gains 2325 g the next week. Find the wrestler's weight gain in kilograms.

12. Find the cost of a beef roast weighing 6700 g if the cost per kilogram is $5.24. Round to the nearest cent.

13. Convert 130 cm^3 to milliliters.

14. Convert 37 ml to liters.

15. Convert 1345 L to kiloliters.

16. Convert 2L 65 ml to liters.

17. One hundred thirty people are going to attend a wedding reception. Assuming that each person drinks 400 ml of wine, how many liters of wine should be purchased?

18. Walking requires 170 Calories per hour. How many hours must you walk to burn off the Calories in pie and ice cream containing 425 Calories? Round to the nearest tenth.

19. Find the weight in kilograms of a 160-pound person. Round to the nearest hundredth.
(1 kg = 2.2 lb)

20. Your height is 154 cm. Find your height in inches.
(1 cm = 0.39 in.)

The circle graph shows a family's monthly expenditures totaling $3250.

1. Find the total amount spent for transportation.

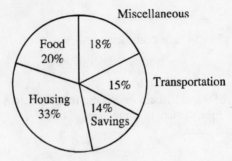

2. Find the ratio, as a fraction in simplest terms, of the amount spent on food to the monthly savings.

Budget for a Monthly
Income of $3250

The double-line graph shows the quarterly profits for a laser company for the years 2000 and 2001.

3. In which quarter of 2000 did the company make the least profit?

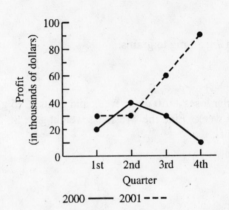

4. What is the difference between the third quarter profits for 2000 and 2001?

5. A taxi driver's tips over a 4-day period were $69, $57, $62, and $59. Find the driver's average daily tip over the 4-day period.

6. Calls to a police station over a 6-day period numbers 54, 62, 51, 67, 74, and 58. Find the median number of calls for the 6-day period.

7. Convert 39 in. to feet.

8. Multiply: $7\frac{3}{4}$ ft $\times 8$

9. Convert 488 oz to pounds.

10. What is the sum of 5 lb 8 oz and 4 lb 10 oz?

11. Convert 10 qt to pints.

12. If a serving contains 1 c, how many servings can be made from 12 gal of punch?

13. Boards 2 ft 6 in., 9 ft 7 in., and 5 ft 11 in. long are needed for a project. What is the total length of the boards?

14. Convert 196 cm to meters.

15. Convert 5917 mg to grams.

16. Convert 192 cm^3 to liters.

17. Find the number of feet in 60 m. (1 m = 3.28 ft)

18. Express 220 m/s in feet per second. (1 m = 3.28 ft)

19. How many meters of fencing are required to enclose a play yard 880 cm long and 650 cm wide?

20. If each serving of coffee is 175 ml, how many liters of coffee are needed to serve 80 people?

Name: _____

Date: _____

1. Place the correct symbol, < or >, between the two numbers:

   $$3 \qquad -4$$

2. Place the correct symbol, < or >, between the two numbers:

   $$-2 \qquad -61$$

3. Evaluate: $|-23|$

4. Add: $23 + (-9)$

5. Find the sum of $6, \ -14, \ -3,$ and 8.

6. Subtract: $-7 - 12$

7. Subtract: $7 - 9 - (-1)$

8. Find the product of 9 and -7.

9. Divide: $-64 \div (-4)$

10. Find the temperature after a rise of 5°C from −12°C.

11. The daily low temperature readings for a 4-day period were as follows: $-12°, -8°, 6°,$ and $2°$. Find the average low temperature for the 4-day period.

12. Add: $-\dfrac{1}{5} + \dfrac{2}{15}$

13. Find the sum of $\dfrac{3}{8}, \ -\dfrac{5}{12},$ and $-\dfrac{1}{4}$.

14. Subtract: $-\dfrac{2}{3} - \dfrac{1}{9}$

15. Subtract: $2\dfrac{1}{4} - 2\dfrac{5}{6}$

16. Multiply: $-\dfrac{2}{7} \times \left(-\dfrac{3}{4}\right)$

17. Find the quotient of $-3\dfrac{2}{3}$ and $1\dfrac{5}{6}$.

18. Subtract: $-3.6 - 5.94$

19. Subtract: $2.3 - (-4.1)$

20. Find the product of -6.5 and -2.01.

21. Divide: $0.32 \div (-1.6)$

22. Simplify: $-(-2)^2 + 12 \div 4$

23. Simplify: $12 - 6 \cdot (3 - 5) \div 4$

24. Write 0.0000604 in scientific notation.

25. The boiling point of xenon is −107.1°C. The melting point of xenon is −111.9°C. What is the difference between the boiling point and the melting point of xenon?

Name: _____

Date: _____

1. Evaluate $ab + ac - bc$ when $a = -2$, $b = 3$, and $c = -4$.

2. Evaluate $\dfrac{b-a}{ab^2}$ when $a = -2$ and $b = 3$.

3. Simplify: $-8x + 3y - 4x - 5y$

4. Simplify: $3y - 2(y - 6)$

5. Is 5 a solution of $y^2 - 2y - 15 = 0$?

6. Solve: $n + 9 = -21$

7. Solve: $-7x = -42$

8. Solve: $-\dfrac{1}{5}x = 3$

9. Solve: $-3x + 7 = -11$

10. Solve: $\dfrac{x}{3} - 5 = 2$

11. An investor uses the formula $A = P + I \cdot P$, where A is the value of an investment after 1 year, P is the original investment, and I is the interest rate for the investment. Find the interest rate for an original investment of $5000 that has a value of $5600 after 1 year.

12. Luis Sanchez earns a base monthly salary of $400 plus 5% commission on total sales. Find the total sales during a month Luis earned $2850. Use the formula $M = S \cdot R + B$, where M is monthly earnings, S is the total sales, R is the commission rate, and B is the base monthly salary.

13. Solve: $-3 = 6y - 12$

14. Solve: $x - 1 = 2 - 2x$

15. Solve: $4(x - 3) + 6 = 10$

16. Translate "the product of m and the sum of twelve and m" into a mathematical expression.

17. Translate "three more than the sum of a number and nine" into a mathematical expression.

18. Translate "three plus one-half of a number is ten" into an equation and solve.

19. The total of eight times a number and fifteen is thirty-one. Find the number.

20. The value of a building lot this year is $78,000. This is three times its value 18 years ago. Find its value 18 years ago.

Name: _____

Date: _____

1. Find the supplement of a 15° angle.

2. A right triangle has a 37° angle. Find the measures of the other two angles.

3. In the figure, $L_1 \parallel L_2$. $\angle y = 105°$. Find $\angle x$.

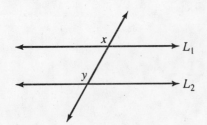

4. In the figure $L_1 \parallel L_2$. $\angle x = 45°$. Find $\angle y$.

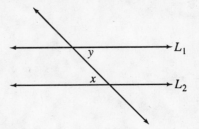

5. Find the circumference of a circle with a radius of 8 cm. Use 3.14 for π.

6. Find the perimeter of the composite figure. Use 3.14 for π.

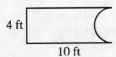

7. A homeowner is putting molding around the ceiling of a room that is 14 ft wide and 22 ft long. At $2.35 per foot, how much will it cost for the molding?

8. Find the area of a right triangle with a base of 4 ft and a height of $\frac{2}{3}$ ft.

9. Find the area of the composite figure. Use 3.14 for π.

10. Find the area of the composite figure. Use 3.14 for π.

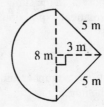

11. A room 12 ft by 16 ft is carpeted. At $18 per square yard, how much does it cost to carpet the room? ($9 \text{ ft}^2 = 1 \text{ yd}^2$)

12. Find the volume of a cube with a side of $3\frac{1}{2}$ in.

13. Find the volume of the solid. The diameter of the cylinder is 3 ft. Use 3.14 for π.

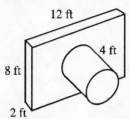

14. How many gallons of water will fill a fish tank that is 18 in. long, 10 in. wide, and 9 in. high? Round to the nearest tenth. ($1 \text{ gal} = 231 \text{ in.}^3$)

15. Find the square root of 82. Round to the nearest thousandth.

16. Find the unknown side of the triangle. Round to the nearest tenth.

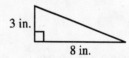

17. A ladder 12 ft long is leaning against a building. How high on the building will the ladder reach when the bottom of the ladder is 5 ft from the building? Round to the nearest tenth.

18. Triangles *ABC* and *DEF* are similar. Find side *BC*.

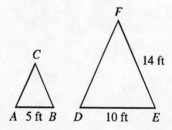

19. A flagpole 14 m high casts a shadow of 8 m. How high is a flagpole that casts a shadow of 10 m?

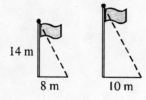

20. In the figure, triangle *ABC* is congruent to triangle *DEF*. Find the length of *DF*.

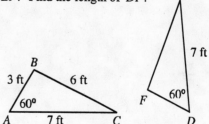

1. Find the sum of -16, -12, and 8.

2. Add: $\dfrac{1}{6}+\left(-\dfrac{8}{9}\right)+\left(-\dfrac{1}{4}\right)$

3. Subtract: $-9-14$

4. Find the difference between 9.2 and -10.46.

5. Find the product of -20 and -7.

6. Multiply: $-\dfrac{3}{8}\times\left(-\dfrac{5}{8}\right)$

7. Find the quotient of 20.8 and -0.04.

8. Simplify: $7\times(3-6)-5$

9. Simplify: $(-5)^2-(2-3)+4\div2\times3$

10. Simplify: $6x^2-8y-x^2+7y$

11. Evaluate $3bc-2a^2$ when $a=2$, $b=3$, and $c=4$.

12. Solve: $8y+7=-17$

13. Solve: $\dfrac{x}{6}=-5$

14. Solve: $z-14=-2$

15. Solve: $6x - 2(x+1) = 3(x+2)$

16. The product of four and a number is twenty-four. Find the number.

17. A plumber charged $125 to install a garbage disposal. This charge included $45 for materials and $20 per hour for labor. How long did it take the plumber to install the garbage disposal?

18. The formula $C = \dfrac{5}{9}(F - 32)$ represents the relationship between the Fahrenheit temperature F and the Celsius temperature C. Find the Fahrenheit temperature when the Celsius temperature is $25°$.

19. In the figure, $L_1 \parallel L_2$. $\angle x = 124°$. Find $\angle y$.

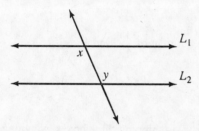

20. Two angles of a triangle measure $42°$ and $75°$. Find the measure of the third angle.

21. Find the perimeter of a rectangle whose length is $3\dfrac{3}{4}$ in. and whose width is $2\dfrac{1}{2}$ in.

22. Find the area of the figure.

23. Find the unknown leg of the right triangle. Round to the nearest tenth.

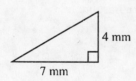

24. Find the volume of a cube with sides of 7.2 cm.

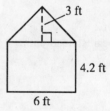

25. In the figure, triangles *ABC* and *DEF* are similar. Find the perimeter of triangle *DEF*.

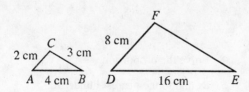

Name: _____

Date: _____

1. Subtract: $82,406 - 37,598$

2. Find 9486 divided by 279.

3. Simplify: $6 - 2 \times 2 + 8 \div 2$

4. A computer programmer earns $750 for working a 40-hour week. The programmer also worked 5 hours of overtime at $28 an hour. What were the programmer's total earnings for the week?

5. Add: $\frac{4}{9} + 2\frac{1}{3}$

6. Subtract: $5\frac{2}{7} - 3\frac{9}{14}$

7. Find the product of $3\frac{1}{5}$ and $\frac{5}{8}$.

8. Find the quotient of $\frac{11}{12}$ and $1\frac{1}{3}$.

9. Simplify: $\left(\frac{3}{4}\right)^2 + \frac{5}{8} \times \frac{1}{2} - \frac{3}{8}$

10. A company is shipping three boxes, weighing $4\frac{1}{3}$ lb, $4\frac{3}{4}$ lb, and $2\frac{1}{8}$ lb. What is the total weight of the shipment?

11. What is 6.8 minus 3.782?

12. Multiply: 3.9×0.11

13. Divide: $8 \div 0.062$
    Round to the nearest hundredth.

14. Convert 0.72 to a fraction.

15. Convert to a decimal: $\frac{7}{30}$
    Round to the nearest thousandth.

16. Write the comparison "15 boards to 12 boards" as a ratio in simplest form using a fraction.

17. Write "$16.75 for 25 notepads" as a unit rate.

18. Solve the proportion: $\frac{4}{n} = \frac{15}{41}$
    Round to the nearest hundredth.

19. The dosage of a medicine is $\frac{1}{2}$ oz for every 75 lb of body weight. How many ounces are required for a person weighing 225 lb?

20. Write $\frac{1}{8}$ as a percent.

21. What is 320% of 16?

22. 48 is what percent of 60?

23. 39.6 is 33% of what number?

24. Marcel correctly answered 75 out of 90 questions on an exam. What percent of the questions were answered correctly? Round to the nearest tenth of a percent.

25. Find the unit cost: 4 lb for $15.96.

26. A $21,600 car is purchased with a 12% down payment. Find the amount to be financed.

27. Vanessa had a checking account balance of $1325.76. She wrote checks for $84.50, $327.85, and $51.22. She deposited $427.86. Find her new checking account balance.

28. The price of heating oil increased from 78¢ per gallon to 97.5¢ per gallon. Find the percent increase in price.

29. The circle graph shows the annual expense of owning and operating a car. Find the amount spent on fuel if the total car expenses for the year were $4200.

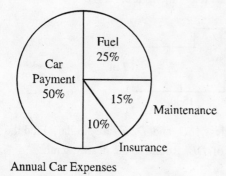

Annual Car Expenses

30. The double-bar graph shows the number of video games sold by a wholesale distributor during the last 4 months of 2000 and 2001. In which month in 2001 were the sales the lowest?

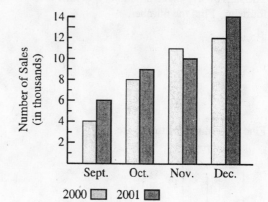

31. Convert 70 oz to pounds.

32. Convert 40 c to quarts.

Name: _____

33. A baby weighs 6 lb 10 oz at birth and weighs 9 lb 2 oz 1 month later. How much weight did the baby gain in the first month?

34. How many 8-inch bricks will be needed for 1 row of a 6-foot brick wall?

35. Convert 2892 m to kilometers.

36. Convert 2.76 L to milliliters.

37. Each student in a chemistry lab uses 250 ml of acid for an experiment. If there are 20 students in the class, how many liters of acid are used?

38. Place the correct symbol, < or >, between the two numbers.
$$5 \qquad -20$$

39. Add: $-\dfrac{2}{7}+\dfrac{1}{2}$

40. Subtract: $-2-(-7)$

41. Find the product of -0.02 and 32.

42. Simplify: $3-6\cdot(-2)+(2-6)$

43. Evaluate $2ab^2+b$ when $a=3$ and $b=-2$.

44. Solve: $y-15=-10$

45. Solve: $5x-12=18$

46. Solve: $4(x-5)-4=-4$

47. The sum of five times a number and nine is fourteen. Find the number.

48. Find the area of the figure.

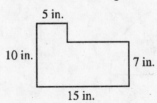

49. Find the volume of the figure.

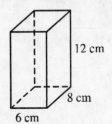

50. Triangles ABC and DEF are similar. Find the length of DE. Round to the nearest tenth.

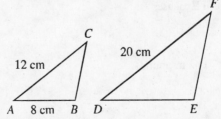

Form C Tests

Free Response

Chapter 1 Test Form C

Name: _____

Date: _____

1. Place the correct symbol, < or >, between the two numbers:

    98   201

2. Write 512,013 in words.

3. Write ten thousand eight hundred ten in standard form.

4. Write 30,290 in expanded form.

5. Round 12,985 to the nearest hundred.

6. Add: 5,617
        + 81,282

7. What is 531,274 plus 60,988 ?

8. William Garfield has a monthly budget of $180 for food, $85 for car expenses, and $80 for entertainment. Find the total amount budgeted for the three items each month.

9. Find the difference between 8631 and 3411.

10. Subtract: 35,021
            − 9,086

11. You had a balance of $1109 in your checking account. You then wrote checks in the amounts of $315 for rent, $112 for insurance, and $87 for utilities. What is your new checking account balance?

12. Find the product of 642 and 9.

13. Multiply: 3049
            × 506

14. A machinist earns $12 per hour. Find the machinist's total pay for a 40-hour work week.

Name: _____

15. Find the quotient of 2058 and 7 .

16. Divide: $9\overline{)20,796}$

17. Divide: $309\overline{)4207}$

18. A computer can store 11,520,000 pieces of information on 8 disks. How many pieces of information can be stored on 1 disk?

19. Write $2\cdot2\cdot2\cdot3\cdot3\cdot5\cdot5$ in exponential notation.

20. Simplify: $4\cdot2^3\cdot7^2$

21. Simplify: $3+2\cdot(12-2)\div4$

22. Simplify: $3\cdot(6-2)+10\div5$

23. Find all the factors of 32 .

24. Find the prime factorization of 105 .

25. Find the prime factorization of 64 .

Name: _____

Date: _____

1. Find the LCM of 14 and 49.

2. Find the GCF of 21 and 35.

3. Express the shaded portion of the circles as an improper fraction.

4. Write $\dfrac{9}{2}$ as a mixed number.

5. Write $7\dfrac{4}{5}$ as an improper fraction.

6. What number must be placed in the numerator so that the following fractions are equivalent?

$$\dfrac{1}{6} = \dfrac{}{48}$$

7. Write $\dfrac{88}{120}$ in simplest form.

8. Add: $\dfrac{7}{8} + \dfrac{5}{8}$

9. Add: $\begin{array}{r} \dfrac{1}{8} \\ + \dfrac{5}{6} \\ \hline \end{array}$

10. Find the total of $3\dfrac{3}{8}$ more than $6\dfrac{5}{12}$.

11. A welder works $1\dfrac{3}{4}$ hours of overtime on Friday, $6\dfrac{3}{4}$ hours on Saturday, and $2\dfrac{1}{2}$ hours on Sunday. How many hours of overtime the welder work in this 3-day period?

12. Subtract: $\dfrac{29}{32} - \dfrac{17}{32}$

13. Find $\dfrac{7}{8}$ decreased by $\dfrac{2}{5}$.

14. Subtract: $\begin{array}{r} 17\dfrac{9}{20} \\ -\ 5\dfrac{17}{25} \\ \hline \end{array}$

15. Marise Carr bought an oil company stock for 83\frac{5}{8}$

per share. The price of the stock lost 16\frac{7}{8}$ during

a 6-month period. Find the price of the stock at the
end of the 6 months.

16. Multiply: $\frac{7}{8} \times \frac{36}{49}$

17. What is $2\frac{3}{5}$ multiplied by $1\frac{5}{12}$?

18. A compact car gets 34 miles on each gallon of
gasoline. How many miles can the car travel on
$12\frac{1}{2}$ gallons of gasoline?

19. Divide: $\frac{16}{27} \div \frac{28}{81}$

20. Find the quotient of $5\frac{3}{4}$ and $2\frac{1}{2}$.

21. Yvette purchased a $2\frac{1}{4}$-carat diamond for $2160.
What was the cost per carat for the stone she
purchased?

22. Place the correct symbol, $<$ or $>$, between the two
numbers: $\frac{17}{24}$ $\frac{23}{32}$

23. Simplify: $25 \cdot \left(\frac{3}{5}\right)^3 \left(\frac{1}{3}\right)^2$

24. Simplify: $\frac{2}{3} + \frac{5}{12} \cdot \frac{3}{10}$

25. Simplify: $\frac{7}{9} - \left(\frac{3}{10}\right)\left(\frac{4}{9}\right) \div \frac{1}{3}$

Chapter 3 Test Form C

Name: _____
Date: _____

1. Write 129.04 in words.

2. Write in standard form: seven and two hundred five ten-thousandths.

3. Round 47.28351 to the nearest thousandth.

4. Round 3792.6974 to the nearest hundredth.

5. Add:
$$\begin{array}{r} 42.97 \\ 162.9 \\ 12.876 \\ +1.093 \end{array}$$

6. Find the sum of 716.23 , 4.913 , and 1200.19 .

7. You have $692.46 in your checking account. You make deposits of $41.30, $122.79, and $98.42. Find the amount in your checking account after making the deposits.

8. Subtract:
$$\begin{array}{r} 20.092 \\ -17.9263 \end{array}$$

9. Find 25.367 less than 108.44 .

10. An electrician earns $3129.60. Deductions from the check are $630.24 for federal tax, $180.92 for state tax, and $43.12 for insurance. Find the electrician's take-home pay.

11. Multiply:
$$\begin{array}{r} 6.21 \\ \times 0.032 \end{array}$$

12. Find the product of 0.93 and 0.027 .

13. A car travels 32.3 miles on each gallon of gas. How far does a car travel on 11.8 gallons of gas? Round to the nearest tenth of a mile.

14. Find 2.192 divided by 0.004 .

15. Divide. Round to the nearest thousandth.

$$34\overline{)5.072}$$

16. You work 40 hours and receive $302. Find your hourly rate of pay.

17. Convert $\frac{7}{18}$ to a decimal. Round to the nearest thousandth.

18. Convert 0.225 to a fraction.

19. Place the correct symbol, < or >, between the two numbers: 0.017   0.17

20. Place the correct symbol, < or >, between the two numbers: $\frac{5}{8}$ 0.6255

Name: _____
Date: _____

1. Divide. Express your answer in remainder form.

   $16\overline{)3476}$

2. Simplify: $3^2 \cdot 7^2$

3. Simplify: $8^2 - 25 + (9 - 4)$

4. Find the LCM of 24 and 40.

5. Write $\dfrac{37}{6}$ as a mixed number.

6. Write $6\dfrac{5}{9}$ as an improper fraction.

7. Find the numerator for an equivalent fraction with the given denominator: $\dfrac{7}{16} = \dfrac{}{96}$

8. Add: $\dfrac{2}{3} + \dfrac{3}{4} + \dfrac{1}{18}$

9. What is $9\dfrac{2}{7}$ increased by $2\dfrac{3}{5}$?

10. Subtract: $5\dfrac{1}{8} - 2\dfrac{1}{3}$

11. Multiply: $\dfrac{3}{35} \times \dfrac{14}{15}$

12. Find the product of $4\dfrac{2}{3}$ and 15.

13. Divide: $\dfrac{7}{9} \div \dfrac{2}{3}$

14. What is $4\dfrac{4}{9}$ divided by $\dfrac{5}{18}$?

15. Simplify: $\left(\dfrac{3}{4}\right)^3 \left(\dfrac{2}{3}\right)^5$

16. Simplify: $\dfrac{3}{7} - \dfrac{1}{2} \cdot \dfrac{4}{7} + \dfrac{3}{4}$

17. Write 58.023 in words.

18. Add: 3.659
            27.08
         + 196.2
         _____

Chapters 1-3 Test C (*continued*)

Name: _____

19. What is the difference between 207.35 and 48.096 ?

20. Multiply: 2.702
 $\times$ 0.58

21. Divide. Round to the nearest thousandth.

$1.26\overline{)30.128}$

22. Convert $\frac{4}{13}$ to a decimal.
Round to the nearest thousandth.

23. Convert 0.015 to a fraction.

24. Place the correct symbol, < or >, between the two numbers: $\frac{15}{26}$ 0.576

25. A 3-day, 25-mile hike is planned. A hiker travels $8\frac{1}{2}$ miles the first day and $7\frac{3}{8}$ miles the second day. How many miles are left to travel on the third day?

26. A painter earns $86 for each day worked. What are the painter's earnings for working $5\frac{1}{2}$ days?

27. Mike worked $2\frac{1}{4}$ hours, $3\frac{3}{4}$ hours, $4\frac{1}{2}$ hours, and $2\frac{1}{2}$ hours overtime last week. How many hours of overtime did Mike work?

28. You received a salary of $260, a commission of $511.35, and a bonus of $310.65. Find your total income.

29. A compact car can be bought for $2875 down and payments of $189.60 each month for 48 months. Find the total cost of the car.

30. Gasoline tax is $0.18 per gallon. Find the number of gallons of gasoline sold in a month in which $3960 was collected in taxes.

Name: _____
Date: _____

1. Write the comparison 3 days to 27 days as a ratio in simplest form using a fraction, a colon (:), and the word TO.

2. Write the comparison 20 feet to 45 feet as a ratio in simplest form using a fraction, a colon (:), and the word TO.

3. Write the comparison 12 cents to 28 cents as a ratio in simplest form using a fraction, a colon (:), and the word TO.

4. Write the comparison 9 people to 36 people as a ratio in simplest form using a fraction, a colon (:), and the word TO.

5. A high school class has an enrollment of 10 freshmen, 5 sophomores, 8 juniors, and 7 seniors. Find the ratio, as a fraction in simplest form, of the number of freshmen to the total class enrollment.

6. A company spends $150,000 a month on salaries out of a total income of $750,000. Find the ratio, as a fraction in simplest form, of the amount spent on salaries to the total income for the month.

7. Write "120 miles on 9 gallons" as a rate in simplest form.

8. Write "84 ounces in 15 vials" as a rate in simplest form.

9. Write "285.6 miles on 10.5 gallons" as a unit rate.

10. Write "1000 meters in 15.2 seconds" as a unit rate. Round to the nearest tenth.

11. You own 275 shares of stock and receive a dividend of $506. Find the dividend per share.

12. 8.4 pounds of meat cost $20.16. What is the cost per pound?

13. Determine if the proportion is true or not true.
$$\frac{2}{9} = \frac{5}{18}$$

14. Determine if the proportion is true or not true.
$$\frac{5}{11} = \frac{20}{44}$$

15. Solve the proportion: $\dfrac{12}{7} = \dfrac{n}{21}$

16. Solve the proportion: $\dfrac{16}{n} = \dfrac{21}{40}$
Round to the nearest tenth.

17. A garden guide suggests spreading 50 pounds of lime on each 1500 square feet of lawn. How much lime is required for a 12,000-square foot lawn?

18. A scale on a map is 1 inch equals $2\frac{1}{2}$ miles. What is the distance between 2 towns that are 8 inches apart on the map?

19. A survey indicates that 3 out of every 8 voters are not interested enough in a local election to vote on election day. How many of the 18,400 registered voters would be expected not to vote?

20. Sales tax on a $380 purchase was $30.40. What would the sales tax be on a $270 purchase?

Chapter 5 Test Form C

Name: _____

Date: _____

1. Write 5% as a decimal.

2. Write 6.8% as a decimal.

3. Write 0.072 as a percent.

4. Write 3.6 as a percent.

5. Write $\frac{3}{5}$ as a percent.

6. Write $1\frac{5}{8}$ as a percent.

7. What is 76% of 24?

8. 0.04% of 52,000 is what number?

9. Which is larger: 115% of 8 or 3.2% of 120?

10. Which is smaller: 0.6% of 1100 or 16% of 60?

11. A customer buys a Kitchen Aid dishwasher for $480 and must pay a sales tax of 5%. What is the total cost of the dishwasher?

12. 2.3% of the electric switches tested by a quality control inspector were defective. If the inspector tested 3000 switches, how many were defective?

13. What percent of 280 is 78.4?

14. 600 is what percent of 900? Round to the nearest hundredth.

15. A student missed 18 out of 120 questions on an economics exam. What percent of the questions did the student answer correctly?

16. A person whose yearly income is $29,250 pays a state income tax of $1755. What percent of the income is the state income tax?

17. 48 is 40% of what number?

18. 369 is 180% of what number?

19. A used car was sold for $8928. This is 72% of the original cost of the car. What was the original cost of the car?

20. A college has an enrollment of 7020 students. This is 108% of last year's enrollment. What was last year's enrollment?

21. 1560 is 13% of what number?

22. What percent of 250 is 75?

23. If a state tax rate is 3.5% and a tax of $21 was paid on a purchase, what was the cost of the purchase?

24. The Szeto family paid an annual interest of $1080 on a tuition loan of $14,400. What was the yearly rate of interest on the loan?

25. It is estimated that 78% of the adult population of a city is registered to vote. If the adult population is 28,400, how many people are registered to vote?

Name: _____
Date: _____

1. Six pounds of almonds cost $22.74. Find the unit cost.

2. Find the most economical purchase: 80 tablets for $3.44, 100 tablets for $4.50, 200 tablets for $8.90, or 250 tablets for $10.50.

3. Apples cost $.89 per pound. Find the total cost of 5 pounds.

4. A new labor contract called for a 3.5% increase in pay for all employees. What is the new wage of an employee who was earning $440 per week?

5. A ticket agent's salary increased from $10.25 an hour to $11.48 per hour. What percent increase does this represent?

6. What is the selling price of a 10-speed bicycle that cost a store $280 if the store uses a markup rate of 45%?

7. A service station pays $1.15 per gallon for premium gasoline. What is the markup per gallon if the station uses a markup rate of 15%? Round to the nearest cent.

8. A ski resort employs 60% fewer people in April than in February. If the resort employs 400 people in February, how many people will be employed in April?

9. The Nasdaq index fell from 1739 to 1667 in one week. What percent decrease is this? Round to the nearest percent.

10. A Sony Camcorder that regularly sells for $950 is on sale for 30% off the regular price. What is the discount?

11. A gold ring that regularly sells for $275 is on sale for 20% off the regular price. What is the sale price?

12. A company purchases a small plane for $85,000 and finances the full amount for 3 years at a simple annual interest rate of 12.5%. Find the simple interest due on the loan.

13. An investment of $2000 pays 9% annual interest compounded monthly. What is the value of the investment after 5 years? Use the Compound Interest Table. Round to the nearest cent.

14. Northeast Mortgage Company requires a borrower to pay $4\frac{1}{2}$ points for a loan. Find the loan origination fee for a loan of $60,000.

15. A house has a mortgage of $80,000 for 20 years at an annual interest rate of 9%. Find the monthly mortgage payment. Use the Monthly Payment Table. Round to the nearest cent.

16. A plumber buys a truck for $12,400. A state license fee of $215 and a sales tax of 5% of the purchase price are required. Find the total cost of the sales tax and license fee.

17. A car loan of $5400 is financed through a credit union at an annual interest rate of 11% for 3 years. Find the monthly car payment. Use the Monthly Payment Table. Round to the nearest cent.

Name: _____

18. A nurse's hourly wage is $16.20. For working the night shift, the nurse's wage is increased by 15%. What is the nurse's hourly wage for working the night shift?

19. Tracy's checkbook balance is $2416.22. She then deposits checks of $89.15 and $1215.44 and writes a check for $2250.00. Find her current checkbook balance.

20. Balance the checkbook shown.

		RECORD ALL CHARGES OR CREDITS THAT AFFECT YOUR ACCOUNT					BALANCE	
NUMBER	DATE	DESCRIPTION OF TRANSACTION	PAYMENT/DEBIT (-)	√ T	FEE (IF ANY) (-)	DEPOSIT/CREDIT (+)	645	59
	3/2	House payment	416 30				229	29
	3/5	Oil bill	129 35				99	94
	3/5	Groceries	79 22				20	72
	3/7	Newspaper	15 40				5	32
	3/8	Deposit				692 00	697	32
	3/10	Dentist	85 00				612	32
	3/12	Car insurance	369 10				243	22
	3/16	Deposit				100 00	343	22
	3/20	Deposit				230 00	573	22

REMEMBER TO RECORD AUTOMATIC PAYMENTS/DEPOSITS ON DATE AUTHORIZED

CHECKING ACCOUNT Monthly Statement		Account Number : 924-297-8	
DATE	Transaction	Amount	Balance
	OPENING BALANCE		645.59
3/5	CHECK	416.30	229.29
3/7	CHECK	129.35	99.94
3/8	INTEREST	3.77	103.71
3/12	CHECK	15.40	88.31
3/12	DEPOSIT	692.00	780.31
3/15	CHECK	369.10	411.21
3/17	DEPOSIT	100.00	511.21
3/30	SERVICE CHARGE	7.00	504.21
3/30	CLOSING BALANCE		504.21

Do the bank statement and the checkbook balance?

Name: _____

Date: _____

1. Write the comparison 15 to 60 as a ratio in simple form using a fraction, a colon (:), and the word TO.

2. The original value of a house was $35,000. The current market price is $75,000. Find the ratio of the increase in price to the original price.

3. Write "288 miles in 12 hours" as a unit rate.

4. A student can read 2040 words in 6 minutes. What is the student's reading speed per minute?

5. Solve the proportion: $\dfrac{n}{76} = \dfrac{3}{4}$

6. A college official estimates that 2 out of 7 college graduates will attend graduate school. At this rate, how many students out of a graduating class of 3500 will attend graduate school?

7. Write 107% as a decimal.

8. Write 64% as a fraction.

9. Write $\dfrac{19}{5}$ as a percent.

10. Write 0.458 as a percent.

Name: _____

11. 25.6% of 45 is what number? Round to the nearest tenth.

12. A company produced 4500 units of its product in May. Production in June decreased by 4%. How many fewer units were produced in June?

13. What percent of 90 is 18?

14. Twenty-five thousand out of 35,000 eligible voters in a town are registered to vote. What percent of the eligible voters are registered? Round to the nearest tenth of a percent.

15. 45 is 9% of what number?

16. In an emissions test of new cars, 52 cars failed. This was 20% of the cars tested. How many cars were tested?

17. Cooking oil costs $2.39 for 26 ounces. Find the cost per ounce. Round to the nearest cent.

18. A department store uses a markup rate of 45%. What is the markup on a shirt that cost the store $24?

19. West Side Jewelers Co. is selling bracelets for 25% off the regular price. What is the sale price of a bracelet that has a regular price of $35?

20. What is the simple interest due on a loan of $83,000 at an annual interest rate of 7.8% for 2 years?

The pictograph shows the number of part-time and full-time students enrolled in the day and evening divisions at a local college. Each figure represents 200 students.

1. How many students are enrolled at the college?

2. What is the ratio of part-time evening students to full-time evening students?

3. What percent of the day students is full time? Round to the nearest tenth of a percent.

Full-time Day Students   𝕀𝕀𝕀𝕀𝕀𝕀

Part-time Day Students   𝕀𝕀𝕀𝕀

Full-time Evening Students   𝕀

Part-time Evening Students   𝕀𝕀𝕀𝕀

The circle graph shows the distribution of an employee's gross monthly income of $3200.

4. Find the employee's monthly savings.

5. What does the employee pay monthly in taxes?

6. How much does the employee deposit monthly into a retirement fund?

MONTHLY INCOME
1: 53% - Take-home Pay
2: 10% - Retirement
3: 15% - Savings
4: 22% - Taxes

The double-bar graph shows the number of cars (in thousands) sold by an automobile manufacturer during the first three months of 2000 and 2001.

7. What were the total 2000 sales for the 3 months shown?

8. What is the difference between the February 2000 sales and the February 2001 sales?

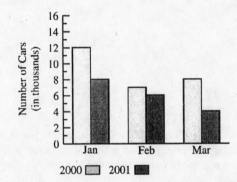

9. A survey of residents of a community asked each resident to rate the performance of their senator. The results were: 20, excellent; 45, good; 15, poor. What was the modal response?

10. In a math class, a set of exams earned the following grades: 5 A's, 7 B's, 12 C's, and 4 D's. If a single student's paper is chosen from this class, what is the probability that it received a C?

Name: _____

The double-line graph shows the weekly attendance at a professional team's football games (in thousands) during September of 2000 and 2001.

11. Find the difference between the 2000 and the 2001 attendance during the third week in September.

12. During which week was 2001 attendance greater than 2000 attendance?

13. What was the total 2000 attendance during September?

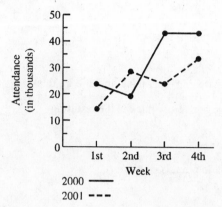
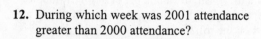

The histogram shows the test scores of 38 students on a history exam.

14. What is the ratio of the number of students who scored between 60 and 70 to the number of students who scored between 70 and 80?

15. How many students had a score of 80 or more?

16. What percent of the students had a score of less than 70? Round to the nearest tenth of a percent.

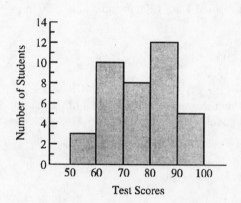

The frequency polygon shows the scores of 39 students who took a final exam in an English course.

17. Find the number of students who scored more than 70 on the exam.

18. What percent of the students scored between 70 and 80? Round to the nearest tenth of a percent.

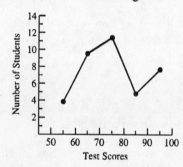

19. The numbers of points scored by a basketball player in the last seven games were 23, 18, 17, 22, 10, 19, and 27. What was the median number of points scored for these six games?

20. The scores on an English exam are shown below. Determine the first quartile of the scores.

93	87	73	85	77	90
78	64	98	63	72	84
83	75	66	92	81	67

1. Convert $2\frac{2}{3}$ yd to feet.

2. Multiply: 3 ft 4 in.

    $\times$ 5

3. Two boards that are $1\frac{3}{8}$ in. thick and $1\frac{2}{3}$ in. thick are nailed together. How thick is the resulting board?

4. You use 27 in. of ribbon off of a roll of ribbon containing 2 yd. How many inches of ribbon are left on the roll?

5. Convert 40 oz to pounds.

6. Convert $2\frac{1}{4}$ tons to pounds.

7. Find the sum of 1 ton 1200 lb and 3 tons 1500 lb.

8. Divide: $(4 \text{ tons } 400 \text{ lb}) \div 3$

9. A case of canned goods contained 24 18-ounce cans. What was the weight in pounds of the case of canned goods?

10. A large wheel of cheese weighed 7 lb 4 oz before a piece weighing 2 lb 6 oz was cut from it. Find the resulting weight of the wheel of cheese.

11. Convert 16 pt to quarts.

12. Convert 18 qt to gallons.

13. Subtract: 5 gal 1 qt − 3 gal 2 qt

14. Add: 3 qt 1 pt

    + 5 qt 1 pt

15. If a coffee mug contains 12 fl oz, how many mugs can be filled from a 6-quart container?

16. If 1 qt of paint will cover 80 sq ft, how many gallons of paint will be required to paint a room with 320 sq ft of wall space?

17. One pound of natural gas will give off 1500 Btu of energy when burned. How many foot-pounds of energy are released when 1.5 lb of natural gas are burned? (1 Btu = 778 ft·lb)

18. Find the energy required to lift a 5400-pound elevator a distance of 75 ft.

19. Convert $4\frac{1}{2}$ hp to foot-pounds per second.

    $\left(1 \text{ hp } = 550 \dfrac{\text{ft} \cdot \text{lb}}{\text{s}}\right)$

20. Find the power in foot-pounds per second needed to raise 300 lb a distance of 12 ft in 30 s.

Name: _____

Date: _____

1. Convert 23.2 km to meters.

2. Convert 432 mm to centimeters.

3. Convert 7 m 89 cm to meters.

4. Convert 2 km 35 m to kilometers.

5. A rectangular garden measures 975 cm long and 625 cm wide. What total length of fencing (in meters) is required to enclose the field?

6. A piece of wood 875 cm long is cut from a 10 m board. Find the length (in meters) of the remaining board.

7. Convert 27 mg to grams.

8. Convert 0.046 kg to grams.

9. Convert 2 kg 470 g to kilograms.

10. Convert 35 g 4 mg to grams.

11. In packing for a trip, a family wants to distribute books weighing 13.8 kg evenly among 6 boxes. What weight of books (in grams) should be placed in each box?

12. A brick weighs 985 g. Find the weight (in kilograms) of a load of 200 bricks.

13. Convert 36 ml to cubic centimeters.

14. Convert 2.05 L to milliliters.

15. Convert 5 L 294 ml to liters.

16. Convert 6 kl 50 L to kiloliters.

17. There are 48 bottles in a case of shampoo. Each bottle contains 250 ml of shampoo. How many liters of shampoo are in 1 case?

18. Gardening requires 260 Calories per hour. How many Calories do you burn up in 15 days of gardening if you garden 2 h each day?

19. Find the number of liters in 10.5 gal of gasoline. Round to the nearest hundredth. (1 L = 1.06 qt)

20. Find the weight in ounces of 415 g of cereal. Round to the nearest hundredth. (28.35 g = 1 oz)

Name: _____

Date: _____

The circle graph shows the annual expenses for a student at a university.

1. Find the ratio of the amount spent for entertainment to the amount spent for clothes.

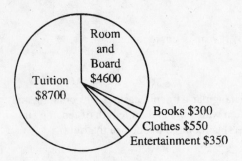

2. What fraction of the total expenditures are the costs of books?

Annual Student Expenses

The histogram shows the salary distribution of 180 recent graduates of a small college.

3. How many graduates earn between $20,000 and $25,000?

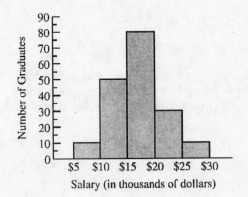

4. What percent of the total graduates earn more than $20,000? Round to the nearest tenth of a percent.

5. A salesperson's commissions during a 3-week period were $112, $152, and $122. Find the salesperson's average weekly commission. Round to the nearest cent.

6. The number of fire alarms answered by a fire house during a 4-week period were 7, 5, 10, and 6. Find the median number of alarms answered during the 4-week period.

7. Convert $4\frac{2}{3}$ yd to feet.

8. What is 12 ft 2 in. decreased by 5 ft 8 in.?

9. Convert 7 lb to ounces.

10. Add: 10 tons 1600 lb
         + 5 tons 500 lb

11. Convert 48 fl oz to cups.

12. A florist recommended that a customer add $\frac{1}{3}$ c of plant food to a floral arrangement every day. How many fluid ounces of plant food had been added at the end of 9 days?

13. Thirty-two bricks, each 8 in. long, are laid end to end to make the base for a wall. Find the length of the wall in feet.

14. Convert 7539 m to kilometers.

15. Convert 1347 g to milligrams.

16. Convert 1.34 L to milliliters.

17. Find the number of pounds in 12 kg. (1 kg = 2.2 lb)

18. Cheese costs $3.65/lb. What is the cost per kilogram? Round to the nearest cent. (1 lb = 0.454 kg)

19. How many people can be vaccinated with 5 L of vaccine if each person receives 8 cm³ of vaccine?

20. A football player weighs 120.3 kg and loses 4550 g during training camp. What is the player's weight, in kilograms, after training camp?

Chapter 10 Test Form C

Name: _____

Date: _____

1. Place the correct symbol, < or >, between the two numbers:

   $$-4 \qquad 5$$

2. Place the correct symbol, < or >, between the two numbers:

   $$0 \qquad -11$$

3. Evaluate: $-\left|-\dfrac{1}{2}\right|$

4. Add: $-21+(-34)$

5. Find the sum of $2, \ -8, \ -4,$ and 3.

6. Subtract: $9-21$

7. Subtract: $-1-(-8)-7$

8. Find the product of 60 and -8.

9. Divide: $-92 \div (-4)$

10. The temperature at 3 P.M. was $19°$ and the temperature at 11 P.M. was $-12°$. Find the difference between the temperatures.

11. The low temperature today was $-2°$. Yesterday the low temperature was $12°$. What was the average low temperature for the 2 days?

12. Add: $\dfrac{7}{12}+\left(-\dfrac{1}{3}\right)$

13. Find the sum of $-1\dfrac{2}{3}$ and $2\dfrac{1}{8}$.

14. Subtract: $-\dfrac{1}{5}-\dfrac{2}{15}$

15. Subtract: $-3\dfrac{5}{8}+\left(-4\dfrac{5}{12}\right)$

16. Multiply: $\dfrac{1}{2}\times\left(-\dfrac{2}{3}\right)\times\left(-\dfrac{6}{7}\right)$

17. Divide: $12 \div \left(-\dfrac{1}{3}\right)$

18. What is the difference between -2.8 and -0.65?

19. Subtract: $9.37-15.56$

20. Find the product of -4.01 and -0.03.

21. Divide: $3.96 \div (-0.022)$

22. Simplify: $(-2)^2 -2(6-4)+2$

23. Simplify: $8-4(-2)^2 -(2-7)$

24. Write 0.000107 in scientific notation.

25. The boiling point of chlorine is $-34.6°C$. The melting point of chlorine is $-100.98°C$. What is the difference between the boiling point and the melting point of chlorine?

1. Evaluate $a^2 - b^2 - c^2$ when $a = -2$, $b = 3$, and $c = -4$.

2. Evaluate $\dfrac{b^2 - a}{2ab}$ when $a = 3$ and $b = -2$.

3. Simplify: $3x - 5y + 4x - 8y$

4. Simplify: $4n - 2(n-1) + 5$

5. Is 2 a solution of $2x(x+3) = x + 12$?

6. Solve: $9 + y = -2$

7. Solve: $-9x = 81$

8. Solve: $\dfrac{3}{4}x = 18$

9. Solve: $-3x - 7 = 11$

10. Solve: $\dfrac{x}{5} - 3 = -6$

11. A loan of $6768 is to be paid in 36 equal monthly installments. Find the monthly payment. Use the formula $L = P \cdot N$, where L is the loan amount, P is the monthly payment, and N is the number of months.

12. The monthly tax paid by a wage earner is $430. The wage earner's monthly income is $1750, and the base monthly tax is $80. Find the wage earner's income tax rate. Use the formula $T = I \cdot R + B$, where T is the monthly tax, I is the monthly income, R is the income tax rate, and B is the base monthly tax.

13. Solve: $5 = 18 - 3x$

14. Solve: $8x - 6 = 5x + 9$

15. Solve: $2x - 3(x-2) = -4$

16. Translate "z divided by the total of three and z" into a mathematical expression.

17. Translate "the quotient of twice a number and two less than the number" into a mathematical expression.

18. Translate "four times a number is negative two hundred" into an equation and solve.

19. Eight decreased by the quotient of a number and three is five. Find the number.

20. Kim Zheng is now making $48,500 a year. This is two times the amount Kim was making 5 years ago. Find Kim's salary 5 years ago.

Name: _____
Date: _____

1. Find the complement of a 76° angle.

2. Two angles of a triangle are 30° and 70°. Find the measure of the third angle of the triangle.

3. In the figure, $L_1 \parallel L_2$. $\angle x = 55°$. Find $\angle y$.

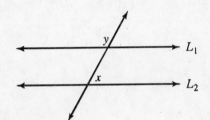

4. In the figure $L_1 \parallel L_2$. $\angle x = 110°$. Find $\angle a + \angle b$.

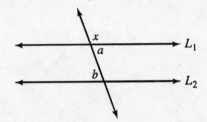

5. Find the perimeter of a square in which the sides are equal to 1 ft 4 in.

6. Find the perimeter of the composite figure.

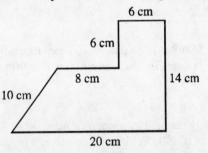

7. Find the number of feet of framing needed to frame a picture that is $3\frac{1}{3}$ by $2\frac{1}{2}$ ft.

8. Find the area of a square with a side of 3.1 m.

9. Find the area of the composite figure. Use 3.14 for π.

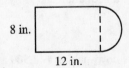

10. A carpet is to be placed in one room and hallway, as shown in the diagram. At $18.50 per square meter, how much will it cost to carpet the area?

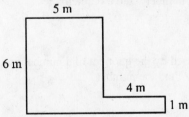

Chapter 12 Test Form C (*continued*)

Name: _____

11. Two rooms, one 12 ft by 16 ft and the other 18 ft by 24 ft, are to be carpeted. Find the total number of square yards of carpet needed. Round to the nearest tenth. ($9 \text{ ft}^2 = 1 \text{ yd}^2$)

12. Find the volume of a sphere with a 6-centimeter radius. Use 3.14 for π.

13. Find the volume of the solid. The diameter of the cylinder is 2 ft. Use 3.14 for π.

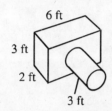

14. An oil storage tank that is in the form of a cylinder is 15 ft high and has a 30-foot diameter. Find the volume of the storage tank. Use 3.14 for π.

15. Find the square root of 130. Round to the nearest thousandth.

16. Find the unknown side of the triangle. Round to the nearest tenth.

17. A car is driven 40 mi east and then 30 mi south. How far is the car from the starting point?

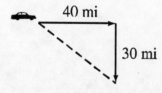

18. Triangles *ABC* and *DEF* are similar. Find side *BC*.

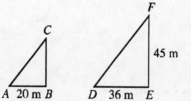

19. A flagpole 4 ft high casts a shadow of 3 ft. How high is a flagpole that casts a shadow of 16 ft? Round to the nearest tenth.

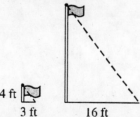

20. In the figure, triangles *ABC* and *DEF* are congruent. Find the measure of $\angle F$.

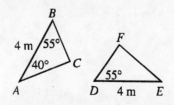

Chapters 10-12 Cumulative Test C

Name: _____
Date: _____

1. Find the sum of -8, 14, and -20.

2. Add: $-\dfrac{3}{8}+\left(-\dfrac{1}{2}\right)$

3. Subtract: $-3-4-(-9)$

4. What is 4.27 decreased by -3.2?

5. Find the product of -40 and -15.

6. Multiply: $\dfrac{3}{5}\times\left(-\dfrac{10}{13}\right)$

7. Find the quotient of -16.8 and -0.4.

8. Simplify: $6-3\times2+(-5)(4)$

9. Simplify: $6\div3\times2-4^2$

10. Evaluate ab^2-c^2 when $a=-1$, $b=3$, and $c=-2$.

11. Simplify: $\dfrac{4}{5}w=20$

12. Simplify: $9y^2-3-3y^2$

13. Solve: $-3x+15=0$

14. Solve: $\dfrac{2}{3}+y=-\dfrac{1}{6}$

Name: _____

15. Solve: $4 - 3(x - 2) = 4(x - 1)$

16. Nine more than a number is one. Find the number.

17. During a sale, a shirt is discounted $12. This is 25% off of its regular price. Find its regular price.

18. The value of a house is $88,000. This is five-fourths of its value last year. Find its value last year.

19. Two angles of a triangle measure 17° and 31°. Find the measure of the third angle.

20. In the figure, $L_1 \parallel L_2$, $\angle x = 73°$. Find $\angle y$.

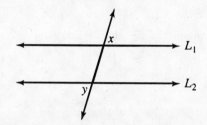

21. Find the perimeter of a square whose sides measure $2\frac{1}{8}$ in.

22. Find the area of the figure.

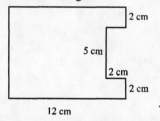

23. Find the volume of a sphere whose radius is 4.2 m. Use 3.14 for π. Round to the nearest hundredth.

24. In the figure, triangles *ABC* and *DEF* are similar. Find the perimeter of triangle *DEF*.

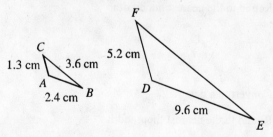

25. Find the unknown leg of the right triangle. Round to the nearest tenth.

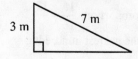

Name: _____

Date: _____

1. Subtract: $4008 - 579$

2. Find 38,997 divided by 619.

3. Simplify: $8 - 2 \times 2 + 3^2 - 5$

4. A car costs \$14,328. A down payment of \$2000 is required. The balance is to be paid in 36 equal payments. What is the monthly car payment? Round to the nearest cent.

5. Add: $\dfrac{2}{5} + 2\dfrac{1}{4}$

6. Subtract: $10\dfrac{1}{3} - 4\dfrac{5}{9}$

7. Find the product of $2\dfrac{5}{7}$ and $3\dfrac{1}{2}$.

8. Divide: $2\dfrac{1}{3} \div 1\dfrac{1}{2}$

9. Simplify: $\left(\dfrac{2}{3}\right)^2 + \dfrac{1}{2} \times \dfrac{1}{3} - \dfrac{2}{9}$

10. Crystal correctly answered $\frac{2}{3}$ of her history test questions. If there were 60 questions on the test, how many did she answer correctly?

11. Find 24.8 minus 1.93.

12. Multiply: 8.15×0.7

13. Divide: $6 \div 0.095$
    Round to the nearest hundredth.

14. Convert 0.6 to a fraction.

15. Convert to a decimal: $\dfrac{8}{17}$
    Round to the nearest thousandth.

16. Write the comparison "\$42 to \$35" as a ratio in simplest form using a fraction.

17. Write "132 tiles for each 11 ft" as a unit rate.

18. Solve the proportion: $\dfrac{15}{16} = \dfrac{12}{n}$
    Round to the nearest hundredth.

19. The sales tax on a $550 purchase is $33. Find the sales tax on a $98 purchase.

20. Write $\dfrac{19}{20}$ as a percent.

21. What is 34.6% of 70?

22. 58 is what percent of 290?

23. 37 is 25% of what number?

24. 84% of the 2500 students at a college voted in the college election. How many students voted in the election?

25. Find the unit cost of 12 lb for $10.68.

26. Which is the more economical purchase: 28 oz of juice for $0.65 or 24 oz of juice for $0.57?

27. A furniture store is selling a sofa for 20% off the regular price. What is the sale price if the sofa regularly sells for $875?

28. A toy store borrowed $85,000 at an annual interest rate of 10.5% for 3 months. Find the simple interest due on the loan.

29. The circle graph shows the distribution of an employee's monthly income of $1875. Find the employee's monthly federal tax.

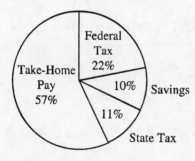

Distribution of Gross Monthly
Income Totaling $1875

30. There are 35 store merchants in the city's square. Their yearly profits are recorded in the histogram. How many merchants make a profit of between $50,000 and $60,000 per year?

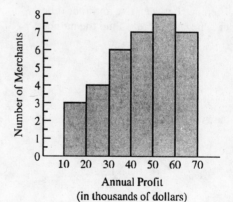

31. Convert 52 in. to feet.

32. Convert $2\dfrac{1}{2}$ gal to cups.

33. If $1\frac{1}{2}$ c of liquid fertilizer are to be mixed with 10 gal of water, how many quarts will be mixed with 80 gal of water?

34. A piece of wire 1 yd 2 ft in length is cut from a 9-yard roll. How much wire remains on the roll?

35. Convert 256 mm to centimeters.

36. Convert 8 m to centimeters.

37. Two pieces of wire are cut from a 20-meter roll. The two pieces measure 825 cm and 650 cm. How much wire remains on the roll?

38. Place the correct symbol, < or >, between the two numbers.

          -19 4

39. Add: $-\frac{1}{3}+\left(-\frac{3}{4}\right)$

40. Find the difference between 12 and -7.

41. Multiply: $-2.4(-3.1)$

42. Simplify: $(-1)^2 - 3 + (4 - 7)$

43. Evaluate $a^2 - b^2$ when $a = 2$ and $b = -3$.

44. Solve: $y - 18 = -7$

45. Solve: $6x - 17 = 19$

46. Solve: $3x + 4(x + 1) = 2(x + 7)$

47. The difference between five and four times a number is negative three. Find the number.

48. Find the area of the figure. Use 3.14 for π.

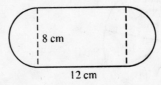

    8 cm

    12 cm

49. Find the volume of the figure.

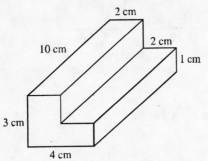

    2 cm
    2 cm
    10 cm
    1 cm
    3 cm
    4 cm

50. Triangles ABC and DEF are similar. Find the length of DF.

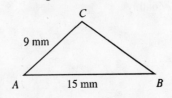

    C
    9 mm
    A 15 mm B
    F
    D 6 mm E

Form D Tests

Free Response

1. Place the correct symbol, < or >, between the two numbers:

   6   12

2. Write 110,347 in words.

3. Write twenty two thousand twenty two in standard form.

4. Write 67,020 in expanded form.

5. Round 325,697 to the nearest hundred.

6. Find the sum of 47,250 and 193,750.

7. Add: 21,375
             19,031
           + 2,996

8. A local high school has an enrollment of 416 freshmen, 367 sophomores, 337 juniors, and 354 seniors. Find the total enrollment of the high school.

9. Subtract: 7395
             − 2164

10. Find the difference between 12,435 and 9677.

11. After a trip of 697 miles, the odometer of your car reads 21,097 miles. What was the odometer reading at the beginning of your trip?

12. Find the product of 807 and 6.

13. Multiply: 276
             × 39

14. An investor receives a check for $419 each month. How much will the investor receive over a 12-month period?

15. Find the quotient of 3360 and 8 .

16. Divide: $4\overline{)5003}$

17. Divide: $57\overline{)23,976}$

18. A business owner makes a down payment of $1750 on a computer server costing $3850. The remaining balance is to be paid in 12 monthly payments. What is the monthly payment?

19. Write $2 \cdot 2 \cdot 7 \cdot 7 \cdot 7 \cdot 9$ in exponential notation.

20. Simplify: $3^3 \cdot 4^2$

21. Simplify: $2^4 \div 4 - 2 \cdot (3 - 1)$

22. Simplify: $3^2 - 3 \cdot (5 - 3) \div 2$

23. Find all the factors of 92 .

24. Find the prime factorization of 88 .

25. Find the prime factorization of 90 .

1. Find the LCM of 18 and 30.

2. Find the GCF of 36 and 45.

3. Express the shaded portion of the circles as a mixed number.

4. Write $\frac{13}{3}$ as a mixed number.

5. Write $4\frac{5}{8}$ as an improper fraction.

6. What number must be placed in the numerator so that the following fractions are equivalent?

$$\frac{7}{9} = \frac{}{72}$$

7. Write $\frac{24}{64}$ in simplest form.

8. Add: $\frac{5}{16} + \frac{3}{16}$

9. Find the total of $\frac{3}{8}$ and $\frac{7}{24}$.

10. Add: $1\frac{5}{8}$
$+ 4\frac{7}{12}$

11. Jon worked 4, $2\frac{1}{2}$, $3\frac{3}{4}$, and $1\frac{3}{4}$ hours during 4 days last week. Find the total hours he worked during the 4-day period.

12. Subtract: $\frac{39}{40} - \frac{27}{40}$

13. What is $\frac{19}{24}$ minus $\frac{11}{16}$?

14. Subtract: $17\frac{4}{9}$
$-11\frac{11}{12}$

15. A patient with high blood pressure is told to lose 25 pounds in the next three months. He loses $8\frac{3}{4}$ pounds the first month and $7\frac{1}{2}$ pounds the second month. How much weight does he need to lose during the third month to meet his goal?

16. Multiply: $\dfrac{16}{25} \times \dfrac{15}{56}$

17. What is $2\frac{3}{8}$ multiplied by $7\frac{5}{9}$?

18. A sales executive has completed $\dfrac{3}{5}$ of an 875-mile business trip. How many miles of the trip remain?

19. Divide: $\dfrac{5}{8} \div 1\frac{3}{5}$

20. What is $6\frac{2}{3}$ divided by $1\frac{2}{3}$?

21. Four hundred fifty people attended a concert at the music center. The center was $\dfrac{3}{4}$ full. What is the capacity of the music center?

22. Place the correct symbol, $<$ or $>$, between the two numbers: $\dfrac{11}{30}$ ___ $\dfrac{7}{12}$

23. Simplify: $\left(\dfrac{2}{3}\right)^6 \left(\dfrac{81}{4}\right)^2$

24. Simplify: $\dfrac{3}{4} + \dfrac{1}{5} \div \dfrac{4}{5}$

25. Simplify: $\left(\dfrac{11}{12} - \dfrac{2}{3}\right) + \dfrac{15}{16} \div \left(\dfrac{1}{2}\right)^3$

Name: _____

Date: _____

1. Write 4.00632 in words.

2. Write twelve and six hundredths in standard form.

3. Round 12.138 to the nearest hundredth.

4. Round 43.0973 to the nearest tenth.

5. Add: 69.94
          9.807
        994.673
        + 95.06

6. Find the total of 34.92 , 6.817 , and 152.9 .

7. Kara Brady bought a math textbook for $39.43, a history text for $43.95, a biology text for $35.61, and an English workbook for $19.45. Find the total cost of the four books.

8. Subtract: 121.63
            − 93.72

9. What is 84.5903 decreased by 9.953 ?

10. Your lunch costs $4.87. An additional cost of $0.29 is added for tax. Find the change you receive from a $10 bill.

11. Multiply: 0.086
             × 0.07

12. Find the product of 16.5 and 0.24 .

13. A motorist averages 56.4 miles per hour while traveling 3.5 hours. Find the total distance traveled during the 3.5 hours.

14. Find the quotient of 0.036 and 12 .

15. Divide. Round to the nearest thousandth.

    $0.076 \overline{)0.02904}$

16. A $563.68 Sony stereo system is bought for a down payment of $100 and 18 equal monthly payments. Find the amount of each monthly payment.

17. Convert $\dfrac{9}{40}$ to a decimal.

18. Convert $0.16\dfrac{2}{3}$ to a fraction.

19. Place the correct symbol, < or >, between the two numbers: 0.72   0.702

20. Place the correct symbol, < or >, between the two numbers: $\dfrac{11}{24}$ 0.45

Name: _____
Date: _____

1. Divide. Express your answer in remainder form.

   $19\overline{)4966}$

2. Simplify: $3 \cdot 4^3 \cdot 5^2$

3. Simplify: $5^2 - 3 \cdot (6 \div 2)$

4. Find the LCM of 28 and 20.

5. Write $\dfrac{52}{7}$ as a mixed number.

6. Write $9\dfrac{2}{7}$ as an improper fraction.

7. Find the numerator for an equivalent fraction with the given denominator: $\dfrac{4}{5} = \dfrac{}{85}$

8. Add: $\dfrac{11}{12} + \dfrac{2}{9} + \dfrac{1}{4}$

9. What is $4\dfrac{1}{7}$ increased by $5\dfrac{9}{10}$?

10. Subtract: $7 - 2\dfrac{5}{8}$

11. Multiply: $\dfrac{7}{9} \times \dfrac{15}{28}$

12. Find the product of 8 and $3\dfrac{3}{4}$.

13. Divide: $\dfrac{11}{12} \div \dfrac{3}{4}$

14. What is $2\dfrac{7}{10}$ divided by $1\dfrac{4}{5}$?

15. Simplify: $\dfrac{1}{2} \cdot \left(\dfrac{3}{5}\right)^2 \cdot \left(\dfrac{2}{9}\right)^2$

16. Simplify: $\dfrac{3}{8} + \dfrac{1}{2} \cdot \dfrac{4}{7}$

17. Write 67.013 in words.

18. Add:
    $\begin{array}{r} 6.059 \\ 29.18 \\ +\,387.2 \\ \hline \end{array}$

19. What is the difference between 10.2 and 7.93 ?

20. Multiply:
$$\begin{array}{r} 6.059 \\ \times\ 0.08 \\ \hline \end{array}$$

21. Divide. Round to the nearest thousandth.

$$0.76\overline{)0.4835}$$

22. Convert $\dfrac{5}{38}$ to a decimal. Round to the nearest thousandth.

23. Convert 0.12 to a fraction.

24. Place the correct symbol, $<$ or $>$, between the two numbers:

$$0.633 \qquad \frac{19}{30}$$

25. You bought a stock at $\$53\dfrac{3}{8}$ per share. Monthly gains for the first 3 months of ownership were $\$\dfrac{3}{4}$, $\$2\dfrac{1}{8}$, and $\$4\dfrac{1}{2}$ per share. Find the value of the stock at the end of the 3 months.

26. A student worked $\dfrac{1}{6}$ of a math assignment incorrectly. How many problems were worked correctly out of the 132 problems assigned?

27. You had a checking account balance of $915.34. You then wrote checks for $131.25, $71.74, and $15.78. Find the new balance in the checking account.

28. A used Volvo can be bought for $1250 down and $168.30 each month for 48 months. Find the total cost of the car.

29. You pay $1086.72 per year in property taxes. You pay the taxes in 12 equal monthly payments. Find the amount of each monthly payment.

30. A state income tax on your business is $900 plus 0.07 times your profit. You made a profit of $72,680 last year. Find the amount of the state income tax you paid.

1. Write the comparison 15 meters to 50 meters as a ratio in simplest form using a fraction, a colon (:), and the word TO.

2. Write the comparison $12 to $36 as a ratio in simplest form using a fraction, a colon (:), and the word TO.

3. Write the comparison 18 ounces to 38 ounces as a ratio in simplest form using a fraction, a colon (:), and the word TO.

4. Write the comparison 80 weeks to 50 weeks as a ratio in simplest form using a fraction, a colon (:), and the word TO.

5. The Rawding family has an income of $4200 per month. The family invests $280 each month in a mutual fund. Find the ratio, as a fraction in simplest form, of the monthly investment in the mutual fund to the total monthly income.

6. A geometry class has an enrollment of 12 freshmen and 22 sophomores. Find the ratio, as a fraction in simplest form, of the number of juniors to the total number of students in the geometry class.

7. Write "$50 earned in 6 hours" as a rate in simplest form.

8. Write "735 trees planted on 7 acres" as a rate in simplest form.

9. Write "232.6 miles in 4.2 hours" as a unit rate. Round to the nearest tenth.

10. Write "1575 trees planted on 15 acres" as a unit rate.

11. David purchased 250 shares of stock for $10,640. What is the cost per share?

12. The cost to produce 50 Casio calculators is $1800. What is the cost to produce one calculator?

13. Determine if the proportion is true or not true.
$$\frac{7}{5} = \frac{35}{25}$$

14. Determine if the proportion is true or not true.
$$\frac{4}{9} = \frac{16}{33}$$

15. Solve the proportion: $\dfrac{5}{18} = \dfrac{16}{n}$

16. Solve the proportion: $\dfrac{n}{13} = \dfrac{74}{52}$
    Round to the nearest tenth.

17. The dosage for a medication is $\frac{1}{8}$ ounce for every 20 pounds of body weight. What would the dosage be for a 144-pound person?

18. If the faculty-student ratio at a local college is 1 to 15, how many faculty would the college have if the student enrollment is 4200?

19. An investor who owns 75 shares of stock receives dividends of $187.50. What dividend would an investor receive who owns 90 shares of the same stock?

20. A mail-order company estimates that it makes errors on 5 out of every 150 orders it fills. How many errors would be expected in a month when 14,400 orders were filled?

Name: _____

Date: _____

1. Write 4.25% as a decimal.

2. Write $16\frac{2}{3}$% as a fraction.

3. Write 0.092 as a percent.

4. Write 2.75 as a percent.

5. Write $\frac{3}{8}$ as a percent.

6. Write $1\frac{7}{5}$ as a percent.

7. What is 52% of 550?

8. 0.36% of 275 is what number?

9. Which is larger: 0.6% of 8 or 0.4% of 10?

10. Which is smaller: 28% of 2000 or 32% of 1800?

11. A candidate received 55.8% of the 320,000 votes cast in an election. How many votes did this candidate receive?

12. A car dealer offers a 6% rebate on a new car costing $15,200. What is the amount of the rebate?

13. What percent of 625 is 75?

14. 300 is what percent of 900%? Round to the nearest hundredth.

15. A survey showed that 700 out of 1600 people interviewed had attended college. What percent of the people interviewed had attended college?

16. A house that was bought in 1972 for $34,000 is valued now at $95,200. What percent of the 1972 price is the present value?

17. 245 is 35% of what number?

18. 164 is 250% of what number?

19. A receptionist makes $11.73 an hour. This is 115% of last year's hourly wage. What was last year's hourly wage?

20. A runner finished a mile in 4.14 minutes. This was 90% of the runner's previous race time. What was the runner's previous race time?

21. 44.8 is 12.8% of what number?

22. What percent of 10 is 18?

23. Christopher Cooper had 40 questions correct on a test. This was 80% of the questions on the test. How many questions were on the test?

24. The monthly interest charge on a credit card balance of $900 is $14.40. What is the monthly rate of interest?

25. A makeup artist has 21% of her monthly paycheck withheld for income tax. How much income tax is withheld from a paycheck of $2280?

1. Fifteen pounds of potatoes cost $4.35. Find the unit cost.

2. Find the most economical purchase: 25 feet for $29.75, 30 feet for $36.30, 40 feet for $46.00, or 50 feet for $58.50.

3. Photocopying costs $.07 per page. Find the total cost of photocopying 400 pages.

4. The average price of gasoline rose from $1.20 to $1.26 in 2 months. What was the percent increase in the price of gasoline?

5. Bionex stock that sold for $43.50 per share increased in price by 2% in a day. What is the new price of the stock?

6. The owner of Russell Home Appliances uses a markup rate of 38% on all air conditioners. What is the markup on an air conditioner that cost the store $290?

7. Cushman Office Supply Co. uses a 42% markup rate. Find the selling price of a filing cabinet that was purchased by the store for $120.

8. A summer resort employs 800 people during the summer season. At the end of the summer season, the resort reduces the number of employees by 80%. What is the decrease in the number of employees?

9. It is estimated that the value of a new car is reduced by 25% after 1 year of ownership. Using this estimate, how much value does a $16,400 new car have after 1 year?

10. A jacket that regularly sells for $140 is on sale for 15% off the regular price. What is the discount?

11. A dress that regularly sells for $112 is on sale for 33% off the regular price. What is the sale price?

12. A credit card company charges a customer 1.75% per month on the customer's unpaid balance. Find the interest owed to the credit card company when the customer's unpaid balance for the month is $2600.

13. A money market fund pays 8% annual interest compounded monthly. What is the value of $10,000 after 20 years in this money market fund? Use the Compound Interest Table.

14. A doctor makes a down payment of 18% of the $180,000 purchase price of an office building. How much is the down payment?

15. A bicycle shop is purchased, and a 25-year mortgage of $95,000 is obtained. The bank charges an annual interest rate of 13%. Find the monthly mortgage payment. Use the Monthly Payment Table. Round to the nearest cent.

16. A license fee of 1.8% of the purchase price of a truck is to be paid on a truck costing $14,950. How much is the license fee for the truck?

17. Eric spent $1364 on gas, oil, and car insurance during a period when his car was driven 12,400 miles. Find the cost per mile for gas, oil, and car insurance.

18. A computer operator's hourly wage is $12.60. For working the evening shift, the operator's wage is increased by 15%. What is the computer operator's hourly wage for working the evening shift?

19. Maria has a checking account balance of $1116.40 before making a deposit of $1560.40. She then writes checks for $892.60, $309.12, and $79.60. Find the current checkbook balance.

20. Balance the checkbook shown.

		RECORD ALL CHARGES OR CREDITS THAT AFFECT YOUR ACCOUNT							
NUMBER	DATE	DESCRIPTION OF TRANSACTION	PAYMENT/DEBIT (-)		√T	FEE (IF ANY) (-)	DEPOSIT/CREDIT (+)	BALANCE	
								1092	07
	2/1	Car payment	159	00				933	07
	2/1	Rent	550	00				383	07
	2/12	Credit card	113	82				269	25
	2/15	Clothing	16	84				252	41
	2/19	Groceries	21	90				230	51
	2/20	Deposit					315 00	545	51
	2/26	Hardware store	72	40				473	11
	2/27	Deposit					475 00	948	11

REMEMBER TO RECORD AUTOMATIC PAYMENTS/DEPOSITS ON DATE AUTHORIZED

CHECKING ACCOUNT Monthly Statement		Account Number : 924-297-8	
DATE	Transaction	Amount	Balance
2/1	OPENING BALANCE		1092.07
2/3	CHECK	550.00	542.07
2/4	CHECK	159.00	383.07
2/15	CHECK	113.82	269.25
2/15	INTEREST	12.32	281.57
2/21	DEPOSIT	315.00	596.57
2/28	DEPOSIT	475.00	1071.57
2/28	SERVICE CHARGE	10.00	1061.57
2/28	CLOSING BALANCE		1061.57

Do the bank statement and the checkbook balance?

Name: _____

Date: _____

1. Write the comparison 27 minutes to 45 minutes as a ratio in simplest form using a fraction, a colon (:), and the word TO.

2. A child measured 36 inches tall last year, and this year the child measures 42 inches. Find the ratio of the child's growth to last year's height.

3. Write "$28 for 17.5 feet of lumber" as a unit rate.

4. A car traveled 350.4 miles on 12 gallons of gasoline. Find the car's gas mileage in miles per gallon.

5. Solve the proportion: $\dfrac{6.5}{52} = \dfrac{n}{4}$

6. It is estimated that 4 out of every 9 students at a certain college have taken a biology course. If 5400 students attend the college, how many have taken a biology course?

7. Write 145% as a decimal.

8. Write 84% as a fraction.

9. Write 0.003 as a percent.

10. Write $\dfrac{11}{8}$ as a percent.

Name: _____

11. 42% of 90 is what number?

12. Fifteen percent of a business budget is spent on utilities. If the business has a yearly budget of $225,000, how much is spent on utilities?

13. What percent of 85 is 17?

14. An antique clock that originally sold for $82 was auctioned for $451. What percent of the original price is the auction price?

15. 79.2 is 120% of what number?

16. A state income tax is 5% of a person's earnings. How much money was earned by a person who paid $1250 in state income tax?

17. Bagels cost $3.89 per dozen. Find the cost of one bagel. Round to the nearest cent.

18. A department store uses a markup rate of 52%. What is the selling price of a pair of jeans that cost the store $32?

19. National Hardware Company is having a 15% off sale. What is the sale price of a can of paint that regularly sells for $22.60?

20. A credit card company charges 1.5% per month on each customer's unpaid balance. Find the interest charged if a customer's unpaid balance for the month is $800.

The pictograph shows the ages of students enrolled at a local community college. Each figure represents 200 students.

1. What is the total enrollment at the college?

2. What percent of the total number of students are 21-25 years old? Round to the nearest tenth of a percent.

18-20 years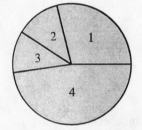

21-25 years

25-35 years

Over 35 years

The circle graph shows the number of students attending the schools of a large city.

3. What is the ratio of the number of students attending elementary school to the number of students attending college?

4. What is the ratio of the number of junior high students to the number of high school students?

5. What is the ratio of the number of high school students to the number of college students?

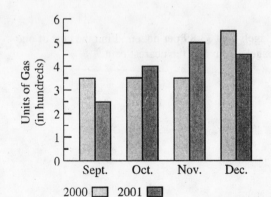

TOTAL SCHOOL ENROLLMENT
1: 21,000 - Elementary School
2:   9,000 - Junior High
3:   8,000 - High School
4: 35,000 - College

The double-bar graph shows the number of units of gas (in hundreds) used during the last four months of 2000 and 2001.

6. Find the ratio of the number of units used in September 2001 to the number of units used in September 2000.

7. Find the total number of units of gas used during the 4 months of 2000.

8. What is the difference between the number of units of gas used in November 2001 and November 2000?

9. A survey of tax returns of the clients of an accounting firm revealed the following: 17 were due a refund, 10 owed less than $50, 21 owed more than $50 but less than $100, 33 owed more than $100 but less than $150, and 42 owed more than $150. What was the modal class?

10. The number of pocket cellular phones sold by a store for the first five months of the year were 34, 28, 31, 36, and 38. What was the mean number of cellular phones sold per month?

The double-line graph shows the number of computer disks (in thousands) sold by a manufacturer during the last four months of 2000 and 2001.

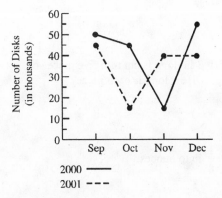

11. What is the difference between October sales for 2000 and 2001?

12. In which month did 2001 sales exceed 2000 sales?

13. What were the total 2001 sales for the 4 months?

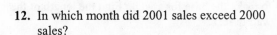

2000 ——

2001 - - -

The histogram shows the distribution of annual rainfall for a city for the last 40 years.

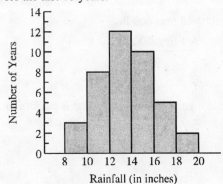

14. Find the number of years in which the total rainfall was between 16 and 20 inches.

15. What percent of the total number of years had rainfall between 8 and 14 inches?

The frequency polygon shows the fuel usage of 64 cars as measured by a research group.

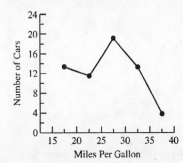

16. What percent of the cars got between 30 and 35 mpg? Round to the nearest tenth of a percent.

17. How many cars got more than 36 mpg?

18. A coin is tossed twice. List all the possible outcomes of the experiment as a sample space.

19. A typing test was given to eight candidates for a clerk-typist position. The results of the tests, in words per minute, were: 78, 62, 72, 63, 56, 74, 80, 67. Find the median number of words per minute.

20. The scores on a nursing license exam are shown at the right. Determine the third quartile of the scores.

97	86	79	65	91	73
78	69	94	67	68	80
89	92	60	82	77	88

1. Convert 20 ft to yards.

2. Find the quotient of 9 ft 8 in. and 4.

3. A board 6 ft 3 in. long is cut into five pieces of equal length. How long is each piece?

4. Fifty-two bricks, each 6 in. long, are laid end to end to make the base for a wall. Find the length of the wall in feet.

5. Convert $3\frac{1}{8}$ lb to ounces.

6. Convert 6500 lb to tons.

7. Subtract: 3 tons 600 lb
            − 1 ton 800 lb

8. Find the total of 3 lb 12 oz and 2 lb 9 oz.

9. A metal ingot weighing 22 lb 8 oz is cut into four equal pieces. Find the weight of each ingot.

10. A baby weighed 7 lb 9 oz at birth. At 3 months of age, the baby weighed 13 lb 2 oz. Find the baby's increase in weight during the 3 months.

11. Convert 24 pt to gallons.

12. Convert $2\frac{1}{2}$ qt to gallons.

13. Subtract: 5 gal
            − 3 gal 3 qt

14. Divide: $5\overline{)3\ \text{gal}\ 3\ \text{qt}}$

15. Sixty people are going to attend a reception. Assume that each person will drink $2\frac{1}{2}$ cups of coffee. How many gallons of coffee should be prepared?

16. There are 24 cans in a case of soft drinks. Each can contains 12 fl oz of soft drink. Find the number of quarts of soft drink in 1 case of soft drinks.

17. Find the energy required to lift a 4800-pound elevator a distance of 80 ft.

18. Six tons are lifted 18 ft. Find the energy required in foot-pounds.

19. Convert $5280\ \dfrac{\text{ft}\cdot\text{lb}}{\text{s}}$ to horsepower.

$$\left(1\ \text{hp} = 550\ \dfrac{\text{ft}\cdot\text{lb}}{\text{s}}\right)$$

20. Find the power in foot-pounds per second needed to raise 80 lb a distance of 15 ft in 5 s.

1. Convert 3792 m to kilometers.

2. Convert 6.8 km to meters.

3. Convert 5 cm 2 mm to millimeters.

4. Convert 72 cm 4 mm to centimeters.

5. A carpenter needs 18 rafters, each 672 cm long. Find the total length (in meters) of rafters needed.

6. Two pieces of wire are cut from a 50-meter roll. The two pieces measure 940 cm and 2180 cm. How much wire (in meters) is left on the roll after the two pieces are cut?

7. Convert 0.06 kg to grams.

8. Convert 4237 mg to grams.

9. Convert 2 kg 467 g to grams.

10. Convert 6 g 84 mg to grams.

11. A football player starts the season weighing 102.5 kg. The player loses 3500 g during the first 2 weeks of practice. Find the weight (in kilograms) of the player after the first 2 weeks of practice.

12. Find the cost of a ham weighing 3200 g if the price per kilogram is $4.45.

13. Convert 0.04 L to milliliters.

14. Convert 9.2 cm^3 to milliliters.

15. Convert 7 kl 100 L to kiloliters.

16. Convert 3 L 412 ml to liters.

17. If one serving of punch contains 250 ml, how many servings can be made from 18.5 L of punch?

18. Housework requires 240 Calories per hour. How many Calories are used in 30 days by doing $1\frac{1}{4}$ h of housework each day?

19. Find the height in meters of a person 5 ft 9 in. Round to the nearest hundredth. (1 m = 3.28 ft)

20. Convert 32.8 L of gasoline to gallons. Round to the nearest hundredth. (1 L = 1.06 qt)

The circle graph shows a family's monthly expenditures totaling $2250.

1. Find the amount spent for food.

2. How much more is spent for miscellaneous expenses than for savings?

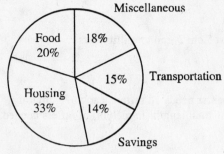

Budget for a Monthly
Income of $2250

The frequency polygon shows annual rainfall at a seaside community during the past 22 years.

3. What is the ratio of the number of years that rainfall was between 5 in. and 6 in. to the total number of years the records were kept?

4. During what percent of the years was the rainfall between 6 in. and 7 in.? Round to the nearest tenth of a percent.

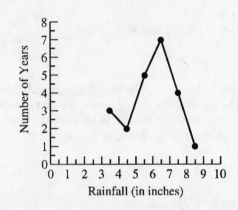

5. Rainfall in a community last summer measured 8.6 in. in June, 4.5 in. in July, and 5.2 in. in August. Find the average rainfall during the 3 months.

6. A carpenter spent 6 days making window boxes. The numbers of boxes built each day were 7, 6, 9, 5, 3, and 10. What was the median number of boxes built per day for the 6 days?

7. Convert 32 in. to feet.

8. What is the sum of 11 ft 5 in. and 7 ft 8 in.?

9. Convert 90 oz to pounds.

10. Subtract: 9 tons 1000 lb
             − 3 tons 1500 lb

11. Convert 36 pt to quarts.

12. A room is partitioned with 6 screens, each $4\frac{1}{2}$ ft long. How many yards of screen are used for the partitions?

13. If a serving of lemonade contains $1\frac{1}{2}$ c, how many servings can be made from 6 gal of lemonade?

14. Convert 56 cm to millimeters.

15. Convert 0.123 kg to grams.

16. Convert 1028 ml to cubic centimeters.

17. Find the number of grams in 8 lb of meat. (1 lb = 454 g)

18. Ice cream costs $2.19/L. Find the cost per quart. Round to the nearest cent. (1 L = 1.06 qt)

19. A veterinarian wants to install a dog run 12 m long and 350 cm wide. What is the length of the fencing required to enclose the dog run?

20. A store buys a 20-kilogram bag of coffee beans and packages the beans into 500-gram bags to sell. How many 500-gram bags can be filled from the 20-kilogram bag?

Name: _____

Date: _____

1. Place the correct symbol, < or >, between the two numbers:

$$-3 \qquad -7$$

2. Place the correct symbol, < or >, between the two numbers:

$$0 \qquad -6$$

3. Evaluate: $-|2|$

4. Add: $24 + (-6)$

5. Find the sum of $-3,\ 14,\ -9$.

6. Subtract: $-16 - 4$

7. Subtract: $6 - 8 - (-3)$

8. Find the product of -10 and 40.

9. Divide: $-27 \div 9$

10. Find the temperature after a rise of $24°C$ from $-5°C$.

11. The high temperature today was $16°$. The high temperature yesterday was $-2°$. What was the average high temperature for the 2 days?

12. Add: $\dfrac{1}{3} + \left(-\dfrac{5}{6}\right)$

13. Find the sum of $-1\dfrac{3}{4}$ and $-2\dfrac{1}{6}$.

14. Subtract: $-6 - \left(-1\dfrac{1}{3}\right)$

15. Subtract: $\dfrac{1}{6} - \left(-\dfrac{2}{5}\right)$

16. Multiply: $\dfrac{7}{15} \times \left(-\dfrac{5}{8}\right)$

17. Divide: $-6\dfrac{1}{2} \div \left(-2\dfrac{1}{2}\right)$

18. What is -16.7 decreased by -13.8?

19. Subtract: $-3.97 - (-2)$

20. Find the product of -0.8 and -5.4.

21. Divide: $5.632 \div (-1.6)$

22. Simplify: $8 - 4 \div 2 - 10 \div 2$

23. Simplify: $4 - 2(6 - 4)^2 \div 4$

24. Write $14,760,000$ in scientific notation.

25. The boiling point of hydrogen is $-252.87°C$. The melting point of hydrogen is $-259.14°C$. Find the difference between the boiling point and the melting point of hydrogen.

Name: _____

Date: _____

1. Evaluate $2ac - (b \div c)$ when $a = 3$, $b = -4$, and $c = 2$.

2. Evaluate $\dfrac{b - a^2}{-2a}$ when $a = -1$ and $b = 4$.

3. Simplify: $3x^2 - x + 5x^2$

4. Simplify: $-6y - 2(4 - y) + 8$

5. Is -3 a solution of $x^2 - 6x + 9 = 0$?

6. Solve: $3 + x = -3$

7. Solve: $-4x = -28$

8. Solve: $-\dfrac{2}{3}x = -24$

9. Solve: $-7x + 5 = -9$

10. Solve: $\dfrac{x}{2} - 3 = -5$

11. The value of an investment after 1 year was $5280. The original investment was $4500. Find the increase in value of the investment. Use the formula $A = P + I$, where A is the value of the investment after 1 year, P is the original investment, and I is the increase in value of the investment.

12. Find the time required for a falling object to increase in velocity from 64 ft/s to 180 ft/s. Use the formula $V = V_0 + 32t$, where V is the final velocity of a falling object, V_0 is the starting velocity of a falling object, and t is the time for the object to fall. Round to the nearest hundredth.

13. Solve: $-3 = 5 - 6y$

14. Solve: $8x + 19 = 3x + 4$

15. Solve: $5(4 - x) + 3x = 24$

16. Translate "the sum of x and the product of fifteen and x" into a mathematical expression.

17. Translate "fifteen times the total of a number and six" into a mathematical expression.

18. Translate "the sum of twelve and a number is four" into an equation and solve.

19. Two more than the product of four and a number is negative fourteen. Find the number.

20. During a sale, a suit is discounted $36. This is 15% off the regular price. Find the regular price.

1. Find the supplement of a 25° angle.

2. Two angles of a triangle are 80° and 33°. Find the measure of the third angle of the triangle.

3. In the figure, $L_1 \parallel L_2$. $\angle x = 160°$. Find $\angle y$.

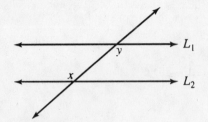

4. In the figure $L_1 \parallel L_2$. $\angle x = 35°$. Find $\angle a + \angle b$.

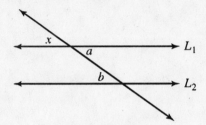

5. Find the perimeter of a square with a side of 35 cm.

6. Find the perimeter of the composite figure.

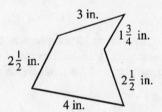

7. Find the length of molding needed to put around a circular table that is $4\frac{2}{3}$ ft in diameter. Use $\frac{22}{7}$ for π.

8. Find the area of a square with a side of $4\frac{1}{3}$ ft.

9. Find the area of the composite figure.

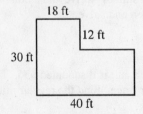

10. Find the cross-sectional area of a redwood tree that is 10 ft in diameter. Use 3.14 for π.

11. Find the area of the composite figure. Use 3.14 for π.

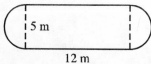

12. Find the volume of a cylinder with a diameter of 4 ft and a height of 5 ft. Use 3.14 for π.

13. Find the volume of the solid.

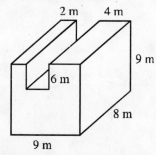

14. A silo that is in the shape of a cylinder is 18 ft in diameter and has a height of 22 ft. Find the volume of the silo. Use 3.14 for π.

15. Find the square root of 98. Round to the nearest thousandth.

16. Find the unknown side of the triangle. Round to the nearest tenth.

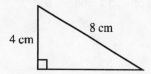

17. A 30-foot cable holds a telephone pole in place. The cable is attached to the telephone pole 20 ft above the ground. Find the distance along the ground from the base of the pole to the cable. Round to the nearest tenth.

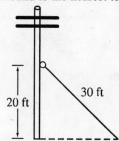

18. Triangles *ABC* and *DEF* are similar. Find side *EF*.

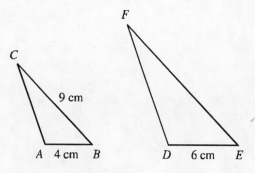

19. A flagpole 20 m high casts a shadow of 12 m. How high is a flagpole that casts a shadow of 9 m? Round to the nearest tenth.

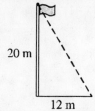

20. In the figure, triangle *ABC* is congruent to triangle *DEF*. Find the length of *EF*.

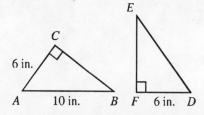

1. Add: $-\dfrac{5}{6}+\dfrac{2}{9}$

2. Find the sum of 18 and -32.

3. Subtract: $-15-25$

4. What is the difference between 9.2 and -4.1.

5. Multiply: $200(-16)$

6. Find the product of $-\dfrac{2}{3}$ and $-\dfrac{5}{7}$.

7. Find the quotient of -25.2 and -0.6.

8. Simplify: $-8+3\times2-(-4)^2$

9. Simplify: $4-2\times7+(3-1)$

10. Evaluate $b\cdot c\div a\cdot c$ when $a=-2$, $b=3$, and $c=4$.

11. Solve: $b-7=-22$

12. Simplify: $6w-v-10w+6v$

13. Solve: $-\dfrac{m}{8}=3$

14. Solve: $2x-4(x+3)=3(x-1)$

Name: _____

15. Solve: $15x - 4 = -49$

16. Five times a number is twenty-four. Find the number.

17. An employee wants to save money to buy a car. If the employee saves $180 each month, and this is 6% of the employee's monthly income, what is the employee's monthly income?

18. A computer system is bought for $2900. A down payment of $290 is made. If the remaining balance is paid in 12 equal payments, find the amount of each payment.

19. In the figure, $L_1 \parallel L_2$. $\angle x = 22°$. Find $\angle y - \angle x$.

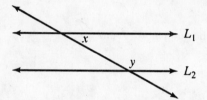

20. Two angles of a triangle measure 105° and 68°. Find the measure of the third angle.

21. Find the circumference of a circle with radius of 8 cm. Use 3.14 for π.

22. Find the area of the figure. Use 3.14 for π.

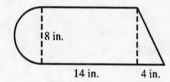

14 in.   4 in.

23. Find the volume of a rectangular solid with a length of 2.3 m, width of 4m, and height of 5.1 m.

24. In the figure, triangles *ABC* and *DEF* are similar. Find the height of triangle *ABC*. Round to the nearest tenth.

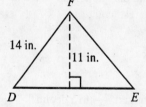

25. Find the unknown leg of the right triangle. Round to the nearest tenth.

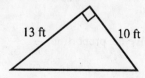

13 ft   10 ft

Name: _____

Date: _____

1. Subtract: $14,208 - 6375$

2. Find $14,624$ divided by 457.

3. Simplify: $6^2 + (8-3) - 4 \times 5$

4. Henrique had a balance of $654 in his checking account before making deposits of $84, $327, and $58. What is the balance in his account after making the deposits?

5. Add: $\dfrac{2}{7} + 1\dfrac{1}{2}$

6. Subtract: $3\dfrac{2}{7} - 1\dfrac{1}{2}$

7. Find the product of $\dfrac{2}{7}$ and $2\dfrac{1}{3}$.

8. Find the quotient of 7 and $1\dfrac{2}{5}$.

9. Simplify: $\dfrac{2}{3} + \dfrac{1}{6} \times \dfrac{3}{4} - \left(\dfrac{1}{2}\right)^2$

10. You bought stock at $45\frac{3}{4}$ per share. It gained $\frac{7}{8}$ a share in the first month and $2\frac{1}{4}$ a share in the second month. What was the value per share at the end of 2 months?

11. Find 9.2 decreased by 4.68.

12. Multiply: 7.5×0.04

13. Find the quotient of 3.4 and 0.26. Round to the nearest tenth.

14. Convert 0.45 to a fraction in simplest terms.

15. Convert $\dfrac{19}{25}$ to a decimal.

16. Write the comparison "27 ft to 63 ft" as a ratio in simplest form using a fraction.

17. Write "$783.75 earned in 15 days" as a unit rate.

18. Solve the proportion: $\dfrac{3}{n} = \dfrac{5}{52}$

Final Exam Form D (*continued*)　　　　Name: _____

19. Forty-five out of 80 people surveyed approved of the mayor's performance. At this rate, how many out of the town population of 14,00 approve of the mayor's performance?

20. Write 1.4 as a percent.

21. What is 160% of 80?

22. 17.5 is what percent of 350 ?

23. 264 is 48% of what number?

24. Last year it snowed 70% of the 120 days of the ski season. How many days did it snow?

25. Find the unit cost of 10 lb for $2.80.

26. A home that was valued at $110,000 last year is now valued at $137,500. Find the percent increase in the value of the house.

27. A music store uses a 45% markup rate. What is the selling price of a CD that cost the store $12?

28. Corrine had a checking account balance of $873.45. She wrote checks for $35.75, $126.83, and $154.67. She deposited $356.74. Find her new checking account balance.

29. The circle graph shows how a family's monthly income of $2600 is budgeted. How much money is budgeted for savings?

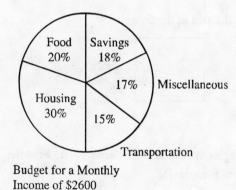

Budget for a Monthly
Income of $2600

30. The double-bar graph shows the number of video games sold by a wholesale distributor during the last four months of 2000 and 2001. In which month were 2001 sales lower than 2000 sales?

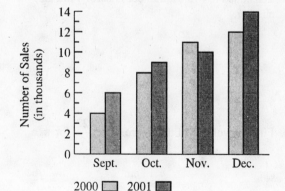

2000 ▢　2001 ▢

31. Convert $3\frac{3}{4}$ lb to ounces.

32. Convert 34 ft to yards.

33. How long must a board be if four pieces, each 1 ft 6 in. long, are to be cut from it?

34. If a book weighs 8 oz, what is the weight of a carton containing 600 copies of the book? Express the answer in pounds.

35. Convert 140 cm to meters.

36. Convert 2500 g to kilograms.

37. A vacationer caught fish weighing 650 g, 1250 g, and 875 g. What was the total weight, in kilograms, of the fish?

38. Place the correct symbol, < or >, between the two numbers.
$$-4 \qquad -7$$

39. Add: $-\dfrac{1}{2} + 2\dfrac{1}{4}$

40. Subtract: $-4 - (-7)$

41. Find the product of $\dfrac{4}{3}$ and $-\dfrac{9}{10}$.

42. Simplify: $-2 + 6 \cdot 3 - (4 - 8)$

43. Evaluate $-2ab + b^2$ when $a = -2$ and $b = -1$.

44. Solve: $3x + 3(x + 2) = 2(x + 1)$

45. Solve: $41 + y = 23$

46. Solve: $-11x + 10 = -12$

47. Ten added to twice a number is zero. Find the number.

48. Find the area of the figure.

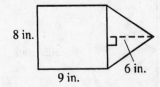

8 in.

9 in.

6 in.

49. Find the volume of the figure. Use $\dfrac{22}{7}$ for π.

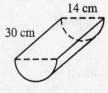

14 cm

30 cm

50. Triangles *ABC* and *DEF* are similar. Find the area of triangle *DEF*.

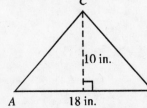

C

10 in.

A   18 in.   *B*

F

D   6 in.   *E*

Form E Tests

Multiple Choice

Chapter 1 Test Form E

Name: _____

Date: _____

1. Which statement is correct?

    a. $92 < 59$ b. $45 < 55$ c. $34 > 57$ d. $0 > 4$

2. Write $10,902$ in words.

    a. One thousand nine hundred two   b. Ten thousand ninety-two
    c. Ten thousand nine hundred two   d. One hundred nine thousand two

3. Write ninety-six thousand four hundred one in standard form.

    a. $96,410$ b. $96,041$ c. $90,641$ d. $96,401$

4. Write $501,803$ in expanded form.

    a. $50,000 + 1000 + 800 + 30$ b. $500,000 + 1000 + 800 + 3$
    c. $500,000 + 800 + 30$ d. $500,000 + 100 + 800 + 30$

5. Round $84,619$ to the nearest hundred.

    a. $84,600$ b. $48,700$ c. $84,620$ d. $84,000$

6. Add: $29,325$
        $+ 150,324$

    a. $79,649$ b. $443,574$
    c. $179,649$ d. $169,639$

7. Add: $27,319 + 16,324 + 9,725$

    a. $53,368$ b. $53,378$ c. $54,378$ d. $54,387$

8. You are leaving for a 3-day vacation. The odometer on your car reads 37,402. You plan to drive 149 miles the first day, 92 miles the second day, and 245 miles the third day. What will your odometer reading be at the end of the trip?

    a. 37,788 miles   b. 38,778 miles   c. 37,877 miles   d. 37,888 miles

9. Subtract: 9899
        $- 4895$

    a. 5004 b. 5104
    c. 5014 d. 4004

10. Find the difference between $92,591$ and $87,015$.

    a. 5596 b. 5576 c. 5656 d. 5976

11. A sales executive has an expense account of $1200. She spends $639 for airfare, $112 for food, and $255 for lodgings. Find the balance remaining in the expense account.

    a. $184   b. $5710   c. $5206   d. $194

12. Find the product of $37,056$ and 4.

    a. $155,224$ b. $144,204$ c. $148,224$ d. $148,204$

13. Multiply: 796

            $\times\,309$

      a. 245,864   **b.** 244,944

      c. 244,864   **d.** 245,964

14. The owner of a marina bought 67 canoes for $515 each. What was the total cost for the 67 canoes?

    a. $34,505   **b.** $35,505   **c.** $35,405   **d.** $34,405

15. Find the quotient of 10,890 and 9 .

    a. 1201   **b.** 1021   **c.** 1210   **d.** 121

16. Divide: $6\overline{)98,741}$

      a. 16,456 r 5   **b.** 16,446 r 5

      c. 14,790 r 1   **d.** 16,440 r 1

17. Divide: $28,938 \div 78$

    a. 371 r 1   **b.** 371   **c.** 368 r 14   **d.** 370

18. A teacher receives a salary of $30,480 per year. Find the teacher's monthly salary if the teacher receives a paycheck each month of the year.

    a. $2440   **b.** $2390   **c.** $2340   **d.** $2540

19. Write $5 \cdot 5 \cdot 5 \cdot 11 \cdot 11 \cdot 11 \cdot 11$ in exponential notation.

    a. $3^5 \cdot 4^{11}$ **b.** $5^3 \cdot 11^4$ **c.** $5^4 \cdot 11^3$ **d.** 55^3

20. Simplify: $2^3 \cdot 5^2$

    a. 100   **b.** 200   **c.** 50   **d.** 60

21. Simplify: $11 - 2(9-1) \div 4$

    a. 7   **b.** 8   **c.** 20   **d.** 18

22. Simplify: $4 \cdot 6 - 6 \div 2$

    a. 18   **b.** 21   **c.** 9   **d.** 0

23. Find all the factors of 27 .

    a. 1, 9, 27   **b.** 1, 3, 9, 27   **c.** 1, 3, 9, 18, 27   **d.** 3, 9, 27

24. Find the prime factorization of 50.

    a. $2 \cdot 5 \cdot 5$ **b.** $5 \cdot 10$ **c.** $2 \cdot 25$ **d.** $2 \cdot 2 \cdot 5 \cdot 5$

25. Find the prime factorization of 40.

    a. $2 \cdot 2 \cdot 2 \cdot 5$ **b.** $2 \cdot 2 \cdot 5 \cdot 5$ **c.** $4 \cdot 10$ **d.** prime

1. Find the LCM of 16 and 28.

   a. 28   **b.** 72   **c.** 112   **d.** 4

2. Find the GCF of 48 and 104.

   a. 624   **b.** 8   **c.** 12   **d.** 6

3. Express the shaded portion of the circles as an improper fraction.

   a. $\dfrac{7}{6}$ **b.** $\dfrac{6}{7}$ **c.** $\dfrac{1}{6}$ **d.** $\dfrac{7}{9}$

4. Write $\dfrac{19}{5}$ as a mixed number.

   a. $3\dfrac{5}{19}$ **b.** $3\dfrac{4}{5}$ **c.** $3\dfrac{3}{5}$ **d.** $4\dfrac{4}{5}$

5. Write $3\dfrac{5}{9}$ as an improper fraction.

   a. $\dfrac{27}{9}$ **b.** $\dfrac{32}{5}$ **c.** $\dfrac{30}{9}$ **d.** $\dfrac{32}{9}$

6. What number must be placed in the numerator so that the following fractions are equivalent? $\dfrac{3}{5} = \dfrac{\ \ \ }{30}$

   a. 18   **b.** 15   **c.** 3   **d.** 6

7. Write $\dfrac{30}{100}$ in simplest form.

   a. $\dfrac{5}{20}$ **b.** $\dfrac{3}{5}$ **c.** $\dfrac{3}{10}$ **d.** $\dfrac{5}{10}$

8. Add: $\dfrac{1}{7} + \dfrac{5}{7} + \dfrac{6}{7}$

   a. $1\dfrac{5}{7}$ **b.** $\dfrac{5}{7}$ **c.** $1\dfrac{3}{7}$ **d.** $\dfrac{3}{7}$

9. Find the total of $\dfrac{2}{3}$, $\dfrac{7}{9}$, and $\dfrac{5}{12}$.

   a. $1\dfrac{1}{6}$ **b.** $1\dfrac{13}{36}$ **c.** $1\dfrac{1}{12}$ **d.** $1\dfrac{31}{36}$

10. Add:

$$3\frac{5}{8}$$
$$+\,2\frac{7}{12}$$

     a. $6\frac{5}{24}$ **b.** $6\frac{5}{48}$

     c. $5\frac{5}{24}$ **d.** $5\frac{29}{48}$

11. Michael Santo bought one share of stock in a computer company for $41\frac{3}{8}$. Monthly gains for the first 3 months of ownership were $\$\frac{7}{8}$, $\$1\frac{1}{2}$, and $\$3\frac{3}{4}$ per share. Find the value of the stock at the end of the 3 months.

    a. $\$47\frac{3}{8}$ **b.** $\$49\frac{1}{2}$ **c.** $\$47\frac{1}{2}$ **d.** $\$46\frac{1}{2}$

12. Subtract: $\dfrac{43}{48}-\dfrac{31}{48}$

    a. $\dfrac{1}{24}$ **b.** $1\frac{1}{12}$ **c.** $\dfrac{1}{2}$ **d.** $\dfrac{1}{4}$

13. Find $\dfrac{7}{15}$ decreased by $\dfrac{11}{45}$.

    a. $\dfrac{1}{5}$ **b.** $\dfrac{2}{9}$ **c.** $\dfrac{3}{48}$ **d.** $\dfrac{11}{90}$

14. Subtract:

$$21\frac{7}{8}$$
$$-\,8\frac{5}{12}$$

     a. $13\frac{11}{24}$ **b.** $12\frac{7}{12}$

     c. $12\frac{11}{12}$ **d.** $13\frac{7}{12}$

15. Mark wants to fence in his backyard during four Saturday afternoons. His yard needs 110 feet of fencing. If he completes $50\frac{1}{2}$ feet the first Saturday, $15\frac{3}{4}$ feet the second Saturday, and $20\frac{1}{4}$ feet the third Saturday, how much fencing must he complete on the fourth Saturday to complete the job?

    a. $23\frac{1}{2}$ feet   **b.** 25 feet   **c.** $30\frac{1}{4}$ feet   **d.** $25\frac{1}{2}$ feet

16. Multiply: $\dfrac{16}{27}\times\dfrac{15}{28}$

    a. $\dfrac{2}{7}$ **b.** $\dfrac{5}{18}$ **c.** $\dfrac{20}{63}$ **d.** $\dfrac{5}{48}$

17. Find the product of 12 and $2\frac{7}{10}$.

    a. $9\frac{3}{10}$ **b.** $32\frac{2}{5}$ **c.** $4\frac{4}{9}$ **d.** $24\frac{7}{10}$

18. Jim saves $\frac{1}{12}$ of his salary each year. His income this year totaled $105,000. How much of his salary did Jim put in savings this year?

    a. $8750   **b.** $880   **c.** $8800   **d.** $10,500

19. Divide: $\frac{4}{11} \div \frac{9}{33}$

    a. $4\frac{1}{3}$ **b.** $2\frac{3}{4}$ **c.** $1\frac{1}{3}$ **d.** $1\frac{3}{4}$

20. Find the quotient of $8\frac{1}{3}$ and $2\frac{2}{3}$.

    a. $5\frac{2}{3}$ **b.** $2\frac{11}{16}$ **c.** $22\frac{2}{9}$ **d.** $3\frac{1}{8}$

21. A 28-foot tree was sawed into logs $3\frac{1}{2}$ feet long. How many logs were sawn from the tree?

    a. 7 logs   **b.** 9 logs   **c.** 8 logs   **d.** 6 logs

22. Which statement is correct?

    a. $\frac{32}{81} = \frac{11}{27}$ **b.** $\frac{32}{81} < \frac{11}{27}$ **c.** $0 > \frac{11}{27}$ **d.** $\frac{32}{81} > \frac{11}{27}$

23. Simplify: $\left(\frac{5}{6}\right)^2 \cdot \left(\frac{3}{10}\right)^3$

    a. $\frac{3}{160}$ **b.** $1\frac{1}{2}$ **c.** $\frac{17}{60}$ **d.** $1\frac{7}{60}$

24. Simplify: $\left(\frac{3}{4} + \frac{5}{8}\right) \div \frac{1}{4}$

    a. $3\frac{1}{4}$ **b.** $4\frac{4}{5}$ **c.** $2\frac{2}{3}$ **d.** $5\frac{1}{2}$

25. Simplify: $\frac{5}{8} - \frac{3}{8} \cdot \left(\frac{2}{3}\right)^2$

    a. $\frac{3}{8}$ **b.** $\frac{11}{24}$ **c.** $\frac{1}{12}$ **d.** $\frac{9}{24}$

Name: _____

Date: _____

1. Write 3046.09 in words.
   - a. Three thousand forty-six and nine tenths
   - b. Three thousand forty-six and nine hundredths
   - c. Three hundred forty-six and nine tenths
   - d. Three hundred forty-six and nine hundredths

2. Write fourteen and seventy-two ten-thousandths.
   - a. 14720
   - b. 14.00072
   - c. 14.072
   - d. 14.0072

3. Round 309.50905 to the nearest thousandth.
   - a. 309.51
   - b. 309.5091
   - c. 309.509
   - d. 309.591

4. Round 4.09723 to the nearest tenth.
   - a. 4.09
   - b. 4.1
   - c. 4.098
   - d. 4.0

5. Add: 361.721
          1238.5234
       +   31.865
   - a. 1631.1004
   - b. 1632.0094
   - c. 1632.1084
   - d. 1632.1094

6. Find the total of 32.4905, 6.0899, 129.567, and 3.05.
   - a. 271.1974
   - b. 170.1974
   - c. 171.1974
   - d. 171.193

7. Joel paid $29.95 for a pair of jeans, $14.95 for a shirt, and $31.49 for a pair of shoes. Find the total cost of the three items.
   - a. $76.39
   - b. $76.49
   - c. $76.59
   - d. $76.69

8. Subtract: 38.778
             −   9.712
   - a. 28.066
   - b. 30.066
   - c. 29.966
   - d. 29.066

9. Find 0.0444 less than 1.392.
   - a. 1.3484
   - b. 1.3476
   - c. 1.3486
   - d. 1.3474

10. You buy two books, one for $18.42 and the other for $26.72. How much change do you receive from a $50 bill?
    - a. $45.14
    - b. $4.86
    - c. $3.86
    - d. $4.76

11. Multiply: 2.341
                   × 2.39

   a. 5.59499   **b.** 5.5949
   c. 5.59599   **d.** 5.5499

12. Find the product of 5.037 and 9.38.

 a. 47247.06   **b.** 4724.706   **c.** 47.24706   **d.** 47.19669

13. You bought 8.3 pounds of steak for \$4.89 per pound. How much change will you receive from a \$50 bill? Round to the nearest cent.

 a. \$9.41   **b.** \$8.66   **c.** \$8.67   **d.** \$9.42

14. Find 115.8 divided by 2.72. Round to the nearest hundredth.

 a. 0.02   **b.** 4.26   **c.** 31.36   **d.** 42.57

15. Divide. Round to the nearest thousandth.

   $0.204\overline{)0.0906}$

   a. 0.444   **b.** 0.424
   c. 0.445   **d.** 4.441

16. You pay \$914.40 per year in life insurance premiums. You pay the premiums in 12 equal monthly payments. Find the amount of each monthly payment.

 a. \$66.20   **b.** \$86.20   **c.** \$7.62   **d.** \$76.20

17. Convert $\dfrac{7}{15}$ to a decimal. Round to the nearest thousandth.

 a. 0.4   **b.** 0.4667   **c.** 0.47   **d.** 0.467

18. Convert 0.36 to a fraction.

 a. $\dfrac{44}{25}$ **b.** $\dfrac{9}{25}$ **c.** $\dfrac{9}{20}$ **d.** $\dfrac{7}{20}$

19. Which statement is correct?
 a. $0.22 = 0.219$ **b.** $0.22 > 0.219$ **c.** $0.22 < 0.219$ **d.** $0 > 0.219$

20. Which statement is correct?
 a. $0.43 > \dfrac{3}{7}$ **b.** $0.43 < \dfrac{3}{7}$ **c.** $0.43 = \dfrac{3}{7}$ **d.** $0.43 < 0$

1. Divide: $12\overline{)21{,}627}$

   a. $1802\,r\,4$ b. $1810\,r\,3$

   c. $1802\,r\,3$ d. $1802\,r\,7$

2. Simplify: $2^4 \cdot 7^2 \cdot 9$

   a. 7056 b. 1008 c. 3528 d. 72

3. Simplify: $20 - (12 \div 4) \cdot 2 + 5$

   a. 39 b. 19 c. 9 d. 17

4. Find the GCF of 18 and 63.

   a. 2 b. 6 c. 9 d. 18

5. Write $\dfrac{49}{8}$ as a mixed number.

   a. $9\dfrac{1}{8}$ b. $7\dfrac{1}{4}$ c. $6\dfrac{1}{4}$ d. $6\dfrac{1}{8}$

6. Write $3\dfrac{3}{7}$ as an improper fraction.

   a. $\dfrac{24}{3}$ b. $\dfrac{24}{7}$ c. $\dfrac{63}{7}$ d. $\dfrac{25}{7}$

7. Find the numerator for an equivalent fraction with the given denominator: $\dfrac{3}{16} = \dfrac{}{48}$

   a. 6 b. 9 c. 12 d. 3

8. Add: $\dfrac{5}{9} + \dfrac{7}{12} + \dfrac{1}{2}$

   a. $1\dfrac{23}{36}$ b. $1\dfrac{13}{36}$ c. $2\dfrac{5}{36}$ d. $1\dfrac{5}{24}$

9. What is $15\dfrac{4}{9}$ increased by $3\dfrac{5}{6}$?

   a. $18\dfrac{5}{18}$ b. $18\dfrac{5}{12}$ c. $19\dfrac{5}{18}$ d. $18\dfrac{1}{2}$

10. Subtract:

    $$\begin{array}{r} 7\dfrac{1}{2} \\ -\,4\dfrac{2}{3} \\ \hline \end{array}$$

    a. $3\dfrac{5}{6}$ b. $2\dfrac{5}{6}$

    c. $2\dfrac{1}{6}$ d. $3\dfrac{1}{3}$

11. Multiply: $\dfrac{15}{35} \times \dfrac{22}{25}$

   a. $\dfrac{2}{55}$ **b.** $1\dfrac{1}{5}$ **c.** $\dfrac{2}{5}$ **d.** $\dfrac{2}{3}$

12. Find the product of $3\dfrac{1}{8}$ and 4 .

   a. $12\dfrac{3}{4}$ **b.** $12\dfrac{1}{2}$ **c.** $12\dfrac{1}{8}$ **d.** 12

13. Divide: $\dfrac{1}{4} \div \dfrac{2}{3}$

   a. $2\dfrac{1}{3}$ **b.** $\dfrac{1}{6}$ **c.** $\dfrac{1}{4}$ **d.** $\dfrac{3}{8}$

14. What is 450 divided by $\dfrac{3}{4}$?

   a. 500 **b.** 650 **c.** 600 **d.** 337

15. Simplify: $\left(\dfrac{5}{8}\right)^3 \cdot \left(\dfrac{16}{5}\right)^2$

   a. $1\dfrac{1}{4}$ **b.** $2\dfrac{1}{2}$ **c.** $\dfrac{2}{5}$ **d.** $6\dfrac{1}{4}$

16. Simplify: $\left(\dfrac{1}{3}\right)^2 + \dfrac{2}{3} - \dfrac{3}{4}$

   a. $\dfrac{1}{36}$ **b.** $\dfrac{1}{4}$ **c.** $\dfrac{1}{9}$ **d.** $\dfrac{1}{17}$

17. Write 9.06 in words.

   a. Nine hundred six   **b.** Nine and six hundredths
   c. Nine and six tenths   **d.** Nine and six thousandths

18. Add:
$$\begin{array}{r} 11 \\ 77.29 \\ +\ 5.0531 \\ \hline \end{array}$$

   a. 92.3531   **b.** 94.3431

   c. 93.3531   **d.** 93.3431

19. What is 85.23 decreased by 45.621 ?

   a. 39.601   **b.** 39.609   **c.** 40.609   **d.** 39.610

20. Multiply: 0.28
                  × 0.6

       a.   1.68   b.   0.0168

       c.   0.168   d.   0.1068

21. Divide. Round to the nearest thousandth.

     $32\overline{)28.15}$

       a.   1.137   b.   0.880

       c.   0.8797   d.   0.9213

22. Convert $\frac{5}{7}$ to a decimal. Round to the nearest thousandth.

     a.   0.714   b.   0.715   c.   1.4   d.   7.142

23. Convert $0.83\frac{1}{3}$ to a fraction.

     a. $\frac{83}{1000}$ b. $\frac{5}{9}$ c. $\frac{83}{100}$ d. $\frac{5}{6}$

24. Which statement is correct?

     a. $0.375 < \frac{3}{8}$ b. $0.375 = \frac{3}{8}$ c. $0.375 > \frac{3}{8}$ d. $0.375 < 0$

25. On a hiking trip, Janice walked $4\frac{1}{2}$ miles the first hour, $2\frac{3}{4}$ miles the second hour, and 3 miles the third hour. How many miles did Janice walk in the 3 hours?

     a. $11\frac{1}{4}$ miles   b. $9\frac{1}{4}$ miles   c. $10\frac{1}{4}$ miles   d. $9\frac{3}{4}$ miles

26. A $7\frac{1}{2}$-pound roast is purchased. If $1\frac{1}{4}$ pounds of fat are trimmed and discarded, how many $\frac{1}{4}$-pound servings can be cut from the remaining meat?

     a.   26   b.   25   c.   20   d.   16

27. A bicyclist travels $5\frac{1}{2}$ miles in 1 hour. How many miles does he travel in 8 hours?

     a.   44 miles   b.   40 miles   c.   42 miles   d.   46 miles

28. A computer technician earns $3741.52. Deductions from the check are $748.31 for federal tax, $187.08 for state tax, and $137.50 for insurance. Find the computer technician's take-home pay.

     a. $2806.13   b. $4814.41   c. $2412.73   d. $2668.63

29. A machine lathe takes 0.044 inch from a bushing that is 1.392 inches thick. Find the resulting thickness of the bushing.

     a.   1.436 in.   b.   1.338 in.   c.   1.248 in.   d.   1.348 in.

30. Last week the local food market purchased a total of 1240.5 pounds of bananas at $0.78 a pound. How much did the market pay for the bananas?

     a. $967.60   b. $966.60   c. $967.59   d. $965.59

Name: _____
Date: _____

1. Write the comparison 16 days to 40 days as a ratio in simplest form.

   a. 5 to 2   b. $\dfrac{2}{7}$ c. $\dfrac{2}{5}$ d. $\dfrac{5}{2}$

2. Write the comparison 3 quarts to 5 quarts as a ratio in simplest form.

   a. $\dfrac{3}{5}$ b. $\dfrac{5}{8}$ c. $\dfrac{3}{8}$ d. $\dfrac{5}{3}$

3. Write the comparison 5 years to 15 years as a ratio in simplest form.

   a. 5:3   b. 5   c. $\dfrac{1}{5}$ d. $\dfrac{1}{3}$

4. Write the comparison 15 yards to 20 yards as a ratio in simplest form.

   a. $\dfrac{3}{4}$ b. $\dfrac{4}{7}$ c. $\dfrac{3}{7}$ d. $\dfrac{4}{3}$

5. The cost of adding a new room to a house was $2300 for labor and $9200 for materials. What is the ratio, as a fraction in simplest form, of the cost of the labor to the total cost of adding the new room?

   a. $\dfrac{1}{4}$ b. $\dfrac{1}{5}$ c. $\dfrac{4}{5}$ d. 5

6. An airplane flies 20,000 miles one morning. It flies 4000 miles that afternoon. What is the ratio, as a fraction in simplest form, of the afternoon mileage to the total mileage for the day?

   a. $\dfrac{2}{3}$ b. $\dfrac{1}{6}$ c. $\dfrac{1}{5}$ d. $\dfrac{1}{3}$

7. Write "$55 for 5 CDs" as a rate in simplest form.

   a. $\dfrac{1 \text{ CD}}{\$11}$ b. $\dfrac{\$55}{5 \text{ CDs}}$ c. 11   d. $\dfrac{\$11}{1 \text{ CD}}$

8. Write "125 miles on 10 gallons" as a rate in simplest form.

   a. $\dfrac{25 \text{ miles}}{5 \text{ gallons}}$ b. $\dfrac{25}{2}$ c. $\dfrac{2 \text{ gallons}}{25 \text{ miles}}$ d. $\dfrac{25 \text{ miles}}{2 \text{ gallons}}$

9. Write "$2210 for 40 shares of stock" as a unit rate.

   a. $55.55/share   b. $55.25/share   c. $55.50/share   d. $55.20/share

10. Write "$9.45 for 5 quarts of oil" as a unit rate.

    a. $1.89/quart   b. $1.88/quart   c. $1.90/quart   d. $1.98/quart

11. You own 220 shares of an electric utility stock and receive a dividend of $334.40. Find the dividend per share.

    a. $1.52   **b.** $2.15   **c.** $1.25   **d.** $1.15

12. Seventy-five yards of fabric cost $240. What is the cost per yard?

    a. $3.36   **b.** $2.80   **c.** $3.30   **d.** $3.20

13. Which proportion is true?

    a. $\dfrac{3}{4} = \dfrac{14}{20}$ **b.** $\dfrac{8}{5} = \dfrac{96}{60}$ **c.** $\dfrac{2}{9} = \dfrac{60}{280}$ **d.** $\dfrac{10}{30} = \dfrac{60}{160}$

14. Which proportion is true?

    a. $\dfrac{7}{18} = \dfrac{17}{56}$ **b.** $\dfrac{5}{13} = \dfrac{23}{82}$ **c.** $\dfrac{9}{17} = \dfrac{32}{67}$ **d.** $\dfrac{3}{11} = \dfrac{27}{99}$

15. Solve: $\dfrac{x}{18} = \dfrac{90}{12}$

    a. 135   **b.** 84   **c.** 7.5   **d.** 134

16. Solve: $\dfrac{n}{30} = \dfrac{4}{25}$

    a. 3.3   **b.** 4.8   **c.** 24   **d.** 6

17. A life insurance policy costs $5.42 for every $1000 of insurance. At this rate, what is the cost for $40,000 worth of life insurance?

    a. $261.80   **b.** $216.80   **c.** $206.80   **d.** $5420

18. Every 10,000 miles, John spends $6.50 to add oil to his car. How much will he have spent after driving 35,000 miles?

    a. $23.50   **b.** $97.50   **c.** $22.75   **d.** $162.50

19. A car can travel 70 miles on 2 gallons of gasoline. How far can the car travel on 14 gallons of gasoline?

    a. 390 miles   **b.** 980 miles   **c.** 490 miles   **d.** 540 miles

20. If 1480 men who wash windows on New York City's skyscrapers, each receiving the same hourly pay, earn a combined total of $41,440 in one hour, how many window washers, working at the same rate, would earn a total of $102,200?

    a. 6056   **b.** 3560   **c.** 3660   **d.** 3650

Name: _____

Date: _____

1. Write 3.02% as a decimal.

   a. 302   **b.** 0.302   **c.** 0.0302   **d.** 30.2

2. Write 66% as a fraction.

   a. $\dfrac{33}{50}$ **b.** $\dfrac{2}{3}$ **c.** $\dfrac{3}{5}$ **d.** $\dfrac{13}{20}$

3. Write 0.034 as a percent.

   a. 3.4%   **b.** 0.34%   **c.** 0.034%   **d.** 0.0034%

4. Write 3.16 as a percent.

   a. 0.316%   **b.** 31.6%   **c.** 0.0316%   **d.** 316%

5. Write $\dfrac{7}{16}$ as a percent. Round to the nearest tenth.

   a. 50%   **b.** 40%   **c.** 43.8%   **d.** 33.5%

6. Write $1\dfrac{5}{8}$ as a percent.

   a. 1.0625%   **b.** 16.25%   **c.** 162.5%   **d.** 1.625%

7. What is 10.8% of 200?

   a. 14.6   **b.** 21.6   **c.** 3.6   **d.** 27.4

8. 42% of 300 is what number?

   a. 126   **b.** 12.6   **c.** 7.14   **d.** 1260

9. Which statement is correct?

   a. 6% of 18 is larger than 3% of 36   **b.** 6% of 18 is smaller than 3% of 36

   c. 6% of 18 is equal to 3% of 36   **d.** 6% of 18 is larger than 18

10. Which statement is correct?

    a. 11.5% of 1200 is larger than 8.6% of 1800   **b.** 11.5% of 1200 is smaller than 8.6% of 1800

    c. 11.5% of 1200 is equal to 8.6% of 1800   **d.** 11.5% of 1200 is smaller than 10

11. What would be the amount of an 8.8% luxury tax on a fur coat valued at $5030?

    a. $442.66   **b.** $446.64   **c.** $444.64   **d.** $442.64

12. A plumber's hourly wage was $16.80 before a raise of 6.5%. What is the new hourly wage? Round to the nearest cent.

    a. $15.71   **b.** $17.89   **c.** $23.30   **d.** $17.45

13. What percent of 3000 is 6?

    a. 0.2%   **b.** 5%   **c.** 0.5%   **d.** 2%

14. What percent of 2.4 is 3.7? Round to the nearest tenth.

    a. 15.4%   **b.** 154.2%   **c.** 1.5%   **d.** 64.9%

15. Penn Co.'s stock is selling for $62.50 a share and pays a dividend of $4 a share. What percent of the stock price is the dividend?

    a. 0.64%   **b.** 64%   **c.** 15.62%   **d.** 6.4%

16. A county registrar of voters found that 582 ballots of the 48,500 ballots cast were incorrectly marked and could not be counted. What percent of the ballots could not be counted?

    a. 0.12%   **b.** 12%   **c.** 83.33%   **d.** 1.2%

17. 392 is 140% of what number?

    a. 280   **b.** 548.8   **c.** 252   **d.** 532

18. 624 is 0.8% of what number?

    a. 7800   **b.** 780   **c.** 78,000   **d.** 0.129

19. A teacher receives a salary of $2322 per month. This is 108% of last year's salary. What was the teacher's salary last year?

    a. $2050   **b.** $2150   **c.** $2250   **d.** $2507.76

20. A city's population this year is 60,000. This is 160% of the city's population 10 years ago. What was the city's population 10 years ago?

    a. 37,500   **b.** 47,500   **c.** 26,666   **d.** 96,000

21. 20 is 125% of what number?

    a. 14   **b.** 16   **c.** 20   **d.** 6.25

22. 4.5% of 2100 is what number?

    a. 2194.5   **b.** 945   **c.** 9.45   **d.** 94.5

23. A state income tax is 9% of that amount earned over $15,000. What state income tax does a person earning $24,500 pay?

    a. $650   **b.** $855   **c.** $1350   **d.** $2205

24. There are 44 grams of acid in a solution that is 11% acid. How many grams of the solution are there?

    a. 400   **b.** 484   **c.** 4.84   **d.** 4

25. At the state university, 1650 of the 5500 students are enrolled in Psychology 101. What percent of the students are enrolled in that class?

    a. 33.3%   **b.** 35%   **c.** 30%   **d.** 25%

1. A nursery is selling 5 flowering shrubs for $17.95. Find the unit cost.

   a. $3.59   b. $3.95   c. $3.35   d. $3.53

2. Find the most economical purchase:

   a. 18 ounces for $5.04   b. 9 ounces for $2.43
   c. 12 ounces for $3.12   d. 24 ounces for $7.20

3. A nut-and-snack mix costs $3.99 per pound. Find the total cost of 4.2 pounds. Round to the nearest cent.

   a. $8.09   b. $0.95   c. $17.67   d. $16.76

4. The cost of a $21 oil change was increased by 7%. What is the cost of an oil change now?

   a. $21.47   b. $22.47   c. $20.47   d. $1.47

5. An industrial plant increased the number of its employees from 3200 to 3680. What was the percent increase in the number of employees? Round to the nearest percent.

   a. 18%   b. 85%   c. 13%   d. 15%

6. A department store buys a sports jacket for $65 and uses a markup rate of 45%. What is the selling price?

   a. $94.25   b. $92.45   c. $95.42   d. $94.52

7. Dinner for four in the hotel dining room costs $86. If the same meal is served in your room, the hotel adds a 27% service charge. What will this dinner for four cost in your room?

   a. $109.22   b. $102.99   c. $113   d. $100.22

8. The price of gold dropped from approximately $540 per ounce to $420 per ounce in 3 months. What percent decrease does this represent? Round to the nearest tenth of a percent.

   a. 20%   b. 28.6%   c. 22.2%   d. 77.8%

9. Last year a company earned a profit of $160,000. This year, because of unexpected losses, the company's profits were 12% less than last year's. What is the profit this year?

   a. $140,800   b. $148,000   c. $144,800   d. $19,200

10. A jogging suit that regularly sells for $56 is on sale for 30% off the regular price. What is the sale price?

    a. $16.80   b. $39.60   c. $32.90   d. $39.20

11. A sofa priced at $875 has been marked down by 36%. What is the discounted price of the sofa?

    a. $650   **b.** $315   **c.** $350   **d.** $560

12. A contractor borrows $80,000 for 9 months at an annual interest rate of 12%. What is the simple interest due on the loan?

    a. $9600   **b.** $8400   **c.** $7200   **d.** $10,200

13. An investment group invests $50,000 in a certificate of deposit that pays 9% annual interest compounded daily. Find the value of the investment after 5 years. Use the Compound Interest Table.

    a. $76,931.20   **b.** $78,411.50   **c.** $77,648.50   **d.** $54,708.00

14. The construction loan for a builder was $2\frac{1}{2}$ points on a loan of $75,000. What was the amount of the loan origination fee?

    a. $1875   **b.** $18,755   **c.** $1785   **d.** $1870

15. A factory that produces bicycles has a 25-year mortgage of $150,000 at an annual interest rate of 7%. Find the monthly mortgage payment. Use the Monthly Payment Table. Round to the nearest cent.

    a. $1231.78   **b.** $997.95   **c.** $1060.17   **d.** $1691.76

16. Raj buys a car for $13,200. He makes a down payment of $2640, and the sales tax is 4% of the purchase price. Find the total cost for the sales tax and the down payment.

    a. $3062.40   **b.** $528   **c.** $3618   **d.** $3168

17. An electric bill totaled $105 for 875 kWh. What was the cost per kilowatt-hour?

    a. $0.11   **b.** $0.10   **c.** $0.12   **d.** $0.13

18. A company that sells heavy equipment pays its sales executives a commission of 8% of all sales over $250,000. During one year a sales executive sold $815,000 worth of heavy equipment. Find the commission earned by the sales executive.

    a. $6520   **b.** $20,000   **c.** $65,200   **d.** $45,200

19. Lila had a checking account balance of $617.84. She deposited checks for $216.25 and $408.77, and she wrote checks in the amount of $399.89 and $125.39. Find the new checking account balance.

    a. $968.36   **b.** $817.49   **c.** $717.58   **d.** $285.08

11. 26% of 19 is what number?

    a. 0.494   **b.** 4.94   **c.** 23.94   **d.** 73.08

12. Eighty-four percent of the people surveyed said they wanted the incumbent city mayor to run again. If 350 people were surveyed, how many said they wanted the incumbent mayor to run for reelection?

    a. 284   **b.** 294   **c.** 29.4   **d.** 292

13. What percent of 50 is 15?

    a. 30%   **b.** 3%   **c.** 300%   **d.** 3.33%

14. A town has a population of 5664, which is 64% of the town's population 10 years ago. What was the town's population ten years ago?

    a. 13,828   **b.** 8880   **c.** 56,640   **d.** 8850

15. 46 is 23% of what number?

    a. 10.58   **b.** 2   **c.** 200   **d.** 50

16. Nicole answered 44 questions on an exam correctly. This was 80% of the total number of exam questions. How many questions were on the exam?

    a. 55   **b.** 35   **c.** 182   **d.** 50

17. Twenty tea bags cost $2.49. Find the cost per bag. Round to the nearest cent.

    a. $1.25   **b.** $0.12   **c.** $1.24   **d.** $0.13

18. Wright's Garden Center uses a markup rate of 35%. What is the selling price of a wheelbarrow that cost the shop $54?

    a. $18.90   **b.** $73.90   **c.** $55.89   **d.** $72.90

19. Nast Jewelers Store is giving a $45 discount on a watch that regularly sells for $150. What is the discount rate?

    a. $33\frac{1}{3}$%   **b.** 30%   **c.** 35%   **d.** 3%

20. A 3-year car loan of $15,280 had a simple interest rate of 7.6%. Find the simple interest on the loan.

    a. $1161.28   **b.** $348.38   **c.** $11,612.80   **d.** $3483.84

The pictograph shows the number of soft drinks sold at a local fast-food restaurant during 4 weeks of the year. Each glass represents 500 soft drinks.

Week 1

Week 2

Week 3

Week 4

1. How many soft drinks were sold during Weeks 1 and 2?
   a. 12 **b.** 6000
   c. 1200 **d.** 600

2. Find the ratio of the number of soft drinks sold during the first week to the number of soft drinks sold during the fourth week.
   a. $\frac{2}{7}$ **b.** $\frac{5}{7}$ **c.** $\frac{6}{7}$ **d.** $\frac{11}{14}$

The circle graph shows the distribution of the 62,000 students enrolled in the schools of a large city.

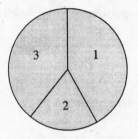

3. How many students are enrolled in high school?
   a. 24,180 **b.** 26,040
   c. 11,780 **d.** 16,460

4. How many students are enrolled in college?
   a. 24,180 **b.** 11,780
   c. 25,180 **d.** 2418

5. How many students attend elementary schools?
   a. 2604 **b.** 26,040
   c. 28,040 **d.** 16,460

TOTAL SCHOOL ENROLLMENT
1: 42% – Elementary School
2: 19% – High School
3: 39% – College

The double bar graph shows the number of shares of stock (in thousands) sold on the Pacific Stock Exchange for the four quarters in 2000 and 2001.

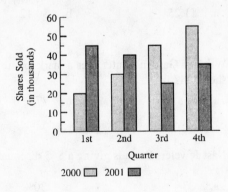

6. What is the difference in the total number of sales during the first and fourth quarters of 2000 and 2001?
   a. 30,000 **b.** 25
   c. 250 **d.** 45,000

7. Find the total shares sold during 2001.
   a. 155,000 **b.** 150,000
   c. 145,000 **d.** 130,000

8. What is the difference in fourth-quarter sales from 2000 and 2001?
   a. 20 **b.** 200
   c. 20,000 **d.** 25,000

9. The cost of seven lunches at a diner were $8.40, $10.44, $11.12, $11.08, $11.24, $7.33, and $9.45. What was the average cost of these lunches? Round to the nearest cent.
   a. $9.45 **b.** $9.87 **c.** $9.86 **d.** $9.85

10. The vertical rise, in feet, for seven ski lifts at a resort are 2050, 980, 900, 1050, 1540, 2010, and 1360. What is the median vertical rise for these ski lifts?
   a. 1230 ft **b.** 1050 ft **c.** 1360 ft **d.** 2050 ft

The double-line graph shows a company's profits (in thousands of dollars) for each quarter of 2000 and 2001.

11. Find the difference between the company's fourth-quarter profits for 2000 and 2001.
    a. $20,000   b. $30,000   c. $10,000   d. $25,000

12. What is the ratio of the first-quarter sales in 2000 to the first-quarter sales in 2001?

    a. $\frac{3}{2}$ b. $\frac{3}{4}$ c. $\frac{2}{5}$ d. $\frac{2}{3}$

13. How much did profits drop from the third quarter of 2001 to the fourth quarter of 2001?
    a. $10,000   b. $15,000   c. $20,000   d. $40,000

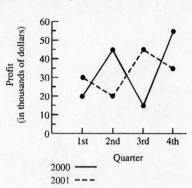

The histogram shows the distribution of salaries of 60 employees of a small manufacturing company.

14. Find the number of employees whose salary is between $30,000 and $48,000.
    a. 21   b. 26   c. 23   d. 35

15. What is the ratio of the number of employees whose salaries are between $30,000 and $36,000 to the number of employees whose salaries are less than $42,000?

    a. $\frac{14}{5}$ b. $\frac{5}{14}$ c. $\frac{5}{19}$ d. $\frac{7}{29}$

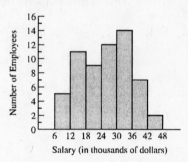

The frequency polygon shows the number of hours of TV watched per week by 68 families.

16. How many families watch between 5 and 15 hours per week?

    a. 8   b. 4   c. 12   d. 14

17. What is the ratio of the number of families who watched less than 5 hours each week to the number of families who watched more than 25 hours each week?
    a. 1:2   b. 3:2   c. 4:3   d. 2:1

18. How many families watched more than 15 hours each week?
    a. 30   b. 35   c. 42   d. 45

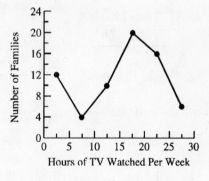

19. Two dice are rolled. What is the probability that the sum of the dots on the upward faces is <u>not</u> 12?

    a. $\frac{1}{36}$ b. $\frac{35}{36}$ c. $\frac{5}{6}$ d. $\frac{10}{36}$

20. The scores of the 14 leaders participating in a college golf tournament are given below. Determine the third quartile of the scores.

80	76	70	71	74	68	72
74	70	70	73	75	69	73

    a. 70   b. 73   c. 74   d. 80

Name: _____

Date: _____

1. Convert $2\frac{1}{4}$ ft to inches.

    a. 37 in.   **b.** 31 in.   **c.** 40 in.   **d.** 27 in.

2. Subtract: 4 yd 1 ft – 1 yd 2 ft

    a. 2 yd 2 ft   **b.** 3 yd 2 ft   **c.** 2 yd 1 ft   **d.** 1 yd 2 ft

3. A plumber used 2 ft 8 in., 2 ft 6 in., and 7 in. of copper tubing to install a sink. Find the total length of copper tubing used.

    a. 4 ft 7 in.   **b.** 5 ft 7 in.   **c.** 4 ft 9 in.   **d.** 5 ft 9 in.

4. Twenty-five yards of material were used for making pleated drapes. How many feet of material were used?

    a. 50 ft   **b.** $8\frac{1}{3}$ ft   **c.** 75 ft   **d.** 100 ft

5. Convert: 82 oz = _____ lb _____ oz

    a. 6 lb 4 oz   **b.** 5 lb 2 oz   **c.** 5 lb 6 oz   **d.** 6 lb 6 oz

6. Convert $3\frac{1}{4}$ lb to ounces.

    a. 44 oz   **b.** 22 oz   **c.** 52 oz   **d.** 33 oz

7. Add: 2 tons 1500 lb
          + 3 tons   700 lb

    a. 6 tons 1200 lb   **b.** 5 tons 1200 lb   **c.** 6 tons 200 lb   **d.** 6 tons 800 lb

8. Subtract: 10 lb 9 oz
              – 6 lb 14 oz

    a. 4 lb 7 oz   **b.** 3 lb 7 oz   **c.** 4 lb 11 oz   **d.** 3 lb 11 oz

9. Hand cream weighing 7 lb 14 oz is divided equally and poured into seven containers. How much hand cream is in each container?

    a. 1 lb 4 oz   **b.** 1 lb 5 oz   **c.** 1 lb 3 oz   **d.** 1 lb 2 oz

10. A can of tuna weighs 6 oz. Find the weight in pounds of a case of tuna containing 48 cans.

    a. 8 lb   **b.** 18 lb   **c.** 4 lb   **d.** 12 lb

11. Convert: 9 qt = _____ gal _____ qt

    a. 2 gal 1 qt   **b.** 2 gal 2 qt   **c.** 1 gal 1 qt   **d.** 2 gal 3 qt

12. Convert 19 pt to quarts.

    a. 38 qt   **b.** $8\frac{1}{2}$ qt   **c.** $9\frac{1}{2}$ qt   **d.** $4\frac{3}{4}$ qt

13. Find the sum of $2\frac{1}{3}$ qt and $1\frac{5}{6}$ qt.

    a. $3\frac{3}{8}$ qt   **b.** $4\frac{3}{8}$ qt   **c.** $3\frac{1}{2}$ qt   **d.** $4\frac{1}{6}$ qt

14. Multiply: $3\frac{1}{5}$ qt × 5

    a. $\frac{9}{10}$ qt   **b.** 15 qt   **c.** 16 qt   **d.** $\frac{4}{5}$ qt

15. If one serving contains $1\frac{1}{2}$ c, how many servings can be made from 6 qt?

    a. 16 servings   **b.** 15 servings   **c.** 12 servings   **d.** 25 servings

16. One bottle of apple juice holds 36 fl oz. How many quarts are in 9 bottles of the apple juice?

    a. $22\frac{1}{2}$ qt   **b.** $10\frac{1}{8}$ qt   **c.** 4 qt   **d.** $3\frac{1}{6}$ qt

17. A construction worker carries 4.5-pound blocks up a 12-foot flight of stairs. How many foot-pounds of energy are required to carry 400 blocks up the stairs?

    a. 4800 ft·lb   **b.** 1800 ft·lb   **c.** 21,600 ft·lb   **d.** 31,600 ft·lb

18. A crane lifts a 1400-pound steel beam to the roof of a building 44 ft high. Find the amount of energy required by the crane in lifting the beam.

    a. 72,600 ft·lb   **b.** 61,600 ft·lb   **c.** 30,800 ft·lb   **d.** 31.82 ft·lb

19. Convert $2\frac{1}{5}$ hp to foot pounds per second. $\left(1\ hp = 550\frac{ft\cdot lb}{s}\right)$

    a. $1210\frac{ft\cdot lb}{s}$ **b.** $1100\frac{ft\cdot lb}{s}$ **c.** $660\frac{ft\cdot lb}{s}$ **d.** $5500\frac{ft\cdot lb}{s}$

20. A motor has a power of $6600\frac{ft\cdot lb}{s}$. Find the horsepower of the motor. $\left(1\ hp = 550\frac{ft\cdot lb}{s}\right)$

    a. 10 hp   **b.** 14 hp   **c.** 16 hp   **d.** 12 hp

Name: _____

Date: _____

1. Convert 164 cm to meters.

   a. 0.164 m   **b.** 16.4 m   **c.** 1.64 m   **d.** 16,400 m

2. Convert 62 mm to centimeters.

   a. 0.62 cm   **b.** 620 cm   **c.** 6.2 cm   **d.** 0.062 cm

3. Convert 2.05 km to meters.

   a. 205 m   **b.** 2050 m   **c.** 20.5 m   **d.** 20,500 m

4. Convert 2 m 65 cm to meters.

   a. 130 cm   **b.** 26.5 cm   **c.** 2.65 m   **d.** 1.35 m

5. Fabric with a length of 7.53 m is cut into three equal pieces. Find the length, in centimeters, of each piece.

   a. 0.251 cm   **b.** 25.1 cm   **c.** 2.51 cm   **d.** 251 cm

6. A picture is 46 cm wide and 75 cm high. Find the length of framing needed to put around the picture.

   a. 1.21 m   **b.** 2.42 m   **c.** 4.84 m   **d.** 48.4 m

7. Convert 2.47 g to milligrams.

   a. 247 mg   **b.** 2470 mg   **c.** 24.7 g   **d.** 0.0247 g

8. Convert 12 mg to grams.

   a. 0.12 g   **b.** 0.012 g   **c.** 1.2 g   **d.** 12,000 g

9. Convert 45 g 126 mg to grams.

   a. 45,126 g   **b.** 46.26 g   **c.** 4512.6 g   **d.** 45.126 g

10. Convert 2 kg 50 g to kilograms.

    a. 2.50 kg   **b.** 250 kg   **c.** 2.050 kg   **d.** 2050 kg

11. A fisherman caught trout weighing 650 g, 1150 g, 390 g, and 890 g. Find the total weight in kilograms of the fish.

    a. 308 kg   **b.** 3.08 kg   **c.** 3080 kg   **d.** 30.8 kg

12. An airline charges $2.50 for each kilogram or part of a kilogram over 15 kg of luggage weight. How much extra must a passenger pay who has two pieces of luggage weighing 9400 g and 8700 g?

    a. $7.75   **b.** $10.00   **c.** $9.25   **d.** $7.50

13. Convert 0.2 L to cubic centimeters.

    a. 200 cm^3 **b.** 0.2 cm^3 **c.** 20 cm^3 **d.** 0.002 cm^3

14. Convert 1296 L to kiloliters.

    a. 1,296,000 kl   **b.** 12.96 kl   **c.** 129.6 kl   **d.** 1.296 kl

15. Convert 12 L 140 ml to liters.

    a. 13.40 L   **b.** 12.014 L   **c.** 12.140 L   **d.** 12,140 L

16. Convert 1 kl 72 L to kiloliters.

    a. 1072 kl   **b.** 1.072 kl   **c.** 172 kl   **d.** 1.72 kl

17. If 400 ml of chlorine are put into a swimming pool each day, how many liters of chlorine are used in 90 days?

    a. 4.44 L   **b.** 360 L   **c.** 3.6 L   **d.** 36 L

18. Canoeing burns 540 Calories per hour. If you paddle three times a week for $1\frac{1}{2}$ h each time, how many Calories will you burn in 4 weeks?

    a. 9720 Calories   **b.** 3240 Calories   **c.** 24,300 Calories   **d.** 929 Calories

19. Ham costs $2.15 per pound. Find the cost per kilogram. Round to the nearest cent. (2.2 lb = 1 kg)

    a. $4.73/kg   **b.** $0.98/kg   **c.** $4.37/kg   **d.** $7.53/kg

20. Express 75 m/s in feet per second. Round to the nearest tenth. (1 m = 3.28 ft)

    a. 264 ft/s   **b.** 22.8 ft/s   **c.** 246 ft/s   **d.** 228.7 ft/s

Name: _____

Date: _____

The circle graph shows a family's monthly expenditures totaling $2250.

1. How much money is saved monthly?
   a. $315
   b. $160.71
   c. $31.50
   d. $337.50

2. Find the ratio of the amount of money saved to the amount spent for transportation.

   a. $\frac{15}{14}$ b. $\frac{5}{7}$ c. $\frac{14}{15}$ d. $\frac{7}{8}$

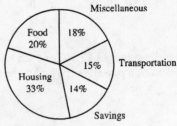

Distribution for a Monthly
Income of $2250

The double-bar graph shows the number of video recorders sold during the first 3 months of 2000 and 2001.

3. Find the difference in March sales for 2000 and 2001.
   a. 200
   b. 1000
   c. 800
   d. 600

4. What percent of 2001's 3-month's sales were made in March? Round to the nearest whole percent.
   a. 47%
   b. 21%
   c. 50%
   d. 44%

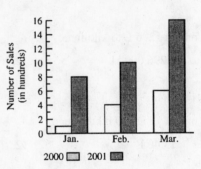

5. A fishing boat caught 100 lb of fish on Monday, 150 lb on Tuesday, 175 lb on Wednesday, and 110 lb on Friday. Find the weight of the average catch.
   a. 134.5 lb   b. 135.25 lb   c. 135 lb   d. 133.75 lb

6. The timed runs, in seconds, for five downhill skiers were 52.1, 55.4, 53.6, 51.5 and 53.9. What was the median time?
   a. 52.8 s   b. 53.3 s   c. 53.6 s   d. 52.1 s

7. Convert 4 yd to inches.
   a. 12 in.   b. 144 in.   c. 36 in.   d. 100 in.

8. Find the product of 2 ft 7 in. and 6.
   a. 15 ft 3 in.   b. 14 ft 10 in.   c. 15 ft 6 in.   d. 15 ft 5 in.

9. Convert 110 oz to pounds.
   a. 6.875 lb   b. 13.75 lb   c. 1.10 lb   d. 11 lb

10. Add: 2 tons   900 lb
         + 5 tons 1200 lb

   a. 8 tons 500 lb   b. 9 tons 100 lb   c. 8 tons 100 lb   d. 8 tons 300 lb

11. Convert $5\frac{1}{2}$ pt to quarts.

    a. 11 qt   **b.** 22 qt   **c.** $2\frac{1}{4}$ qt   **d.** $2\frac{3}{4}$ qt

12. A piece of wire 12 ft 8 in. long is cut from a roll containing 60 ft of wire. How much wire remains on the roll?

    a. 46 ft 8 in.   **b.** 48 ft 4 in.   **c.** 47 ft 2 in.   **d.** 47 ft 4 in.

13. Four farmers came to the co-op with bags of grain to sell. The four bags weighed 6 lb 2 oz, 4 lb 9 oz, 5 lb 3 oz, and 9 lb 8 oz. What was the total weight of the four bags of grain?

    a. 15 lb 6 oz   **b.** 24 lb 6 oz   **c.** 24 lb 22 oz   **d.** 25 lb 6 oz

14. Convert 6.24 m to centimeters.

    a. 62.4 cm   **b.** 624 cm   **c.** 0.624 cm   **d.** 6240 cm

15. Convert 2754 g to kilograms.

    a. 275,400 kg   **b.** 27.54 kg   **c.** 2.754 kg   **d.** 275.4 kg

16. Convert 4 L 50 ml to cubic centimeters.

    a. 4.5 cm^3 **b.** 45 cm^3 **c.** 4050 cm^3 **d.** 405 cm^3

17. Find the number of quarts in 7 L. (1 L = 1.06 qt)

    a. 7.42 qt   **b.** 74.2 qt   **c.** 0.742 qt   **d.** 742 qt

18. Gasoline costs $1.20/gal. Find the cost per liter (1 L = 1.06 qt). Round to the nearest cent.

    a. $1.13/L   **b.** $0.28/L   **c.** $0.32/L   **d.** $0.30/L

19. On a day's fishing trip, fish weighing 750 g, 500 g, and 380 g were caught. What was the total weight of the fish in kilograms?

    a. 16.3 kg   **b.** 1.630 kg   **c.** 163 kg   **d.** 17.8 kg

20. A multivitamin tablet has 50 mg of phosphorus. If there are 75 vitamins in a bottle, how many grams of phosphorus are in the bottle?

    a. 3.75 g   **b.** 375 g   **c.** 37.5 g   **d.** 0.37 g

Name: _____

Date: _____

1. Which statement is correct?

   a. $-3 < -4$ **b.** $-3 > -4$ **c.** $-7 > 6$ **d.** $-2 > 0$

2. Which statement is correct?

   a. $-7 > 0$ **b.** $-7 < 6$ **c.** $-7 > 6$ **d.** $-7 = 7$

3. Evaluate $-|-3|$ and $-|4|$.

   a. -3 and -4 **b.** -3 and 4 **c.** 3 and 4 **d.** 3 and -4

4. Add: $-8 + 3$

   a. 11 **b.** -5 **c.** 5 **d.** -11

5. Find the sum of -5, -7, and -12.

   a. -14 **b.** 24 **c.** 14 **d.** -24

6. Subtract: $-7 - 2$

   a. -9 **b.** -5 **c.** 5 **d.** 14

7. Subtract: $3 - 5 - 2$

   a. -4 **b.** 1 **c.** -1 **d.** -10

8. Find the product of -7 and 4.

   a. -28 **b.** -3 **c.** 28 **d.** 3

9. Multiply: $(-2) \times (-4) \times 8$

   a. -64 **b.** 64 **c.** 0 **d.** 16

10. Find the temperature after a rise of $12°C$ from $-5°C$.

    a. $7°C$ **b.** $-17°C$ **c.** $-7°C$ **d.** $17°C$

11. The temperature at 4 P.M. was $12°$. The temperature at 3 A.M. was $-6°$. Find the difference between the temperatures.

    a. $6°$ **b.** $20°$ **c.** $14°$ **d.** $18°$

12. Add: $-\dfrac{5}{6} + \left(-\dfrac{2}{3}\right)$

    a. $-1\dfrac{1}{2}$ **b.** 1 **c.** $1\dfrac{1}{2}$ **d.** $-\dfrac{7}{9}$

13. Add: $2\dfrac{1}{6} + \left(-1\dfrac{3}{4}\right)$

    a. $\dfrac{7}{12}$ **b.** $1\dfrac{7}{12}$ **c.** $-\dfrac{5}{12}$ **d.** $\dfrac{5}{12}$

14. Subtract: $\dfrac{3}{4} - \left(-2\dfrac{1}{2}\right)$

    a. $-1\dfrac{3}{4}$ **b.** $3\dfrac{1}{2}$ **c.** $3\dfrac{1}{4}$ **d.** $-3\dfrac{1}{4}$

15. Subtract: $-\dfrac{3}{7} - \left(-\dfrac{2}{3}\right)$

    a. $-\dfrac{23}{21}$ **b.** $-\dfrac{1}{4}$ **c.** $-\dfrac{2}{7}$ **d.** $\dfrac{5}{21}$

16. Multiply: $-8 \times \left(-\dfrac{5}{12}\right)$

    a. $19\dfrac{1}{5}$ **b.** $3\dfrac{1}{3}$ **c.** $3\dfrac{3}{4}$ **d.** $-3\dfrac{1}{3}$

17. Find the quotient of $-\dfrac{3}{5}$ and 2.

    a. $-\dfrac{3}{10}$ **b.** $-3\dfrac{1}{3}$ **c.** $3\dfrac{1}{3}$ **d.** $\dfrac{3}{10}$

18. What is -3.1 decreased by 1.6?

    a. -4.7 **b.** 1.5 **c.** -1.5 **d.** 4.7

19. Multiply: $0.002 \times (-6.3)$

    a. 0.0126 **b.** 0.00126 **c.** -0.0126 **d.** -0.00126

20. Find the product of -2.56 and 29.2.

    a. -58.112 **b.** 58.112 **c.** -74.752 **d.** 74.752

21. Divide: $-4.5 \div (-0.03)$

    a. -150 **b.** 150 **c.** 15 **d.** 1.5

22. Simplify: $3 - (-2)^2 + (-3) \div (-1)$

    a. 8 **b.** 1 **c.** 2 **d.** -1

23. Simplify: $15 \div (-3) + 8 - 4(6 - 4)$

    a. -15 **b.** -5 **c.** 15 **d.** 5

24. Write 0.00000356 in scientific notation.

    a. 3.56×10^{-7} **b.** 3.56×10^{5} **c.** 3.56×10^{-5} **d.** 3.56×10^{-6}

25. On February 21, 1918, the temperature in Granville, North Dakota, rose to 10°C from -36.11°C. Find the difference between these two temperatures.

    a. 46.11°C   **b.** -26.11°C   **c.** 26.11°C   **d.** -46.11°C

Name: _____

Date: _____

1. Evaluate $2ac - b^2 + c$ when $a = -2$, $b - 4$, and $c = -1$.

    a. -18 **b.** -13 **c.** -12 **d.** 18

2. Evaluate $4ab - a^2b$ when $a = -2$ and $b = -1$.

    a. 4 **b.** -3 **c.** -8 **d.** 12

3. Simplify: $8ab - 5ac - 9ab$

    a. $-ab - 5ac$ **b.** $-17ab - 5ac$ **c.** $ab - 5ac$ **d.** $17ab - 5ac$

4. Simplify: $3x - 2(4 - x) + 2x$

    a. $7x - 4$ **b.** $4x - 8$ **c.** $7x + 4$ **d.** $7x - 8$

5. Which number is a solution of $3x - 5 = 5x + 7$?

    a. 6 **b.** 3 **c.** -6 **d.** -3

6. Solve: $x - 9 = -4$

    a. -5 **b.** 5 **c.** 13 **d.** -13

7. Solve: $-11x = -77$

    a. 7 **b.** -7 **c.** $\dfrac{1}{7}$ **d.** $-\dfrac{1}{7}$

8. Solve: $-\dfrac{x}{3} = -9$

    a. 27 **b.** -27 **c.** $\dfrac{1}{3}$ **d.** 3

9. A new car has a sticker price of \$18,425. After one year of ownership, the value of the car has depreciated to \$9500. Find the amount of the depreciation by using the formula $V = N - D$, where V is the value of the car now, N is the original value, and D is the depreciation.

    a. \$9825   **b.** \$8925   **c.** \$9500   **d.** \$9925

10. Solve: $3 - 5x = 8$

    a. 2 **b.** -1 **c.** 1 **d.** -2

11. Solve: $\frac{3}{4}x - 2 = 7$

   a. $6\frac{3}{4}$ b. -12 c. 6   d. 12

12. Solve: $-7 = -3 + 2x$

   a. -5 b. $-\frac{21}{2}$ c. -2 d. 2

13. Find the Celsius temperature when the Fahrenheit temperature is $-40°$. Use the formula $F = \frac{9}{5}C + 32$, where F is the Fahrenheit temperature and C is the Celsius temperature.

   a. $-4\frac{4}{9}°C$ b. $40°C$ c. $-30°C$ d. $-40°C$

14. Solve: $3x - 5 = x - 4$

   a. $\frac{1}{4}$ b. $-2\frac{1}{4}$ c. $\frac{1}{2}$ d. $-\frac{1}{4}$

15. Solve: $-3x - 4(2 - x) = -5$

   a. $-\frac{3}{4}$ b. 3   c. $-1\frac{1}{3}$ d. -13

16. Translate "t decreased by the quotient of t and four" into a mathematical expression.

   a. $t - \frac{t}{4}$ b. $t - \frac{4}{t}$ c. $\frac{t - 4}{t}$ d. $\frac{4 - t}{4}$

17. Translate "the product of three and the sum of a number and two" into a mathematical expression.

   a. $(3 + n) \cdot 2$ b. $3(n + 2)$ c. $3n + 2$ d. $3 + 2n$

18. Translate "4 less than three times a number is seven" into an equation and solve.

   a. 17   b. 21   c. $2\frac{3}{4}$ d. $3\frac{2}{3}$

19. The difference between four and twice a number is ten. Find the number.

   a. 7   b. -7 c. -3 d. 3

20. One fifth of a department store's floor space is used for a 2525-square-foot display of sporting goods. How many square feet of floor space are there in the entire store?

   a. $12,225 \text{ ft}^2$ b. 505 ft^2 c. $12,505 \text{ ft}^2$ d. $12,625 \text{ ft}^2$

1. Find the complement of a 72° angle.

   a. 28°　　　　　b. 108°　　　　　c. 180°　　　　　d. 18°

2. Two angles of a triangle are 48° and 57°. Find the measure of the third angle of the triangle.

   a. 85°　　　　　b. 95°　　　　　c. 75°　　　　　d. 65°

3. In the figure, $L_1 \parallel L_2$. $\angle x = 85°$. Find $\angle x + \angle y$.

   a. 95°　　　　　b. 85°

   c. 180°　　　　d. 275°

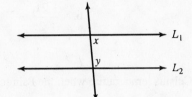

4. In the figure, $L_1 \parallel L_2$. $\angle x = 21°$. Find $\angle a + \angle b$.

   a. 158°　　　　b. 318°

   c. 42°　　　　　d. 108°

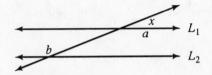

5. Find the perimeter of a rectangle with a length of 4 ft 5 in. and a width of 3 ft.

   a. 7 ft 5 in.　　　b. 14 ft 5 in.　　　c. 14 ft 10 in.　　　d. 10 ft 5 in.

6. Find the perimeter of the composite figure. Use 3.14 for π.

   a. 22.14 cm　　　b. 22.44 cm

   c. 18.38 cm　　　d. 20.56 cm

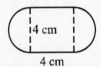

7. A rectangular lot 60 ft by 110 ft is fenced with redwood. At $7.15 per foot, how much does it cost to fence the lot?

   a. $2431　　　　b. $1215.50　　　c. $3853.14　　　d. $2631

8. Find the area of a circle with a diameter of 6 in. Use 3.14 for π.

   a. 28.26 in.^{2}　　　b. 113.04 in.^{2}　　　c. 354.95 in.^{2}　　　d. 88.74 in.^{2}

9. Find the area of the composite figure. Use 3.14 for π.

   a. 11.44 cm^2　　　b. 45.76 cm^2

   c. 22.88 cm^2　　　d. 73.12 cm^2

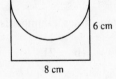

10. Find the area between the two rectangles.

    a. 56 in.^{2}　　　b. 54 in.^{2}

    c. 150 in.^{2}　　　d. 96 in.^{2}

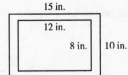

11. A yard measures 55 ft by 20 ft. How much would it cost to install sod on the yard if the cost for sod is $6.25 for 50 ft^2?

    a. $687.50　　　b. $343.75　　　c. $6875　　　d. $137.50

Chapter 12 Test Form E (*continued*)

Name: _____

12. Find the volume of a cylinder with a diameter of 40 cm and a height of 60 cm. Use 3.14 for π.

   a. 75,360 cm³   **b.** 37,680 cm³   **c.** 301,440 cm³   **d.** 57,360 cm³

13. Find the volume of the solid. The radius of the cylinder is 3 m. Use 3.14 for π.

   a. 407.065 m³   **b.** 484.78 m³

   c. 739.12 m³   **d.** 428.26 m³

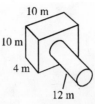

14. Find the volume of a spherical melon that has a 6-inch diameter. Use 3.14 for π.

   a. 37.68 in.³   **b.** 63.585 in.³   **c.** 113.04 in.³   **d.** 150.72 in.³

15. Find the square root of 31. Round to the nearest thousandth.

   a. 5.658   **b.** 5.568   **c.** 5.586   **d.** 5.657

16. Find the unknown side of the triangle. Round to the nearest tenth.

   a. 10.5 in.   **b.** 9.4 in.
   c. 12 in.   **d.** 8.5 in.

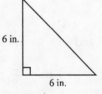

17. A fence that costs $4.50 per foot is built around a plot. How much does it cost to fence the plot?

   a. $585   **b.** $675
   c. $607.50   **d.** $630

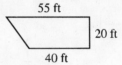

18. Triangles *ABC* and *DEF* are similar. Find side *BC*. Round to the nearest tenth.

   a. 6.4 m   **b.** 15 m
   c. 9.6 m   **d.** 10.2 m

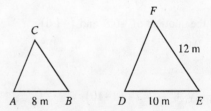

19. Triangles *ABC* and *DEF* are similar. The height of triangle *ABC* is 3 in. Find the area of triangle *DEF*.

   a. 36 in.²   **b.** 6 in.²
   c. 9 in.²   **d.** 72 in.²

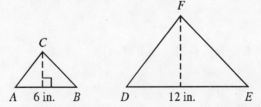

20. In the figure, triangles *ABC* and *DEF* are congruent. Find the measure of ∠*F*.

   a. 67°   **b.** 47°
   c. 49°   **d.** 23°

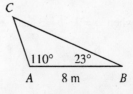

Name: _____
Date: _____

1. Find the sum of 64 and −24.

   a. −88
   b. 40
   c. 88
   d. −40

2. Add: $-\dfrac{3}{8}+\dfrac{1}{2}$

   a. $\dfrac{1}{8}$
   b. $-\dfrac{1}{8}$
   c. $-\dfrac{7}{8}$
   d. $\dfrac{7}{8}$

3. What is 46 decreased by 71?

   a. −25
   b. 25
   c. 118
   d. −118

4. Subtract: $1.4-\left(-3.5\right)$

   a. 2.1
   b. −2.1
   c. 4.9
   d. −4.9

5. Find the product of 8 and −3.

   a. 24
   b. $-\dfrac{3}{8}$
   c. −24
   d. 5

6. Multiply: $-\dfrac{3}{4}\times\left(-\dfrac{4}{8}\right)$

   a. $\dfrac{3}{8}$
   b. $\dfrac{1}{4}$
   c. $-\dfrac{3}{8}$
   d. $1\dfrac{1}{2}$

7. Find the quotient of −0.8 and $\left(-1.6\right)$.

   a. 0.05
   b. 0.5
   c. −5
   d. −0.5

8. Simplify: $8^2-3\times7+\left(8-10\right)$

   a. 425
   b. 41
   c. 45
   d. 38

9. Simplify: $\left(-3\right)^2\times2-8\div\left(-4\right)$

   a. 16
   b. $\dfrac{5}{2}$
   c. $-\dfrac{5}{2}$
   d. 20

10. Evaluate $c^2-\left(a^2+b\right)$ when $a=2$, $b=3$, and $c=4$.

    a. 9
    b. 7
    c. −1
    d. 8

11. Simplify: $2x - 3y - 5y + 2x$

    a. $-4x - 8y$ **b.** $4x + 8y$ **c.** $4x - 2y$ **d.** $4x - 8y$

12. Solve: $x - 7 = -12$

    a. 5   **b.** -19 **c.** 19   **d.** -5

13. Solve: $\dfrac{x}{2} = -3$

    a. -1 **b.** -5 **c.** -6 **d.** 6

14. Solve: $-5x - 11 = 4$

    a. -3 **b.** $1\dfrac{2}{5}$ **c.** 3   **d.** $-1\dfrac{2}{5}$

15. Solve: $3x - 4 = 2x + 6$

    a. 2   **b.** 10   **c.** -2 **d.** -10

16. The total of 15 and a number is 6. Find the number.

    a. -21 **b.** 9   **c.** -9 **d.** 21

17. Find the Celsius temperature when the Fahrenheit temperature is 104°. Use the formula $F = \dfrac{9}{5}C + 32$, where F is the Fahrenheit temperature and C is the Celsius temperature.

    a. 85°   **b.** 129.6°   **c.** 30°   **d.** 40°

18. A cement contractor charges $36 for travel expenses plus $42 for each cubic yard of cement. How many cubic yards of cement can be purchased for $372?

    a. 6.95 yd³   **b.** 8 yd³   **c.** 7.81 yd³   **d.** 9.2 yd³

19. Two angles of a triangle measure 78° and 88°. Find the measure of the third angle.

    a. 194°   **b.** 140°   **c.** 14°   **d.** 190°

20. In the figure, $L_1 \parallel L_2$. $\angle x = 123°$. Find $\angle y$.

a. 57°   b. 237°

c. 33°   d. 67°

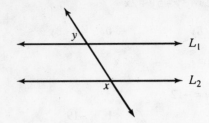

21. Find the perimeter of a square whose sides are 5.4 in.

a. 2.16 in.   b. 21.6 in.   c. 10.8 in.   d. 29.16 in.

22. Find the area of the figure.

a. 93 in.^{2} b. 126 in.^{2}

c. 72 in.^{2} d. 83 in.^{2}

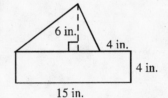

6 in.

4 in.

4 in.

15 in.

23. Find the volume of a cylinder with a radius of 3.4 cm and a height of 9 cm. Use $\dfrac{22}{7}$ for π.

Round to the nearest hundredth.

a. 326.98 cm^3 b. 192.21 cm^3 c. 36.34 cm^3 d. 82.72 cm^3

24. Find the unknown leg of the right triangle. Round to the nearest tenth.

a. 27.5 ft   b. 4 ft

c. 15.8 ft   d. 17.4 ft

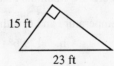

15 ft

23 ft

25. In the figure, triangles *ABC* and *DEF* are similar. Find the length of side *DE*.

a. 35 in.   b. $1\dfrac{2}{7}$ in.

c. 5 in.   d. $1\dfrac{2}{5}$ in.

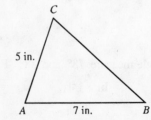

C

5 in.

A   7 in.   B

F

1 in.

D   E

1. Subtract: $22{,}173 - 17{,}621$
   - **a.** 4552
   - **b.** 4525
   - **c.** 5452
   - **d.** 4452

2. Find $10{,}395$ divided by 27.
   - **a.** 405
   - **b.** 385
   - **c.** 383
   - **d.** 144

3. Simplify: $7 + 3 \times 2 - (4 - 1) + 4^2$
   - **a.** 33
   - **b.** 1
   - **c.** 26
   - **d.** 28

4. You withdraw $135 from your savings account, which had totaled $846. What is your new savings account balance?
   - **a.** $729
   - **b.** $711
   - **c.** $709
   - **d.** $693

5. Add: $3\dfrac{1}{8} + 2\dfrac{1}{3}$
   - **a.** $5\dfrac{2}{11}$
   - **b.** $5\dfrac{3}{4}$
   - **c.** $\dfrac{1}{24}$
   - **d.** $5\dfrac{11}{24}$

6. Subtract: $6\dfrac{1}{2} - 3\dfrac{5}{6}$
   - **a.** 3
   - **b.** $2\dfrac{2}{3}$
   - **c.** $3\dfrac{2}{3}$
   - **d.** $2\dfrac{1}{3}$

7. Find the product of $2\dfrac{5}{6}$ and $1\dfrac{1}{5}$.
   - **a.** $3\dfrac{2}{5}$
   - **b.** $2\dfrac{6}{11}$
   - **c.** $2\dfrac{1}{5}$
   - **d.** $2\dfrac{13}{16}$

8. Divide: $1\dfrac{3}{4} \div 2\dfrac{1}{3}$
   - **a.** $\dfrac{3}{4}$
   - **b.** $4\dfrac{1}{12}$
   - **c.** $1\dfrac{1}{3}$
   - **d.** $\dfrac{3}{8}$

9. Simplify: $\left(\dfrac{2}{3} + \dfrac{1}{4}\right) - \dfrac{1}{2} \div \dfrac{1}{6}$
   - **a.** $-2\dfrac{1}{12}$
   - **b.** $2\dfrac{1}{6}$
   - **c.** $\dfrac{1}{12}$
   - **d.** $2\dfrac{1}{12}$

10. A piece of ribbon $4\dfrac{1}{3}$ ft long is cut from a 12-foot roll of ribbon. How much ribbon remains on the roll?
    - **a.** $6\dfrac{2}{3}$ ft
    - **b.** $8\dfrac{2}{3}$ ft
    - **c.** $7\dfrac{2}{3}$ ft
    - **d.** $8\dfrac{1}{3}$ ft

11. Find 1.6 decreased by 0.08.

    a. 0.128   **b.** 1.68   **c.** 0.20   **d.** 1.52

12. Multiply: 0.02×0.006

    a. 0.12   **b.** 0.012   **c.** 0.00012   **d.** 0.0012

13. Find the quotient of 8.4 and 0.25.

    a. 33.6   **b.** 3.36   **c.** 336   **d.** 0.336

14. Convert 0.018 to a fraction.

    a. $\dfrac{9}{50}$ **b.** $\dfrac{3}{125}$ **c.** $\dfrac{9}{500}$ **d.** $\dfrac{6}{125}$

15. Convert to a decimal: $\dfrac{19}{31}$ Round to the nearest thousandth.

    a. 0.594   **b.** 0.59   **c.** 0.61   **d.** 0.613

16. Write 84 to 36 as a ratio in simplest form using a fraction.

    a. $\dfrac{7}{3}$ **b.** $\dfrac{2}{3}$ **c.** $\dfrac{9}{21}$ **d.** $\dfrac{3}{7}$

17. Write "119 miles on 6.8 gallons" as a unit rate.

    a. 18.5 mi/gal   **b.** 17.7 mi/gal   **c.** 17.5 mi/gal   **d.** 18.3 mi/gal

18. Solve the proportion: $\dfrac{8}{n} = \dfrac{45}{37}$ Round to the nearest hundredth.

    a. $n = 9.73$ **b.** $n = 65.78$ **c.** $n = 6.49$ **d.** $n = 6.58$

19. If a car used 18 gal of gas on a 405-mile trip, how much gas will it use on a 180-mile trip?

    a. 40.5 gal   **b.** 16 gal   **c.** 6 gal   **d.** 8 gal

20. Write 0.025 as a percent.

    a. 0.25%   **b.** 2.5%   **c.** 0.0025%   **d.** 25%

21. What is 22% of 150?

    a. 330   **b.** 3.3   **c.** 33   **d.** 1.83

22. 27 is what percent of 250?

    a. 10.8%   **b.** 1.8%   **c.** 9.26%   **d.** 92.6%

23. 72 is 45% of what number?

    a. 160   **b.** 625   **c.** 32.4   **d.** 32.9

Final Exam Form E (*continued*)

Name: _____

24. Eighty-two out of 4000 circuit boards tested were found to be defective. What percent of the boards were defective?

    a. 20.5%   b. 2.05%   c. 48.8%   d. 0.0205%

25. A jar of 32 pickles sells for $4.16. Find the unit cost.

    a. $0.13 per pickle   b. $0.21 per pickle   c. $0.28 per pickle   d. $0.12 per pickle

26. An insurance agent receives a yearly salary of $15,000 plus 40% of the cost of an insurance policy. How much does the agent earn in a year when the policies sold cost $80,000.

    a. $32,000   b. $47,000   c. $18,200   d. $6000

27. An electrician earned $36,000 this year, an increase from the $32,000 salary earned last year. What is the percent increase in the electrician's salary?

    a. 88.8%   b. 11.25%   c. 12.5%   d. 11.11%

28. A department store uses a markup rate of 40%. Find the selling price of a lamp that cost the store $75.

    a. $30   b. $115   c. $105   d. $45

29. The circle graph shows how a family's monthly income of $2600 is budgeted. How much money does the family spend on food each month?

    a. $520   b. $550
    c. $468   d. $390

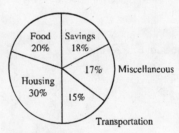

Budget for a Monthly
Income of $2600

30. The double-line graph compares two employees' quarterly sales for 2001. In which quarters did Employee 1 have more sales than Employee 2?

    a. 1st and 2nd   b. 2nd and 3rd
    c. 3rd and 4th   d. 1st and 4th

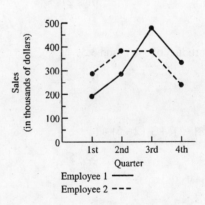

31. Convert $6\frac{2}{3}$ yd to feet.

    a. 80 ft   b. 20 ft   c. $2\frac{1}{3}$ ft   d. 22 ft

32. Convert 3 qts to ounces.

    a. 16 oz   b. 96 oz   c. 12 oz   d. 48 oz

33. A baby weighed 7 lb 8 oz at birth. At 1 month of age, the baby weighed 9 lb 2 oz. Find the baby's weight gain in that month.
    a.   1 lb 10 oz   b.   1 lb 2 oz   c.   2 lb 6 oz   d.   2 lb 8 oz

34. How much wood must be cut from a 12-foot board to make a 10 ft 8 in. shelf?
    a.   1 ft 8 in.   b.   2 ft 8 in.   c.   2 ft 4 in.   d.   1 ft 4 in.

35. Convert 3250 g to kilograms.
    a.   32.5 kg   b.   325 kg   c.   0.325 kg   d.   3.25 kg

36. Convert 2 L to cubic centimeters.
    a.   2000 cm^3 b.   1000 cm^3 c.   200 cm^3 d.   4000 cm^3

37. Find the cost of a roast weighing 2350 g if the price per kilogram is $3.80.
    a. $89.30   b. $7.93   c. $8.93   d. $9.03

38. Which statement is correct?
    a. $-9 > -4$ b. $-4 > -9$ c. $-4 < -9$ d. $-4 > 0$

39. Find the sum of $-\dfrac{2}{3}$ and $\dfrac{3}{4}$.
    a. $\dfrac{1}{12}$ b. $-1\dfrac{5}{12}$ c. $1\dfrac{5}{12}$ d. $-\dfrac{1}{12}$

40. What is 12 decreased by 9?
    a.   4   b.   21   c. -3 d.   3

41. Find the product of -1.2 and 3.5.
    a.   2.3   b. -4.2 c.   4.7   d.   4.2

42. Simplify: $(-2)^2 + 3 \cdot (2 - 5)$
    a. -13 b.   5   c. -5 d.   6

43. Evaluate $a^2 - 2ab$ when $a = 2$ and $b = 3$.
    a. -8 b.   8   c. -10 d.   10

44. Solve: $y - 17 = -10$
    a.   27   b. -27 c. -7 d.   7

45. Solve: $5x - 2 = 7$

    a. $\dfrac{9}{5}$ **b.** 1   **c.** $\dfrac{5}{9}$ **d.** 4

46. Solve: $18 + 2(x - 9) = 3(x - 10)$

    a. -30 **b.** 6   **c.** 30   **d.** -6

47. Translate "three times a number added to eight is thirty-five" into an equation and solve.

    a. 27   **b.** $4\dfrac{3}{8}$ **c.** 9   **d.** 24

48. Find the area of the figure. Use 3.14 for π.

    a. 10.28 in.^{2} **b.** 16.56 in.^{2}

    c. 29.12 in.^{2} **d.** 7.14 in.^{2}

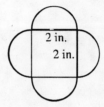

49. Find the volume of the figure. Use 3.14 for π.

    a. 150.72 cm^3 **b.** 226.08 cm^3

    c. 228.08 cm^3 **d.** 236.08 cm^3

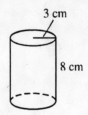

50. Triangles *ABC* and *DEF* are similar. Find the perimeter of triangle *DEF*.

    a. 25.6 cm   **b.** 24 cm

    c. 33.6 cm   **d.** 32 cm

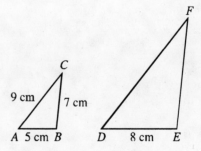

Form F Tests

Multiple Choice

Chapter 1 Test Form F

Name: _____

Date: _____

1. Which statement is correct?

   a. $4 > 9$ **b.** $12 < 14$ **c.** $5 > 7$ **d.** $8 < 3$

2. Write $42,023$ in words.

   a. Four thousand two hundred twenty-three   **b.** Four hundred two thousand twenty-three

   c. Four hundred twenty thousand twenty-three   **d.** Forty-two thousand twenty-three

3. Write twenty-eight thousand thirty-five in standard form.

   a. 2835   **b.** $28,035$ **c.** $20,835$ **d.** $28,305$

4. Write $56,060$ in expanded form.

   a. $56,000 + 600$ **b.** $55,000 + 600 + 60$

   c. $56,000 + 60$ **d.** $50,000 + 6,000 + 60$

5. Round $87,053$ to the nearest ten.

   a. $87,050$ **b.** $87,100$ **c.** $87,060$ **d.** $87,000$

6. Find the sum of $23,417$ and $16,281$.

   a. $18,598$ **b.** $39,698$ **c.** $38,698$ **d.** $37,688$

7. Add:
$$
\begin{array}{r}
18,314 \\
1,973 \\
+\ 54,896 \\
\hline
\end{array}
$$

   a. $75,083$ **b.** $73,183$

   c. $75,183$ **d.** $73,083$

8. The attendance at a Friday night movie was 272. The attendance on Saturday was 213, and the attendance on Sunday afternoon was 186. Find the total attendance for the three showings.

   a. 571   **b.** 661   **c.** 671   **d.** 761

9. Find 1768 decreased by 547.

   a. 2315   **b.** 1221   **c.** 1212   **d.** 221

10. Subtract:
$$
\begin{array}{r}
62,469 \\
-\ 31,802 \\
\hline
\end{array}
$$

   a. $30,567$ **b.** $30,657$

   c. $31,667$ **d.** $30,667$

11. At the beginning of a trip, the odometer of your car read 31,026 miles. At the end of the trip, the odometer read 32,014 miles. Find the number of miles traveled during the trip.

   a. 988   **b.** 888   **c.** 982   **d.** 998

12. Find the product of 5129 and 7.

   a. $34,913$ **b.** $35,903$ **c.** $35,904$ **d.** $34,813$

13. Multiply: 416
                  $\times\,73$

         a.   31,368   **b.**   30,368

         c.   30,248   **d.**   30,348

14. Your travel club account has a total of 52,000 points. Each hotel stay deducts 32 points. How many points do you have left after 34 visits?

    a.   50,912   **b.**   50,976   **c.**   58,844   **d.**   50,192

15. Find the quotient of 41,280 and 3.

    a.   13,422   **b.**   1376   **c.**   13,760   **d.**   13,660

16. Divide: $8\overline{)10,086}$

         a.   1250 r 6   **b.**   1285 r 6

         c.   1010 r 6   **d.**   1260 r 6

17. Divide: $35\overline{)6720}$

         a.   189 r 5   **b.**   192

         c.   182   **d.**   19 r 2

18. A teacher receives a salary of $28,080 per year. Find the teacher's monthly salary if the teacher receives a paycheck each month of the year.

    a. $2440   **b.** $2540   **c.** $2390   **d.** $2340

19. Write $5\cdot5\cdot7\cdot7\cdot7\cdot7$ in exponential notation.

    a. $5^2\cdot7^3$ **b.** $5\cdot7^6$ **c.** $5^2\cdot7$ **d.** $5^2\cdot7^4$

20. Simplify: $4^2\cdot3^3\cdot8$

    a.   576   **b.**   3456   **c.**   1152   **d.**   1576

21. Simplify: $6^2-12\div(19-13)$

    a.   10   **b.**   34   **c.**   32   **d.**   4

22. Simplify: $20-(12\div4)\cdot2+5$

    a.   19   **b.**   9   **c.**   39   **d.**   18

23. Find all the factors of 34.

    a.   1, 2, 17, 34   **b.**   1, 7, 17, 34   **c.**   1, 17, 34   **d.**   2, 17, 34

24. Find the prime factorization of 42.

    a. $1\cdot2\cdot4$ **b.** $2\cdot3\cdot7$ **c.** $1\cdot4\cdot2$ **d.** $1\cdot2\cdot3\cdot7$

25. Find the prime factorization of 64.

    a. $2\cdot32$ **b.** $2\cdot2\cdot16$ **c.** $2\cdot2\cdot2\cdot2\cdot2$ **d.** $2\cdot2\cdot2\cdot2\cdot2\cdot2$

1. Find the LCM of 11 and 12.

   a. 12   **b.** 3   **c.** 121   **d.** 132

2. Find the GCF of 18 and 54.

   a. 8   **b.** 9   **c.** 6   **d.** 18

3. Express the shaded portion of the circles as an improper fraction.

   a. $\dfrac{2}{5}$ **b.** $\dfrac{1}{2}$ **c.** $\dfrac{5}{2}$ **d.** $\dfrac{3}{2}$

4. Write $\dfrac{16}{5}$ as a mixed number.

   a. $3\dfrac{1}{5}$ **b.** $2\dfrac{1}{5}$ **c.** $3\dfrac{5}{16}$ **d.** $3\dfrac{4}{5}$

5. Write $3\dfrac{5}{9}$ as an improper fraction.

   a. $\dfrac{17}{9}$ **b.** $\dfrac{24}{9}$ **c.** $\dfrac{32}{9}$ **d.** $\dfrac{59}{9}$

6. What number must be placed in the numerator so that the following fractions are equivalent? $\dfrac{2}{3} = \dfrac{}{45}$

   a. 30   **b.** 18   **c.** 36   **d.** 42

7. Write $\dfrac{64}{144}$ in simplest form.

   a. $\dfrac{4}{9}$ **b.** $\dfrac{9}{16}$ **c.** $\dfrac{8}{12}$ **d.** $\dfrac{8}{32}$

8. Add: $\dfrac{7}{8} + \dfrac{3}{8} + \dfrac{1}{8}$

   a. $\dfrac{11}{24}$ **b.** $1\dfrac{1}{2}$ **c.** $1\dfrac{3}{8}$ **d.** $\dfrac{8}{11}$

9. Find the total of $\dfrac{1}{2}$, $\dfrac{2}{5}$, and $\dfrac{7}{15}$.

   a. $\dfrac{4}{75}$ **b.** $1\dfrac{11}{30}$ **c.** $1\dfrac{4}{15}$ **d.** $1\dfrac{11}{60}$

10. Add:
$$4\frac{1}{5}$$
$$+3\frac{5}{7}$$

    a. $7\frac{32}{35}$ **b.** $7\frac{6}{35}$

    c. $7\frac{1}{2}$ **d.** $7\frac{28}{35}$

11. A recipe for salad dressing calls for $3\frac{1}{2}$ tablespoons of safflower oil, $7\frac{1}{4}$ tablespoons of olive oil and $5\frac{1}{3}$ tablespoons of fresh lemon juice. How many tablespoons are in the completed salad dressing?

    a. $15\frac{1}{24}$ **b.** $15\frac{1}{3}$ **c.** $16\frac{1}{3}$ **d.** $16\frac{1}{12}$

12. Subtract: $\frac{7}{16} - \frac{3}{16}$

    a. $\frac{11}{16}$ **b.** $\frac{1}{4}$ **c.** $\frac{3}{16}$ **d.** $\frac{1}{5}$

13. What is $\frac{11}{12}$ minus $\frac{5}{8}$?

    a. $\frac{6}{7}$ **b.** $\frac{1}{8}$ **c.** $\frac{7}{24}$ **d.** $\frac{6}{4}$

14. Subtract:
$$41\frac{5}{7}$$
$$-26\frac{8}{15}$$

    a. $25\frac{19}{105}$ **b.** $14\frac{4}{15}$

    c. $15\frac{3}{15}$ **d.** $15\frac{19}{105}$

15. A 12-mile race has two checkpoints. The first checkpoint is $3\frac{5}{8}$ miles from the starting point. The second checkpoint is $4\frac{1}{2}$ miles from the first checkpoint. How many miles is it from the second checkpoint to the finish line?

    a. $3\frac{7}{8}$ **b.** $3\frac{3}{8}$ **c.** $6\frac{3}{8}$ **d.** $4\frac{5}{8}$

16. Multiply: $\frac{18}{35} \times \frac{14}{27}$

    a. $\frac{2}{15}$ **b.** $\frac{4}{15}$ **c.** $\frac{27}{105}$ **d.** $\frac{4}{5}$

17. What is $3\frac{1}{6}$ multiplied by $4\frac{2}{7}$?

    a. $12\frac{4}{7}$ **b.** $12\frac{2}{13}$ **c.** $12\frac{2}{42}$ **d.** $13\frac{4}{7}$

18. The Andersen family has an income of \$1896 each month. The family spends $\frac{1}{3}$ of its income each month on housing. How much income is left each month after spending $\frac{1}{3}$ of it on housing?

    a. \$1264   **b.** \$816   **c.** \$1422   **d.** \$632

19. Divide: $\dfrac{11}{18} \div \dfrac{22}{3}$

    a. $4\dfrac{13}{27}$ **b.** 12   **c.** $\dfrac{1}{12}$ **d.** $\dfrac{3}{8}$

20. Find the quotient of $\dfrac{2}{15}$ and $4\dfrac{1}{5}$.

    a. $1\dfrac{1}{3}$ **b.** $\dfrac{2}{63}$ **c.** $13\dfrac{4}{25}$ **d.** $1\dfrac{1}{15}$

21. Marcel Thompson purchased $4\dfrac{1}{2}$ ounces of gold for \$2340. What was the price of 1 ounce?

    a. \$520   **b.** \$720   **c.** \$380   **d.** \$260

22. Which statement is correct?

    a. $\dfrac{7}{18} < \dfrac{11}{30}$ **b.** $\dfrac{7}{18} < 0$ **c.** $\dfrac{7}{18} = \dfrac{11}{30}$ **d.** $\dfrac{7}{18} > \dfrac{11}{30}$

23. Simplify: $\left(\dfrac{1}{3}\right)^3 \cdot \left(\dfrac{3}{2}\right)^4$

    a. $\dfrac{1}{2}$ **b.** $\dfrac{1}{128}$ **c.** $\dfrac{3}{16}$ **d.** $\dfrac{1}{16}$

24. Simplify: $\left(\dfrac{5}{6} + \dfrac{3}{8}\right) \div \dfrac{3}{4}$

    a. $1\dfrac{11}{18}$ **b.** $\dfrac{16}{21}$ **c.** $\dfrac{11}{18}$ **d.** $1\dfrac{5}{24}$

25. Simplify: $\dfrac{3}{8} + \left(\dfrac{5}{12} - \dfrac{2}{9}\right) \div \dfrac{1}{3}$

    a. $\dfrac{9}{24}$ **b.** $\dfrac{23}{29}$ **c.** $\dfrac{23}{24}$ **d.** 23

Name: _____
Date: _____

1. Write 16.0709 in words.

   a. Sixteen and seven hundred nine thousandths   **b.** Sixteen and seventy-nine ten-thousandths

   c. Sixteen and seven hundred nine ten-thousandths   **d.** Sixteen and seventy-nine thousandths

2. Write in standard form: fifty and ninety-three ten-thousandths

   a. 50.0093   **b.** 50.093   **c.** 50.93   **d.** 50.0903

3. Round 56.435974 to the nearest thousandth.

   a. 56.43560   **b.** 56.43597   **c.** 56.436   **d.** 56.4360

4. Round 54.8975 to the nearest hundredth.

   a. 54.90   **b.** 54.80   **c.** 54.898   **d.** 54.897

5. Add: 2594.3765
          293.073
       + 997.67

   a. 3885.1085   **b.** 3875.0195
   c. 2885.1185   **d.** 3885.1195

6. Find the total of 18.7186, 78.1493, 106, and 4.2916.

   a. 107.2695   **b.** 202.2195   **c.** 207.1595   **d.** 187.2685

7. Sabrina Mathews has $962.44 in her checking account. She makes deposits of $144.13, $516.97, and $29.30. Find the amount in her checking account after making the deposits.

   a. $1662.84   **b.** $1652.84   **c.** $1652.74   **d.** $1552.74

8. Subtract: 9.15
            − 5.173

   a. 4.987   **b.** 4.977
   c. 3.987   **d.** 3.977

9. Find 2.18 less than 6.6578.

   a. 4.4778   **b.** 6.4398   **c.** 6.6360   **d.** 4.5778

10. At the beginning of a trip, the odometer of your car reads 23,021.4 miles. At the end of the trip, the odometer reads 24,329.7 miles. Find the number of miles traveled during the trip.

    a. 1318.3   **b.** 1308.3   **c.** 1208.3   **d.** 1318.7

11. Multiply: 16.9
      × 0.074

  a. 1.2506 **b.** 1.2416
  c. 12.506 **d.** 12.406

12. Find the product of 6.4 and 0.159.

  a. 6.241 **b.** 1.0176 **c.** 40.252 **d.** 0.10176

13. A 3-minute telephone call to a nearby town is \$1.05. Each additional minute costs \$0.34. Find the cost of a 24-minute telephone call.

  a. \$8.16 **b.** \$9.51 **c.** \$8.76 **d.** \$8.19

14. Find 5.230 divided by 0.025.

  a. 20.92 **b.** 209.2 **c.** 2092 **d.** 211.5

15. Divide. Round to the nearest hundredth.

  $0.908\overline{)16.092}$

  a. 16.62 **b.** 17.72
  c. 177.22 **d.** 1.77

16. A computer programmer receives an annual salary of \$46,107.84 in 12 equal monthly payments. Find the programmer's monthly income.

  a. \$3842.29 **b.** \$5532.94 **c.** \$3842.32 **d.** \$5342.32

17. Convert $\dfrac{3}{11}$ to a decimal. Round to the nearest thousandth.

  a. 0.273 **b.** 0.237 **c.** 0.263 **d.** 3.67

18. Convert 0.96 to a fraction.

  a. $\dfrac{24}{25}$ **b.** $\dfrac{4}{5}$ **c.** $\dfrac{3}{5}$ **d.** $\dfrac{19}{25}$

19. Which statement is correct?

  a. $1.509 < 1.51$ **b.** $1.509 = 1.51$ **c.** $1.509 > 1.51$ **d.** $1.509 < 0$

20. Which statement is correct?

  a. $0.28 < \dfrac{7}{25}$ **b.** $0.28 = \dfrac{7}{25}$ **c.** $0.28 > \dfrac{7}{25}$ **d.** $0.28 < 0$

Chapters 1-3 Cumulative Test F

Name: _____
Date: _____

1. Divide: $514\overline{)20{,}046}$

        a. 309   **b.** 39
        c. 3.9   **d.** 49

2. Simplify: $2 \cdot 5^3 \cdot 11$

   a. 2750   **b.** 330   **c.** 550   **d.** 176

3. Simplify: $4 \cdot 6 + 2^2 - 3$

   a. 55   **b.** 28   **c.** 49   **d.** 25

4. Find the LCM of 27, 18, and 12.

   a. 108   **b.** 3   **c.** 54   **d.** 81

5. Write $\dfrac{75}{4}$ as a mixed number.

   a. $19\dfrac{1}{4}$ **b.** $18\dfrac{1}{2}$ **c.** $18\dfrac{3}{4}$ **d.** $18\dfrac{1}{4}$

6. Write $2\dfrac{1}{7}$ as an improper fraction.

   a. $\dfrac{3}{7}$ **b.** $\dfrac{13}{7}$ **c.** $\dfrac{9}{7}$ **d.** $\dfrac{15}{7}$

7. Find the numerator for an equivalent fraction with the given denominator: $\dfrac{9}{17} = \dfrac{}{51}$

   a. 36   **b.** 45   **c.** 27   **d.** 18

8. Add: $\dfrac{3}{7} + \dfrac{4}{35} + \dfrac{3}{10}$

   a. $\dfrac{59}{70}$ **b.** $\dfrac{5}{26}$ **c.** $\dfrac{6}{7}$ **d.** $\dfrac{58}{70}$

9. What is $6\dfrac{3}{7}$ increased by $1\dfrac{2}{3}$?

   a. $7\dfrac{2}{21}$ **b.** $8\dfrac{4}{21}$ **c.** $8\dfrac{2}{21}$ **d.** $8\dfrac{1}{7}$

10. Subtract: $5\dfrac{2}{3} - 2\dfrac{7}{9}$

   a. $3\dfrac{8}{9}$ **b.** $2\dfrac{8}{9}$ **c.** $3\dfrac{1}{9}$ **d.** $2\dfrac{1}{9}$

11. Multiply: $\dfrac{10}{9} \times \dfrac{18}{55}$

   a. $\dfrac{1}{11}$ **b.** $\dfrac{20}{55}$ **c.** $\dfrac{36}{101}$ **d.** $\dfrac{4}{11}$

12. Find the product of $3\dfrac{2}{3}$ and $2\dfrac{2}{11}$.

    a. $7\dfrac{1}{17}$ **b.** $8\dfrac{1}{17}$ **c.** 8   **d.** 9

13. Divide: $\dfrac{3}{7} \div \dfrac{5}{21}$

    a. $1\dfrac{4}{5}$ **b.** $\dfrac{5}{49}$ **c.** 2   **d.** $\dfrac{2}{7}$

14. What is 56 divided by $2\dfrac{2}{3}$?

    a. 21   **b.** 12   **c.** 16   **d.** 18

15. Simplify: $8 \cdot \left(\dfrac{3}{4}\right)^2 \cdot \left(\dfrac{2}{3}\right)^3$

    a. $\dfrac{3}{4}$ **b.** $1\dfrac{1}{3}$ **c.** $2\dfrac{2}{3}$ **d.** $5\dfrac{1}{5}$

16. Simplify: $\dfrac{3}{4} \cdot \left(\dfrac{5}{6} + \dfrac{2}{9}\right) \div \dfrac{19}{2}$

    a. $\dfrac{5}{12}$ **b.** $\dfrac{7}{36}$ **c.** $\dfrac{7}{20}$ **d.** $\dfrac{1}{12}$

17. Write 14.931 in words.
    a. Fourteen and nine hundred thirty-one thousandths
    b. Fourteen and nine tenths and three hundredths and one thousandth
    c. Fourteen thousand nine hundred thirty-one
    d. Fourteen and nine hundred thirty-one ten-thousandths

18. Add:
$$\begin{array}{r} 39.724 \\ 4.01 \\ +\ 0.329 \end{array}$$

    a. 44.063   **b.** 33.063
    c. 43.063   **d.** 33.053

19. What is 348.97 decreased by 63.881?

    a. 285.081   **b.** 285.089   **c.** 285.079   **d.** 285.086

20. Multiply:
$$\begin{array}{r} 0.039 \\ \times\ 4.8 \end{array}$$

    a. 18.72   **b.** 1.872
    c. 0.19   **d.** 0.1872

21. Divide. Round to the nearest thousandth.

$0.9\overline{)0.0717}$

   a. 0.080   **b.** 0.079
   c. 0.008   **d.** 7.967

22. Convert $\frac{8}{9}$ to a decimal. Round to the nearest thousandth.

   a. 0.888   **b.** 0.89   **c.** 0.889   **d.** 1.125

23. Convert $0.11\frac{1}{9}$ to a fraction.

   a. $\frac{11}{100}$ **b.** $\frac{1}{9}$ **c.** $\frac{119}{1000}$ **d.** $\frac{1}{900}$

24. Which statement is correct?

   a. $0.1875 = \frac{3}{16}$ **b.** $0.1875 < \frac{3}{16}$ **c.** $0.1875 > \frac{3}{16}$ **d.** $0.1875 < 0$

25. On a recent trip, you stopped three times for gas, buying $8\frac{3}{10}$ gallons, $11\frac{1}{2}$ gallons, and $10\frac{4}{5}$ gallons. Find the total amount of gas purchased.

   a. $29\frac{4}{5}$ gallons   **b.** $29\frac{3}{10}$ gallons   **c.** $30\frac{3}{10}$ gallons   **d.** $30\frac{3}{5}$ gallons

26. A land developer purchased $8\frac{5}{6}$ acres of land for a building project. Two and one-half acres were set aside for a park. How many $\frac{1}{3}$-acre parcels of developed land can be sold?

   a. 16   **b.** 27   **c.** 24   **d.** 19

27. If the sun sets $1\frac{1}{3}$ minutes earlier each day in December, how many minutes earlier will it set on December 31 than on November 30?

   a. $40\frac{1}{3}$ minutes   **b.** 40 minutes   **c.** $41\frac{1}{3}$ minutes   **d.** 41 minutes

28. An electrician earns $3129.60. Deductions from the check are $630.24 for federal tax, $180.92 for state tax, and $43.12 for insurance. Find the electrician's take-home pay.

   a. $2275.32   **b.** $854.28   **c.** $2272.72   **d.** $2375.22

29. A carpenter uses a plane to take 0.125 inch from a 0.75-inch board. How thick is the board now?

   a. 0.875 inch   **b.** 0.7375 inch   **c.** 0.5 inch   **d.** 0.625 inch

30. A tax of $25.10 is paid on each camera sold by a store. This month the total tax bill paid on cameras was $1054.20. How many cameras were sold this month?

   a. 40   **b.** 45   **c.** 42   **d.** 39

1. Write the comparison 6 meters to 5 meters as a ratio in simplest form.

    a. $\dfrac{1}{5}$ **b.** $\dfrac{5}{6}$ **c.** $\dfrac{6}{5}$ **d.** $\dfrac{1}{3}$

2. Write the comparison 4 days to 12 days as a ratio in simplest form.

    a. $\dfrac{1}{3}$ **b.** $3:1$ **c.** $\dfrac{1}{4}$ **d.** 3

3. Write the comparison 15 inches to 25 inches as a ratio in simplest form.

    a. $\dfrac{3}{7}$ **b.** $\dfrac{5}{3}$ **c.** $\dfrac{3}{5}$ **d.** $\dfrac{3}{4}$

4. Write the comparison 42 ounces to 24 ounces as a ratio in simplest form.

    a. $\dfrac{4}{7}$ **b.** $\dfrac{7}{4}$ **c.** $\dfrac{3}{2}$ **d.** $\dfrac{2}{1}$

5. Sandy weighed 120 pounds in the ninth grade. She weighed 160 pounds when she graduated from high school. What is the ratio, as a fraction in simplest form, of the amount of increase in her weight to her weight in the ninth grade?

    a. $\dfrac{3}{4}$ **b.** $\dfrac{1}{4}$ **c.** $\dfrac{1}{3}$ **d.** $\dfrac{1}{12}$

6. Twenty-four hundred voters in a small town registered as independents and 8400 voters registered along a party line. Find the ratio, as a fraction in simplest form, of the number of party-line voters to the total number of registered voters.

    a. $\dfrac{2}{9}$ **b.** $\dfrac{7}{9}$ **c.** $\dfrac{2}{7}$ **d.** $\dfrac{7}{2}$

7. Write "6 pounds for 66 cents" as a rate in simplest form.

    a. $\dfrac{11 \text{ cents}}{1 \text{ pound}}$ **b.** $\dfrac{3 \text{ pounds}}{33 \text{ cents}}$ **c.** $\dfrac{1 \text{ pound}}{11 \text{ cents}}$ **d.** $\dfrac{1}{11}$

8. Write "14 supports for every 6 feet" as a rate in simplest form.

    a. $\dfrac{14 \text{ supports}}{6 \text{ feet}}$ **b.** $\dfrac{7 \text{ supports}}{3 \text{ feet}}$ **c.** $\dfrac{3 \text{ feet}}{7 \text{ supports}}$ **d.** $\dfrac{7}{3}$

9. Write "$8.58 for 22 slices of Swiss cheese" as a unit rate.

    a. $0.42/slice   **b.** $0.39/slice   **c.** $0.429/slice   **d.** $0.43/slice

10. Write "5600 words on 20 pages" as a unit rate.

    a. 180 words/page   **b.** 280   **c.** 208 words/page   **d.** 280 words/page

11. Kelly purchased 150 shares of stock for $4147.50. What was the cost per share?

    a. $26.75   **b.** $26.57   **c.** $27.65   **d.** $26.65

12. The Coburn family purchased a 260-pound side of beef for $320 and had it packaged. During the packaging, 60 pounds of beef were discarded as waste. What was the cost per pound of the packaged beef?

    a. $1.23   **b.** $1.70   **c.** $1.60   **d.** $1.50

13. Which proportion is true?

    a. $\dfrac{14}{21} = \dfrac{4}{7}$ **b.** $\dfrac{3}{7} = \dfrac{15}{35}$ **c.** $\dfrac{3}{8} = \dfrac{15}{35}$ **d.** $\dfrac{4}{7} = \dfrac{16}{35}$

14. Which proportion is true?

    a. $\dfrac{8}{1} = \dfrac{60}{6}$ **b.** $\dfrac{65}{5} = \dfrac{13}{1}$ **c.** $\dfrac{5}{15} = \dfrac{1}{4}$ **d.** $\dfrac{11}{15} = \dfrac{44}{64}$

15. Solve: $\dfrac{16}{n} = \dfrac{15}{78}$

    a. 83.2   **b.** 63.2   **c.** 3.08   **d.** 73.12

16. Solve: $\dfrac{9}{n} = \dfrac{13}{5}$ Round to the nearest hundredth.

    a. 3.46   **b.** 3.64   **c.** 23.40   **d.** 7.22

17. A $2 sales tax is charged for a $40 purchase. At this rate, what is the sales tax for an $85 purchase?

    a. $5.25   **b.** $4.15   **c.** $4.25   **d.** $3.74

18. A car can travel 65 miles on 2 gallons of gasoline. How far can the car travel on 14 gallons of gasoline?

    a. 448 miles   **b.** 454 miles   **c.** 455 miles   **d.** 525 miles

19. A bank demands a monthly loan payment of $9.85 for each $1000 borrowed. At this rate, what is the monthly payment on a $12,000 loan?

    a. $98.20   **b.** $108.20   **c.** $128.20   **d.** $118.20

20. To get the best results from exercising on a treadmill, it is recommended that you walk at a rate of $2\frac{1}{2}$ miles per hour for 30 minutes 4 times a week. If you follow the recommendation, how many miles will you walk in a week?

    a. 10 miles   **b.** 5 miles   **c.** 30 miles   **d.** 15 miles

Name: _____

Date: _____

1. Write 0.09% as a decimal.

   a. 0.0009   **b.** 0.009   **c.** 0.09   **d.** 0.9

2. Write $62\frac{1}{2}\%$ as a fraction.

   a. $\dfrac{311}{500}$ **b.** $\dfrac{5}{8}$ **c.** $\dfrac{125}{2}$ **d.** $\dfrac{62.5}{100}$

3. Write 0.004 as a percent.

   a. 0.04%   **b.** 0.4%   **c.** 0.00004%   **d.** 0.004%

4. Write 0.455 as a percent.

   a. 0.0455%   **b.** 0.00445%   **c.** 45.5%   **d.** 0.455%

5. Write $\dfrac{21}{25}$ as a percent.

   a. 84%   **b.** 8.4%   **c.** 0.084%   **d.** 0.84%

6. Write $1\frac{3}{4}$ as a percent.

   a. 1.75%   **b.** 175%   **c.** 0.175%   **d.** $1\frac{3}{4}\%$

7. What is 34% of 170?

   a. 112.2   **b.** 227.8   **c.** 500   **d.** 57.8

8. 54.4% of 270 is what number?

   a. 49.63   **b.** 14.69   **c.** 145.88   **d.** 146.88

9. Which statement is correct?

   a. 16% of 2000 is larger than 15% of 2500   **b.** 16% of 2000 is smaller than 15% of 2500

   c. 16% of 2000 is equal to 15% of 2500   **d.** 16% of 2000 is larger than 400

10. Which statement is correct?

    a. 0.2% of 100 is larger than 2% of 10   **b.** 0.2% of 100 is smaller than 2% of 10

    c. 0.2% of 100 is equal to 2% of 10   **d.** 0.2% of 100 is larger than 1

11. A soft-drink company uses 12% of its $90,000 budget for advertising. What amount of the budget is spent for advertising?

    a. $10,800   **b.** $9800   **c.** $12,500   **d.** $7500

12. Mark is buying a $240 jacket on "lay away." The store wants 20% down. How much will Mark have to pay as a deposit?

    a. $48   **b.** $20   **c.** $192   **d.** $2

Name: _____

13. What percent of 20 is 46?

    a. 23%   **b.** 2.3%   **c.** 230%   **d.** 43.5%

14. What percent of 8.7 is 5.2? Round to the nearest tenth.

    a. 6%   **b.** 59.8%   **c.** 1.67%   **d.** 60.8%

15. A jar is filled with 460 jelly beans. 161 of the jelly beans are red. What percent of the jelly beans in the jar are red?

    a. 35%   **b.** 28.5%   **c.** 45%   **d.** 25%

16. The Veiga family has an income of $2640 each month and spends $792 a month for payments on a house. What percent of the monthly income is spent for house payments?

    a. 3%   **b.** 30%   **c.** 27%   **d.** 33.3%

17. 6080 is 76% of what number?

    a. 4620.8   **b.** 10700.8   **c.** 800   **d.** 8000

18. 888 is 120% of what number?

    a. 106.56   **b.** 666   **c.** 740   **d.** 1100

19. This year a sanitation worker receives a wage of $15.41 an hour. This is 115% of last year's wage. What is the increase in the hourly wage over last year?

    a. $2.01   **b.** $13.40   **c.** $14.41   **d.** $17.72

20. A mechanic estimates that a tire still has 8000 miles of useful tread life. This is 20% of the original useful tread life of the tire. What was the tire's original useful tread life?

    a. 40,000 miles   **b.** 50,000 miles   **c.** 30,000 miles   **d.** 1600 miles

21. 1344 is 84% of what number?

    a. 1128.9   **b.** 160   **c.** 6.06   **d.** 1600

22. What is 0.4% of 250?

    a. 1   **b.** 10   **c.** 100   **d.** 625

23. It cost $320 to repair your automobile. Of this cost, 65% was for parts and 35% was for labor. What was the cost for labor?

    a. $102   **b.** $112   **c.** $913.29   **d.** $208

24. At a resort city, the sun did not shine for 45 days out of 360 days. Find the percent of days the sun did shine.

    a. 88.5%   **b.** 87.5%   **c.** 11.5%   **d.** 12.5%

25. There are 17.81 grams of fat in one ounce of hazelnuts. This is 130% of the number of grams of fat in one ounce of pistachios. How many grams of fat are in one ounce of pistachios?

    a. 23.68 grams   **b.** 12.7 grams   **c.** 23.15 grams   **d.** 13.7 grams

Name: _____

Date: _____

1. Six light bulbs cost $4.98. Find the cost of one light bulb.

    a. $0.38   **b.** $0.83   **c.** $0.77   **d.** $0.85

2. Find the most economical purchase:

    a. 2.5 pounds for $4.22   **b.** 4.2 pounds for $6.93
    c. 3.7 pounds for $6.36   **d.** 5.1 pounds for $7.91

3. If Troy earns $10.20 an hour, what does he earn in $\frac{1}{4}$ hour? Round to the nearest cent.

    a. $2.05   **b.** $2.50   **c.** $2.55   **d.** $40.80

4. A manufacturer of calculators increased its monthly output of 3000 calculators by 12%. What is the amount of increase?

    a. 330 calculators   **b.** 3360 calculators   **c.** 630 calculators   **d.** 360 calculators

5. The average price of a refrigerator rose from $500 to $585 in 2 years. What was the percent increase in the price of the refrigerator?

    a. 15%   **b.** 14.5%   **c.** 17%   **d.** 20%

6. Jane got a new job, which increased her present weekly salary of $324 by 20%. What is her new weekly salary?

    a. $344.00   **b.** $388.80   **c.** $648.80   **d.** $388.88

7. A gas station pays $1.05 per gallon for gasoline. The gas station uses a markup rate of 12%. Find the selling price of 1 gallon of gasoline. Round to the nearest cent.

    a. $1.16   **b.** $1.28   **c.** $1.18   **d.** $0.13

8. The stock market index fell from 7945.26 to 7442.08 during October 1997. What percent decrease does this represent? Round to the nearest tenth of a percent.

    a. 6.8%   **b.** 1.1%   **c.** 1.6%   **d.** 6.3%

9. Barnes and Noble sells a $25 best-selling book for $17.50. What percentage decrease does this represent?

    a. 30%   **b.** 25%   **c.** 70%   **d.** 33%

10. A sleep sofa that regularly sells for $649 is on sale for 35% off the regular price. What is the sale price?

    a. $421.58   **b.** $421.85   **c.** $433.00   **d.** $227.15

11. A ski parka that regularly sells for $112 is on sale for 24% off the regular price. What is the sale price?

    a. $85.12   b. $81.52   c. $85.21   d. $26.88

12. A bank agrees to finance the construction of a new store. The $36,000 loan is for 18 months with an annual simple interest rate of 10.5%. What is the simple interest due on the loan?

    a. $3780   b. $5760   c. $5670   d. $3428

13. An investment of $2500 pays 9% annual interest compounded quarterly. What is the value of this investment after 10 years? Use the Compound Interest Table. Round to the nearest cent.

    a. $6087.97   b. $5918.41   c. $78,523.55   d. $3123.01

14. The mortgage on a real estate investment is $150,000. The buyer paid a loan origination fee of $2\frac{3}{4}$ points. How much is the loan origination fee?

    a. $275   b. $4125   c. $3125   d. $4215

15. A family bought a $112,000 home with a down payment of $10,000. They were able to obtain a mortgage for 25 years at 12%. Find their monthly mortgage payment. Use the Monthly Payment Table. Round to the nearest cent.

    a. $1074.28   b. $1179.60   c. $1049.18   d. $1152.04

16. A contractor purchases a truck for $9200 and must pay a sales tax of 6% of the purchase price. Find the sales tax.

    a. $5648   b. $425   c. $525   d. $552

17. The financial ledger for the first nine months of the year showed the total expenses for a small office. Rent was $7470, electricity was $997.40, telephone service was $385.45, and secretarial services were $8640.90. What was the average monthly expense for this office?

    a. $1934.75   b. $1492.75   c. $1943.75   d. $4373.44

18. The Booster Club has a total of $240.12 in their checking account before they wrote checks for $50.46 and $96.21. After another fund-raiser, they deposited $812.80. Find the Booster Club's new checking account balance.

    a. $906.25   b. $285.87   c. $1002.46   d. $1199.59

19. Tim Lee had a checking account balance of $792.40 before writing checks of $64.35 and $514.20 and making a deposit of $304.70. Find his current checking account balance.

    a. $588.55   b. $518.55   c. $508.55   d. $581.55

Chapter 6 Test F (*continued*)

Name: _____

20. Balance the checkbook shown.

		RECORD ALL CHARGES OR CREDITS THAT AFFECT YOUR ACCOUNT						

NUMBER	DATE	DESCRIPTION OF TRANSACTION	PAYMENT/DEBIT (-)	√T	FEE (IF ANY) (-)	DEPOSIT/CREDIT (+)	BALANCE 496 12	
	6/3	Car payment	289 76				206	36
	6/6	Credit card	117 30				89	06
	6/10	Hardware store	15 50				73	56
	6/15	Deposit				406 32	479	88
	6/17	Groceries	53 82				426	06
	6/22	Paint	80 00				346	06
	6/29	Deposit				150 00	496	06
	6/30	Phone bill	87 29				408	77

REMEMBER TO RECORD AUTOMATIC PAYMENTS/DEPOSITS ON DATE AUTHORIZED

CHECKING ACCOUNT Monthly Statement		Account Number : 924-297-8	
DATE	Transaction	Amount	Balance
6/1	OPENING BALANCE		496.12
6/5	CHECK	289.76	206.36
6/16	DEPOSIT	406.32	612.68
6/16	CHECK	117.30	495.38
6/20	CHECK	53.82	441.56
6/21	INTEREST	6.04	447.60
6/22	CHECK	15.50	432.10
6/29	SERVICE CHARGE	7.00	425.10
6/30	CLOSING BALANCE		425.10

Do the bank statement and the checkbook balance?

   a. Yes   **b.** No

Name: _____

Date: _____

1. Write the comparison 81 pints to 99 pints as a ratio in simplest form.

   a. $\dfrac{11}{9}$

   b. $\dfrac{8}{9}$

   c. $\dfrac{9}{10}$

   d. $\dfrac{9}{11}$

2. A vitamin tablet contains 60 milligrams of vitamin C and 80 milligrams of potassium. What is the ratio of the number of grams of potassium to the number of grams of vitamin C?

   a. $\dfrac{4}{3}$

   b. $\dfrac{1}{3}$

   c. $\dfrac{3}{4}$

   d. $\dfrac{3}{1}$

3. Write "$9150 for 6 months" as a unit rate.

   a. $9150/6 months

   b. $3050/2 months

   c. $1525/month

   d. $1535/month

4. If a worker at Burger King earned $188.50 for working 32.5 hours, find the worker's earnings per hour.

   a. $8.50/hour

   b. $5.80/hour

   c. $5.15/hour

   d. $6.75/hour

5. Solve the proportion: $\dfrac{21}{n} = \dfrac{36}{15}$

   a. 8.3

   b. 8.75

   c. 87.5

   d. 48

6. A bank demands a loan payment of $17.95 for every $1000 borrowed. At this rate, what is the monthly payment for a $12,000 loan?

   a. $2154.00

   b. $215.40

   c. $21.54

   d. $225.40

7. Write 67.5% as a decimal.

   a. 6.75

   b. 6750

   c. 0.675

   d. 0.0675

8. Write 64% as a fraction.

   a. $\dfrac{16}{25}$

   b. $\dfrac{2}{5}$

   c. $\dfrac{1}{5}$

   d. $\dfrac{4}{5}$

9. Write 1.07 as a percent.

   a. 0.00107%

   b. 107%

   c. 1.07%

   d. 10.7%

10. Write $\dfrac{15}{60}$ as a percent.

    a. 0.25%

    b. 40%

    c. 25%

    d. 4%

11. 1.5% of 5600 is what number?

    a. 840   **b.** 84   **c.** 8400   **d.** 3733.3

12. Quality control inspectors found that 0.15% of the circuit boards inspected were defective. If 4000 circuit boards were inspected, how many were found to be defective?

    a. 0.6   **b.** 600   **c.** 60   **d.** 6

13. What percent of 9000 is 2745?

    a. 30.5%   **b.** 3.05%   **c.** 305%   **d.** 3.28%

14. The auctioneer started the bidding on a pair of antique vases at $80,000. If the vases sold at the auction for $120,000, what percent of the selling price was the starting price?

    a. 33.3%   **b.** 66.7%   **c.** 150%   **d.** 80%

15. 5.34 is 6% of what number?

    a. 0.3204   **b.** 890   **c.** 89   **d.** 8.9

16. A salesclerk's wage this year is $8.69 an hour. This is 110% of last year's wage. Find last year's wage.

    a. $7.90   **b.** $9.56   **c.** $12.65   **d.** $7.09

17. Six plastic hangers sell for $1.12. What is the unit price? Round to the nearest cent.

    a. $0.06   **b.** $0.19   **c.** $0.16   **d.** $0.18

18. A produce market uses a 45% markup rate. Find the selling price of a cantaloupe that cost the market $0.80.

    a. $1.26   **b.** $0.36   **c.** $0.34   **d.** $1.16

19. A stereo that regularly sells for $620 has been discounted at a rate of 15%. What is the sale price?

    a. $527   **b.** $537   **c.** $713   **d.** $93

20. A car dealer offers a loan for a new $26,500 Chevrolet. The loan is for the full amount of the car, has an annual simple interest rate of 8.5%, and is for a period of three years. Find the total amount of simple interest to be paid on the loan.

    a. $67,575   **b.** $675.75   **c.** $6757.50   **d.** $2252.50

The pictograph shows the number of hamburgers sold at a local fast-food restaurant during different times in 1 day. Each hamburger represents 50 hamburgers sold.

1. What was the total number of hamburgers sold during the times shown?

   a. 650   b. 950   c. 850   d. 700

2. Find the ratio of the number of hamburgers sold between 11 and 1 o'clock to the number of hamburgers sold between 4 and 7 o'clock.

   a. $\frac{11}{13}$ b. $\frac{13}{11}$ c. $\frac{12}{11}$ d. $\frac{15}{11}$

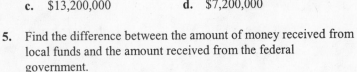

Before 11:00

11:00 - 1:00

1:00 - 4:00

4:00 - 7:00

The circle graph shows the sources of income for a community college that has a total budget of $24,000,000.

3. How much money does the college receive from federal funds?

   a. $13,200,000   b. $7,200,000
   c. $3,600,000   d. $6,300,000

4. Find the amount of money the college received from the state government.

   a. $14,200,000   b. $1,320,000
   c. $13,200,000   d. $7,200,000

5. Find the difference between the amount of money received from local funds and the amount received from the federal government.

   a. $360,000   b. $3,200,000
   c. $13,200,000   d. $3,600,000

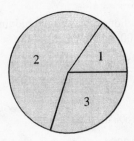

SOURCES OF INCOME
1: 15% - Federal Government
2: 55% - State Government
3: 30% - Local Funds

The double-bar graph shows a company's monthly profits (in thousands of dollars) during the first four months of 2000 and 2001.

6. Find the difference between the 2000 and 2001 profits for the month of March.

   a. $3000   b. $300   c. $1500   d. $2500

7. What were the total profits for 2001 for the 4 months shown?

   a. $50,000   b. $5100   c. $51,000   d. $48,000

8. In which month did the 2000 profits exceed the 2001 profits?

   a. January   b. February
   c. April   d. March

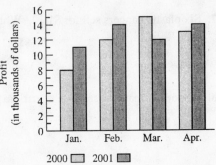

2000 □ 2001 ■

9. A coin is tossed three times. What is the probability of getting heads on all three tosses?

   a. $\frac{1}{3}$ b. $\frac{1}{6}$ c. $\frac{1}{8}$ d. $\frac{3}{8}$

10. The salaries of six executives of a computer company are $87,000, $62,400, $54,600, $66,000, $75,400, and $59,000. Find the median salary of the six executives.

    a. $62,400   b. $66,000   c. $67,400   d. $64,200

11. The number of vacation days taken last year by each of the employees of a firm was recorded. The box-and-whisker plot represents the data. Determine the third quartile of this data.

4 7   14   20   26

   a. 4 days   b. 7 days   c. 14 days   d. 20 days

The double-line graph shows the number of shares of stock (in thousands) traded on the New York Stock Exchange for each of five days in 2000 and 2001.

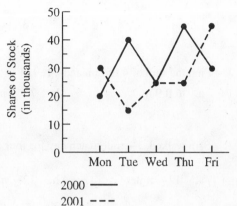

2000 ——
2001 - - - -

12. Find the total number of shares of stock sold on the Fridays of 2000 and 2001.

   a. 65,000 shares   b. 70,000 shares
   c. 75,000 shares   d. 80,000 shares

13. On what day were sales the same in both 2000 and 2001?

   a. Wednesday   b. Friday
   c. Tuesday   d. Monday

14. What is the ratio of Friday 2000's sales to Friday 2001's sales?

   a. $\frac{2}{3}$ b. $\frac{4}{9}$ c. $\frac{9}{5}$ d. $\frac{3}{5}$

The histogram shows the number of hours of television watched each week by 54 people.

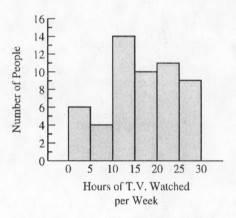

15. How many people watch between 15 and 30 hours of television each week?

   a. 21 people   b. 11 people
   c. 30 people   d. 18 people

16. How many people watched less than 10 hours of television each week?

   a. 10   b. 24   c. 8   d. 12

17. What is the ratio of the number of people who watched less than 5 hours of television a week to the number who watched more than 25 hours of television a week?

   a. $\frac{3}{2}$ b. $\frac{2}{3}$ c. $\frac{2}{5}$ d. $\frac{1}{3}$

The frequency polygon shows the annual snowfall in a mountain community during the past 50 years.

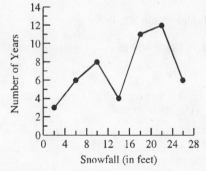

18. Find the number of years in which the annual snowfall was between 0 feet and 12 feet.

   a. 21 years   b. 17 years
   c. 9 years   d. 15 years

19. During what percentage of the years was the snowfall between 8 and 12 feet?

   a. 16%   b. 6.25%   c. 18%   d. 20%

20. Motor vehicle accident reports were recorded by the traffic department of a city's police force. The data shows the cause of accidents as follows: 9, speeding; 12, failure to yield the right of way; 2, running a red light; 3, following too closely; 1, an improper turn; 11, other causes. What was the modal cause of accidents?

   a. Failure to yield   b. 12   c. Running a red light   d. 2
   right of way

Name: _____
Date: _____

1. Convert 96 in. to yards.

    a. 8 yd **b.** $1\frac{1}{3}$ yd **c.** $2\frac{2}{3}$ yd **d.** 3 yd

2. Find the sum of 4 ft 4 in. and 2 ft 9 in.

    a. 6 ft 9 in. **b.** 7 ft 1 in. **c.** 7 ft 3 in. **d.** 8 in.

3. Sam walked $3\frac{1}{3}$ miles each day for four days. Find the total number of miles walked in the four days.

    a. $12\frac{1}{4}$ miles **b.** $12\frac{1}{3}$ miles **c.** $9\frac{1}{3}$ miles **d.** $13\frac{1}{3}$ miles

4. A homeowner needs 486 ft of fencing to fence his property. How many yards of fencing are needed?

    a. 1458 yd **b.** 272 yd **c.** 152 yd **d.** 162 yd

5. Convert $5\frac{1}{2}$ tons to pounds.

    a. 11,000 lb **b.** 9000 lb **c.** 13,000 lb **d.** 10,000 lb

6. Convert 100 oz to pounds.

    a. $6\frac{1}{4}$ lb **b.** $7\frac{1}{2}$ lb **c.** $8\frac{1}{3}$ lb **d.** 8 lb

7. Divide: $4\overline{)10\text{ lb }8\text{ oz}}$

    a. 2 lb 14 oz **b.** 2 lb 12 oz **c.** 2 lb 7 oz **d.** 2 lb 10 oz

8. Multiply 1 ton 800 lb by 3.

    a. 4 tons 400 lb **b.** 3 tons 1400 lb **c.** 4 tons 1400 lb **d.** 3 tons 800 lb

9. A bookstore received 250 workbooks, each weighing 8 oz. Find the total weight in pounds of the 250 workbooks.

    a. 166.7 lb **b.** 150 lb **c.** 125 lb **d.** 100 lb

10. Each day Alice drinks $7\frac{2}{5}$ glasses of water. How many glasses of water does Alice drink in a year? (Use a 365-day year.)

    a. 1022 glasses **b.** 1350 glasses **c.** 2701 glasses **d.** 2555 glasses

11. Convert 12 c to pints.

    a. 3 pt   **b.** 6 pt   **c.** 24 pt   **d.** 9 pt

12. Convert 42 pt to gallons.

    a. 21 gal   **b.** $10\frac{1}{2}$ gal   **c.** 17 gal   **d.** $5\frac{1}{4}$ gal

13. Divide 7 gal 2 qt by 3.

    a. 2 gal 2 qt   **b.** 2 gal 1 qt   **c.** 3 gal 2 qt   **d.** 2 gal 1 qt

14. Subtract: $6\frac{1}{2}$ gal

                $-2\frac{7}{8}$ gal

    a. $3\frac{3}{8}$ gal   **b.** $4\frac{3}{8}$ gal   **c.** $4\frac{5}{8}$ gal   **d.** $3\frac{5}{8}$ gal

15. A can of tomato juice contains 26 fl oz. Find the number of quarts of tomato juice in a case of 12 cans.

    a. $19\frac{1}{2}$ qt   **b.** $9\frac{3}{4}$ qt   **c.** $4\frac{7}{8}$ qt   **d.** $8\frac{3}{4}$ qt

16. A caterer plans to prepare two cups of coffee for each of 24 guests at a dinner party. How many gallons of coffee will need to be brewed?

    a. 4 gallons   **b.** 6 gallons   **c.** 3 gallons   **d.** 12 gallons

17. A furnace is rated at 37,500 Btu per hour. How many foot-pounds of energy are released by the furnace in 1 h? (1 Btu = 778 ft · lb)

    a. 48.2 ft · lb   **b.** 37,500 ft · lb   **c.** 29,175 ft · lb   **d.** 29,175,000 ft · lb

18. A furnace is rated at 26,500 Btu per hour. How many foot-pounds of energy are released by the furnace in 1 h? (1 Btu = 778 ft · lb)

    a. 2,617,000 ft · lb   **b.** 206,170 ft · lb   **c.** 20,617,000 ft · lb   **d.** 26,500 ft · lb

19. Find the power in foot-pounds per second needed to raise 2 tons a distance of 30 ft in 60 s.

    a. $3000\frac{\text{ft} \cdot \text{lb}}{\text{s}}$ **b.** $2000\frac{\text{ft} \cdot \text{lb}}{\text{s}}$ **c.** $1000\frac{\text{ft} \cdot \text{lb}}{\text{s}}$ **d.** $400\frac{\text{ft} \cdot \text{lb}}{\text{s}}$

20. A motor has a power of $3850\frac{\text{ft} \cdot \text{lb}}{\text{s}}$. Find the horsepower of the motor. $\left(1 \text{ hp} = 550\frac{\text{ft} \cdot \text{lb}}{\text{s}}\right)$

    a. 7 hp   **b.** 3.5 hp   **c.** 14.29 hp   **d.** 14 hp

Name: _____

Date: _____

1. Convert 0.052 m to centimeters.

   a. 520 cm   **b.** 52 cm   **c.** 5.2 cm   **d.** 0.00052 cm

2. Convert 17.2 mm to centimeters.

   a. 172 cm   **b.** 1.72 cm   **c.** 0.172 cm   **d.** 1.72 cm

3. Convert 7 m 65 cm to centimeters.

   a. 7065 cm   **b.** 7.65 cm   **c.** 765 cm   **d.** 7.065 cm

4. Convert 10 km 4 m to kilometers.

   a. 10.4 km   **b.** 10.04 km   **c.** 104 km   **d.** 10.004 km

5. A piece 420 cm long is cut from a board 6.3 m long. Find the length of the remaining piece.

   a. 1.8 m   **b.** 0.18 cm   **c.** 4.485 m   **d.** 2.1 m

6. A bookcase 240 cm long has three shelves. Find the cost of the shelves when the price of the lumber is $12.50 per meter.

   a. $30   **b.** $90   **c.** $60   **d.** 7.20m

7. Convert 627 g to kilograms.

   a. 62.7 kg   **b.** 6.27 kg   **c.** 0.627 kg   **d.** 627,000 kg

8. Convert 4.27 kg to grams.

   a. 427 g   **b.** 0.00427 g   **c.** 4270 g   **d.** 42.7 g

9. Convert 32 g 14 mg to grams.

   a. 32.014 g   **b.** 3214 g   **c.** 32.14 g   **d.** 32,014 g

10. Convert 3 kg 64 g to kilograms.

    a. 364 kg   **b.** 3.64 kg   **c.** 3064 kg   **d.** 3.064 kg

11. Find the cost of a roast weighing 7400 g if the price per kilogram is \$4.49. Round to the nearest cent.

    a. \$31.23   **b.** \$28.63   **c.** \$31.43   **d.** \$33.23

12. Four hundred grams of grass seed are used for every 100 m^2 of lawn. Find the amount of seed needed, in kilograms, to cover 3000 m^2.

    a. 75 kg   **b.** 1.2 kg   **c.** 12 kg   **d.** 120 kg

13. Convert 0.04 L to cubic centimeters.

    a. 0.00004 cm^3 **b.** 40 cm^3 **c.** 0.04 cm^3 **d.** 400 cm^3

14. Convert 1.02 kl to liters.

    a. 1020 L   **b.** 10.2 L   **c.** 102 L   **d.** 0.00102 L

15. Convert 9 L 91 ml to liters.

    a. 991 L   **b.** 9.91 L   **c.** 9091 L   **d.** 9.091 L

16. Convert 6 L 814 ml to milliliters.

    a. 6.814 ml   **b.** 60.814 ml   **c.** 6814 ml   **d.** 60.814 ml

17. A hospital buys 45 L of flu vaccine. How many people can be immunized if each person receives 3 cm^3 of vaccine?

    a. 15,000 people   **b.** 1500 people   **c.** 13,500 people   **d.** 1350 people

18. Find the cost of running a 60-watt stereo set for 60 h at 9.3¢ per kilowatt-hour. Round to the nearest cent.

    a. \$334.80   **b.** 33¢   **c.** 23¢   **d.** 43¢

19. Express 55 mi/h in kilometers per hour. Round to the nearest hundredth. (1.61 km = 1 mi)

    a. 8.85 km/h   **b.** 88.55 km/h   **c.** 34.16 km/h   **d.** 78.55 km/h

20. A bag of road salt weighs 6.2 kg. Find the weight in pounds. (2.2 lb = 1 kg)

    a. 12.84 lb   **b.** 1.5 lb   **c.** 13.64 lb   **d.** 12.4 lb

The circle graph shows the annual expenses for a student at a university.

1. What percent of the total expenses are spent on clothes and entertainment? Round to the nearest tenth of a percent.
   a. 62%
   b. 6.2%
   c. 6.21%
   d. 0.062%

2. Find the ratio of the amount spent for books to the amount spent for clothes.

   a. $\dfrac{11}{6}$
   b. $\dfrac{5}{11}$
   c. $\dfrac{7}{12}$
   d. $\dfrac{6}{11}$

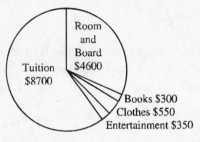

Annual Student Expenses

The double-line graph shows quarterly profits for a laser company for the years 2000 and 2001.

3. What is the difference in third-quarter profits for 2000 and 2001?
   a. $3000
   b. $40,000
   c. $30,000
   d. $30

4. Find the total sales for 2001.
   a. $220,000
   b. $210,000
   c. $120,000
   d. $100,000

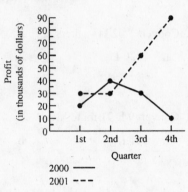

5. A student has scores of 86, 82, 78, 84, and 80 on five math tests this semester. What is the average grade for the tests?
   a. 81.5
   b. 80.5
   c. 82
   d. 81.25

6. The number of fish caught per day in a small lake over a 7-day period were 15, 10, 12, 17, 14, 9, and 13. Find the median number of fish caught per day over the 7-day period.
   a. 12 fish
   b. 13.4 fish
   c. 12.5 fish
   d. 13 fish

7. Convert 13 ft to inches.
   a. 156 in.
   b. 130 in.
   c. 39 in.
   d. 165 in.

8. Subtract: 16 yd
   − 9 yd 1 ft

   a. 7 yd 1 ft
   b. 6 yd 11 ft
   c. 6 yd 2 ft
   d. 6 yd 9 ft

9. Convert 168 oz to pounds.
   a. 14 lb
   b. 10.5 lb
   c. 16.8 lb
   d. 21 lb

10. Add: 6 tons   700 lb
              + 8 tons 1500 lb

   a. 16 tons 200 lb   **b.** 17 tons   **c.** 15 tons 100 lb   **d.** 15 tons 200 lb

11. Convert 6 pt to fluid ounces.
   a. 96 fl oz   **b.** 192 fl oz   **c.** 144 fl oz   **d.** 72 fl oz

12. If a serving of coffee contains 10 fl oz, how many quarts of coffee are needed to serve 64 people?
   a. 20 qt   **b.** 8 qt   **c.** 3 qt   **d.** 12 qt

13. Jack bought three bunches of bananas weighing 1 lb 3 oz, 9 oz, 1 lb 5 oz, and 2 lb 1 oz. Find the total weight of the bananas Jack purchased.
   a. 5 lb 18 oz   **b.** 5 lb 2 oz   **c.** 5 lb 6 oz   **d.** 4 lb 18 oz

14. Convert 6860 m to kilometers.
   a. 686 km   **b.** 686,000 km   **c.** 6.860 km   **d.** 68.6 km

15. Convert 0.72 kg to grams.
   a. 72 g   **b.** 0.0072 g   **c.** 7200 g   **d.** 720 g

16. Convert 2 L 45 ml to liters.
   a. 24.5 L   **b.** 2.45 L   **c.** 245 L   **d.** 2.045 L

17. Find the number of inches in 40 cm. (1 cm = 0.39 in.)
   a. 156 in.   **b.** 15.6 in.   **c.** 1.56 in.   **d.** 102.6 in.

18. Bases on a baseball diamond are 27.439 m apart. How far apart are they in feet? Round to the nearest whole number. (1 m = 3.28 ft)
   a. 84 ft   **b.** 90 ft   **c.** 89 ft   **d.** 120 ft

19. A swimming pool requires 225 g of chlorine added to the water twice a week. How many kg of chlorine are required for a 12-week summer?
   a. 5.4 kg   **b.** 2.7 kg   **c.** 54 kg   **d.** 0.27 kg

20. A football field is 300 ft long. What is the length in cm? (1 ft = 30.5 cm)
   a. 9150 cm   **b.** 91.5 cm   **c.** 983.6 cm   **d.** 915 cm

Name: _____

Date: _____

1. Which statement is correct?

   a. $-5 < 0$ **b.** $-5 < -7$ **c.** $-7 > -3$ **d.** $-9 > 4$

2. Which statement is correct?

   a. $3 < -50$ **b.** $3 = -50$ **c.** $3 > -50$ **d.** $3 < 0$

3. Evaluate $-|24|$ and $|-3|$.

   a. -24 and -3 **b.** -24 and 3 **c.** 24 and 3 **d.** 24 and -3

4. Add: $-5 + (-12)$

   a. 7 **b.** 17 **c.** -17 **d.** -7

5. Find the sum of 8, 3, and -14.

   a. -3 **b.** 3 **c.** 2 **d.** -2

6. Subtract: $8 - (-11)$

   a. -19 **b.** 3 **c.** 19 **d.** -3

7. Subtract: $-8 - (-3) - (-12)$

   a. -1 **b.** 7 **c.** -23 **d.** -7

8. Find the product of -8 and -3.

   a. 11 **b.** 24 **c.** -24 **d.** -11

9. Divide: $-108 \div 18$

   a. -1944 **b.** -10 **c.** 6 **d.** -6

10. Find the temperature after a rise of 6°C from -1°C.

    a. 5°C   **b.** -5°C   **c.** -7°C   **d.** 7°C

11. The daily low temperature readings for a 3-day period were 12°, -2°, and -4°. Find the average low temperature for this period.

    a. 2°   **b.** 3°   **c.** -2°   **d.** -3°

12. Add: $8\frac{2}{3} + \left(-4\frac{1}{6}\right)$

    a. $3\frac{1}{3}$ **b.** $4\frac{1}{2}$ **c.** $4\frac{1}{3}$ **d.** $\frac{1}{2}$

13. Add: $-\frac{7}{12} + \frac{3}{4}$

    a. $\frac{1}{6}$ **b.** $\frac{5}{12}$ **c.** $-1\frac{1}{3}$ **d.** $\frac{1}{12}$

14. Subtract: $\dfrac{5}{8} - \dfrac{11}{12}$

   a. $-1\dfrac{15}{24}$ **b.** $\dfrac{7}{24}$ **c.** $1\dfrac{15}{24}$ **d.** $-\dfrac{7}{24}$

15. Subtract: $-\dfrac{5}{6} - \left(-\dfrac{1}{4}\right)$

   a. $\dfrac{7}{12}$ **b.** $-\dfrac{7}{12}$ **c.** $\dfrac{5}{24}$ **d.** $-\dfrac{5}{24}$

16. Multiply: $-\dfrac{1}{3} \times \dfrac{3}{4}$

   a. $\dfrac{3}{7}$ **b.** $\dfrac{1}{4}$ **c.** $-\dfrac{1}{4}$ **d.** $-\dfrac{3}{7}$

17. Find the quotient of $-2\dfrac{1}{3}$ and $\dfrac{2}{3}$.

   a. $-1\dfrac{5}{9}$ **b.** $-3\dfrac{1}{2}$ **c.** $4\dfrac{1}{2}$ **d.** $-4\dfrac{1}{2}$

18. What is 6.82 decreased by 30.2?

   a.   37.02   **b.**   −23.38   **c.**   23.38   **d.**   −37.02

19. Multiply: $-4.2 \times (-9.4)$

   a.   −36.08   **b.**   36.08   **c.**   −39.48   **d.**   39.48

20. Find the product of -4.02 and -6.9.

   a.   −27.738   **b.**   2.87   **c.**   −10.92   **d.**   27.738

21. Divide: $18.56 \div (-3.2)$

   a.   4.8   **b.**   5.8   **c.**   −5.8   **d.**   −4.8

22. Simplify: $5 - (-6) - (2)^3 \cdot 5$

   a.   −41   **b.**   245   **c.**   41   **d.**   −29

23. Simplify: $8 - 3(4 - 6)^2 \div 3$

   a. $-\dfrac{4}{3}$ **b.**   −4   **c.**   4   **d.** $6\dfrac{2}{3}$

24. Write $29,300,000$ in scientific notation.

   a. 2.93×10^7 **b.** 29.3×10^7 **c.** 29.3×10^8 **d.** 293×10^5

25. The record low temperature of $-128.6°F$ was recorded at the Soviet Antarctica station Vostok in 1983. The lowest official temperature in North America is $-81°F$, recorded in 1947 in Yukon. Find the difference between the lowest temperature ever recorded in North America and the lowest temperature recorded in the world.

   a.   62.4°F   **b.**   47.6°F   **c.**   209.6°F   **d.**   120.5°F

Name: _____

Date: _____

1. Evaluate $ab - ac + bc$ when $a = -2$, $b = 3$, and $c = -4$.

   a. -2 b. -10 c. -26 d. 14

2. Evaluate $b^3 - 4a$ when $a = -1$ and $b = -2$.

   a. -12 b. -4 c. 12 d. -6

3. Simplify: $-7xy + 3xy - 4xy$

   a. $-14xy$ b. $-8xy$ c. $-4xy - 4$ d. 0

4. Simplify: $3 - 2(4 - z) - 5z$

   a. $-5 - 3z$ b. $-4 - 6z$ c. $4 - 6z$ d. $5 - 3z$

5. Which number is a solution of $3(x - 7) = 4x - 30$?

   a. 6 b. -9 c. -6 d. 9

6. Solve: $y - 5 = -7$

   a. 12 b. -12 c. -2 d. 2

7. Solve: $-3x = 21$

   a. -7 b. -63 c. 24 d. 18

8. Solve: $-\dfrac{1}{3}x = 6$

   a. 18 b. -18 c. -2 d. 2

9. On a 483-mile trip, a student averaged 23 mi/gal. Find the number of gallons of gasoline used. Use the formula $D = M \cdot G$, where D is distance, M is miles per gallon, and G is the number of gallons.

   a. 19 gal   b. 25 gal   c. 21 gal   d. 29 gal

10. Solve: $7 - 5x = -3$

   a. $\dfrac{4}{5}$ b. $1\dfrac{1}{4}$ c. -2 d. 2

11. Solve: $\dfrac{x}{6} - 3 = -2$

    a. 6   **b.** −3   **c.** $-\dfrac{1}{6}$ **d.** −6

12. Solve: $-7 = 2 - 5x$

    a. 1   **b.** −4   **c.** $\dfrac{9}{5}$ **d.** 0

13. Find the cost per unit during a week when the total cost was \$8200, the number of units produced was 200, and the fixed costs were \$1200. Use the formula $T = U \cdot N + F$, where T is the total cost, U is the cost per unit, N is the number of units made, and F is the fixed cost.

    a. \$35   **b.** \$25   **c.** \$30   **d.** \$40

14. Solve: $2x - 9 = 11 - 5x$

    a. $-\dfrac{2}{3}$ **b.** $\dfrac{2}{7}$ **c.** $-6\dfrac{2}{3}$ **d.** $2\dfrac{6}{7}$

15. Solve: $-x + 2(3 - 2x) = 12$

    a. −2   **b.** −1   **c.** $-1\dfrac{1}{5}$ **d.** 6

16. Translate "the difference between c and the product of eight and c" into a mathematical expression.

    a. $8c - c$ **b.** $c - 8c$ **c.** $c(c - 8)$ **d.** $c(c) - 8$

17. Translate "the quotient of twice a number and the cube of the number" into a mathematical expression.

    a. $\dfrac{(2n)^3}{n}$ **b.** $\dfrac{n^2}{3n}$ **c.** $\dfrac{n^3}{2n}$ **d.** $\dfrac{2n}{n^3}$

18. Translate "the sum of a number divided by three and nine is three" into an equation and solve.

    a. −18   **b.** 12   **c.** 36   **d.** −2

19. The product of a number plus six and three is equal to twelve. Find the number.

    a. −6   **b.** 10   **c.** 2   **d.** −2

20. This year the Community Music School's enrollment increased by 36 students. This is 45% more students than were enrolled last year. How many students were enrolled last year?

    a. 80 students   **b.** 16 students   **c.** 20 students   **d.** 65 students

1. Find the supplement of a 47° angle.
   a. 133°   b. 313°   c. 43°   d. 33°

2. Two angles of a triangle are 22° and 17°. Find the measure of the third angle of the triangle.
   a. 111°   b. 68°   c. 141°   d. 158°

3. In the figure, $L_1 \parallel L_2$. $\angle x = 37°$. Find $\angle y$.
   a. 37°   b. 53°
   c. 127°   d. 39°

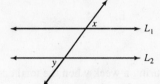

4. In the figure, $L_1 \parallel L_2$. $\angle x = 112°$. Find $\angle a + \angle b$.
   a. 136°   b. 68°
   c. 224°   d. 248°

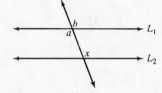

5. Find the perimeter of a rectangle with a length of 4 m and a width of 2.8 m.
   a. 12 m   b. 27.2 m   c. 6.8 m   d. 13.6 m

6. Find the perimeter of the composite figure. The distance between the parallel lines is 4 in. Use 3.14 for π.
   a. 26.56 in.   b. 18.38 in.
   c. 22.44 in.   d. 22.14 in.

7 in.

7. How much binding is needed to bind the outside of a circular rug that is 8 m in diameter? Use 3.14 for π.
   a. 12.56 m   b. 25.12 m   c. 50.24 m   d. 31.40 m

8. Find the area of a rectangle with a length of 4.8 cm and a width of 3.5 cm.
   a. 16.8 cm^2 b. 16.8 cm^3 c. 8.4 cm^2 d. 8.4 cm^3

9. Find the area of the composite figure.
   a. 130 ft^2 b. 96 ft^2
   c. 148 ft^2 d. 168 ft^2

2 ft

12 ft

8 ft

20 ft

10. Carpeting was ordered to cover a floor that is 15 ft long and 11 ft wide. The cost of the carpeting is $8.40 per sq. ft. How much will the carpeting cost?
    a. $436.80   b. $107.40   c. $1386   d. $693

11. How much hardwood flooring is needed to cover the roller rink? Use 3.14 for π.
    a. 22,850 ft^2 b. 157,850 ft^2
    c. 614 ft^2 d. 78,925 ft^2

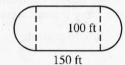

100 ft

150 ft

12. Find the volume of a rectangular solid with a length of $1\frac{3}{4}$ ft, a width of $2\frac{2}{5}$ ft, and a height of 5 ft.

    a.   6 ft³   **b.**   21 ft³   **c.** $8\frac{1}{4}$ ft³   **d.** $1\frac{1}{5}$ ft³

13. Find the volume of the solid.

    a.   98 m³   **b.**   120 m³

    c.   144 m³   **d.**   108 m³

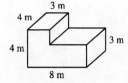

14. The foundation for a new house measures 25 ft long, 20 ft wide, and is $7\frac{1}{2}$ ft high. Find the volume of the foundation.

    a.   375 ft³   **b.**   1875 ft³   **c.**   175 ft³   **d.**   3750 ft³

15. Find the square root of 28. Round to the nearest thousandth.

    a.   5.196   **b.**   5.385   **c.**   5.292   **d.**   5.099

16. Find the unknown side of the triangle. Round to the nearest tenth.

    a.   11.3 ft   **b.**   12.6 ft

    c.   8 ft   **d.**   9.3 ft

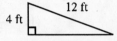

17. A fence is built around a plot. At $5.80 per meter, how much did it cost to fence the plot?

    a. $324.80   **b.** $313.20

    c. $295.80   **d.** $319.00

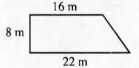

18. Triangles *ABC* and *DEF* are similar. Find side *AC*. Round to the nearest tenth.

    a.   14 ft   **b.**   7 ft

    c.   7.7 ft   **d.**   10.5 ft

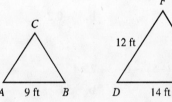

19. Triangles *ABC* and *DEF* are similar. The height of triangle *DEF* is 6 cm. Find the area of triangle *ABC*.

    a.   21 cm²   **b.**   14.7 cm²

    c.   29.4 cm²   **d.**   30 cm²

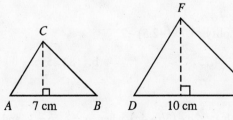

20. In the figure, triangles *ABC* and *DEF* are congruent. Find the measure of ∠*E*.

    a.   35°   **b.**   90°

    c.   55°   **d.**   125°

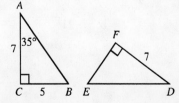

Name: _____

Date: _____

1. Find the sum of −42 and 18.

    a. −24   **b.** 60   **c.** 24   **d.** −60

2. Add: $-\dfrac{7}{9}+\left(-\dfrac{1}{3}\right)$

    a. $1\dfrac{1}{9}$ **b.** $-1\dfrac{1}{9}$ **c.** $\dfrac{4}{9}$ **d.** $-\dfrac{4}{9}$

3. Subtract: $-7-22-(-5)$

    a. 34   **b.** −29   **c.** −10   **d.** −24

4. What is 12.96 decreased by 18.05?

    a. −31.01   **b.** 31.01   **c.** −5.09   **d.** 5.09

5. Find the product of −8 and −13.

    a. −104   **b.** $\dfrac{8}{13}$ **c.** −21   **d.** 104

6. Multiply: $\left(-\dfrac{2}{3}\right)\times\left(-\dfrac{3}{16}\right)$

    a. $\dfrac{9}{32}$ **b.** $\dfrac{1}{8}$ **c.** $-\dfrac{1}{8}$ **d.** $3\dfrac{5}{9}$

7. Find the quotient of 16 and −0.8 .

    a. 20   **b.** −0.2   **c.** −20   **d.** −2

8. Simplify: $30-(-5)^2-6-3+2\times4$

    a. −8   **b.** 54   **c.** 4   **d.** 192

9. Simplify: $4.7\times(-2.5)-7$

    a. 4.75   **b.** 82.25   **c.** −18.75   **d.** −44.65

10. Evaluate $2a-(3b+4c)$ when $a=2$, $b=3$, and $c=4$.

    a. 21   **b.** −21   **c.** 29   **d.** −29

11. Simplify: $z - y + 3z - 10y$

    a. $4z - 11y$ **b.** $2z - 11y$ **c.** $4z + 11y$ **d.** $4z - 9y$

12. Solve: $9 + x = 11$

    a. 2   **b.** -2 **c.** -20 **d.** 20

13. Solve: $-\dfrac{x}{2} = 12$

    a. $-\dfrac{1}{6}$ **b.** 6   **c.** -24 **d.** 12

14. Solve: $4x - 7 = 9$

    a. 4   **b.** $\dfrac{1}{2}$ **c.** 12   **d.** -2

15. Solve: $8 - 2x = 7x - 10$

    a. -2 **b.** -4 **c.** 2   **d.** 4

16. Translate "five more than one-fourth of a number is eight" into an equation and solve.

    a. 52   **b.** -12 **c.** 27   **d.** 12

17. Find the time required for a falling object to increase in velocity from 20 ft/s to 100 ft/s. Use the formula $V = V_0 + 32t$, where V is the final velocity of a falling object, V_0 is the starting velocity of a falling object, and t is the time for the object to fall.

    a. 2.5 s   **b.** 3 s   **c.** 1.5 s   **d.** 2 s

18. A travel company offers a cruise package at $3800. A deposit of $270 is required. The balance is to be paid in 10 monthly installments. Find the monthly payment.

    a. $380   **b.** $353   **c.** $530   **d.** $350

19. Two angles of a triangle measure 37° and 54°. Find the measure of the third angle.

    a. 89°   **b.** 197°   **c.** 99°   **d.** 79°

20. In the figure, $L_1 \parallel L_2$. $\angle x = 166°$. Find $\angle y$.

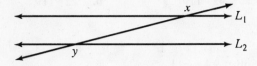

    a. 24°   **b.** 166°

    c. 14°   **d.** 346°

21. Find the perimeter of a rectangle whose length is 2 ft 7 in. and whose width is 10 in.

    a. 3 ft 5 in.   **b.** 5 ft 10 in.   **c.** 6 ft 10 in.   **d.** 10 ft 6 in.

22. Find the area of the figure. Use 3.14 for π.

    a. 338 cm^2 **b.** 87.25 cm^2

    c. 103.5 cm^2 **d.** 126.5 cm^2

23. Find the volume of a cube with sides 3.4 m.

    a. 34.309 m^3 **b.** 10.2 m^3 **c.** 9.2 m^3 **d.** 39.304 m^3

24. Find the unknown leg of the right triangle. Round to the nearest tenth.

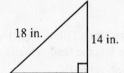

    a. 22.8 in.   **b.** 15.2 in.

    c. 11.3 in.   **d.** 128 in.

25. In the figure, triangles *ABC* and *DEF* are similar. Find the length of side *DE*.

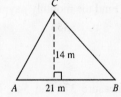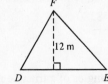

    a. 18 m   **b.** 16 m

    c. 14 m   **d.** 20 m

1. Subtract: $340,859 - 57,026$
   - **a.** $283,933$
   - **b.** $283,833$
   - **c.** $283,283$
   - **d.** $238,833$

2. Find 18,360 divided by 18.
   - **a.** 120
   - **b.** 102
   - **c.** 1120
   - **d.** 1020

3. Simplify: $5^2 - 3 \cdot (4 \div 2)$
   - **a.** 44
   - **b.** 14
   - **c.** 4
   - **d.** 19

4. A security guard receives a total of $1578 per month. Deductions from the check are $363 for taxes, $82 for social security, and $37 for insurance. Find the guard's take-home pay.
   - **a.** 2060
   - **b.** 996
   - **c.** 1096
   - **d.** 1196

5. Add: $3\frac{2}{7} + 4\frac{1}{14}$
   - **a.** $7\frac{5}{14}$
   - **b.** $7\frac{3}{14}$
   - **c.** $7\frac{3}{21}$
   - **d.** $7\frac{1}{2}$

6. Subtract: $4\frac{2}{9} - \frac{2}{3}$
   - **a.** $3\frac{9}{14}$
   - **b.** $4\frac{4}{9}$
   - **c.** $3\frac{5}{9}$
   - **d.** $1\frac{11}{14}$

7. Find the product of $\frac{5}{14}$ and $1\frac{1}{5}$.
   - **a.** $\frac{14}{25}$
   - **b.** $\frac{3}{7}$
   - **c.** $\frac{1}{10}$
   - **d.** $\frac{2}{7}$

8. Divide: $3\frac{5}{8} \div 4\frac{1}{7}$
   - **a.** $\frac{7}{9}$
   - **b.** $\frac{7}{8}$
   - **c.** $\frac{5}{6}$
   - **d.** $\frac{8}{9}$

9. Simplify: $\frac{7}{8} - \frac{1}{6} \cdot \frac{3}{8} + \left(\frac{1}{2}\right)^2$
   - **a.** $1\frac{1}{16}$
   - **b.** $\frac{33}{64}$
   - **c.** $1\frac{1}{8}$
   - **d.** $1\frac{3}{16}$

10. A package contains 18 oz of cereal. How many $1\frac{1}{2}$-ounce portions can be served from this package?
    - **a.** 16
    - **b.** 14
    - **c.** 12
    - **d.** 10

Final Exam Form F (*continued*)

Name: _____

11. Find 25.8 decreased by 0.936.

    a. 24.864   b. 25.864   c. 26.736   d. 248.64

12. Multiply: 8.1×0.003

    a. 0.243   b. 2.43   c. 24.3   d. 0.0243

13. Find the quotient of 7 and 0.13. Round to the nearest hundredth.

    a. 0.05   b. 53.85   c. 0.54   d. 5.39

14. Convert 0.024 to a fraction.

    a. $\dfrac{6}{125}$ b. $\dfrac{6}{25}$ c. $\dfrac{3}{155}$ d. $\dfrac{3}{125}$

15. Convert $\dfrac{9}{16}$ to a decimal. Round to the nearest hundredth.

    a. 0.56   b. 0.563   c. 0.60   d. 0.600

16. Write the comparison "120 ft to 84 ft" as a ratio in simplest form using a fraction.

    a. $\dfrac{5}{4}$ b. $\dfrac{10}{7}$ c. $\dfrac{5}{3}$ d. $\dfrac{10}{9}$

17. Write "1476 miles in 18 hours" as a unit rate.

    a. 83 mi/h   b. 62 mi/h   c. 80.2 mi/h   d. 82 mi/h

18. Solve the proportion: $\dfrac{11}{15} = \dfrac{8}{n}$ Round to the nearest hundredth.

    a. 10.91   b. 1.09   c. 10.90   d. 1.91

19. A painter painted 18 ft of a wall in 20 min. How long will it take him to paint 63 ft of the wall?

    a. 70 min   b. 56.7 min   c. 5.7 min   d. 7 min

20. Write 0.0003 as a percent.

    a. 30%   b. 3%   c. 0.3%   d. 0.03%

21. What is 80% of 16.25?

    a. 1300   b. 1.3   c. 130   d. 13

22. 3.7 is what percent of 18.5?

    a. 2%   b. 20%   c. 5%   d. 50%

23. 495 is 55% of what number?

    a. 90   b. 900   c. 9000   d. 272.25

24. 3520 of the students at a college live in dormitories. This is 64% of the total number of students at the school. How many students attend the college?

    a. 5550 students   **b.** 2252 students   **c.** 5500 students   **d.** 55,000 students

25. Find the unit cost of $65.88 for 12 boards.

    a. $4.49   **b.** $5.49   **c.** $6.49   **d.** $7.49

26. A sales representative receives a commission of 12% of the weekly sales. Find the commission earned in a week when sales totaled $380.

    a. $47.60   **b.** $4.56   **c.** $45.60   **d.** $45.80

27. A land developer borrows $92,000 for five months at a 10.5% annual simple interest rate. Find the simple interest due on the loan.

    a. $966   **b.** $9660   **c.** $8050   **d.** $4025

28. A garden nursery is selling off its stock at a 45% discount. Find the sale price of a tree that regularly sells for $80.

    a. $36   **b.** $38   **c.** $42   **d.** $44

29. The double-bar graph shows the number of video games sold by a wholesale distributor during the last four months of 2000 and 2001. What is the difference between 2000 and 2001 October sales?

    a. 1   **b.** 1000

    c. 100   **d.** 10

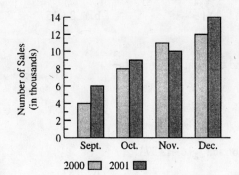

30. The circle graph shows the annual expense of owning and operating a car. How much is spent annually on fuel if the total expenses for the year are $4300?

    a. $1057   **b.** $107.50

    c. $645   **d.** $1075

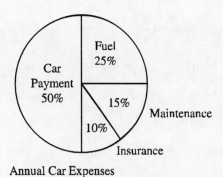

Annual Car Expenses

31. Convert 50 oz to pounds.

    a. 6.125 lb   **b.** 4.125 lb   **c.** 3.125 lb   **d.** 5 lb

32. Convert 14 qt to gallons.

    a. 7 gal   **b.** 1 gal 6 qt   **c.** 3 gal 2 qt   **d.** 2 gal 2 qt

Final Exam Form F (*continued*)

Name: _____

33. A yard was enclosed with twelve sections of fencing. Each section was 8 ft 2 in. long. What is the entire length of the fence enclosing the yard?

    a. 94 ft   **b.** 98 ft   **c.** 96 ft   **d.** 98.4 ft

34. There are 24 cans in a case of soft drinks. Each can contains 10 oz of soft drink. Find the number of 1-cup servings in the case.

    a. 30 servings   **b.** 40 servings   **c.** 15 servings   **d.** 20 servings

35. Convert 45.5 m to centimeters.

    a. 4550 cm   **b.** 455 cm   **c.** 0.455 cm   **d.** 45,500 cm

36. Convert 3 L to milliliters.

    a. 300 ml   **b.** 3000 ml   **c.** 6000 ml   **d.** 600 ml

37. If a serving is 200 ml, how many people can receive one serving from 18 one-liter bottles of soda?

    a. 400 people   **b.** 9 people   **c.** 45 people   **d.** 90 people

38. Which statement is correct?

    a. $-11 > -8$ **b.** $8 > 15$ **c.** $-8 > -11$ **d.** $-3 > 0$

39. Find the total of $-\dfrac{3}{8}$ and $\dfrac{3}{4}$.

    a. $\dfrac{3}{8}$ **b.** $-\dfrac{3}{4}$ **c.** $\dfrac{3}{4}$ **d.** $-\dfrac{3}{8}$

40. Subtract: $-16 - (-37)$

    a. 21   **b.** 53   **c.** -21 **d.** -53

41. Multiply: $1\dfrac{2}{5} \times \left(-4\dfrac{1}{6}\right)$

    a. $1\dfrac{1}{6}$ **b.** $5\dfrac{5}{6}$ **c.** $-5\dfrac{5}{6}$ **d.** $-1\dfrac{1}{6}$

42. Simplify: $3xy + 4x - 4xy$

    a. $4x$ **b.** $3x^2y$ **c.** $4x + xy$ **d.** $-xy + 4x$

43. Evaluate $2a^2 + ab$ when $a = -2$ and $b = 3$.

    a. -2 **b.** 2   **c.** 14   **d.** -14

44. Solve: $x - \dfrac{4}{9} = \dfrac{2}{9}$

    a. $\dfrac{2}{3}$ **b.** $\dfrac{1}{3}$ **c.** $-\dfrac{2}{3}$ **d.** $-\dfrac{1}{3}$

45. Solve: $-6 + 10x = -4$

    a.   1   **b.** $\dfrac{1}{5}$ **c.** -1 **d.** $-\dfrac{1}{5}$

46. Solve: $x + 4(x-3) = 2(x-6) + 9$

    a.   3   **b.**   2   **c.**   0   **d.**   5

47. Translate "eight decreased by a number is three" into an equation and solve.

    a.   11   **b.** -5 **c.** -11 **d.**   5

48. Find the area of the figure.

    a.   152 in.^{2} **b.**   116 in.^{2}

    c.   126 in.^{2} **d.**   118 in.^{2}

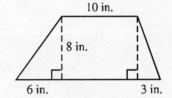

49. Find the volume of the figure.

    a.   204 in.^{3} **b.**   244 in.^{3}

    c.   224 in.^{3} **d.**   184 in.^{3}

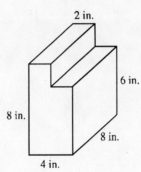

50. Triangles *ABC* and *DEF* are similar. Find the perimeter of triangle *DEF*.

    a.   22 m   **b.**   13 m

    c.   11 m   **d.**   9 m

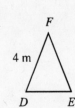

Form G Tests

Multiple Choice

Name: _____
Date: _____

1. Which statement is correct?

   a. $198 > 207$ **b.** $14 > 16$ **c.** $0 < 4$ **d.** $9 < 6$

2. Write $819,048$ in words.

   a. Eight hundred nineteen thousand forty-eight   **b.** Eighty-one thousand nine hundred forty-eight
   c. Eight hundred nine thousand forty-eight   **d.** Eight million nineteen thousand forty-eight

3. Write one hundred-nine thousand three hundred seventy-six in standard form.

   a. 19,376   **b.** 190,376   **c.** 109,376   **d.** 193,076

4. Write $105,006$ in expanded form.

   a. $10,000 + 5000 + 6$ **b.** $100,000 + 5000 + 6$
   c. $100,000 + 50,000 + 6$ **d.** $100,000 + 500 + 6$

5. Round $478,724$ to the nearest thousand.

   a. 478,000   **b.** 479,000   **c.** 470,000   **d.** 480,000

6. Find the sum of $12,397$ and $28,912$.

   a. 42,319   **b.** 40,209   **c.** 41,309   **d.** 30,209

7. Add: 22,457
           18,103
         + 3,698

   a. 44,258   **b.** 43,258
   c. 44,248   **d.** 44,268

8. Your paycheck shows deductions of $175 for savings, $149 for taxes, and $29 for insurance. Find the total of the three deductions.

   a. $363   **b.** $352   **c.** $343   **d.** $353

9. Find the difference between 8969 and 7954.

   a. 1005   **b.** 1105   **c.** 1015   **d.** 915

10. Subtract: 92,398
             − 8,465

    a. 83,933   **b.** 82,933
    c. 83,923   **d.** 83,723

11. Tanya Stewart purchased a new car that cost $12,495 and made a down payment of $1250. Find the amount that remains to be paid.

    a. $13,745   **b.** $12,745   **c.** $11,745   **d.** $11,245

12. Find the product of 2397 and 6.

    a. 13,272   **b.** 13,282   **c.** 14,382   **d.** 14,372

13. Multiply: 697
           × 403

     a. 279,881   **b.** 280,791

     c. 179,861   **d.** 280,891

14. A manufacturer of General Electric microwave ovens now has 2650 ovens in stock. The company manufactures 28 ovens each hour. How many ovens will be in stock 24 hours from now?

     a. 672   **b.** 3322   **c.** 1978   **d.** 3132

15. Find the quotient of $41,280$ and 3.

     a. 13,422   **b.** 1376   **c.** 13,760   **d.** 13,660

16. Divide: $7\overline{)1655}$

     a. 24 r 5   **b.** 123 r 1

     c. 236 r 3   **d.** 308 r 6

17. Divide: $11,689 \div 76$

     a. 153 r 61   **b.** 152 r 61

     c. 178 r 62   **d.** 153 r 62

18. An electrician receives $864 for 36 hours of work. What is the electrician's hourly wage?

     a. $24   **b.** $32   **c.** $26   **d.** $22

19. Write $5 \cdot 5 \cdot 5 \cdot 7 \cdot 7 \cdot 11 \cdot 11$ in exponential notation.

     a. $5^3 \cdot 7^2 \cdot 11^2$ **b.** $5^2 \cdot 7^2 \cdot 11^2$ **c.** $5 \cdot 7^2 \cdot 11^2$ **d.** $5 \cdot 7 \cdot 11^7$

20. Simplify: $3^3 \cdot 9^2$

     a. 162   **b.** 2187   **c.** 342   **d.** 729

21. Simplify: $4^2 - 16 \div (8 - 4)$

     a. 0   **b.** 12   **c.** 4   **d.** 8

22. Simplify: $15 - (16 \div 4) \cdot 3 + 3$

     a. 6   **b.** 36   **c.** 11   **d.** 15

23. Find all the factors of 70.

     a. 1, 2, 5, 7, 10, 14, 28, 35, 70   **b.** 2, 5, 7, 10, 14, 35

     c. 1, 2, 5, 7, 10, 14, 35, 70   **d.** 1, 2, 10, 14, 70

24. Find the prime factorization of 108.

     a. $2 \cdot 2 \cdot 3 \cdot 3 \cdot 3$ **b.** $2 \cdot 3 \cdot 3 \cdot 3 \cdot 5$ **c.** $2 \cdot 2 \cdot 2 \cdot 2 \cdot 5$ **d.** $2 \cdot 2 \cdot 2 \cdot 3 \cdot 3$

25. Find the prime factorization of 98.

     a. $2 \cdot 7 \cdot 7$ **b.** $2 \cdot 2 \cdot 7$ **c.** $2 \cdot 49$ **d.** $7 \cdot 14$

1. Find the LCM of 4, 8, and 10.

   a. 20   **b.** 120   **c.** 80   **d.** 40

2. Find the GCF of 40 and 125.

   a. 10   **b.** 8   **c.** 40   **d.** 5

3. Express the shaded portion of the circles as an improper fraction.

   a. $\dfrac{11}{4}$ **b.** $2\dfrac{3}{4}$ **c.** $\dfrac{9}{4}$ **d.** $2\dfrac{1}{4}$

4. Write $\dfrac{17}{3}$ as a mixed number.

   a. $6\dfrac{1}{3}$ **b.** $5\dfrac{2}{3}$ **c.** $5\dfrac{1}{3}$ **d.** $4\dfrac{5}{17}$

5. Write $6\dfrac{2}{5}$ as an improper fraction.

   a. $\dfrac{12}{5}$ **b.** $\dfrac{32}{5}$ **c.** $\dfrac{32}{2}$ **d.** $\dfrac{23}{5}$

6. What number must be placed in the numerator so that the following fractions are equivalent? $\dfrac{2}{9} = \dfrac{}{45}$

   a. 11   **b.** 2   **c.** 20   **d.** 10

7. Write $\dfrac{30}{80}$ in simplest form.

   a. $\dfrac{3}{8}$ **b.** $\dfrac{6}{16}$ **c.** $\dfrac{15}{40}$ **d.** $\dfrac{2}{3}$

8. Add: $\dfrac{5}{13} + \dfrac{8}{13} + \dfrac{2}{13}$

   a. $1\dfrac{1}{13}$ **b.** $\dfrac{12}{13}$ **c.** $1\dfrac{2}{13}$ **d.** $\dfrac{15}{69}$

9. Find the total of $\dfrac{5}{12}$, $\dfrac{3}{16}$, and $\dfrac{11}{24}$.

   a. $1\dfrac{17}{24}$ **b.** $1\dfrac{1}{16}$ **c.** $\dfrac{7}{16}$ **d.** $\dfrac{19}{52}$

10. Add:

$$4\frac{5}{6}$$
$$+3\frac{2}{9}$$

   a. $7\frac{7}{15}$ **b.** $7\frac{17}{18}$

   c. $8\frac{1}{3}$ **d.** $8\frac{1}{18}$

11. Each week day, a high school teacher spends $5\frac{1}{4}$ hours teaching, $2\frac{2}{3}$ hours correcting papers and preparing lesson plans, and $1\frac{1}{4}$ hours eating. Find the total amount of time spent on these activities.

   a. $9\frac{5}{6}$ hours   **b.** $9\frac{1}{6}$ hours   **c.** $9\frac{1}{12}$ hours   **d.** $10\frac{5}{12}$ hours

12. Subtract: $\frac{22}{25}-\frac{12}{25}$

   a. $\frac{2}{5}$ **b.** $\frac{3}{10}$ **c.** $\frac{9}{25}$ **d.** $\frac{4}{5}$

13. What is $\frac{13}{15}$ decreased by $\frac{3}{5}$?

   a. 1 **b.** $\frac{2}{3}$ **c.** $\frac{1}{2}$ **d.** $\frac{4}{15}$

14. Subtract:

$$16\frac{7}{9}$$
$$-3\frac{14}{15}$$

   a. $12\frac{13}{15}$ **b.** $13\frac{7}{15}$

   c. $12\frac{38}{45}$ **d.** $13\frac{38}{45}$

15. Two painters are painting a house. In 1 day, one painter paints $\frac{1}{3}$ of the house while the other paints $\frac{2}{5}$ of the house. How much of the job remains to be done?

   a. $\frac{4}{15}$ **b.** $\frac{5}{8}$ **c.** $\frac{3}{8}$ **d.** $\frac{1}{2}$

16. Multiply $\frac{17}{9}$ times $\frac{13}{24}$.

   a. 220 **b.** $1\frac{5}{221}$ **c.** $\frac{1}{21}$ **d.** $1\frac{5}{216}$

17. What is $2\frac{3}{8}$ multiplied by $4\frac{2}{7}$?

   a. $9\frac{5}{8}$ **b.** $8\frac{3}{28}$ **c.** $8\frac{6}{56}$ **d.** $10\frac{5}{28}$

18. Samantha reads $\frac{3}{4}$ of a Sunday newspaper containing 264 pages. How many pages remain to be read?

   a. 33 pages   **b.** 66 pages   **c.** 132 pages   **d.** 198 pages

19. Divide: $\frac{8}{15} \div \frac{4}{5}$

   a. $\frac{2}{3}$ **b.** $\frac{3}{5}$ **c.** $\frac{32}{75}$ **d.** $\frac{4}{5}$

20. Find the quotient of $4\frac{3}{4}$ and $2\frac{3}{8}$.

   a. $2\frac{3}{8}$ **b.** $3\frac{1}{21}$ **c.** 2   **d.** $11\frac{9}{32}$

21. Heidi Derosier cooked a roast weighing $12\frac{1}{3}$ pounds. After $3\frac{2}{3}$ pounds of fat were trimmed, the roast was cut into $\frac{1}{3}$ -pound servings. How many servings were cut from the roast?

   a. 29   **b.** 24   **c.** 26   **d.** 18

22. Which statement is correct?

   a. $\frac{7}{8} = \frac{17}{22}$ **b.** $\frac{7}{8} < \frac{17}{22}$ **c.** $\frac{7}{8} > \frac{17}{22}$ **d.** $\frac{7}{8} < 0$

23. Simplify: $\left(\frac{3}{8}\right)^2 \left(\frac{32}{45}\right)$

   a. $\frac{2}{5}$ **b.** $\frac{4}{15}$ **c.** $\frac{1}{5}$ **d.** $\frac{1}{10}$

24. Simplify: $\left(\frac{5}{6}\right)^2 \div \left(\frac{3}{4} - \frac{2}{9}\right)$

   a. $\frac{95}{216}$ **b.** $1\frac{6}{19}$ **c.** $1\frac{1}{19}$ **d.** $1\frac{11}{19}$

25. Simplify: $\frac{4}{5} - \frac{2}{3}\left(\frac{1}{4} - \frac{1}{5}\right)$

   a. $\frac{23}{30}$ **b.** $\frac{13}{30}$ **c.** $\frac{1}{20}$ **d.** $\frac{17}{20}$

Name: _____
Date: _____

1. Write 2.0418 in words.
   a. Two and four thousand one hundred eighty thousandths
   b. Two and four thousand eighteen thousandths
   c. Two and four hundred eighteen thousandths
   d. Two and four hundred eighteen ten-thousandths

2. Write in standard form: fifteen and three hundredths
   a. 15.3   b. 15.03   c. 15.003   d. 15.0003

3. Round 139.72064 to the nearest thousandth.

   a. 139.721   b. 139.720   c. 139.72   d. 139.7206

4. Round 33.49397 to the nearest ten-thousandth.
   a. 33.49   b. 33.494   c. 33.493   d. 33.4940

5. Add: 66.09
           7.325
          166.9
   +   7.43   a. 246.755   b. 247.635
   _____   c. 247.745   d. 249.655

6. Find the sum of 83.812 , 4.7 , 147.898 , and 79.39 .
   a. 316.8   b. 314.87   c. 361.8   d. 315.8

7. Your homeowner's insurance payment is $407.89, your phone bill is $72.18, and your water-and-sewer bill is $58.40. Find the total of these payments.
   a. $539.47   b. $538.37   c. $538.47   d. $539.27

8. Subtract: 109.516
             − 85.937   a. 23.581   b. 23.579
             _____   c. 24.579   d. 23.578

9. What is 19.53 decreased by 8.92 ?
   a. 10.41   b. 10.61   c. 10.74   d. 11.41

10. A sales executive has an expense account of $750. He spends $116.97 for transportation, $49.32 for food, and $216.70 for lodging. Find the balance that remains in the expense account after transportation, food, and lodging.
    a. $382.99   b. $366.99   c. $367.01   d. $382.01

11. Multiply: 8.75
    × 0.0039

   a.   0.034125   **b.**   3.4125
   c.   0.34125   **d.**   0.33115

12. Find the product of 119.2 and 0.0046 .

   a.   0.55832   **b.**   0.54832   **c.**   548.32   **d.**   5.4832

13. A 30-inch television can be bought for $200 down and payments of $49.75 each month for 12 months. Find the total cost of the television.

   a. $979   **b.** $879   **c.** $797   **d.** $897

14. Divide: $8.2\overline{)98.4}$

   a.   1.2   **b.**   0.12
   c.   12   **d.**   120

15. Divide. Round to the nearest thousandth.

$$7.4\overline{)87.603}$$

   a.   1.1084   **b.**   11.838
   c.   11.828   **d.**   11.084

16. A Whirlpool refrigerator is bought for $693.56. The down payment is $100, and the balance is to be paid off in 4 equal monthly payments. Find the amount of each monthly payment.

   a. $49.46   **b.** $148.39   **c.** $173.39   **d.** $593.56

17. Convert $\dfrac{7}{17}$ to a decimal. Round to the nearest thousandth.

   a.   0.411   **b.**   0.402   **c.**   0.412   **d.**   4.02

18. Convert $0.22\dfrac{1}{2}$ to a fraction.

   a. $\dfrac{9}{40}$ **b.** $\dfrac{3}{20}$ **c.** $\dfrac{11}{50}$ **d.** $\dfrac{23}{100}$

19. Which statement is correct?

   a. $3.017 < 3.17$ **b.** $0 > 3.17$ **c.** $3.117 > 3.17$ **d.** $3.10 > 3.107$

20. Which statement is correct?

   a. $0.45 = \dfrac{5}{11}$ **b.** $0.45 < \dfrac{5}{11}$ **c.** $0.45 > \dfrac{5}{11}$ **d.** $0.45 < 0$

Name: _____
Date: _____

1. Divide: $69\overline{)73,508}$

   a. $165\,r\,23$ b. $995\,r\,13$
   c. $1065\,r\,23$ d. $1065\,r\,13$

2. Simplify: $3^2 \cdot 9^3$
   a. 6561   b. 6563   c. 4374   d. 2187

3. Simplify: $10 - 2(8-3) + 4^2$
   a. 4   b. 16   c. 7   d. 10

4. Find the LCM of 34 and 8.
   a. 272   b. 2   c. 136   d. 34

5. Write $\dfrac{59}{7}$ as a mixed number.

   a. $8\dfrac{3}{7}$ b. $9\dfrac{5}{7}$ c. $8\dfrac{1}{7}$ d. $9\dfrac{3}{7}$

6. Write $3\dfrac{5}{8}$ as an improper fraction.

   a. $\dfrac{29}{4}$ b. $\dfrac{29}{8}$ c. $\dfrac{29}{5}$ d. $\dfrac{15}{8}$

7. Find the numerator for an equivalent fraction with the given denominator: $\dfrac{4}{15} = \dfrac{}{90}$

   a. 24   b. 4   c. 16   d. 6

8. Add: $\dfrac{1}{8} + \dfrac{2}{5} + \dfrac{7}{40}$

   a. $\dfrac{14}{20}$ b. $\dfrac{27}{40}$ c. $\dfrac{29}{40}$ d. $\dfrac{7}{10}$

9. Find the total of $8\dfrac{1}{3}$ and $4\dfrac{5}{6}$.

   a. 13   b. $13\dfrac{1}{6}$ c. $12\dfrac{5}{6}$ d. $15\dfrac{1}{6}$

10. Subtract: $14\dfrac{2}{9} - 3\dfrac{5}{6}$

   a. $11\dfrac{7}{18}$ b. $10\dfrac{7}{18}$ c. $11\dfrac{11}{18}$ d. $10\dfrac{1}{2}$

11. Multiply: $\dfrac{9}{10} \cdot \dfrac{13}{18}$

     a. $\dfrac{13}{30}$ **b.** $\dfrac{13}{20}$ **c.** $\dfrac{13}{10}$ **d.** $\dfrac{39}{90}$

12. Find the product of $4\dfrac{1}{3}$ and $3\dfrac{2}{5}$.

     a. $14\dfrac{11}{15}$ **b.** $12\dfrac{2}{15}$ **c.** $1\dfrac{3}{5}$ **d.** $\dfrac{24}{15}$

13. Divide: $\dfrac{11}{15} \div \dfrac{22}{45}$

     a. $\dfrac{1}{10}$ **b.** $\dfrac{2}{3}$ **c.** $2\dfrac{1}{2}$ **d.** $1\dfrac{1}{2}$

14. What is $3\dfrac{3}{4}$ divided by $\dfrac{5}{16}$?

     a. $\dfrac{1}{12}$ **b.** $\dfrac{1}{8}$ **c.** 8 **d.** 12

15. Simplify: $4 \cdot \left(\dfrac{3}{2}\right)^3 \left(\dfrac{1}{6}\right)^2$

     a. $\dfrac{3}{16}$ **b.** $\dfrac{1}{8}$ **c.** $\dfrac{3}{8}$ **d.** $2\dfrac{2}{3}$

16. Simplify: $\dfrac{2}{3} - \dfrac{3}{8} \cdot \left(\dfrac{2}{3} - \dfrac{4}{9}\right)$

     a. $\dfrac{1}{36}$ **b.** $\dfrac{7}{12}$ **c.** $\dfrac{7}{84}$ **d.** $\dfrac{5}{12}$

17. Write 12.0049 in words.
     a. Twelve and forty-nine ten-thousandths
     b. Twelve and forty-nine hundredths
     c. Twelve and forty-nine thousandths
     d. Twelve thousand forty-nine

18. Add: 97.01
         8.456
     + 0.09

     a. 105.556   **b.** 105.456
     c. 105.546   **d.** 105.466

19. What is 32.007 decreased by 11.9235?

     a. 2.00835   **b.** 20.0835   **c.** 20.0935   **d.** 43.9305

Name: _____

20. Multiply: 0.76
　　　　　　　× 0.31

　　　a. 23.56　　　　　　**b.** 0.2456
　　　c. 2.356　　　　　　**d.** 0.2356

21. Divide. Round to the nearest thousandth.

　　　0.3)‾24.95‾

　　　a. 83.167　　　　　　**b.** 8.317
　　　c. 831.667　　　　　**d.** 0.832

22. Convert $\frac{13}{18}$ to a decimal. Round to the nearest thousandth.

　a. 0.72　　　　**b.** 0.7222　　　　**c.** 0.7　　　　**d.** 0.722

23. Convert 0.024 to a fraction.

　a. $\frac{1}{8}$　　　　**b.** $\frac{3}{25}$　　　　**c.** $\frac{9}{25}$　　　　**d.** $\frac{3}{125}$

24. Which statement is correct?

　a. $\frac{1}{3} < 0.32$　　　　**b.** $\frac{1}{3} > 0.32$　　　　**c.** $\frac{1}{3} = 0.32$　　　　**d.** $\frac{1}{3} < 0$

25. A city received $3\frac{1}{2}$ inches of rain in April, $5\frac{1}{2}$ inches in May, and $4\frac{3}{4}$ inches in June. Find the total rainfall for the 3 months.

　a. $12\frac{3}{4}$ inches　　**b.** $13\frac{1}{4}$ inches　　**c.** $13\frac{3}{4}$ inches　　**d.** 13 inches

26. One-sixth of a shipment of videotapes was defective. If there were 480 videotapes in the shipment, how many videotapes were not defective?

　a. 400 video tapes　　**b.** 80 video tapes　　**c.** 390 video tapes　　**d.** 410 video tapes

27. A company spends $\frac{3}{8}$ of its monthly income on employee salaries. During the month of May, the company spent $162,000 on monthly salaries. How much income did the company receive during the month of May?

　a. $60,750　　**b.** $259,200　　**c.** $316,000　　**d.** $432,000

28. A computer analyst receives a salary of $15.50 per hour for a 40-hour week, and $23.25 per hour for overtime work. If the analyst worked 44 hours last week, what was the analyst's income?

　a. $613　　**b.** $713　　**c.** $93　　**d.** $1023

29. The odometer of your car reads 32,067.4 miles. You drive 167.4 miles on Thursday, 65.2 miles on Friday, and 17.9 miles on Saturday. Find the odometer reading at the end of the 3 days.

　a. 32,118.8　　**b.** 32,317.9　　**c.** 32,318.8　　**d.** 32,306.9

30. If you pay your yearly oil bill of $914.40 in 12 equal monthly payments, what is the amount of each monthly payment?

　a. $86.20　　**b.** $7.62　　**c.** $66.20　　**d.** $76.20

1. Write the comparison 12 feet to 58 feet as a ratio in simplest form.

    a. $\dfrac{3}{29}$ **b.** $\dfrac{12}{58}$ **c.** $\dfrac{29}{6}$ **d.** $\dfrac{6}{29}$

2. Write the comparison 14 cents to 30 cents as a ratio in simplest form.

    a. $\dfrac{8}{15}$ **b.** $\dfrac{7}{15}$ **c.** $15:7$ **d.** $\dfrac{15}{7}$

3. Write the comparison 70 quarts to 30 quarts as a ratio in simplest form.

    a. $\dfrac{7}{3}$ **b.** $\dfrac{7}{5}$ **c.** $3:1$ **d.** $\dfrac{3}{7}$

4. Write the comparison 6 liters to 10 liters as a ratio in simplest form.

    a. $\dfrac{2}{5}$ **b.** $\dfrac{5}{3}$ **c.** $1\dfrac{2}{5}$ **d.** $\dfrac{3}{5}$

5. A portable compact disc player sold for $100. Two years later, the same compact disc player sold for $75. Find the ratio, as a fraction in simplest form, of the original price of the compact disc player to its price two years later.

    a. $\dfrac{4}{3}$ **b.** $\dfrac{3}{4}$ **c.** $\dfrac{5}{4}$ **d.** $\dfrac{4}{5}$

6. Sixty-five thousand people attended the Comet's football game on Sunday, and seventy-five thousand attended their game on the following Sunday. Find the ratio, as a fraction in simplest form, of the attendance on the first Sunday to the total attendance at both games.

    a. $\dfrac{4}{7}$ **b.** $\dfrac{13}{28}$ **c.** $\dfrac{15}{28}$ **d.** $\dfrac{28}{13}$

7. Write "12 children in 5 families" as a rate in simplest form.

    a. $\dfrac{12 \text{ children}}{5 \text{ familes}}$ **b.** $\dfrac{5 \text{ families}}{12 \text{ children}}$ **c.** $\dfrac{6 \text{ children}}{2 \text{ families}}$ **d.** $\dfrac{12}{5}$

8. Write "1250 miles in 4 hours" as a rate in simplest form.

    a. $\dfrac{625 \text{ miles}}{2 \text{ hours}}$ **b.** $\dfrac{1250 \text{ miles}}{4 \text{ hours}}$ **c.** $\dfrac{2 \text{ hours}}{625 \text{ miles}}$ **d.** $\dfrac{625}{2}$

9. Write "$1875 for 25 chairs" as a unit rate.

    a. $73/chair   **b.** $75   **c.** $75/chair   **d.** $77/chair

10. Write "275 feet in 11 seconds" as a unit rate.

    a. 275 feet/11 seconds   **b.** 25 seconds/foot   **c.** 25   **d.** 25 feet/second

Name: _____

11. A company's cost to produce 100 calculators was $3200. The company sold the calculators to a retail store for $4500. What was the company's profit on each calculator?

    a. $1300   **b.** $13   **c.** $32   **d.** $45

12. A medical technician earns $34,068 in 12 months. What are the medical technician's monthly earnings?

    a. $2845   **b.** $2283   **c.** $2839   **d.** $2893

13. Which proportion is true?

    a. $\dfrac{65}{90} = \dfrac{13}{18}$ **b.** $\dfrac{6}{9} = \dfrac{60}{80}$ **c.** $\dfrac{7}{35} = \dfrac{14}{80}$ **d.** $\dfrac{5}{14} = \dfrac{30}{72}$

14. Which proportion is true?

    a. $\dfrac{24}{32} = \dfrac{120}{150}$ **b.** $\dfrac{8}{10} = \dfrac{89}{100}$ **c.** $\dfrac{30}{70} = \dfrac{90}{140}$ **d.** $\dfrac{30}{42} = \dfrac{5}{7}$

15. Solve: $\dfrac{7}{n} = \dfrac{12}{15}$ Round to the nearest hundredth.

    a. 0.18   **b.** 5.60   **c.** 8.75   **d.** 25.71

16. Solve: $\dfrac{13}{50} = \dfrac{20}{n}$ Round to the nearest tenth.

    a. 75.9   **b.** 76.9   **c.** 76.92   **d.** 60.5

17. The scale on a map is 1 inch equals 20 miles. What is the distance between two points that are $3\frac{1}{4}$ inches apart on the map?

    a. 55 miles   **b.** 65 miles   **c.** 64 miles   **d.** 85 miles

18. Polls showed that 71 out of every 100 people believed that the company should be the central issue in a presidential campaign. At this rate, how many people out of 40,000 polled believed the same thing?

    a. 28,400 people   **b.** 28,000 people   **c.** 2840 people   **d.** 27,400 people

19. A stock investment of 80 shares paid a dividend of $92.80. At this rate, what dividend would be paid for 200 shares of stock?

    a. $242   **b.** $18,560   **c.** $222   **d.** $232

20. An investor had 200 shares of stock in a company before the company declared a stock split of 3 shares for every 2 owned. How many shares of stock does the investor have after the stock split?

    a. 133   **b.** 150   **c.** 300   **d.** 350

Name: _____

Date: _____

1. Write 7.17% as a decimal.

   a. 7170 b. 0.717 c. 0.0717 d. 7.17

2. Write $37\frac{1}{2}$% as a fraction.

   a. $\frac{75}{2}$ b. $\frac{3}{4}$ c. $\frac{3}{8}$ d. $\frac{1}{3}$

3. Write 0.185 as a percent.

   a. 18.5% b. 0.00185% c. 1.85% d. 0.0185%

4. Write 7.6 as a percent.

   a. 76% b. 760% c. 0.076% d. 0.76%

5. Write $\frac{3}{8}$ as a percent.

   a. 0.00375% b. 0.375% c. 38% d. 37.5%

6. Write $2\frac{5}{6}$ as a percent. Round to the nearest tenth.

   a. 2.8% b. 28.3% c. 283.3% d. 2833.3%

7. What is 41.7% of 83?

   a. 34.611 b. 24.611 c. 14.611 d. 34.62

8. 11.75% of 24,000 is what number?

   a. 2042.6 b. 2820 c. 1830 d. 3820

9. Which statement is correct?

   a. 20% of 150 is larger than 200% of 15 b. 20% of 150 is smaller than 200% of 15
   c. 20% of 150 is equal to 200% of 15 d. 20% of 150 is less than 5

10. Which statement is correct?

    a. 1.2% of 15 is larger than 2.8% of 7 b. 1.2% of 15 is smaller than 2.8% of 7
    c. 1.2% of 15 is equal to 2.8% of 7 d. 1.2% of 15 is larger than 2

11. A department store has 150 employees and must hire an additional 20% for the holiday season. What is the total number of employees needed for the holiday season?

    a. 170 b. 180 c. 130 d. 30

12. A quality control inspector found that 2.4% of 2000 calculators were defective. How many of the calculators were defective?

    a. 480 b. 58 c. 120 d. 48

13. What percent of 5.5 is 22?

    a. 200%   **b.** 27.5%   **c.** 400%   **d.** 40%

14. What percent of 88 is 47? Round to the nearest tenth.

    a. 53.5%   **b.** 5.3%   **c.** 53.4%   **d.** 187.2%

15. A job candidate answered 18 out of 180 exam questions incorrectly. What percent of the questions did the candidate answer correctly?

    a. 90%   **b.** 10%   **c.** 95%   **d.** 87.5%

16. Misty received a dividend of $240 on an investment of $2000. What percent of the investment is the dividend?

    a. 12%   **b.** 1.2%   **c.** 88%   **d.** 8%

17. 35.5 is 28.4% of what number?

    a. 115   **b.** 135   **c.** 0.80   **d.** 125

18. 144 is 180% of what number?

    a. 8   **b.** 800   **c.** 81   **d.** 80

19. A used Jeep was purchased for $9810. This was 45% of what it cost new. What did the jeep cost new?

    a. $14,224.50   **b.** $17,836.36   **c.** $21,800   **d.** $4414.50

20. A typist made errors on four words on a typing test. This was 2.5% of the total number of words typed. How many words were typed?

    a. 160   **b.** 120   **c.** 80   **d.** 140

21. 110.4 is 120% of what number?

    a. 0.92   **b.** 92   **c.** 132.48   **d.** 230.4

22. What percent of 6000 is 30?

    a. 0.5%   **b.** 0.4%   **c.** 5%   **d.** 50%

23. A charity organization collected $40,000. It spent 15% of that amount for administrative expenses. How much of the amount collected was spent for administrative expenses?

    a. $7000   **b.** $6000   **c.** $5000   **d.** $26,666.67

24. A computer malfunctioned 19 hours out of a total of 500 hours of computer operation. What percent of the total time of operation was the computer malfunctioning?

    a. 38%   **b.** 3.8%   **c.** 2.8%   **d.** 26.32%

25. This year's total rainfall in a valley town was 48 inches. This was 120% of last year's total rainfall. What was last year's total rainfall?

    a. 56 inches   **b.** 40 inches   **c.** 24 inches   **d.** 42 inches

1. A 12-foot ash plank costs $35.40. Find the unit cost.

   a. $3.95/foot　　　　**b.** $2.97/foot　　　　**c.** $2.95/foot　　　　**d.** $2.59/foot

2. Which is the most economical purchase?

   a. 4 pounds for $5.25　　　　　　　**b.** 5.2 pounds for $6.75
   c. 5.8 pounds for $8.25　　　　　　　**d.** 9.3 pounds for $12.00

3. Romano cheese costs $3.89 per pound. Find the total cost of $\frac{1}{3}$ pound. Round to the nearest cent.

   a. $11.67　　　　**b.** $1.82　　　　**c.** $1.28　　　　**d.** $1.30

4. A Firefighter's Union negotiated a new contract calling for a 6.5% increase in pay. What is the new wage of a firefighter who was making $680 per week?

   a. $724.20/week　　　　**b.** $915.90/week　　　　**c.** $686.50/week　　　　**d.** $44.20/week

5. The value of an $8000 investment increased by $1200. What percent increase does this represent?

   a. 25%　　　　**b.** 15%　　　　**c.** 20%　　　　**d.** 16%

6. The markup on a power saw that cost a hardware store $245 is $98. What markup rate does this represent?

   a. 25%　　　　**b.** 30%　　　　**c.** 40%　　　　**d.** 35%

7. The Court House Athletic Club pro shop uses a markup rate of 35% on tennis rackets that cost the shop $220.00. What is the selling price?

   a. $77　　　　**b.** $143　　　　**c.** $297　　　　**d.** $255

8. The Trinity College bookstore sold 4500 math books during the fall semester. The bookstore sold 540 fewer math books in the spring semester. What was the percent decrease in the number of math books sold?

   a. 88%　　　　**b.** 11%　　　　**c.** 10.9%　　　　**d.** 12%

9. A computer's price dropped from $2150 to $1247. Find the percent decrease in price.

   a. 42%　　　　**b.** 58%　　　　**c.** 24%　　　　**d.** 48%

10. A stereo that regularly sells for $890 is on sale for 40% off the regular price. What is the sale price?

    a. $356　　　　**b.** $543　　　　**c.** $534　　　　**d.** $643

11. A snowboard that regularly sells for $339 is on sale for 30% off the regular price. What is the discount?

    a. $260.77   **b.** $440.70   **c.** $101.70   **d.** $237.30

12. A hardware store borrows $60,000 at a 16% annual simple interest rate for 9 months. What is the simple interest due on the loan?

    a. $7200   **b.** $9600   **c.** $6400   **d.** $86,400

13. Liberty Investment Co. deposits $120,000 in a trust account that pays 9% annual interest compounded daily. Find the value of this investment after 1 year. Use the Compound Interest Table.

    a. $131,299.20   **b.** $131,043.60   **c.** $184,634.40   **d.** $129,600

14. Western City Bank requires a down payment of 7.5% of the $65,000 purchase price of a town house condominium. Find the amount of the mortgage.

    a. $48,750   **b.** $4875   **c.** $60,125   **d.** $50,125

15. A rancher purchases some land for $360,000 and makes a down payment of $80,000. The bank charges an annual interest rate of 9% on the rancher's 30-year mortgage. Find the monthly mortgage payment. Use the Monthly Payment Table. Round to the nearest cent.

    a. $2896.63   **b.** $2349.76   **c.** $2252.94   **d.** $643.70

16. An insurance executive buys a sports car for $26,500 and makes a down payment of 22% of the purchase price. Find the amount financed.

    a. $22,500   **b.** $22,670   **c.** $5830   **d.** $20,670

17. A truck is purchased for $12,000 with a down payment of $1500. The balance is financed for 3 years at an annual interest rate of 8%. Find the monthly payment. Use the Monthly Payment Table. Round to the nearest cent.

    a. $329.03   **b.** $376.04   **c.** $474.89   **d.** $374.22

18. A sales representative receives a salary of $13,000 per year plus a commission of 6% of all sales over $150,000. During one year, the representative's total sales were $575,000. Find the representative's total earnings for the year.

    a. $47,500   **b.** $46,400   **c.** $26,000   **d.** $38,500

19. The business checking account for a clothing store showed a balance of $3412.66 before making deposits of $614.33 and $1416.29. The store manager then wrote checks for $504.73, $216.82, and $1083.57. Find the current checkbook balance.

    a. $3638.61   **b.** $3683.61   **c.** $3683.16   **d.** $3638.16

20. Balance the checkbook shown.

NUMBER	DATE	DESCRIPTION OF TRANSACTION	PAYMENT/DEBIT (-)	√T	FEE (IF ANY) (-)	DEPOSIT/CREDIT (+)	BALANCE 645 59
	7/1	Rent	410 30				235 29
	7/3	Electric bill	129 35				105 94
	7/10	Car Insurance	79 22				26 72
	7/15	Water bill	15 40				11 32
	7/17	Deposit				590 00	601 32
	7/23	Doctor	85 00				516 32
	7/24	Baseball tickets	32 00				484 32
	7/30	Deposit				200 00	684 32

RECORD ALL CHARGES OR CREDITS THAT AFFECT YOUR ACCOUNT

REMEMBER TO RECORD AUTOMATIC PAYMENTS/DEPOSITS ON DATE AUTHORIZED

CHECKING ACCOUNT Monthly Statement Account Number : 924-297-8

DATE	Transaction	Amount	Balance
7/1	OPENING BALANCE		645.59
7/5	CHECK	410.30	235.29
7/6	CHECK	129.35	105.94
7/17	CHECK	15.40	90.54
7/18	DEPOSIT	590.00	680.54
7/21	CHECK	79.22	601.32
7/29	INTEREST	3.66	604.98
7/31	SERVICE CHARGE	10.00	594.98
7/31	CLOSING BALANCE		594.98

Do the bank statement and the checkbook balance?

    a. Yes   **b.** No

1. Write the comparison 78 donations to 42 donations as a ratio in simplest form.

   a. $\dfrac{13}{7}$ **b.** $\dfrac{78}{42}$ **c.** $\dfrac{13}{6}$ **d.** $\dfrac{7}{13}$

2. A video store rented 415 videos on Friday and 520 videos on Saturday. Find the ratio of the number of rentals on Friday to the number of rentals on Saturday.

   a. $\dfrac{83}{140}$ **b.** $\dfrac{104}{83}$ **c.** $\dfrac{83}{104}$ **d.** $\dfrac{85}{104}$

3. Write "2880 miles in 5 days" as a unit rate.

   a. $\dfrac{2880\ \text{miles}}{5\ \text{days}}$ **b.** 57.6 miles/day   **c.** 576 miles/day   **d.** 2880 miles/day

4. A cardiogram of a patient's heartbeat recorded 252 heartbeats in 3.5 minutes. What is the patient's heartbeat per minute?

   a. 7.2 heartbeats/minute   **b.** 720 heartbeats/minute

   c. 74 heartbeats/minute   **d.** 72 heartbeats/minute

5. Solve the proportion: $\dfrac{19}{n} = \dfrac{54}{135}$

   a. 4.75   **b.** 47.5   **c.** 475   **d.** 49.5

6. A stock investment of 125 shares paid a dividend of $462.50. At this rate, what dividend would be paid on 240 shares of stock?

   a. $888   **b.** $88.80   **c.** $8880   **d.** $240.89

7. Write 93% as a decimal.

   a. 9.3   **b.** 0.93   **c.** 930   **d.** 0.093

8. Write 36% as a fraction.

   a. $\dfrac{9}{25}$ **b.** $\dfrac{7}{20}$ **c.** $\dfrac{9}{20}$ **d.** $\dfrac{8}{25}$

9. Write 2.34 as a percent.

   a. 23,400%   **b.** 0.234%   **c.** 23.4%   **d.** 234%

10. Write $\dfrac{5}{4}$ as a percent.

    a. 120%   **b.** 125%   **c.** 25%   **d.** 80%

Name: _____

11. 7.9% of 120 is what number?

    a. 9.48   **b.** 94.8   **c.** 0.948   **d.** 948

12. The China Star restaurant does 35% more business on Friday night than it does on Thursday night. If the restaurant's receipts on Thursday night totaled $1560, what was the total of the receipts on Friday night?

    a. $546   **b.** $54.60   **c.** $2160   **d.** $2106

13. What percent of 55 is 11?

    a. 20%   **b.** 10%   **c.** 500%   **d.** 5%

14. Spectrum Inc.'s stock is trading at $45 and pays a dividend of $2.25. What percent of the stock price is the dividend?

    a. 20%   **b.** 0.05%   **c.** 50%   **d.** 5%

15. 418 is 110% of what number?

    a. 459.8   **b.** 380   **c.** 263.2   **d.** 38

16. A used car was purchased for $6705. This was 45% of the new car cost. Find the new car cost.

    a. $14,900   **b.** $9722.25   **c.** $12,190.91   **d.** $3017.25

17. Sugar costs $1.89 for a 5-pound bag. Find the cost of 1 pound of sugar. Round to the nearest cent.

    a. $0.37   **b.** $0.38   **c.** $0.04   **d.** $0.36

18. The markup on a necklace that costs a jeweler $280 is $112. What markup rate does this represent?

    a. 20%   **b.** 25%   **c.** 30%   **d.** 40%

19. The Tampa Athletic Club has discounted its regular membership rates by 10%. What is the price of a membership that regularly costs $265?

    a. $26.50   **b.** $238.50   **c.** $237.50   **d.** $239.50

20. The Wilsons built an addition to their convenience store. They financed $75,000 for 18 months at an annual simple interest rate of 9.5%. Find the interest due on the loan.

    a. $6637.50   **b.** $4750   **c.** $10,687.50   **d.** $12,825

The pictograph shows the number of compact discs sold at a music store during 1 month. Each disc represents 20 discs sold.

1. How many discs were sold during the second week?

   a. 7
   b. 140
   c. 700
   d. 120

2. How many more discs were sold during the third week than were sold during the first week?

   a. 40
   b. 20
   c. 1
   d. 10

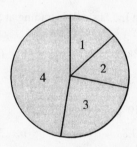

Week 1

Week 2

Week 3

Week 4

The circle graph shows the annual expenses of owning and operating a car.

3. Find the ratio of the cost of maintenance to the car payments.

   a. $\frac{2}{7}$
   b. $\frac{13}{42}$
   c. $\frac{5}{9}$
   d. $\frac{18}{35}$

4. What is the ratio of insurance costs to the cost of maintenance?

   a. $\frac{12}{13}$
   b. $\frac{5}{4}$
   c. $\frac{13}{12}$
   d. $\frac{9}{5}$

5. Find the ratio of the annual cost of fuel to the annual car payments.

   a. $\frac{18}{25}$
   b. $\frac{16}{35}$
   c. $\frac{7}{15}$
   d. $\frac{18}{35}$

ANNUAL CAR EXPENSES
1: $ 600 - Maintenance
2: $ 650 - Insurance
3: $1080 - Fuel
4: $2100 - Car Payments

The double-bar graph shows the number of cars (in hundreds) sold each quarter by a car dealership in 2000 and 2001.

6. Find the total number of cars sold in the third and fourth quarters of 2001.

   a. 750
   b. 850
   c. 900
   d. 800

7. What was the total number of cars sold in 2001?

   a. 1400
   b. 14,500
   c. 1450
   d. 14,000

8. Find the difference between the first quarter sales in 2000 and 2001.

   a. 1000
   b. 1500
   c. 100
   d. 2000

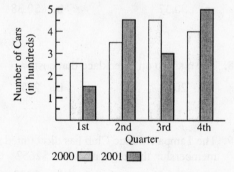

9. The commissions received by a sales representative for the last five months were: $2500, $3000, $1700, $3300, and $3000. What is the median commission earned for these five months?

   a. $2700
   b. $2750
   c. $3000
   d. $3300

10. Luis received grades of 92, 88, 84, 95, 73, 86, and 84 on seven physics exams. Find the mean grade of his physics exams.

    a. 83.5
    b. 87.2
    c. 86.4
    d. 86

The double-line graph shows the quarterly sales (in thousands of dollars) for a grocery store for the years 2000 and 2001.

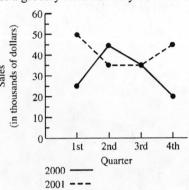

11. In which quarter in 2000 did the grocery store have the lowest sales?

    a. 2nd   **b.** 3rd   **c.** 4th   **d.** 1st

12. In which quarter were 2000 sales and 2001 sales equal?

    a. 2nd   **b.** 3rd   **c.** 4th   **d.** 1st

13. Find the ratio of first quarter 2000 sales to first quarter 2001 sales.

    a. $\dfrac{1}{2}$ **b.** $\dfrac{4}{9}$ **c.** $\dfrac{9}{7}$ **d.** $\dfrac{1}{1}$

The histogram shows the energy bills of 34 customers.

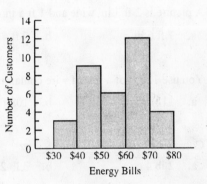

14. What is the ratio of the number of customers whose energy bill was between $60 and $70 to the total number of customers?

    a. $\dfrac{12}{35}$ **b.** $\dfrac{11}{34}$ **c.** $\dfrac{1}{2}$ **d.** $\dfrac{6}{17}$

15. What percent of the customers had bills between $70 and $80? Round to the nearest tenth of a percent.

    a. 11.8%   **b.** 8.8%   **c.** 13.2%   **d.** 10.3%

The frequency polygon shows the speeds of 52 cars on a highway.

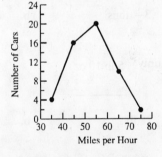

16. Find the number of cars traveling between 50 and 70 miles per hour.

    a. 28   **b.** 30   **c.** 32   **d.** 36

17. What percent of the cars were traveling between 50 and 60 miles per hour? Round to the nearest tenth of a percent.

    a. 37.5%   **b.** 38.5%   **c.** 36.5%   **d.** 34.7%

18. Two dice are rolled. What is the probability that the sum of the dots on the upward faces is <u>not</u> 3?

    a. $\dfrac{1}{18}$ **b.** $\dfrac{17}{18}$ **c.** $\dfrac{5}{36}$ **d.** $\dfrac{35}{36}$

19. A survey of the candidates for a masters degree was conducted to determine political affiliation. The responses were: 257, Republican; 274, Democrat; 122, Independent; 402, other. What was the modal political affiliation?

    a. Republican   **b.** Democrat   **c.** Independent   **d.** Other

20. The box-and-whiskers plot represents data taken from selling prices of homes, in thousands of dollars, in a certain zip code. Determine the first quartile of this data.

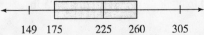

    a. $149,000   **b.** $175,000   **c.** $222,000   **d.** $260,000

Name: _____
Date: _____

1. Convert 75 in. to feet.

   a. $6\frac{1}{2}$ ft

   b. $6\frac{1}{4}$ ft

   c. $6\frac{3}{10}$ ft

   d. $6\frac{1}{3}$ ft

2. Add: $3\frac{1}{3}$ yd

   $+2\frac{1}{2}$ yd

   _____

   a. $4\frac{5}{6}$ yd

   b. $6\frac{5}{6}$ yd

   c. $5\frac{5}{6}$ yd

   d. $\frac{5}{6}$ yd

3. A picture is 2 ft 3 in. wide and 1 ft 5 in. high. Find the length of framing needed to put around the picture.

   a. 7 ft 6 in.

   b. 7 ft 4 in.

   c. 3 ft 8 in.

   d. 6 ft 8 in.

4. You use 120 ft of a roll of wire containing 76 yd of wire. How many feet of wire are left on the roll?

   a. 118 ft

   b. 108 ft

   c. 75 ft

   d. 90 ft

5. Convert: 40 oz = _____ lb _____ oz

   a. 2 lb 4 oz

   b. 3 lb 2 oz

   c. 3 lb 4 oz

   d. 2 lb 8 oz

6. Convert 6750 lb to tons.

   a. $3\frac{1}{2}$ tons

   b. $4\frac{1}{4}$ tons

   c. $3\frac{3}{4}$ tons

   d. $3\frac{3}{8}$ tons

7. Multiply: 5 lb 10 oz

   $\times$ 5

   _____

   a. 28 lb 2 oz

   b. 29 lb 2 oz

   c. 26 lb 2 oz

   d. 28 lb 12 oz

8. What is $5\frac{3}{8}$ lb decreased by $2\frac{2}{3}$ lb?

   a. $2\frac{7}{24}$ lb

   b. $2\frac{17}{24}$ lb

   c. $3\frac{17}{24}$ lb

   d. $7\frac{23}{24}$ lb

9. A case of canned pears contains 24 14-ounce cans. Find the weight in pounds of the case of canned pears.

   a. 27.4 lb

   b. 9.3 lb

   c. 18 lb

   d. 21 lb

10. Find the weight in pounds of 50 packaged CDs. Each CD weighs 4 oz.

    a. 200 lb

    b. 16.7 lb

    c. 10 lb

    d. 12.5 lb

11. Convert $1\frac{1}{4}$ pt to fluid ounces.

   a. $2\frac{1}{2}$ fl oz   b.   10 fl oz   c.   20 fl oz   d.   15 fl oz

12. Convert: 15 pt = _____ qt _____ pt

   a.   7 qt 1 pt   b.   7 qt 2 pt   c.   6 qt 3 pt   d.   6 qt 1 pt

13. Find the quotient of $6\frac{3}{8}$ gal and 3.

   a. $2\frac{1}{3}$ gal   b. $2\frac{1}{8}$ gal   c. $2\frac{1}{2}$ gal   d. $6\frac{1}{2}$ gal

14. Add: 5 gal 1 qt
          + 2 gal 3 qt
          _____

   a.   8 gal   b.   9 gal   c.   8 gal 1 qt   d.   7 gal 3 qt

15. A school cafeteria sold 180 cartons of milk in one school day. Each carton contained 1 c of milk. How many quarts of milk were sold that day?

   a.   90 qt   b. $22\frac{1}{2}$ qt   c.   45 qt   d.   30 qt

16. A farmer can buy a 50-gallon barrel of gasoline for $58.50. The pump price of the gasoline is $1.49 per gallon. How much does the farmer save by buying the 50-gallon barrel of gasoline?

   a. $8   b. $16   c. $74.50   d. $12

17. A furnace is rated at 30,000 Btu per hour. How many foot-pounds of energy are released by the furnace in 1 h? (1 Btu = 778 ft · lb)

   a.   23,340,000 ft · lb   b.   30,000 ft · lb   c.   23,340 ft · lb   d.   38.56 ft · lb

18. One pound of natural gas will give off 1500 Btu of energy when burned. How many foot-pounds of energy are released when 1 lb of natural gas is burned? (1 Btu = 778 ft · lb)

   a.   1.93 ft · lb   b.   167,000 ft · lb   c.   1500 ft · lb   d.   1,167,000 ft · lb

19. Find the power in foot-pounds per second needed to raise 350 lb a distance of 80 ft in 15 s. Round to the nearest tenth.

   a. $2916.7\,\frac{\text{ft} \cdot \text{lb}}{\text{s}}$ b. $342.9\,\frac{\text{ft} \cdot \text{lb}}{\text{s}}$ c. $1866.7\,\frac{\text{ft} \cdot \text{lb}}{\text{s}}$ d. $65.6\,\frac{\text{ft} \cdot \text{lb}}{\text{s}}$

20. A motor has a power of $2200\,\frac{\text{ft} \cdot \text{lb}}{\text{s}}$. Find the horsepower of the motor. $\left(1\ \text{hp} = 550\,\frac{\text{ft} \cdot \text{lb}}{\text{s}}\right)$

   a.   2.5 hp   b.   4 hp   c.   3.5 hp   d.   5 hp

Name: _____
Date: _____

1. Convert 5.16 km to meters.

    a. 516 m

    b. 5160 m

    c. 51.6 m

    d. 51,600 m

2. Convert 2196 m to kilometers.

    a. 2.196 km

    b. 2,196,000 km

    c. 21.96 km

    d. 219.6 km

3. Convert 5 m 6 mm to meters.

    a. 5.6 m

    b. 5.06 km

    c. 50.6 m

    d. 5.006 m

4. Convert 7 m 62 cm to meters.

    a. 7.62 m

    b. 762 m

    c. 7.062 m

    d. 70.62 m

5. Two pieces of wire fence are cut from an 80-meter roll. The two pieces measure 1260 cm and 2485 cm. How much wire fence is left on the roll after the two pieces are cut?

    a. 425.5 m

    b. 42.55 m

    c. 525.5 m

    d. 32.55 m

6. A hiker can walk 6250 m in 1 h. How many kilometers can the hiker walk in 2.5 h?

    a. 13.5 km

    b. 15.625 km

    c. 125 km

    d. 156.25 km

7. Convert 3.2567 g to milligrams.

    a. 0.032567 mg

    b. 325.67 mg

    c. 3256.7 mg

    d. 32,567 mg

8. Convert 6550 g to kilograms.

    a. 65,500 kg

    b. 655.0 kg

    c. 65.50 kg

    d. 6.550 kg

9. Convert 3 kg 47 g to kilograms.

    a. 3.47 kg

    b. 3.047 kg

    c. 347 kg

    d. 30.47 kg

10. Convert 32 g 416 mg to grams.

    a. 32.416 g

    b. 32.0416 g

    c. 32,416 g

    d. 320,416 g

11. Two hundred fifty grams of fertilizer are used to fertilize each tree in an apple orchard. How many kilograms of fertilizer are required to fertilize 250 trees?

     a. 62.5 kg   **b.** 625 kg   **c.** 6.25 kg   **d.** 100 kg

12. A building block weighs 1900 g. Find the weight in kilograms of a load of 400 building blocks.

     a. 660 kg   **b.** 436 kg   **c.** 210.5 kg   **d.** 760 kg

13. Convert 580 L to kiloliters.

     a. 5.80 kl   **b.** 580,000 kl   **c.** 0.580 kl   **d.** 58,000 kl

14. Convert 325 cm^3 to milliliters.

     a. 3.25 ml   **b.** 325 ml   **c.** 32,500 ml   **d.** 32.5 ml

15. Convert 2L 142 ml to liters.

     a. 2.142 L   **b.** 21.42 L   **c.** 2142 L   **d.** 214.2 L

16. Convert 3 L 75 ml to milliliters.

     a. 3075 ml   **b.** 3.75 ml   **c.** 3.075 ml   **d.** 30.75 ml

17. A health food restaurant served 180 glasses of organic vegetable juice on Saturday. Each glass contains 250 ml of juice. How many liters of organic vegetable juice were sold on Saturday?

     a. 950 L   **b.** 45 L   **c.** 450 L   **d.** 90 L

18. An electric heater uses 1800 W per hour. Electricity costs 9.5¢ per kilowatt-hour. Find the cost of using the electric heater for 6 h. Round to the nearest cent.

     a. $1.07   **b.** $1.06   **c.** $1.03   **d.** $0.17

19. Paint costs $10.45 per gallon. Find the cost per liter. Round to the nearest cent. (1 L = 1.06 qt)

     a. $2.64/L   **b.** $39.43/L   **c.** $2.77/L   **d.** $2.46/L

20. Express 9 km/h in miles per hour. Round to the nearest tenth. (1.61 km = 1 mi)

     a. 55.9 mi/h   **b.** 5.59 mi/h   **c.** 14.49 mi/h   **d.** 9.59 mi/h

Name: _____
Date: _____

The circle graph shows a family's monthly expenditures totaling $2250.

1. How much money does the family spend on savings each month?
    a. $450   b. $475
    c. $395   d. $315

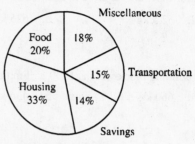

2. Find the ratio of the monthly transportation costs to monthly food expenditures.

    a. $\frac{3}{4}$ b. $\frac{3}{5}$ c. $\frac{4}{5}$ d. $\frac{4}{3}$

Budget for a Monthly
Income of $2250

The histogram shows the salary distribution of 180 recent graduates of a small college.

3. How many graduates earned less than $15,000?
    a. 70   b. 60
    c. 50   d. 140

4. What percent of the graduates earned less than $15,000? Round to the nearest tenth of a percent.
    a. 5.6%   b. 66.7%
    c. 33.3%   d. 27.8%

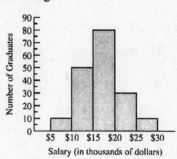

5. Lobsters caught in a series of traps weighed 6.2 lb, 5.3 lb, 7.1 lb, and 4.8 lb. Find the average weight of the lobsters.
    a. 5.75 lb   b. 5.85 lb   c. 5.95 lb   d. 6 lb

6. The vertical rises, in feet, for eight ski lifts at a resort are 1100, 2050, 980, 900, 1050, 1540, 2010, and 1360. What is the median vertical rise for these ski lifts?
    a. 1230 ft   b. 975 ft   c. 1374 ft   d. 2050 ft

7. Convert 1890 in. to yards.
    a. $25\frac{3}{4}$ yd   b. 53 yd   c. $52\frac{1}{2}$ yd   d. $55\frac{3}{4}$ yd

8. Multiply: 5 ft 10 in.
              $\times \quad\quad 6$

    a. 36 ft   b. 34 ft 8 in.   c. 34 ft 6 in.   d. 35 ft

9. Convert $1\frac{3}{4}$ ton to pounds.
    a. 1750 lb   b. 7000 lb   c. 3500 lb   d. 1075 lb

10. What is 11 lb 12 oz increased by 6 lb 6 oz?
    a. 18 lb 2 oz   b. 18 lb 6 oz   c. 18 lb 8 oz   d. 20 lb

11. Convert 48 fl oz to pints.

    a. 6 pt   **b.** 3 pt   **c.** $1\frac{1}{2}$ pt   **d.** 4 pt

12. Two pieces of ribbon, each 10 in. long, are cut from a larger piece of ribbon 1 yd long. In feet and inches, how much ribbon remains of the original piece?

    a. 1 ft 12 in.   **b.** 1 ft 4 in.   **c.** 2 ft 8 in.   **d.** 1 ft 8 in.

13. Boxes being packed for a move weigh 8 lb 12 oz, 20 lb 4 oz, and 15 lb 10 oz. What is the total weight of the boxes?

    a. 44 lb 10 oz   **b.** 45 lb   **c.** 45 lb 4 oz   **d.** 44 lb 12 oz

14. Convert 182.5 cm to meters

    a. 1825 m   **b.** 18.25 m   **c.** 0.01825 m   **d.** 1.825 m

15. Convert 171 mg to grams.

    a. 0.171 g   **b.** 17.1 g   **c.** 1.71 g   **d.** 1710 g

16. Convert 2076 cm^3 to liters.

    a. 2.076 L   **b.** 2076 L   **c.** 20.76 L   **d.** 207.6 L

17. Find the number of meters in 30 ft of track. (1 ft = 0.305 m)

    a. 91.5 m   **b.** 1.01 m   **c.** 9.15 m   **d.** 98.4 m

18. Motor oil costs $1.80/qt. Find the cost per liter. Round to the nearest cent. (1 L = 1.06 qt)

    a. $1.90/L   **b.** $1.89/L   **c.** $1.60/L   **d.** $1.91/L

19. A child grew 9 cm last year and 13 cm the year before that. If the child measured 189 cm 2 years ago, how tall is the child now?

    a. 2.15 m   **b.** 2.11 m   **c.** 2.92 m   **d.** 1.11 m

20. If one serving of lemonade is 150 ml, how many liters of lemonade are required to serve 100 people?

    a. 1.5 L   **b.** 150 L   **c.** 15 L   **d.** 0.15 L

1. Which statement is correct?
   a. $-5 < -12$ b. $-5 = -12$ c. $0 > -5$ d. $-12 > -5$

2. Which statement is correct?
   a. $8 > 11$ b. $0 < -3$ c. $5 < -6$ d. $0 > -3$

3. Evaluate $|-16|$ and $-|7|$.
   a. -16 and -7 b. -16 and 7 c. 16 and -7 d. 16 and 7

4. Find the sum of -15, 9, and -12.
   a. -12 b. -6 c. -36 d. -18

5. Add: $16 + (-12) + 2$
   a. 2 b. 6 c. -6 d. -2

6. Subtract: $20 - (-10)$
   a. -30 b. 30 c. 10 d. -10

7. Subtract: $-8 - (-3) - (-12)$
   a. -1 b. -23 c. 7 d. -7

8. Find the product of 25 and -5.
   a. -5 b. 125 c. -125 d. 5

9. Divide: $-280 \div (-20)$
   a. 14 b. 5600 c. 1.4 d. -14

10. Find the temperature after a fall of $22°C$ from $6°C$.
    a. $28°C$ b. $-28°C$ c. $-16°C$ d. $16°C$

11. The high temperature today was $8°C$. Yesterday the high temperature was $-2°C$. Find the average high temperature for the 2 days.
    a. $-3°C$ b. $3°C$ c. $5°C$ d. $-5°C$

12. Find the sum of $\frac{3}{8}$ and $-\frac{1}{6}$.
    a. $\frac{13}{24}$ b. $-\frac{5}{24}$ c. $\frac{5}{24}$ d. $-\frac{13}{24}$

13. Add: $-\frac{5}{16} + \left(-\frac{7}{24}\right)$
    a. $-\frac{19}{48}$ b. $-\frac{29}{48}$ c. $-\frac{1}{48}$ d. $\frac{1}{48}$

14. Subtract: $\frac{3}{5} - \left(-\frac{3}{4}\right)$

    a. $1\frac{7}{20}$ **b.** $\frac{3}{20}$ **c.** $-\frac{3}{20}$ **d.** $-1\frac{7}{20}$

15. Subtract: $-1\frac{3}{4} - \left(-\frac{5}{4}\right)$

    a. $\frac{1}{2}$ **b.** $-\frac{1}{2}$ **c.** 3 **d.** -3

16. Multiply: $-\frac{5}{8} \cdot \left(-\frac{4}{35}\right)$

    a. 14 **b.** $-\frac{2}{7}$ **c.** $-\frac{1}{14}$ **d.** $\frac{1}{14}$

17. Find the quotient of 4 and $-3\frac{1}{2}$.

    a. -14 **b.** $-\frac{7}{8}$ **c.** $-1\frac{1}{7}$ **d.** $-1\frac{2}{7}$

18. What is -8.4 decreased by -2.3 ?

    a. 10.70 **b.** -10.70 **c.** -6.1 **d.** 6.1

19. Multiply: -3.2×0.16

    a. -2 **b.** 2 **c.** 0.517 **d.** -0.512

20. Find the product of 0.15 and -1.3 .

    a. -0.195 **b.** 0.195 **c.** -1.95 **d.** -0.0195

21. Divide: $-83.3 \div (-7)$

    a. -10.9 **b.** -11.9 **c.** -12.9 **d.** 11.9

22. Simplify: $16 \cdot 3 \div (8-2) - 5$

    a. 3 **b.** 48 **c.** 6 **d.** 9

23. Simplify: $16 - 4 \cdot (-2)^2 - (8-10)^2$

    a. 4 **b.** 44 **c.** 28 **d.** -4

24. Write $270,000,000$ in scientific notation.

    a. 2.7×10^{-7} **b.** 2.7×10^{7} **c.** 2.7×10^{8} **d.** 2.7×10^{-8}

25. The boiling point of helium is $-268.934°C$. The melting point of helium is $-272.2°C$. Find the difference between the boiling point and the melting point of helium.

    a. $59.734°C$ **b.** $41.7341°C$ **c.** $14.734°C$ **d.** $3.266°C$

Name: _____

Date: _____

1. Evaluate $3c \div a - b^2$ when $a = -1$, $b = -2$, and $c = -4$.
   a. -3　　　　b. -16　　　　c. 16　　　　d. 8

2. Evaluate $-a^2 + bc + c^2$ when $a = -3$, $b = -6$, and $c = 2$.
   a. 1　　　　b. -17　　　　c. 25　　　　d. 7

3. Simplify: $8y - 2z - 8y - 10z$
   a. $16y - 12z$　　　　b. $6y - 18z$　　　　c. $-12z$　　　　d. $12z$

4. Simplify: $3x + 2(2 - x) + 2$
   a. $x + 4$　　　　b. $x + 6$　　　　c. $2x + 6$　　　　d. $2x + 4$

5. Which number is a solution of $2x^2 - 6x = 5x - 15$?
   a. 3　　　　b. -5　　　　c. -3　　　　d. 5

6. Solve: $y + 18 = -7$
   a. -11　　　　b. 11　　　　c. 25　　　　d. -25

7. Solve: $-12x = 3$
   a. $\dfrac{1}{4}$　　　　b. $-\dfrac{1}{4}$　　　　c. -9　　　　d. 15

8. Solve: $\dfrac{5}{8}x = 25$
   a. 5　　　　b. $15\dfrac{5}{8}$　　　　c. 40　　　　d. 25

9. A hardware store sells a chainsaw for \$189. The chainsaw has a markup of \$65. Find the cost of the chainsaw. Use the formula $S = C + M$, where S is the selling price, C is the cost, and M is the markup.
   a. \$128　　　　b. \$114　　　　c. \$254　　　　d. \$124

10. Solve: $-2x + 3 = -5$
    a. -1　　　　b. -4　　　　c. 1　　　　d. 4

11. Solve: $6x - 9 = -27$

    a. $-\dfrac{1}{2}$ **b.** -3 **c.** -6 **d.** $\dfrac{1}{2}$

12. Solve: $-13 = 6 - x$

    a. -7 **b.** 7 **c.** -19 **d.** 19

13. The monthly tax paid by a wage earner is $474. The wage earner's monthly tax rate is 22%, and the base monthly tax is $100. Find the wage earner's monthly income. Use the formula $T = I \cdot R + B$, where T is the monthly tax, I is the monthly income, R is the income tax rate, and B is the base monthly tax.

    a. $2609   **b.** $1700   **c.** $822.80   **d.** $1500

14. Solve: $5x - 4 = 2x - 13$

    a. -3 **b.** $-2\dfrac{3}{7}$ **c.** $-1\dfrac{2}{7}$ **d.** 3

15. Solve: $3 - 2(x - 4) = 3(3 - x)$

    a. 10 **b.** -4 **c.** 20 **d.** -2

16. Translate "the product of three and the sum of eight more than z" into a mathematical expression.

    a. $z(3 + 8)$ **b.** $3(8) + z$ **c.** $3(z + 8)$ **d.** $3z + 8$

17. Translate "the sum of three more than a number and five-sixth of the number" into a mathematical expression.

    a. $\dfrac{n + 8}{6}$ **b.** $3 + \left(n + \dfrac{5}{6}\right)$ **c.** $(n + 3) + \dfrac{5}{6}n$ **d.** $\dfrac{5n}{6} + 3$

18. Translate "the ratio of a number to five is twelve" into an equation and solve.

    a. $2\dfrac{2}{5}$ **b.** 60 **c.** $\dfrac{5}{12}$ **d.** 40

19. Six more than the quotient of a number and three is equal to twelve. Find the number.

    a. 18 **b.** 2 **c.** 6 **d.** 12

20. J and P Tackle Shop sells fishing rods for $48 each. This price includes the store's cost for the fishing rod plus a markup rate of 35%. Find the store's cost for a fishing rod.

    a. $16.80   **b.** $31.20   **c.** $64.80   **d.** $29.40

1. Find the complement of a 43° angle
   a. 57°   b. 47°   c. 147°   d. 137°

2. Two angles of a triangle are 13° and 38°. Find the measure of the third angle of the triangle.
   a. 129°   b. 99°   c. 149°   d. 49°

3. In the figure, $L_1 \parallel L_2$. $\angle x = 143°$. Find $\angle y$.
   a. 217°   b. 37°
   c. 77°   d. 143°

   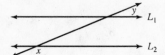

4. In the figure, $L_1 \parallel L_2$. $\angle x = 137°$. Find $\angle a + \angle b$.
   a. 137°   b. 86°
   c. 276°   d. 274°

   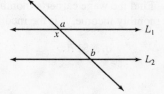

5. Find the perimeter of a triangle with sides 82 cm, 34 cm, and 75 cm.
   a. 191 cm   b. 181 cm   c. 201 cm   d. 211 cm

6. Find the perimeter of the composite figure. Use 3.14 for π.
   a. 32 ft   b. 35 ft
   c. 36.5 ft   d. 23 ft

   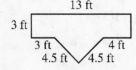

7. Find the length of weather stripping needed to put around a rectangular window that is 3 ft 4 in. wide and 4 ft 8 in. high.
   a. 15 ft   b. 16 ft 4 in.   c. 16 ft   d. 15 ft 4 in.

8. Find the area of a circle with a diameter of 15 in. Use 3.14 for π.
   a. 62.8 in.^{2} b. 176.625 in.^{2} c. 78.6 in.^{2} d. 1256.6 in.^{2}

9. Find the area of the 3-ft boundary around the swimming pool.
   a. 324 ft^2 b. 1188 ft^2
   c. 234 ft^2 d. 442 ft^2

   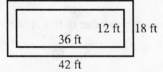

10. Find the area of the composite figure.
    a. 64 m^2 b. 84 m^2
    c. 56 m^2 d. 66 m^2

11. A rectangular roof measures 40 ft by 18 ft. Shingles for the roof cost $44.50 per 100 square feet. Find the cost to purchase shingles for the roof.
    a. $51.62   b. $320.40   c. $1617.98   d. $3204

12. Find the volume of a rectangular solid with a length of 2.8 m, a width of 1.4 m, and a height of 2.5 m.

    a. 12.6 m³   **b.** 6.3 m³   **c.** 9.8 m³   **d.** 5.88 m³

13. Find the volume of the solid. The radius of the cylinder is 7 cm. Use 3.14 for π.

    a. 2251.04 cm³   **b.** 750.58 cm³

    c. 1064.82 cm³   **d.** 2251.74 cm³

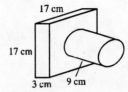

14. A mini motor-home has a water tank that is in the shape of a rectangular solid. The tank has a length of 40 in., a width of 18 in., and a height of 16 in. How many gallons will the water tank hold? Round to the nearest tenth. (1 gal = 231 in.³)

    a. 49.9 gal   **b.** 38.7 gal   **c.** 64.2 gal   **d.** 44.1 gal

15. Find the square root of 67. Round to the nearest thousandth.

    a. 8.7118   **b.** 8.124   **c.** 8.246   **d.** 8.185

16. Find the unknown side of the triangle. Round to the nearest tenth.

    a. 8 in.   **b.** 13.9 in.
    c. 17.9 in.   **d.** 11.5 in.

17. Find the length of the ramp used to roll barrels up to a 4-foot loading platform. Round to the nearest tenth.

    a. 5 ft   **b.** 9.8 ft
    c. 13 ft   **d.** 10.2 ft

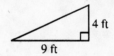

18. Triangles *ABC* and *DEF* are similar. The height of triangle *ABC* is 3 cm. Find the height of triangle *DEF*.

    a. 1 cm   **b.** 6 cm
    c. 1.5 cm   **d.** 5 cm

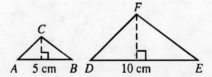

19. Triangles *ABC* and *DEF* are similar. Find the perimeter of triangle *DEF*.

    a. 16 m   **b.** 115.5 m
    c. 36 m   **d.** 19 m

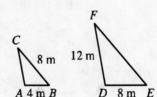

20. In the figure, triangles *ABC* and *DEF* are congruent. Find the measure of *EF*.

    a. 11   **b.** 5
    c. 13   **d.** 12

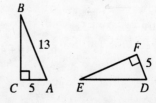

Name: _____
Date: _____

1. Find the sum of -50 and -18.

   a. -32 **b.** 32 **c.** 68 **d.** -68

2. Add: $-\dfrac{7}{22}+\left(-\dfrac{2}{11}\right)$

   a. $\dfrac{1}{2}$ **b.** $\dfrac{3}{22}$ **c.** $-\dfrac{1}{2}$ **d.** $-\dfrac{3}{22}$

3. Find the difference between -22 and 6.

   a. -28 **b.** 28 **c.** -16 **d.** 16

4. Subtract: $10.27-(-1.06)$

   a. 9.81 **b.** 9.21 **c.** 11.33 **d.** 10.93

5. Find the product of -30 and -2.

   a. 60 **b.** 15 **c.** -32 **d.** -60

6. Multiply: $\dfrac{2}{7}\cdot\left(-\dfrac{3}{4}\right)$

   a. $\dfrac{3}{14}$ **b.** $-\dfrac{8}{21}$ **c.** $-\dfrac{3}{14}$ **d.** $-1\dfrac{2}{7}$

7. Find the quotient of 0.505 and -0.5.

   a. -10.1 **b.** 1.01 **c.** -0.101 **d.** -1.01

8. Simplify: $7-\left(3^{2}\right)\cdot 5$

   a. -10 **b.** 38 **c.** 10 **d.** -38

9. Simplify: $(-9)^{2}\cdot\left(-\dfrac{1}{3}\right)-11$

   a. 38 **b.** 16 **c.** -38 **d.** -16

10. Simplify: $6y-z-2y+5z$

   a. $4y+5z$ **b.** $4y+4z$ **c.** $8y+5z$ **d.** $8y+6z$

11. Evaluate $a^2 + 2ab - c^2$ when $a = 2$, $b = 3$, and $c = 4$.

   a. 20   **b.** 14   **c.** 0   **d.** 10

12. Solve: $9x - 5 = -2$

   a. $-\dfrac{7}{9}$ **b.** $\dfrac{1}{3}$ **c.** -6 **d.** -16

13. Solve: $18 - x = -9$

   a. -3 **b.** -27 **c.** 27   **d.** 3

14. Solve: $3(4 + 2x) - 7x = 2(x + 5)$

   a. $\dfrac{2}{3}$ **b.** 2   **c.** $\dfrac{7}{3}$ **d.** $\dfrac{22}{3}$

15. Solve: $2x + 3(x + 1) = 4(x + 7)$

   a. $\dfrac{25}{9}$ **b.** $\dfrac{11}{9}$ **c.** 11   **d.** 25

16. On a 1485-mile trip, a sales executive used 45 gal of gas. Find the miles traveled per gallon. Use the formula $D = M \cdot G$, where D is the distance, M is the miles per gallon, and G is the number of gallons.

   a. 37 mi/gal   **b.** 33 mi/gal   **c.** 27 mi/gal   **d.** 35 mi/gal

17. Translate "three less than four times a number is thirteen" into an equation and solve.

   a. 4   **b.** $2\dfrac{1}{2}$ **c.** -3 **d.** -4

18. A roofing contractor charges $250 plus $180 for each 100 ft² of roofing installed. How many square feet of roofing are installed if the charge is $2410?

   a. $1478\ \text{ft}^2$ **b.** $3888\ \text{ft}^2$ **c.** $1200\ \text{ft}^2$ **d.** $1339\ \text{ft}^2$

19. In the figure, $L_1 \parallel L_2$. $\angle x = 73°$. Find $\angle y$.

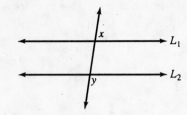

   a. 17°   **b.** 107°
   c. 73°   **d.** 253°

20. Two angles of a triangle measure 12° and 75°. Find the measure of the third angle.

   a. 93°   **b.** 273°   **c.** 103°   **d.** 97°

21. Find the circumference of a circle with a diameter of 48 cm. Use 3.14 for π.

   a. 24 cm   **b.** 73.56 cm   **c.** 178.32 cm   **d.** 150.72 cm

22. Find the area of the figure.

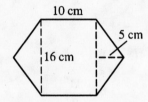

   a. 200 cm²   **b.** 120 cm²
   c. 100 cm²   **d.** 240 cm²

23. Find the volume of a sphere with a radius of 3 in. Use 3.14 for π.

   a. 113.04 in.³   **b.** 114.04 in.³   **c.** 110.06 in.³   **d.** 115.14 in.³

24. Find the unknown leg of the right triangle. Round to the nearest tenth.

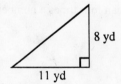

   a. 14.8 yd   **b.** 6.8 yd
   c. 12.5 yd   **d.** 13.6 yd

25. In the figure, triangles *ABC* and *DEF* are similar.
Find the perimeter of triangle *DEF* .

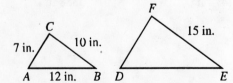

   a. 45 in.   **b.** 43.5 in.
   c. 38.5 in.   **d.** 40.5 in.

Final Exam Form G

Name: _____
Date: _____

1. Subtract: $21,008 - 769$
   a. $21,231$
   b. $20,299$
   c. $20,239$
   d. $20,339$

2. Find $17,136$ divided by 42.
   a. 408
   b. 48
   c. 714
   d. 480

3. Simplify: $8 + 6 \cdot 3 - (4 + 5)$
   a. 17
   b. 33
   c. 19
   d. 34

4. Your bank account had a balance of $852 before you wrote checks for $27, $36, and $435. What is your bank account balance after writing the checks?
   a. $454
   b. $364
   c. $1350
   d. $354

5. Add: $4\frac{2}{3} + 3\frac{2}{5}$
   a. $7\frac{4}{5}$
   b. $8\frac{3}{5}$
   c. $8\frac{1}{15}$
   d. $7\frac{4}{15}$

6. Find 8 decreased by $1\frac{3}{4}$.
   a. $4\frac{4}{7}$
   b. $7\frac{1}{4}$
   c. $9\frac{3}{4}$
   d. $6\frac{1}{4}$

7. Multiply: $2\frac{2}{5} \cdot 3\frac{1}{12}$
   a. $7\frac{3}{5}$
   b. $6\frac{4}{5}$
   c. $7\frac{2}{5}$
   d. $7\frac{1}{5}$

8. Divide: $\frac{2}{5} \div 2\frac{2}{3}$
   a. $1\frac{1}{15}$
   b. $6\frac{2}{3}$
   c. $\frac{3}{20}$
   d. $\frac{1}{5}$

9. Simplify: $\frac{1}{3} + \frac{2}{9} \cdot \frac{1}{2} + \left(\frac{1}{2}\right)^2$
   a. $\frac{19}{36}$
   b. $\frac{25}{36}$
   c. $\frac{27}{36}$
   d. $\frac{23}{36}$

10. A 50-acre parcel of land is being divided into $2\frac{1}{2}$-acre sections for building homes. How many sections will there be on the parcel of land?
    a. 20 sections
    b. 25 sections
    c. 18 sections
    d. 27 sections

11. Subtract: $137.8 - 2.95$
   a. 108.3   b. 134.85   c. 135.25   d. 10.83

12. Find the product of 5.2 and 0.04.
   a. 0.208   b. 130   c. 13   d. 2.08

13. Find the quotient of 6 and 0.45. Round to the nearest tenth.
   a. 11.1   b. 2.7   c. 13.3   d. 0.1

14. Convert 0.095 to a fraction.
   a. $\frac{19}{20}$ b. $\frac{19}{200}$ c. $\frac{19}{250}$ d. $\frac{19}{25}$

15. Convert $\frac{21}{32}$ to a decimal.
   a. 1.52   b. 0.65625   c. 65.625   d. 15.2

16. Write the comparison "72 in. to 26 in." as a ratio in simplest form using a fraction.
   a. $\frac{3}{1}$ b. $\frac{9}{4}$ c. $\frac{36}{13}$ d. $\frac{8}{3}$

17. Write "157.5 miles in 3 hours" as a unit rate.
   a. 52.5 miles/hour   b. 53.5 miles/hour   c. 52.25 miles/hour   d. 52.7 miles/hour

18. Solve the proportion: $\frac{11}{n} = \frac{40}{3}$ Round to the nearest thousandth.
   a. 146.67   b. 0.825   c. 10.91   d. 13.33

19. A houseplant has been growing at the rate of 1.5 in. every 12 days. At this rate, how much will the plant grow in 28 days?
   a. 0.64 in.   b. 3.5 in.   c. 224 in.   d. 35 in.

20. Write 15.92 as a percent.
   a. 1.592%   b. 15.92%   c. 1592%   d. 0.1592%

21. What is $33\frac{1}{3}\%$ of 63?
   a. 21   b. 21.3   c. 2.1   d. 180

22. 13.44 is what percent of 140?
   a. 10.42%   b. 18.816%   c. 9.6%   d. 104.167%

23. 61.5 is 82% of what number?
   a. 750   b. 7.5   c. 75   d. 133.33

24. A car dealer offers new car buyers a 5% rebate on some new car models. What rebate would a new car buyer receive on a car that cost $14,800?

   a. $1406   **b.** $592   **c.** $14,060   **d.** $740

25. Find the unit cost of $15.60 for 15 lb.

   a. $1.02/lb   **b.** $10.40/lb   **c.** $1.04/lb   **d.** $1.40/lb

26. Dean's Bookstore uses a markup rate of 45%. Find the selling price of a cookbook that cost the store $20.

   a. $9   **b.** $0.90   **c.** $20.90   **d.** $29

27. A shoe clerk receives a weekly salary of $200 plus a 6% commission on sales. Find the clerk's salary during a week when sales totaled $4800.

   a. $488   **b.** $288   **c.** $300   **d.** $1000

28. A credit card company charges a customer 1.6% interest per month on the customer's unpaid balance. Find the interest owed when the customer's unpaid balance for the month is $850.

   a. $13.60   **b.** $1.36   **c.** $136   **d.** $14.60

29. The circle graph shows the distribution of an employee's monthly income of $1875. Find the amount paid in federal tax.

   a. $392.70   **b.** $206.25

   c. $412.50   **d.** $852.27

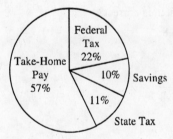

Distribution of Gross Monthly
Income Totaling $1875

30. There are 35 store merchants in the city's square. Their yearly profits are recorded in the histogram. How many merchants had an annual profit of $40,000 or more?

   a. 13   **b.** 22

   c. 15   **d.** 28

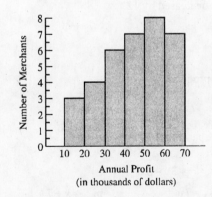

31. Convert 18 fl oz to cups.

   a. $2\frac{1}{4}$ c   **b.** 3 c   **c.** $1\frac{4}{5}$ c   **d.** $1\frac{1}{2}$ c

32. Convert $6\frac{1}{2}$ tons to pounds.

   a. 1300 lb   **b.** 6500 lb   **c.** 650 lb   **d.** 13,000 lb

33. How many feet of fencing are needed to enclose a rectangular yard that is 12 ft 8 in. long and 14 ft 10 in. wide?

    a. 54 ft 10 in.   **b.** 56 ft 6 in.   **c.** 55 ft   **d.** 52 ft

34. A full can of soda weighs 13 oz. Find the weight in pounds of 24 full cans of soda.

    a. 8.67 lb   **b.** 19.5 lb   **c.** 29.54 lb   **d.** 39 lb

35. Convert 12 kg to grams.

    a. 120 g   **b.** 0.012 g   **c.** 12,000 g   **d.** 1,200 g

36. Convert 765 cm to meters.

    a. 76.5 m   **b.** 7650 m   **c.** 7.65 m   **d.** 76,500 m

37. A chemistry experiment requires 15 ml of acid. How many liters are used when 120 students perform this experiment?

    a. 1.8 L   **b.** 18 L   **c.** 0.18 L   **d.** 180 L

38. Which statement is correct?

    a. $-10 > -8$ **b.** $-10 = -8$ **c.** $-10 > 0$ **d.** $-10 < -8$

39. Add: $2\dfrac{3}{4} + \left(-\dfrac{7}{8}\right)$

    a. $-1\dfrac{7}{8}$ **b.** $2\dfrac{7}{8}$ **c.** $1\dfrac{7}{8}$ **d.** $2\dfrac{1}{8}$

40. Find -5 decreased by 12.

    a. 5   **b.** -30 **c.** 20   **d.** -20

41. Find the product of $-\dfrac{2}{3}$ and $-\dfrac{1}{2}$.

    a. $1\dfrac{1}{6}$ **b.** $-\dfrac{1}{2}$ **c.** $1\dfrac{1}{3}$ **d.** $\dfrac{1}{3}$

42. Simplify: $4x + 3y - 8x - 10y$

    a. $-4x - 7y$ **b.** $4x + 7y$ **c.** $12x + 13y$ **d.** $-12x - 13y$

43. Evaluate $2b^2 - a - b$ when $a = -2$ and $b = 3$.

    a. 13   **b.** 15   **c.** 17   **d.** 19

44. Solve: $y - 12 = -15$

    a. 3   **b.** -3 **c.** 27   **d.** -27

45. Solve: $4x - 6 = 2$

    a. -2 **b.** 2 **c.** $\dfrac{1}{2}$ **d.** $-\dfrac{1}{2}$

46. Solve: $5x - 2(x - 4) = 10(x - 2)$

    a. 4 **b.** -4 **c.** $1\dfrac{5}{7}$ **d.** $2\dfrac{2}{13}$

47. Translate "one less than three times a number is eight" into an equation and solve.

    a. 3 **b.** -3 **c.** $2\dfrac{1}{3}$ **d.** 5

48. Find the area of the figure. Use 3.14 for π.

    a. 257.04 cm^2 **b.** 54.84 cm^2
    c. 64.26 cm^2 **d.** 65.26 cm^2

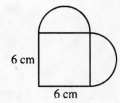

49. Find the volume of the figure. Use $\dfrac{22}{7}$ for π.

    a. $44{,}580$ mm^3 **b.** $41{,}780$ mm^3
    c. $40{,}580$ mm^3 **d.** $41{,}580$ mm^3

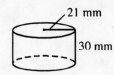

50. Triangles *ABC* and *DEF* are similar. Find the length of *EF*.

    a. 20 in.   **b.** 22 in.
    c. 24 in.   **d.** 12 in.

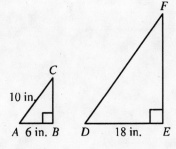

Form H Tests

Multiple Choice

1. Which statement is correct?
   - **a.** $101 < 85$
   - **b.** $72 > 98$
   - **c.** $3 > 18$
   - **d.** $12 < 20$

2. Write $800,410$ in words.
   - **a.** Eighty-four thousand ten
   - **b.** Eight hundred four thousand ten
   - **c.** Eight hundred forty thousand ten
   - **d.** Eight hundred thousand four hundred ten

3. Write forty-four thousand three hundred two in standard form.
   - **a.** $44,032$
   - **b.** 4302
   - **c.** $44,320$
   - **d.** $44,302$

4. Write $50,780$ in expanded form.
   - **a.** $50,000 + 700 + 80$
   - **b.** $50,000 + 7000 + 80$
   - **c.** $500,000 + 70,000 + 80$
   - **d.** $5000 + 700 + 80$

5. Round $875,168$ to the nearest thousand.
   - **a.** $870,000$
   - **b.** $880,000$
   - **c.** $875,000$
   - **d.** $876,000$

6. Find the sum of $20,317$ and $10,231$.
   - **a.** $30,530$
   - **b.** $30,548$
   - **c.** $31,538$
   - **d.** $30,458$

7. Add: $44,824$
           $398,765$
         $+ 72,214$
   - **a.** $515,803$
   - **b.** $515,793$
   - **c.** $504,793$
   - **d.** $504,803$

8. Dr. Carlson treated 17 patients on Monday, 27 on Tuesday, 19 on Wednesday, 37 on Thursday, and 25 on Friday. How many patients did the doctor see during the week?
   - **a.** 124
   - **b.** 135
   - **c.** 125
   - **d.** 115

9. Find the difference between 3095 and 2080.
   - **a.** 1115
   - **b.** 1015
   - **c.** 1105
   - **d.** 1005

10. Subtract: $40,507$
              $- 10,618$
    - **a.** $30,989$
    - **b.** $29,989$
    - **c.** $29,889$
    - **d.** $30,111$

11. A teacher receives a salary $2542 per month. Deductions from the check are $381 for taxes, $203 for retirement, and $56 for insurance. Find the teacher's take-home pay.
    - **a.** $1912
    - **b.** $2002
    - **c.** $1802
    - **d.** $1902

12. Find the product of $32,419$ and 7.
    - **a.** $214,833$
    - **b.** $226,933$
    - **c.** $214,873$
    - **d.** $226,803$

13. Multiply: 796
                    × 309

        a. 244,864   **b.** 244,944
        c. 245,964   **d.** 245,864

14. A truck driver earns \$14 per hour. Find the truck driver's pay for a 36-hour work week.

    a. \$504   **b.** \$484   **c.** \$420   **d.** \$180

15. Find the quotient of 16,709 and 7 .

    a. 2401   **b.** 2244   **c.** 956   **d.** 2387

16. Divide: $6\overline{)38,029}$

        a. 6034 r 1   **b.** 6671 r 3
        c. 6334 r 5   **d.** 6338 r 1

17. Divide: $7350 \div 35$

        a. 203 r 25   **b.** 103 r 25
        c. 210   **d.** 21

18. A clothing manufacturer produces and boxes 225 shirts each hour. Five shirts are put in each box. How many boxes can be produced in 1 hour?

    a. 45   **b.** 41   **c.** 65   **d.** 51

19. Write $2 \cdot 2 \cdot 2 \cdot 2 \cdot 3 \cdot 3 \cdot 5$ in exponential notation.

    a. $2^4 \cdot 3 \cdot 5$ **b.** $2^4 \cdot 3^2 \cdot 5$ **c.** $2^3 \cdot 3^2 \cdot 5$ **d.** $2^3 \cdot 3^3 \cdot 5$

20. Simplify: $5 \cdot 3^4 \cdot 2^3$

    a. 540   **b.** 480   **c.** 15,552   **d.** 3240

21. Simplify: $5 + 3 \cdot (7 - 5)$

    a. 16   **b.** 12   **c.** 24   **d.** 11

22. Simplify: $2^3 + 8 \div (3 - 1)$

    a. 12   **b.** 10   **c.** 8   **d.** 6

23. Find all the factors of 55.

    a. 1, 3, 5, 11, 55   **b.** 1, 5, 11, 55   **c.** 5, 11   **d.** 5, 11, 55

24. Find the prime factorization of 24.

    a. $2 \cdot 12$ **b.** $3 \cdot 8$ **c.** $2 \cdot 2 \cdot 2 \cdot 3$ **d.** $2 \cdot 2 \cdot 3$

25. Find the prime factorization of 120.

    a. $2 \cdot 2 \cdot 30$ **b.** $2 \cdot 2 \cdot 2 \cdot 15$ **c.** $2 \cdot 2 \cdot 2 \cdot 3 \cdot 5$ **d.** $2 \cdot 2 \cdot 6 \cdot 5$

Name: _____

Date: _____

1. Find the LCM of 6, 8, and 18.

   a. 72   **b.** 24   **c.** 48   **d.** 36

2. Find the GCF of 30 and 48.

   a. 9   **b.** 2   **c.** 6   **d.** 240

3. Express the shaded portion of the circles as an improper fraction.

   a. $\dfrac{5}{6}$ **b.** $\dfrac{11}{6}$ **c.** $\dfrac{1}{6}$ **d.** $\dfrac{7}{6}$

4. Write $\dfrac{21}{5}$ as a mixed number.

   a. $5\dfrac{3}{5}$ **b.** $4\dfrac{3}{5}$ **c.** $5\dfrac{1}{5}$ **d.** $4\dfrac{1}{5}$

5. Write $7\dfrac{2}{5}$ as an improper fraction.

   a. $\dfrac{37}{3}$ **b.** $\dfrac{70}{5}$ **c.** $\dfrac{37}{7}$ **d.** $\dfrac{37}{5}$

6. What number must be placed in the numerator so that the following fractions are equivalent? $\dfrac{11}{12} = \dfrac{}{60}$

   a. 55   **b.** 50   **c.** 66   **d.** 44

7. Write $\dfrac{50}{75}$ in simplest form.

   a. $\dfrac{2}{25}$ **b.** $\dfrac{2}{3}$ **c.** $\dfrac{10}{15}$ **d.** $\dfrac{3}{4}$

8. Add: $\dfrac{2}{9} + \dfrac{8}{9} + \dfrac{5}{9}$

   a. $1\dfrac{6}{9}$ **b.** $\dfrac{15}{27}$ **c.** $\dfrac{17}{18}$ **d.** $1\dfrac{5}{18}$

9. Add: $\dfrac{2}{3} + \dfrac{4}{5} + \dfrac{3}{10}$

   a. $\dfrac{1}{2}$ **b.** $1\dfrac{5}{6}$ **c.** $1\dfrac{23}{30}$ **d.** $\dfrac{9}{30}$

10. What is $2\frac{1}{8}$ more than $5\frac{3}{10}$?

    a. $7\frac{1}{6}$ **b.** $7\frac{3}{10}$ **c.** $7\frac{2}{5}$ **d.** $7\frac{17}{40}$

11. A baby weighs $8\frac{1}{3}$ pounds at birth. The baby gains $1\frac{3}{8}$ pounds the first month and $1\frac{3}{4}$ pounds the second month. Find the total weight of the baby after 2 months.

    a. $11\frac{5}{12}$ pounds   **b.** $\frac{5}{6}$ pounds   **c.** $10\frac{1}{2}$ pounds   **d.** $11\frac{11}{24}$ pounds

12. Subtract: $\frac{49}{72} - \frac{25}{72}$

    a. $\frac{12}{31}$ **b.** $\frac{1}{3}$ **c.** $\frac{1}{4}$ **d.** $\frac{3}{4}$

13. What is the difference between $\frac{5}{8}$ and $\frac{1}{5}$?

    a. $\frac{17}{40}$ **b.** $1\frac{1}{3}$ **c.** $\frac{33}{40}$ **d.** $\frac{1}{3}$

14. Subtract:

$$\begin{array}{r} 23 \\ -5\frac{9}{17} \\ \hline \end{array}$$

    a. $17\frac{9}{17}$ **b.** $18\frac{9}{17}$

    c. $17\frac{8}{17}$ **d.** $18\frac{8}{17}$

15. A $3\frac{1}{2}$-foot piece of wood is cut from an $8\frac{3}{8}$-foot board. How much of the board is left?

    a. $5\frac{3}{8}$ feet   **b.** $5\frac{1}{4}$ feet   **c.** $4\frac{7}{8}$ feet   **d.** $4\frac{5}{8}$ feet

16. Multiply: $\frac{27}{35} \times \frac{20}{81}$

    a. $\frac{4}{21}$ **b.** $\frac{11}{63}$ **c.** $\frac{4}{7}$ **d.** $\frac{5}{21}$

17. What is $6\frac{1}{2}$ multiplied by $4\frac{3}{4}$?

    a. $28\frac{1}{4}$ **b.** $30\frac{7}{8}$ **c.** $25\frac{1}{4}$ **d.** $29\frac{7}{8}$

18. A car travels $16\frac{2}{3}$ miles on each gallon of gasoline. How many miles can the car travel on $14\frac{7}{10}$ gallons of gasoline?

    a. 245   **b.** 224   **c.** 264   **d.** 235

19. Divide: $\frac{11}{18} \div \frac{7}{9}$

    a. $\frac{2}{3}$ **b.** $\frac{1}{4}$ **c.** $\frac{13}{14}$ **d.** $\frac{11}{14}$

20. Find the quotient of $2\frac{3}{8}$ and $1\frac{3}{4}$.

    a. $\frac{2}{3}$ **b.** $2\frac{1}{2}$ **c.** $1\frac{5}{14}$ **d.** $1\frac{2}{3}$

21. A car used $12\frac{1}{10}$ gallons of gasoline on a 484-mile trip. How many miles did the car travel on one gallon of gasoline?

    a. 36 miles   **b.** 40 miles   **c.** 34 miles   **d.** 38 miles

22. Which statement is correct?

    a. $\frac{11}{15} > \frac{18}{25}$ **b.** $\frac{11}{15} = \frac{18}{25}$ **c.** $\frac{11}{15} < \frac{18}{25}$ **d.** $0 > \frac{18}{25}$

23. Simplify: $\left(\frac{8}{9}\right)^3 \left(\frac{3}{4}\right)^2$

    a. $1\frac{5}{27}$ **b.** $\frac{32}{81}$ **c.** $\frac{4}{81}$ **d.** $\frac{16}{27}$

24. Simplify: $\left(\frac{1}{3}\right)^2 + \frac{2}{9} - \frac{1}{6}$

    a. $\frac{1}{9}$ **b.** $\frac{2}{9}$ **c.** $\frac{5}{6}$ **d.** $\frac{1}{6}$

25. Simplify: $\frac{3}{4} \cdot \left(\frac{5}{6} + \frac{2}{9}\right) \div \frac{19}{2}$

    a. $\frac{7}{20}$ **b.** $\frac{7}{36}$ **c.** $\frac{5}{12}$ **d.** $\frac{1}{12}$

1. Write 1.042 in words.
    - **a.** One and forty-two thousandths
    - **b.** One and forty-two hundredths
    - **c.** One and forty-two ten-thousandths
    - **d.** One thousand forty two

2. Write twenty-four and seven ten-thousandths in standard form.
    - **a.** 24.0007
    - **b.** 24.07
    - **c.** 24.007
    - **d.** 240.07

3. Round 16.0597 to the nearest thousandth.
    - **a.** 16.0598
    - **b.** 16.060
    - **c.** 16.05
    - **d.** 16.059

4. Round 81.720439 to the nearest hundred-thousandth.
    - **a.** 81.72044
    - **b.** 81.7204
    - **c.** 81.720
    - **d.** 81.72

5. Add: 21.73
           3.215
        + 104.7
    - **a.** 129.535
    - **b.** 129.635
    - **c.** 64.35
    - **d.** 129.645

6. Find the sum of 8.763 , 13.02 , 1037.5 , and 6.87 .
    - **a.** 952.506
    - **b.** 1056.153
    - **c.** 1066.153
    - **d.** 2112.7

7. Your electric bill is $95.73, your gas bill is $64.29, and your water bill is $52.56. Find the total of the three bills.
    - **a.** $202.58
    - **b.** $212.58
    - **c.** $213.58
    - **d.** $203.67

8. Subtract: 123.007
             − 16.9045
    - **a.** 106.1025
    - **b.** 105.1935
    - **c.** 106.0925
    - **d.** 105.1035

9. What is 6.93007 decreased by 2.9804 ?
    - **a.** 3.95957
    - **b.** 3.94067
    - **c.** 4.94967
    - **d.** 3.94967

10. Matt had a balance of $2139.00 in his checking account. He then wrote checks for $132.45, $97.39 and $139.12. Find the new checking account balance.
    - **a.** $1909.16
    - **b.** $1770.04
    - **c.** $1670.16
    - **d.** $2507.96

Name: _____

11. Multiply: 23.92
$$\times\ 7.05$$

a. 168.636   b. 168.36
c. 1685.26   d. 158.536

12. Find the product of 43.86 and 17.09 .
a. 7495.664   b. 749.5674   c. 749.4664   d. 60.95

13. A state income tax on the business you own is $800 plus 0.08 times your profit. You made a profit of $96,420 last year. Find the amount of income tax you owed for last year.
a. $8513.60   b. $7713.60   c. $8313.60   d. $8314.50

14. Find the quotient of 104.52 and 8.04 .
a. 130   b. 13   c. 1.3   d. 0.13

15. Divide. Round to the nearest thousandth.

$2.19\overline{)10.321}$

a. 4.713   b. 3.162
c. 5.194   d. 2.437

16. A service station collects $0.23 in taxes on each gallon of gasoline sold. Find the number of gallons of gasoline sold during a month in which $11,155 was collected in taxes.
a. 2566   b. 34,859   c. 50,239   d. 48,500

17. Convert $3\frac{7}{8}$ to a decimal.
a. 3.875   b. 3.675   c. 0.875   d. 0.258

18. Convert 2.15 to a fraction.
a. $2\frac{1}{5}$ b. $2\frac{3}{40}$ c. $2\frac{3}{20}$ d. $2\frac{1}{15}$

19. Which statement is correct?
a. $0.0382 = 0.102$ b. $0.0382 < 0.102$ c. $0.0382 > 0.102$ d. $0.0382 < 0$

20. Which statement is correct?
a. $0.39 > \frac{5}{13}$ b. $0.39 = \frac{5}{13}$ c. $0.39 < \frac{5}{13}$ d. $0.39 < 0$

Name: _____
Date: _____

1. Divide: $36\overline{)25,816}$

    a.   716 r 40   **b.**   709 r 2

    c.   717 r 4   **d.**   712 r 4

2. Simplify: $5^3 \cdot 2^2$

    a.   60   **b.**   500   **c.**   250   **d.**   972

3. Simplify: $16 - 5(4-2) + 3^2$

    a.   31   **b.**   15   **c.**   121   **d.**   33

4. Find the LCM of 12, 15, and 45.

    a.   3   **b.**   90   **c.**   180   **d.**   360

5. Write $\dfrac{33}{4}$ as a mixed number.

    a. $8\dfrac{3}{4}$ **b.** $7\dfrac{1}{4}$ **c.** $6\dfrac{3}{4}$ **d.** $8\dfrac{1}{4}$

6. Write $6\dfrac{1}{3}$ as an improper fraction.

    a. $\dfrac{17}{3}$ **b.** $\dfrac{19}{3}$ **c.** $\dfrac{23}{6}$ **d.** $\dfrac{13}{3}$

7. Find the numerator for an equivalent fraction with the given denominator: $\dfrac{5}{19} = \dfrac{}{95}$

    a.   25   **b.**   19   **c.**   5   **d.**   30

8. Add: $\dfrac{2}{3} + \dfrac{4}{5} + \dfrac{1}{2}$

    a. $2\dfrac{1}{30}$ **b.** $1\dfrac{27}{30}$ **c.** $1\dfrac{29}{30}$ **d.** $1\dfrac{5}{6}$

9. What is $7\dfrac{7}{10}$ increased by $10\dfrac{4}{15}$?

    a. $17\dfrac{13}{15}$ **b.** $17\dfrac{2}{5}$ **c.** $17\dfrac{29}{30}$ **d.** $18\dfrac{1}{30}$

10. Subtract: $4\dfrac{3}{4} - 2\dfrac{1}{6}$

    a. $2\dfrac{7}{12}$ **b.** $2\dfrac{1}{6}$ **c.** $2\dfrac{2}{5}$ **d.** $2\dfrac{11}{12}$

11. Multiply: $\dfrac{7}{12} \times \dfrac{8}{9}$

   a. $\dfrac{14}{27}$ **b.** $\dfrac{14}{29}$ **c.** $\dfrac{7}{27}$ **d.** $\dfrac{28}{27}$

12. Find the product of $4\dfrac{2}{3}$ and 18 .

   a. 54 **b.** $\dfrac{7}{27}$ **c.** $\dfrac{7}{18}$ **d.** 84

13. Divide: $\dfrac{5}{17} \div \dfrac{15}{68}$

   a. $2\dfrac{5}{17}$ **b.** $1\dfrac{3}{17}$ **c.** $1\dfrac{1}{3}$ **d.** $2\dfrac{2}{3}$

14. What is $4\dfrac{2}{3}$ divided by $2\dfrac{1}{10}$?

   a. $2\dfrac{2}{13}$ **b.** $2\dfrac{2}{9}$ **c.** $9\dfrac{4}{5}$ **d.** $\dfrac{9}{20}$

15. Simplify: $4\left(\dfrac{1}{6}\right)^2\left(\dfrac{3}{2}\right)^3$

   a. $\dfrac{3}{16}$ **b.** $\dfrac{1}{2}$ **c.** $\dfrac{3}{8}$ **d.** $\dfrac{4}{9}$

16. Simplify: $\left(\dfrac{2}{3}\right)^2 \div \left(\dfrac{1}{2} + \dfrac{2}{3}\right)$

   a. $\dfrac{4}{7}$ **b.** $\dfrac{8}{21}$ **c.** $\dfrac{14}{27}$ **d.** $\dfrac{20}{27}$

17. Write 5.078 in words.
   a. Five and seventy-eight ten-thousandths
   b. Five thousand seventy-eight
   c. Five and seventy-eight hundredths
   d. Five and seventy-eight thousandths

18. Add: 1.0593
             0.00417
        + 21.32

   a. 22.38347   **b.** 22.371347
   c. 22.37347   **d.** 22.375

19. What is 36.801 decreased by 9.7223 ?
   a. 27.0777   **b.** 37.0787   **c.** 27.0687   **d.** 27.0787

20. Multiply: 43.7

$$\underline{\times\ 2.3}$$

      a. 101.51   **b.** 1005.1

      c. 99.51   **d.** 100.51

21. Divide. Round to the nearest thousandth.

$$0.46\overline{)1.188}$$

      a. 25.826   **b.** 2.583

      c. 0.0258   **d.** 2.582

22. Convert $\frac{5}{9}$ to a decimal. Round to the nearest thousandth.

    a. 0.556   **b.** 0.555   **c.** 5.556   **d.** 0.56

23. Convert $0.02\frac{1}{2}$ to a fraction.

    e. $\frac{1}{400}$ **f.** $\frac{1}{50}$ **g.** $\frac{1}{40}$ **h.** $\frac{1}{250}$

24. Which statement is correct?

    a. $0.58 > \frac{7}{12}$ **b.** $0.583 = \frac{7}{12}$ **c.** $0.58 < \frac{7}{12}$ **d.** $0.583 > \frac{7}{12}$

25. A ski resort received $9\frac{1}{2}$ inches of snow in October, $12\frac{1}{4}$ inches in November, and $22\frac{3}{4}$ inches in December. Find the total snowfall during the 3 months.

    a. $42\frac{1}{2}$ inches   **b.** $43\frac{1}{2}$ inches   **c.** 45 inches   **d.** $44\frac{1}{2}$ inches

26. One-tenth of a shipment of $12\frac{1}{2}$ pounds of machine screws contained unusable screws. How many pounds of screws were usable?

    a. $11\frac{1}{4}$ **b.** $10\frac{3}{4}$ **c.** 11   **d.** $1\frac{1}{4}$

27. The Vaslet family saves $\frac{1}{12}$ of its monthly income. If the family's income this month is $2940, how much will the family put into savings?

    a. $408.16   **b.** $352.80   **c.** $245   **d.** $235

28. A phone call costs $0.99 for the first 5 minutes and $0.12 for each additional minute. How much does a 20-minute call cost.

    a. $3.12   **b.** $3.39   **c.** $2.40   **d.** $2.79

29. Your house payment is $620.27, your car payment is $323.30, and your electric bill is $86.00. Find the total of the three payments.

    a. $1019.57   **b.** $1029.57   **c.** $1019.47   **d.** $1029.47

30. You bought 8.3 pounds of fish for $22.41. Find the cost of 1 pound of fish.

    a. $2.70   **b.** $2.60   **c.** $2.07   **d.** $3.68

1. Write the comparison 25¢ to 20¢ as a ratio in simplest form.

    a. $\dfrac{3}{5}$ b. $\dfrac{4}{5}$ c. $\dfrac{5}{4}$ d. $\dfrac{2}{3}$

2. Write the comparison 2 years to 12 years as a ratio in simplest form.

    a. $\dfrac{1}{6}$ b. $\dfrac{1}{2}$ c. 6:1   d. $\dfrac{1}{7}$

3. Write the comparison 50 words per minute to 30 words per minute as a ratio in simplest form.

    a. $\dfrac{3}{5}$ b. $\dfrac{5}{3}$ c. 0.6   d. 3:5

4. Write the comparison 6 days to 12 days as a ratio in simplest form.

    a. 1:2   b. $\dfrac{1}{2}$ c. $\dfrac{6}{12}$ d. 6:12

5. The cost to build a patio is $2750 for materials and $1250 for labor. Find the ratio, as a fraction in simplest form, of the labor costs to the cost of materials.

    a. $\dfrac{11}{16}$ b. $\dfrac{5}{16}$ c. $\dfrac{11}{5}$ d. $\dfrac{5}{11}$

6. Greg bought 100 shares of stock for $15 per share. During a 3-month period, the price of the stock rose to $24 per share. Find the ratio, as a fraction in simplest form, of the increase in price to the original price of the stock.

    a. $\dfrac{3}{5}$ b. $\dfrac{3}{8}$ c. $\dfrac{5}{8}$ d. $\dfrac{5}{3}$

7. Write "5 ounces for $1600" as a rate in simplest form.

    a. $\dfrac{\$320}{1 \text{ ounce}}$ b. $\dfrac{5 \text{ ounces}}{\$1600}$ c. $\dfrac{1 \text{ ounce}}{\$320}$ d. $\dfrac{1}{320}$

8. Write "84¢ for 8 bars of soap" as a rate in simplest form.

    a. $\dfrac{21}{2}$ b. $\dfrac{21¢}{2 \text{ bars}}$ c. $\dfrac{84¢}{8 \text{ bars}}$ d. $\dfrac{2 \text{ bars}}{21¢}$

9. Write "463.2 miles on 12 gallons of gasoline" as a unit rate.

    a. 38.6 miles/gallon   b. 36.8 miles/gallon   c. 36.8   d. 38.6 gallons/mile

10. Write "$434 earned in 35 hours" as a unit rate.

    a. $12.20/hour   b. $12.40/hour   c. $12.80/hour   d. $16.40/hour

11. A $60,000 life insurance policy costs $428.40 per year. Find the cost per $1000 worth of life insurance.

    a. $7.14   **b.** $7.41   **c.** $7.31   **d.** $7.04

12. You own 250 shares of a technology stock and receive a dividend of $200. Find the dividend per share.

    a. $1.25   **b.** $5.00   **c.** $0.80   **d.** $0.50

13. Which proportion is true?

    a. $\dfrac{8}{15} = \dfrac{94}{160}$ **b.** $\dfrac{7}{12} = \dfrac{84}{144}$ **c.** $\dfrac{5}{18} = \dfrac{14}{60}$ **d.** $\dfrac{7}{9} = \dfrac{44}{63}$

14. Which proportion is true?

    a. $\dfrac{7}{8} = \dfrac{50}{56}$ **b.** $\dfrac{3}{4} = \dfrac{24}{32}$ **c.** $\dfrac{3}{8} = \dfrac{18}{50}$ **d.** $\dfrac{3}{10} = \dfrac{14}{40}$

15. Solve: $\dfrac{14}{n} = \dfrac{5}{8}$

    a. 20.4   **b.** 8.75   **c.** 2.857   **d.** 22.4

16. Solve: $\dfrac{6}{25} = \dfrac{7}{n}$ Round to the nearest hundredth.

    a. 1.68   **b.** 21.43   **c.** 1.92   **d.** 29.17

17. A dosage for medication is $\frac{1}{2}$ ounce for every 60 pounds of body weight. At this rate, what is the dosage for a person weighing 150 pounds?

    a. $1\dfrac{1}{4}$ ounces   **b.** $1\dfrac{3}{4}$ ounces   **c.** 1.5 ounces   **d.** 2 ounces

18. A scale on a map is 1 inch for every 10 miles. What is the distance between 2 points that measure $5\frac{1}{2}$ inches apart on the map?

    a. 5.5 miles   **b.** 55 miles   **c.** 65 miles   **d.** 52.5 miles

19. An automobile recall was based on testing that showed 31 steering defects per 1000 cars. At this rate, how many defects would be found in 25,000 cars?

    a. 725   **b.** 755   **c.** 7750   **d.** 775

20. A motor home travels 90 miles on 8 gallons of gasoline. How far can the motor home travel on 15 gallons of gasoline?

    a. 48 miles   **b.** 168.75 miles   **c.** 138 miles   **d.** 133.33 miles

Name: _____
Date: _____

1. Write 73% as a decimal.

    a. 0.073   **b.** 7300   **c.** 7.3   **d.** 0.73

2. Write $4\frac{1}{3}\%$ as a fraction.

    a. $4\frac{1}{3}$ **b.** $\frac{13}{300}$ **c.** $\frac{13}{100}$ **d.** $\frac{1}{3}$

3. Write 0.03 as a percent.

    a. 3%   **b.** 0.3%   **c.** 30%   **d.** 0.003%

4. Write 2.11 as a percent.

    a. 0.0211%   **b.** 211%   **c.** 21.1%   **d.** 0.211%

5. Write $\frac{3}{11}$ as a percent. Round to the nearest tenth of a percent.

    a. 0.3%   **b.** 2.7%   **c.** 27.3%   **d.** 272.7%

6. Write $1\frac{2}{9}$ as a percent. Round to the nearest tenth of a percent.

    a. 122.2%   **b.** 1.2%   **c.** 12.2%   **d.** $1\frac{2}{9}$

7. What is 5.03% of 530?

    a. 24.659   **b.** 28.09   **c.** 266.59   **d.** 26.659

8. 13.75% of 4000 is what number?

    a. 55   **b.** 550   **c.** 5500   **d.** 450

9. Which statement is correct?

    a. 5% of 85 is larger than 15% of 115   **b.** 5% of 85 is smaller than 15% of 115
    c. 5% of 85 is equal to 15% of 115   **d.** 5% of 85 is smaller than zero

10. Which statement is correct?

    a. 5.4% of 6 is larger than 10.8% of 12   **b.** 5.4% of 6 is smaller than 10.8% of 12
    c. 5.4% of 6 is equal to 10.8% of 12   **d.** 5.4% of 6 is smaller than zero

11. A company uses 7.5% of its $80,000 budget for advertising. What amount of the budget is spent for advertising?

    a. $1066.67   **b.** $8000   **c.** $6000   **d.** $4000

12. A foreign car dealer offers new buyers a 5% rebate on a new car that costs $12,800. What is the amount of the rebate?

    a. $256   **b.** $2560   **c.** $640   **d.** $390.60

13. What percent of 50 is 12.5?

   a. 25%   **b.** 20%   **c.** 12.5%   **d.** $\frac{1}{2}$%

14. What percent of 40 is 73? Round to the nearest tenth of a percent.

   a. 1.7%   **b.** 18.3%   **c.** 182.5%   **d.** 55.8%

15. An appliance store sold 36 of the 50 bread makers it had in stock. What percent of the bread makers in stock did the company sell?

   a. 28%   **b.** 46%   **c.** 64%   **d.** 72%

16. A teacher has an income of $28,500 and pays $3135 in income tax. What percent of the income is the income tax?

   a. 11%   **b.** 13%   **c.** 9%   **d.** 9.09%

17. 11 is 22% of what number?

   a. 40   **b.** 60   **c.** 200   **d.** 50

18. 4.56 is 28.5% of what number?

   a. 13   **b.** 16   **c.** 1.3   **d.** 15

19. A wheat farmer averaged 44 bushels of wheat per acre for the current harvest. This is 80% of last year's crop. Find the average number of bushels of wheat per acre obtained last year.

   a. 65 bushels   **b.** 45 bushels   **c.** 55 bushels   **d.** 35.2 bushels

20. A store advertises an electronic keyboard for $240. This is 120% of the price at a competitor's store. What is the price at the competitor's store?

   a. $120   **b.** $200   **c.** $244   **d.** $288

21. 58 is 116% of what number?

   a. 67.28   **b.** 55   **c.** 60   **d.** 50

22. What is 5.25% of 1500?

   a. 78.75   **b.** 157.5   **c.** 7.875   **d.** 787.5

23. A clothing store reduced the price of a leather jacket to $180, which was 80% of the original price. What was the original price?

   a. $270   **b.** $225   **c.** $244   **d.** $144

24. A calculator can be purchased for $68, which is 40% of the cost 3 years ago. What was the cost of the calculator 3 years ago?

   a. $160   **b.** $170   **c.** $180   **d.** $27.20

25. A marketing survey showed that 312 out of the 400 people surveyed liked a new commercial. What percent of the people surveyed liked the new commercial?

   a. 22%   **b.** 128%   **c.** 68%   **d.** 78%

Name: _____

Date: _____

1. Twelve pounds of screws for sheet rock cost $3.48. Find the unit cost.

   a. $0.29/pound   **b.** $0.63/pound   **c.** $0.18/pound   **d.** $0.36/pound

2. Find the most economical purchase.

   a. 20 ounces for $8   **b.** 48 ounces for $15.36
   c. 36 ounces for $13.68   **d.** 24 ounces for $8.64

3. Oranges cost $.79 per pound. Find the total cost for 4.2 pounds of oranges. Round to the nearest cent.

   a. $2.33   **b.** $3.23   **c.** $3.32   **d.** $4.32

4. A machinist's salary this year is $32,000. This salary will increase by 9% next year. What will the salary be next year?

   a. $38,440   **b.** $34,880   **c.** $2880   **d.** $36,440

5. At the start of a speed-reading course, Craig's reading speed was 250 words per minute. His speed increased 40% during the course. What was his reading speed at the end of the course?

   a. 350 wpm   **b.** 320 wpm   **c.** 100 wpm   **d.** 380 wpm

6. The Hanson Farm stand uses a markup rate of 60% on a jar of honey that costs $1.20. What is the selling price?

   a. $0.72   **b.** $1.60   **c.** $1.80   **d.** $1.92

7. A department store uses a 30% markup rate. Find the selling price of a dryer that was purchased by the store for $165.

   a. $49.50   **b.** $215.40   **c.** $214.50   **d.** $274.50

8. Due to a large rice harvest, the price of rice dropped from $3.10 per bushel to $2.48 per bushel. Find the percent decrease in the price of rice.

   a. 25%   **b.** 20%   **c.** 60%   **d.** 16%

9. A wool suit dropped in price from $369 to $221.40. Find the percent decrease in price.

   a. 60%   **b.** 44%   **c.** 40%   **d.** 35%

10. A hardware store is selling shovels that regularly sell for $29.95 at 40% off the regular price. What is the sale price?

    a. $17.97   **b.** $18.97   **c.** $11.98   **d.** $17.79

11. A motorcycle that regularly sells for $10,800 is on sale for 10% off the regular price. What is the discount?

    a. $108   **b.** $1000   **c.** $800   **d.** $1080

12. Arrowhead Trucking Company borrows $90,000 at a 9.5% annual rate for 24 months. What is the simple interest due on the loan?

    a. $1710   **b.** $8550   **c.** $17,100   **d.** $20,520

13. Ian invests $8000 in his company's retirement account that pays 11% annual interest compounded semiannually. Find the value of the investment after 5 years. Use the Compound Interest Table.

    a. $13,665.12   **b.** $13,763.44   **c.** $23,342.08   **d.** $13,864.88

14. A house is purchased for $110,000. The lender requires a down payment of 20%. Find the down payment.

    a. $2200   **b.** $2000   **c.** $22,000   **d.** $88,000

15. The Evans purchased a beach house and obtained a $65,000 mortgage for 20 years at an annual interest rate of 8%. Find the monthly mortgage payment. Use the monthly payment table. Round to the nearest cent.

    a. $542.69   **b.** $543.69   **c.** $501.68   **d.** $5436.86

16. A used truck is purchased for $8500. A down payment of $1600 is made. The balance is financed for 4 years at an annual interest rate of 8%. Find the monthly payment on the loan. Use the Monthly Payment Table. Round to the nearest cent.

    a. $143.75   **b.** $155.25   **c.** $207.51   **d.** $168.45

17. A $6550 used car is purchased with a down payment of $1200. The balance is financed for 3 years at an annual rate of 11%. Find the monthly car payment. Use the Monthly Payment Table. Round to the nearest cent.

    a. $151.62   **b.** $185.46   **c.** $230.28   **d.** $175.15

18. A carpet salesperson receives $500 per month plus 2% commission on sales over $25,000. During the month, the salesperson sold $84,000 worth of carpets. Find the salesperson's total earnings for the month.

    a. $1680   **b.** $1180   **c.** $1860   **d.** $1650

19. Beth had a checking account balance of $1024.03. She wrote checks for $18.12, $122.31, and $632.40 and deposited $782. Find her new checking account balance.

    a. $251.20   **b.** $1033.20   **c.** $1014.86   **d.** $1015.08

20. Balance the checkbook shown.

NUMBER	DATE	DESCRIPTION OF TRANSACTION	PAYMENT/DEBIT (-)		√ T	FEE (IF ANY) (-)	DEPOSIT/CREDIT (+)		BALANCE	
		RECORD ALL CHARGES OR CREDITS THAT AFFECT YOUR ACCOUNT							$ 545	96
	1/2	Mortgage payment	$ 214	35	$		$		331	61
	1/10	Loan payment	113	58					218	03
	1/11	Drug store	16	04					201	99
	1/15	Cable T.V.	21	35					180	64
	1/16	Deposit					216	00	396	64
	1/20	Deposit					500	00	896	64
	1/25	Clothing	116	25					780	39
	1/30	Theatre tickets	70	00					710	39

REMEMBER TO RECORD AUTOMATIC PAYMENTS/DEPOSITS ON DATE AUTHORIZED

CHECKING ACCOUNT Monthly Statement		Account Number : 924-297-8	
DATE	Transaction	Amount	Balance
1/1	OPENING BALANCE		545.96
1/4	CHECK	214.35	331.61
1/13	CHECK	113.58	218.03
1/17	CHECK	21.35	196.68
1/17	DEPOSIT	216.00	412.68
1/21	DEPOSIT	500.00	912.68
1/29	CHECK	116.25	796.43
1/30	INTEREST	7.80	804.23
1/31	CLOSING BALANCE		804.23

Do the bank statement and the checkbook balance?

a. Yes **b.** No

Name: _____
Date: _____

1. Write the comparison 112 miles to 30 miles as a ratio in simplest form.

   a. $\dfrac{56}{15}$ **b.** $\dfrac{14}{5}$ **c.** $\dfrac{22}{5}$ **d.** $\dfrac{15}{56}$

2. A company received 230 phone calls on Monday and 190 phone calls on Wednesday. Find the ratio of Wednesday's phone calls to Monday's phone calls.

   a. $\dfrac{19}{25}$ **b.** $\dfrac{23}{19}$ **c.** $\dfrac{19}{23}$ **d.** $\dfrac{25}{19}$

3. Write "980.4 gallons in 17.2 minutes" as a unit rate.

   a. 980.4 gallons/17.2 minutes   **b.** 5.7 gallons/minute

   c. 57 gallons/minute   **d.** 570 gallons/minute

4. The cost of producing 3000 cassette tapes is $8010. What is the production cost per tape?

   a. $26.70   **b.** $2.67   **c.** $0.27   **d.** $2.76

5. Solve the proportion: $\dfrac{44}{12} = \dfrac{n}{8}$ Round to the nearest hundredth.

   a. 29.33   **b.** 0.47   **c.** 2.18   **d.** 66

6. Eight out of every 10 public employees in a certain city are residents of the city. If there are 1500 public employees in the city, how many of these employees are residents of the city?

   a. 1875   **b.** 1400   **c.** 120   **d.** 1200

7. Write 0.3% as a decimal.

   a. 0.003   **b.** 0.3   **c.** 0.03   **d.** 30

8. Write 12% as a fraction.

   a. $\dfrac{4}{25}$ **b.** $\dfrac{3}{20}$ **c.** $\dfrac{3}{25}$ **d.** $\dfrac{1}{5}$

9. Write $\dfrac{12}{15}$ as a percent.

   a. 1.3%   **b.** 80%   **c.** 60%   **d.** 85%

10. Write 0.09 as a percent.

    a. 0.9%   **b.** 90%   **c.** 9%   **d.** 0.09%

11. 14% of 756 is what number?

　　a.　10.58　　　　　　b.　5400　　　　　　c.　185.185　　　　　d.　105.84

12. Because of frost, a farmer lost 15% of the seedlings that had been planted. If 460 seedlings had been planted, how many were lost?

　　a.　39.1　　　　　　b.　391　　　　　　　c.　6.9　　　　　　　d.　69

13. What percent of 720 is 144?

　　a.　50%　　　　　　b.　20%　　　　　　　c.　500%　　　　　　d.　30%

14. A real estate salesperson received a commission of $6250 on the sale of a $125,000 property. What percent of the sale price is the commission?

　　a.　50%　　　　　　b.　0.5%　　　　　　　c.　5%　　　　　　　d.　20%

15. 1.26 is 2.8% of what number?

　　a.　45　　　　　　　b.　4.5　　　　　　　c.　0.45　　　　　　d.　2.22

16. The Walwood Diesel Company spent $13,400 on utilities in 1 year. This was 8% of the company's total expenses. What were the company's total expenses that year?

　　a.　$167,500　　　　b.　$1,675,000　　　c.　$16,750　　　　d.　$1072

17. An 11-ounce container of ginger costs $35.31. Find the cost of 2 ounces of ginger. Round to the nearest cent.

　　a.　$3.21　　　　　　b.　$4.18　　　　　　c.　$6.42　　　　　d.　$8.24

18. National Electronics Company uses a markup rate of 40%. What is the selling price of a copier that cost the store $280?

　　a.　$112　　　　　　b.　$291.20　　　　　c.　$402　　　　　　d.　$392

19. A microwave oven that regularly sells for $230 has been discounted $92. What is the discount rate?

　　a.　4%　　　　　　　b.　40%　　　　　　　c.　25%　　　　　　d.　2.5%

20. A farmer borrowed $105,000 for 8 months at an annual interest rate of 11.5%. What is the simple interest due on the loan?

　　a.　$9660　　　　　　b.　$15,094　　　　　c.　$8050　　　　　d.　$12,075

The pictograph shows the amount of gasoline sold by a service station over a holiday weekend. Each barrel represents 1000 gallons of gasoline.

1. How many gallons of gasoline were sold during the 3-day period?
   a. 10,000   b. 1000
   c. 100,000   d. 100

Friday

Saturday

Sunday

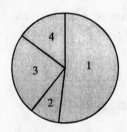

2. Find the ratio of the number of gallons sold on Friday to the number of gallons sold on Sunday.

   a. $\frac{5}{9}$ b. $\frac{5}{8}$ c. $\frac{5}{7}$ d. $\frac{6}{7}$

The circle graph shows how a business spends its annual income of $25,000,000.

3. Find the total amount spent annually for salaries and advertising.
   a. $13,000,000   b. $6,000,000
   c. $6,250,000   d. $15,250,000

4. How much is spent annually on operating costs?
   a. $5,000,000   b. $7,000,000
   c. $6,250,000   d. $6,000,000

5. How much more is spent annually for supplies than for advertising?
   a. $1,500,000   b. $150,000
   c. $15,000,000   d. $6,000,000

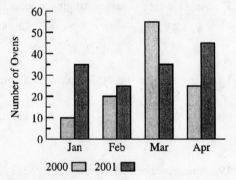

BUSINESS EXPENSES
1: 52% - Salaries
2: 9% - Advertising
3: 24% - Operational Costs
4: 15% - Supplies

The double-bar graph shows the number of microwave ovens sold during the first 4 months of 2000 and 2001.

6. What is the difference between the first two months' sales for 2000 and 2001?
   a. 20   b. 25   c. 30   d. 5

7. In which month did 2000 sales exceed 2001 sales?
   a. March   b. January
   c. April   d. February

8. How many microwave ovens were sold during the first four months of 2000?
   a. 100   b. 110   c. 1100   d. 120

9. The number of miles driven during each of 5 days of a business trip was 110, 72, 66, 145, and 92. Find the average number of miles driven each day.

   a. 97   b. 95   c. 98.25   d. 92

10. The number of books lent by a local library during a 6-day period was 718, 644, 319, 547, 634, and 814. Find the median number of books lent.

    a. 644   b. 639   c. 612   d. 635

The double-line graph shows the number of watches (in hundreds) sold at a jewelry store for the four quarters of 2000 and 2001.

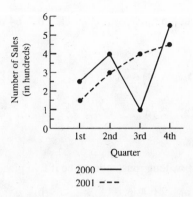

11. Find the difference between the number of watches sold during the third quarters of 2000 and 2001.
    a. 100   b. 400   c. 200   d. 300

12. During which quarter did 2000 sales equal 2001 sales?

    a. 1st   b. 2nd   c. 3rd   d. None

13. Find the ratio of the second quarter 2000 sales to second quarter 2001 sales.

    a. $\frac{4}{5}$ b. $\frac{3}{4}$ c. $\frac{4}{3}$ d. $\frac{5}{4}$

The frequency polygon shows the hourly wages of 43 employees of a cabinet shop.

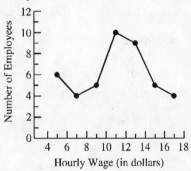

14. Find the number of employees whose hourly wage is between $10 and $14.
    a. 19   b. 9   c. 10   d. 15

15. What is the ratio of the number of employees whose hourly wage is between $4 and $6 to the number of employees whose hourly wage is more than $16?

    a. $\frac{2}{3}$ b. $\frac{3}{4}$ c. $\frac{3}{2}$ d. $\frac{4}{3}$

The histogram shows a mountain community's annual snowfall during the past 54 years.

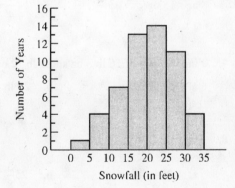

16. Find the number of years in which the annual snowfall was between 20 and 30 feet.

    a. 25   b. 14   c. 11   d. 27

17. During what percentage of the years was the snowfall between 20 and 25 feet? Round to the nearest tenth of a percent.
    a. 2.7%   b. 25.9%   c. 3.7%   d. 28.1%

18. During how many years was the snowfall less than 20 feet?
    a. 28   b. 25   c. 26   d. 29

19. A coin is tossed twice. What is the probability of getting at least one heads?

    a. $\frac{3}{4}$ b. 1   c. $\frac{1}{2}$ d. $\frac{1}{4}$

20. The cholesterol levels for 14 heart patients are recorded below. Determine the third quartile of these cholesterol levels.

250	300	190	325	280	270	200
210	340	290	240	320	190	310

a. 2400   b. 275   c. 305   d. 310

Name: _____
Date: _____

1. Convert $5\frac{1}{3}$ ft to inches.

   a. 52 in.   **b.** 64 in.   **c.** 16 in.   **d.** 72 in.

2. Divide: $4\overline{)6\text{ yd }2\text{ ft}}$

   a. 2 yd   **b.** 1 yd 1 ft   **c.** 1 yd 3 ft   **d.** 1 yd 2 ft

3. How long must a board be if five pieces, each 1 ft 8 in. long, are to be cut from the board?

   a. 7 ft 4 in.   **b.** 6 ft 4 in.   **c.** 8 ft 4 in.   **d.** 8 ft 8 in.

4. A shrub takes up $7\frac{1}{2}$ ft of space along a fence. How many shrubs will it take to occupy 450 ft along the fence?

   a. 90 shrubs   **b.** 60 shrubs   **c.** 30 shrubs   **d.** 120 shrubs

5. Convert 128 ounces to pounds.

   a. $10\frac{2}{3}$ lb   **b.** 8 lb   **c.** 6 lb   **d.** 9 lb

6. Convert $1\frac{3}{16}$ lb to ounces.

   a. 15 oz   **b.** $14\frac{1}{4}$ oz   **c.** 17 oz   **d.** 19 oz

7. Find the sum of 16 lb 3 oz and 9 lb 12 oz.

   a. 24 lb 15 oz   **b.** 25 lb 15 oz   **c.** 7 lb 9 oz   **d.** 25 lb 14 oz

8. Multiply: $5\frac{3}{8}$ lb $\times$ 5

   a. $26\frac{7}{8}$ lb   **b.** $25\frac{3}{8}$ lb   **c.** $27\frac{7}{8}$ lb   **d.** $26\frac{3}{8}$ lb

9. Four students spent their vacation panning for gold. How much did each student receive if they found 1 lb 3 oz of gold and the price of gold was $380 per ounce?

   a. $1805   **b.** $1140   **c.** $1600   **d.** $2755

10. A book weighing 2 lb 3 oz is mailed at the postage rate of $0.15 per ounce. Find the cost of mailing the book.

    a. $5.25   **b.** $2.86   **c.** $4.94   **d.** $5.98

11. Convert $1\frac{3}{4}$ gal to pints.

   a. 18 pt   **b.** 16 pt   **c.** 12 pt   **d.** 14 pt

12. Convert 17 qt to gallons.

   a. $4\frac{1}{2}$ gal   **b.** $4\frac{1}{4}$ gal   **c.** $2\frac{1}{8}$ gal   **d.** $8\frac{1}{2}$ gal

13. What is 5 gal 2 qt decreased by 2 gal 3 qt?

   a. 3 gal 1 qt   **b.** 2 gal 1 qt   **c.** 2 gal 3 qt   **d.** 3 gal 3 qt

14. Multiply: 5 qt 3 pt
   $$\times \quad 4$$

   a. $21\frac{1}{2}$ qt   **b.** 26 qt   **c.** 20 qt 3 pt   **d.** 23 qt

15. A coffee cup holds 6 fl oz of coffee. How many cups can be filled with 3 qt of coffee?

   a. 96 c   **b.** 8 c   **c.** 20 c   **d.** 16 c

16. An automobile supply store sells oil in 5-gallon cans for $27.90 or by the quart for $1.89 per quart. How much can be saved by buying the 5-gallon can of oil?

   a. $9.90   **b.** $11.70   **c.** $4.25   **d.** $9.45

17. Find the energy required to lift a 3600-pound truck a distance of 7 ft.

   a. $25,200$ ft·lb   **b.** $27,800$ ft·lb   **c.** 4300 ft·lb   **d.** $35,720$ ft·lb

18. One pound of methane will give off 1000 Btu of energy when burned. How many foot-pounds of energy are released when 1 lb of methane is burned? (1 Btu = 778 ft·lb)

   a. 778,000 ft·lb   **b.** 1000 ft·lb   **c.** 78,000 ft·lb   **d.** 1.29 ft·lb

19. Find the power in foot-pounds per second needed to raise 900 lb a distance of 30 ft in 20 s.

   a. $1650\dfrac{\text{ft}\cdot\text{lb}}{\text{s}}$ **b.** $600\dfrac{\text{ft}\cdot\text{lb}}{\text{s}}$ **c.** $1200\dfrac{\text{ft}\cdot\text{lb}}{\text{s}}$ **d.** $1350\dfrac{\text{ft}\cdot\text{lb}}{\text{s}}$

20. A motor has a power of $11,550\dfrac{\text{ft}\cdot\text{lb}}{\text{s}}$. Find the horsepower of the motor. $\left(1 \text{ hp} = 550\dfrac{\text{ft}\cdot\text{lb}}{\text{s}}\right)$

   a. 7 hp   **b.** 21 hp   **c.** 18 hp   **d.** 23 hp

Chapter 9 Test Form H

1. Convert 720.5 cm to meters.
   a. 0.725 m
   b. 7.205 m
   c. 72,050 m
   d. 72.05 m

2. Convert 3216 cm to meters.
   a. 3.216 m
   b. 32.16 m
   c. 321.6 m
   d. 321,600 m

3. Convert 2 km 58 m to kilometers.
   a. 2.058 km
   b. 20.58 km
   c. 2.58 km
   d. 2.0058 km

4. Convert 5 m 25 cm to meters.
   a. 50.25 m
   b. 5.205 m
   c. 5.25 m
   d. 5.025 m

5. A student walked 2100 m to school. After school the student walked 650 m to town before walking 1800 m home. Find the total distance walked.
   a. 3.90 km
   b. 455 m
   c. 4.55 km
   d. 3.55 km

6. A carpenter is installing six shelves, each 264 cm long. Find the total length of material needed to build the shelves.
   a. 158.4 cm
   b. 158.4 m
   c. 14.74 m
   d. 15.84 m

7. Convert 5320 g to kilograms.
   a. 5.320 kg
   b. 532.0 kg
   c. 53.20 kg
   d. 53,200 kg

8. Convert 0.8 g to milligrams.
   a. 0.08 mg
   b. 80 mg
   c. 0.008 mg
   d. 800 mg

9. Convert 3 g 42 mg to milligrams.
   a. 3042 mg
   b. 342 mg
   c. 30.42 mg
   d. 0.0342 mg

10. Convert 42 g 617 mg to grams.
    a. 42.617 g
    b. 0.42617 g
    c. 426.17 g
    d. 42,617 g

11. Four people are going on a backpacking trip. Their gear weighs 82,200 g. How much weight in kilograms will each person carry if the gear is divided equally?

    a. 205.5 kg   **b.** 20.55 kg   **c.** 2.055 kg   **d.** 21.45 kg

12. At birth a baby weighs 4550 g. At the age of 8 months, the baby weighs 8780 g. Find the increase in weight during the 8-month period.

    a. 13.75 kg   **b.** 4.65 kg   **c.** 4.23 kg   **d.** 6.30 kg

13. Convert 782 L to kiloliters.

    a. 78,200 kl   **b.** 7.82 kl   **c.** 782,000 kl   **d.** 0.782 kl

14. Convert 675 cm^3 to milliliters.

    a. 67.5 ml   **b.** 6.75 ml   **c.** 675 ml   **d.** 67,500 ml

15. Convert 5 L 89 ml to liters.

    a. 58.9 L   **b.** 0.00589 L   **c.** 5.89 L   **d.** 5.089 L

16. Convert 1 L 749 ml to milliliters.

    a. 174.9 ml   **b.** 17.49 ml   **c.** 1749 ml   **d.** 1.749 ml

17. Eight liters of face cream are bought for $12.50 per liter. The face cream is repackaged in 200-milliliter bottles and sold for $4 per bottle. Find the profit on the 8 L of face cream.

    a. $30   **b.** $260   **c.** $60   **d.** $120

18. An oven uses 600 W of energy per hour. During 1 week the oven is used for 12 h. Electricity costs 10.2¢ per kilowatt-hour. Find the cost of using the oven. Round to the nearest cent.

    a. $73.44   **b.** 72¢   **c.** 74¢   **d.** 73¢

19. Turkey costs $0.85 per pound. Find the cost per kilogram. Round to the nearest cent. (2.2 lb = 1 kg)

    a. $1.87/kg   **b.** $1.78/kg   **c.** $0.42/kg   **d.** $0.83/kg

20. Gasoline costs 39.2¢ per liter. Find the cost per gallon. Round to the nearest cent. (1 L = 1.06 qt)

    a. $1.47/gal   **b.** $1.48/gal   **c.** $1.38/gal   **d.** $1.66/gal

The circle graph shows the annual expenses for a student at a university.

1. Find the ratio of the expenditure for books to the cost of entertainment.

   a. $\dfrac{1}{5}$ **b.** $\dfrac{6}{7}$ **c.** $\dfrac{6}{70}$ **d.** $\dfrac{5}{7}$

2. What percent of the total budget was spent on entertainment? Round to the nearest tenth of a percent.

   a. 24.1%   **b.** 2.4%   **c.** 2.1%   **d.** 3.8%

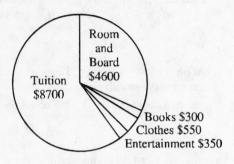

Annual Student Expenses

The frequency polygon shows the annual rainfall at a seaside community during the past 22 years.

3. During what percent of the years was the rainfall between 3 in. and 4 in.? Round to the nearest tenth of a percent.

   a. 13.6%   **b.** 7.3%

   c. 14%   **d.** 13.8%

4. During how many years was the rainfall more than 7 in.?

   a. 5 years   **b.** 7 years

   c. 14 years   **d.** 12 years

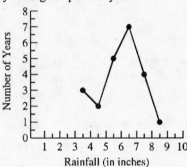

5. Newborn babies at a hospital weighed 7.6 lb, 6.8 lb, 7.2 lb, 8.1 lb, and 8.8 lb. Find the average weight of the newborns.

   a. 7.6 lb   **b.** 8.1 lb   **c.** 7.4 lb   **d.** 7.7 lb

6. Over a 5-day period, traffic on a one-way street was counted. On the first day 84 cars went down the street. Over the next 4 days, 110, 98, 72, and 106 cars were counted. Find the median number of cars using the street for the 5-day period.

   a. 110 cars   **b.** 98 cars   **c.** 94 cars   **d.** 92 cars

7. Convert 39 ft to yards.

   a. $6\dfrac{3}{4}$ yd   **b.** $3\dfrac{1}{4}$ yd   **c.** $19\dfrac{1}{2}$ yd   **d.** 13 yd

8. What is 5 ft 9 in. increased by 4 ft 5 in.?

   a. 10 ft 2 in.   **b.** 9 ft 2 in.   **c.** 10 ft 4 in.   **d.** 10 ft 6 in.

9. Convert 18 lb to ounces.

   a. 216 oz   **b.** 180 oz   **c.** 144 oz   **d.** 288 oz

10. Subtract: 5 tons 1600 lb
                  − 2 tons 1800 lb

    a. 3 tons 200 lb   **b.** 2 tons 1800 lb   **c.** 3 tons 1800 lb   **d.** 2 tons 1600 lb

11. Convert 4 qt to cups.

    a. 8 c   **b.** 32 c   **c.** 16 c   **d.** $\frac{1}{4}$ c

12. How much fencing is needed to surround a rectangular field that is 20 yd 1 ft long and 15 yd 2 ft wide?

    a. 70 yd   **b.** $70\frac{1}{2}$ yd   **c.** 72 yd   **d.** 76 yd

13. Three pieces of fish weighing 1 lb 4 oz, 12 oz, and 1 lb 8 oz are purchased for a dinner. What is the total weight of the fish?

    a. 5 lb   **b.** 4 lb   **c.** 3 lb 6 oz   **d.** 3 lb 8 oz

14. Convert 46.9 mm to centimeters.

    a. 4.69 cm   **b.** 0.469 cm   **c.** 469 cm   **d.** 4690 cm

15. Convert 436 mg to grams.

    a. 43.6 g   **b.** 0.436 g   **c.** 0.0436 g   **d.** 4.36 g

16. Convert 480 ml to liters.

    a. 0.48 L   **b.** 4.8 L   **c.** 48 L   **d.** 480 L

17. Find the number of grams in 24 oz of soda. (28.35 g = 1 oz)

    a. 68.04 g   **b.** 6.804 g   **c.** 1.18 g   **d.** 680.4 g

18. Express 44 km/h in miles per hour. Round to the nearest tenth. (1.61 km = 1 mi)

    a. 27.3 mi/h   **b.** 28 mi/h   **c.** 70.8 mi/h   **d.** 25.3 mi/h

19. A large roast weighing 3120 g is to be cut into three smaller roasts. How much will each smaller roast weigh if the large roast is divided equally?

    a. 1.40 kg   **b.** 104 kg   **c.** 1.040 kg   **d.** 10.4 kg

20. A plumber needs three pieces of pipe for a project. The three pieces need to be 125 cm, 85 cm, and 95 cm long. How many total meters of pipe does the plumber need?

    a. 3.5 m   **b.** 3 m 50 cm   **c.** 30.5 m   **d.** 3.05 m

1. Which statement is correct?

   a. $5 < -5$ **b.** $0 < -5$ **c.** $-7 > -5$ **d.** $-5 > -7$

2. Which statement is correct?

   a. $-8 < 1$ **b.** $-5 > 0$ **c.** $-8 > 1$ **d.** $-3 < -11$

3. Evaluate $-\left|-\dfrac{1}{2}\right|$ and $-\left|\dfrac{1}{5}\right|$.

   a. $\dfrac{1}{2}$ and $-\dfrac{1}{5}$ **b.** $-\dfrac{1}{2}$ and $\dfrac{1}{5}$ **c.** $\dfrac{1}{2}$ and $\dfrac{1}{5}$ **d.** $-\dfrac{1}{2}$ and $-\dfrac{1}{5}$

4. Find the sum of 32, -14, -12, and 4.

   a. 10 **b.** 2 **c.** 8 **d.** -8

5. Add: $-23 + 40$

   a. -17 **b.** 63 **c.** 17 **d.** -63

6. Subtract: $-6 - (-10)$

   a. 4 **b.** 16 **c.** -4 **d.** -16

7. Subtract: $-4 - (-10) - 3$

   a. -11 **b.** -17 **c.** -3 **d.** 3

8. Find the product of -5, -4, and 8.

   a. -160 **b.** 12 **c.** -1 **d.** 160

9. Divide: $288 \div (-16)$

   a. 18 **b.** -18 **c.** 4608 **d.** -36

10. Find the temperature after a rise of 11°C from −20°C.

    a. $9°C$ **b.** $31°C$ **c.** $-9°C$ **d.** $-31°C$

11. The daily low temperature readings for a 3-day period were −6°, 8°, and 4°. Find the average low temperature for the period.

    a. $-2°$ **b.** $3°$ **c.** $2°$ **d.** $-3°$

12. Find the sum of $\dfrac{7}{8}$ and $-\dfrac{5}{12}$.

    a. $-\dfrac{11}{24}$ **b.** $1\dfrac{7}{24}$ **c.** $-\dfrac{11}{12}$ **d.** $\dfrac{11}{24}$

13. Add: $-1\dfrac{3}{8} + \left(-2\dfrac{1}{4}\right)$

    a. $-1\dfrac{1}{8}$ **b.** $\dfrac{7}{8}$ **c.** $-3\dfrac{5}{8}$ **d.** $2\dfrac{3}{8}$

14. Subtract: $\dfrac{3}{8} - \left(-\dfrac{1}{4}\right)$

    a. $\dfrac{1}{8}$ **b.** $\dfrac{5}{8}$ **c.** $-\dfrac{5}{8}$ **d.** $-\dfrac{1}{8}$

15. Subtract: $\dfrac{7}{12} - \dfrac{2}{3}$

    a. $\dfrac{5}{4}$ **b.** $-\dfrac{5}{4}$ **c.** $\dfrac{1}{12}$ **d.** $-\dfrac{1}{12}$

16. Multiply: $1\dfrac{7}{8} \cdot \left(-\dfrac{5}{13}\right)$

    a. $-\dfrac{75}{104}$ **b.** $-4\dfrac{1}{2}$ **c.** $4\dfrac{1}{2}$ **d.** $\dfrac{25}{32}$

17. Find the quotient of 4 and $-3\dfrac{1}{2}$.

    a. $-1\dfrac{2}{7}$ **b.** $-\dfrac{7}{8}$ **c.** -14 **d.** $-1\dfrac{1}{7}$

18. What is -3.4 decreased by 2.85?

    a. 6.25 **b.** 0.55 **c.** -0.55 **d.** -6.25

19. Multiply: $-1.8 \cdot (-4.7)$

    a. 6.5 **b.** -6.5 **c.** 8.46 **d.** -8.46

20. Find the product of -0.07 and -0.002.

    a. 0.0014 **b.** -0.00014 **c.** 0.00014 **d.** -0.0014

21. Divide: $0.7844 \div (-21.2)$

    a. -0.037 **b.** -0.0037 **c.** 0.037 **d.** -0.37

22. Simplify: $3 + 7(2-5)^2 \div 3$

    a. 30 **b.** 24 **c.** 10 **d.** 15

23. Simplify: $2 - 8(-3)^2 - (-4)$

    a. -66 **b.** 58 **c.** 54 **d.** 2.3

24. Write 0.0000278 in scientific notation.

    a. 2.78×10^{-6} **b.** 2.78×10^{-5} **c.** 2.78×10^{6} **d.** 2.78×10^{5}

25. On January 19, 1892, the temperature in Fort Assiniboine, Montana rose to $2.78°C$ from $-20.56°C$ in a period of only 15 min. Find the difference between these two temperatures.

    a. $23.34°C$ **b.** $17.781°C$ **c.** $1.185°C$ **d.** $-17.78°C$

Name: _____

Date: _____

1. Evaluate $b^2 + c^2 - abc$ when $a = 3$, $b = -1$, and $c = 5$.

   a. 41   b. -10   c. 11   d. -39

2. Evaluate $b^2 - 2(-a + c)$ when $a = 3$, $b = 2$, and $c = -2$.

   a. 6   b. 8   c. 14   d. -6

3. Simplify: $-5ab + 6b + 3ab$

   a. $6ab + 6b$ b. $-9ab$ c. $6ab - 3b$ d. $-2ab + 6b$

4. Simplify: $-2n + 3(n - 4) + 5$

   a. $-6n - 17$ b. $5n - 1$ c. $n - 7$ d. $n + 4$

5. Which number is a solution of $3(x - 2) = 14 - 7x$?

   a. $\dfrac{4}{5}$ b. 2   c. -2   d. -4

6. Solve: $x + 5 = -5$

   a. -10   b. 10   c. 0   d. -25

7. Solve: $-12y = 60$

   a. $-\dfrac{1}{5}$ b. 5   c. -5   d. $\dfrac{1}{5}$

8. Solve: $-\dfrac{x}{5} = 5$

   a. 25   b. -1   c. 1   d. -25

9. The value of an investment in silver after 1 year was $12,280. The original investment was $9000. Find the increase in value during the year. Use the formula $A = P + I$, where A is the value of the investment after 1 year, P is the original investment, and I is the increase in value of the investment.

   a. $3280   b. $21,280   c. $3180   d. $3260

10. Solve: $3x - 7 = 11$

   a. 6   b. 4   c. $1\dfrac{1}{3}$ d. $3\dfrac{1}{3}$

11. Solve: $2(x-1)-3 = -3x+2$

    a. $1\dfrac{2}{5}$ **b.** $-1\dfrac{2}{5}$ **c.** $\dfrac{1}{5}$ **d.** $\dfrac{5}{7}$

12. Solve: $20 = -4+3c$

    a. $\dfrac{16}{3}$ **b.** -8 **c.** 8 **d.** $-\dfrac{16}{3}$

13. A sales executive earns a base monthly salary of \$800 plus a 6% commission on total sales. Find the total sales during a month the executive earned \$3500. Use the formula $M = S \cdot R + B$, where M is the monthly earnings, S is total sales, R is the commission rate, and B is the base monthly salary.

    a. \$71,667   **b.** \$4500   **c.** \$45,000   **d.** \$35,000

14. Solve: $5x-9 = 2x-3$

    a. $1\dfrac{5}{7}$ **b.** 2 **c.** -2 **d.** $-1\dfrac{5}{7}$

15. Solve: $2+5(x-3) = 2(2x+1)$

    a. 15 **b.** $1\dfrac{2}{3}$ **c.** $-1\dfrac{2}{3}$ **d.** 3

16. Translate "the total of y and the quotient of y and five" into a mathematical expression.

    a. $y+\dfrac{5}{y}$ **b.** $\dfrac{y+5}{y}$ **c.** $\dfrac{y}{y}+5$ **d.** $y+\dfrac{y}{5}$

17. Translate "the quotient of ten times a number and the number" into a mathematical expression.

    a. $\dfrac{10n}{n}$ **b.** $\dfrac{n}{10}+n$ **c.** $10n+\dfrac{1}{n}$ **d.** $\dfrac{n}{10n}$

18. Translate "a number decreased by five is seven" into an equation and solve.

    a. 7 **b.** 5 **c.** 12 **d.** -2

19. Seven less than one-half of a number is eight. Find the number.

    a. 4 **b.** 30 **c.** 15 **d.** 14

20. This month's salary for a car sales representative was \$2600. This includes the representative's base monthly salary of \$800 plus a 4% commission on total sales. Find the representative's total sales for the month.

    a. \$60,000   **b.** \$104   **c.** \$45,000   **d.** \$85,000

1. Find the supplement of a 17° angle.

   a. 73°   **b.** 103°   **c.** 163°   **d.** 83°

2. Two angles of a triangle are 24° and 38°. Find the measure of the third angle of the triangle.

   a. 88°   **b.** 118°   **c.** 38°   **d.** 138°

3. In the figure, $L_1 \parallel L_2$ $\angle x = 82°$. Find $\angle y$.

   a. 164°   **b.** 82°

   c. 98°   **d.** 68°

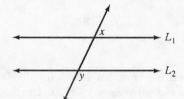

4. In the figure, $L_1 \parallel L_2$. $\angle x = 174°$. Find $\angle a + \angle b$.

   a. 12°   **b.** 348°

   c. 186°   **d.** 36°

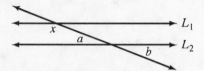

5. Find the perimeter of a triangle with sides 2 ft 3 in., 3 ft 4 in., and 4 ft 6 in.

   a. 10 ft 3 in.   **b.** 10 ft 1 in.   **c.** 9 ft 1 in.   **d.** 10 ft 11 in.

6. Find the perimeter of the composite figure.

   a. 280 cm   **b.** 180 cm

   c. 220 cm   **d.** 120 cm

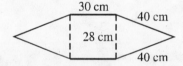

7. The dimensions of a living room are 28 ft by 18 ft. At $2.15 per foot for wall baseboards, how much does it cost to purchase baseboard for the living room? Subtract 10 feet for doorways.

   a. $77.40   **b.** $197.80   **c.** $1083.60   **d.** $176.30

8. Find the area of a circle with a radius of 12 cm. Use 3.14 for π.

   a. 31.4 cm^2 **b.** 226 cm^2 **c.** 452.16 cm^2 **d.** 314 cm^2

9. Find the total area of the national forest with the dimensions shown in the diagram below.

   a. 496 mi^2 **b.** 376 mi^2

   c. 434 mi^2 **d.** 344 mi^2

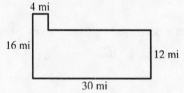

10. Find the area between the two rectangles.

    a. 608 ft^2 **b.** 2272 ft^2

    c. 688 ft^2 **d.** 580 ft^2

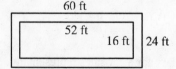

11. Find the volume of a rectangular solid with a length of 9 in., a width of 5 in., and a height of 6 in.

    a. 230 in.^{3} **b.** 540 in.^{3} **c.** 62.80 in.^{3} **d.** 270 in.^{3}

Name: _____

12. Tile is to be placed in an entryway, as shown below. At $5.75 per square foot, how much does it cost to tile the entryway?

    a. $661.25   **b.** $718.75

    c. $741.75   **d.** $603.75

13. Find the volume of the solid. The diameter of the cylinder is 4 ft. Use 3.14 for π.

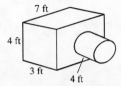

    a. 109.12 ft^3 **b.** 134.24 ft^3

    c. 536.96 ft^3 **d.** 284.96 ft^3

14. An oil storage tank that is in the shape of a cylinder is 5 m high and has a 6-meter radius. Find the volume of the oil storage tank. Use 3.14 for π.

    a. 741.3 m^3 **b.** 565.2 m^3 **c.** 3391.2 m^3 **d.** 141.3 m^3

15. Find the square root of 74. Round to the nearest thousandth.

    a. 8.602   **b.** 8.206   **c.** 8.660   **d.** 8.544

16. Find the unknown side of the triangle. Round to the nearest tenth.

    a. 5 ft   **b.** 15.8 ft

    c. 11.2 ft   **d.** 9.2 ft

17. Find the length of the ramp used to roll barrels up to a 3-foot loading platform. Round to the nearest tenth.

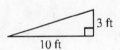

    a. 7 ft   **b.** 11.2 ft

    c. 10.4 ft   **d.** 13 ft

18. Triangles *ABC* and *DEF* are similar. The height of triangle *DEF* is 4 cm. Find the area of triangle *ABC*.

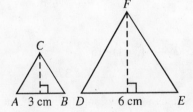

    a. 1.5 cm^2 **b.** 2 cm^2

    c. 6 cm^2 **d.** 3 cm^2

19. Triangles *ABC* and *DEF* are similar. Find the perimeter of triangle *DEF*.

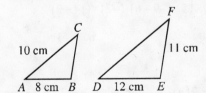

    a. 34.7 cm   **b.** 25.3 cm

    c. 15 cm   **d.** 38 cm

20. In the figure, triangles *ABC* and *DEF* are congruent. Find the measure of *DF*.

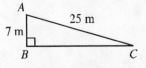
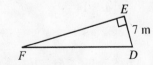

    a. 24 m   **b.** 25 m

    c. 7 m   **d.** 25.961 m

Name: _____
Date: _____

1. Find the sum of −35 and −12.
   - **a.** −47
   - **b.** 47
   - **c.** −23
   - **d.** 23

2. Add: $\dfrac{3}{4} + \left(-\dfrac{5}{12}\right)$
   - **a.** $-\dfrac{1}{3}$
   - **b.** $1\dfrac{1}{6}$
   - **c.** $-1\dfrac{1}{6}$
   - **d.** $\dfrac{1}{3}$

3. Subtract: $-44 - (-8)$
   - **a.** 36
   - **b.** −36
   - **c.** −52
   - **d.** 52

4. Subtract: $-2.1 - (-6.8)$
   - **a.** 8.9
   - **b.** 4.7
   - **c.** −4.7
   - **d.** −8.9

5. Find the product of −100 and −25.
   - **a.** −2500
   - **b.** 2500
   - **c.** 4
   - **d.** −4

6. Multiply: $-\dfrac{4}{9} \cdot \dfrac{15}{17}$
   - **a.** $\dfrac{20}{51}$
   - **b.** $-\dfrac{20}{41}$
   - **c.** $-\dfrac{12}{51}$
   - **d.** $-\dfrac{20}{51}$

7. What is −0.008 divided by −0.2 ?
   - **a.** 0.04
   - **b.** −0.04
   - **c.** 0.004
   - **d.** 0.4

8. Simplify: $5 \cdot 2^2 + 6 \cdot (3-1) - 15$
   - **a.** 17
   - **b.** 37
   - **c.** 19
   - **d.** 29

9. Simplify: $15 \div (-9+6) \cdot (-2) \div (14-9)$
   - **a.** −4
   - **b.** −1
   - **c.** 4
   - **d.** 2

10. Evaluate $2(a+b) - 3ac$ when $a=2$, $b=3$, and $c=4$.
    - **a.** 14
    - **b.** −34
    - **c.** 36
    - **d.** −14

11. Simplify: $6x - 2(3-x) - 2x$
    - **a.** $6x - 3$
    - **b.** $6x + 6$
    - **c.** $6x - 6$
    - **d.** $4x - 6$

12. Solve: $y + 7 = -41$

   a. 48   **b.** 34   **c.** −48   **d.** −34

13. Solve: $2(3 - 5x) + 6x = 3(x + 4)$

   a. $-\dfrac{6}{7}$ **b.** 6   **c.** $-2\dfrac{4}{7}$ **d.** −6

14. Solve: $12 - 3x = 15$

   a. 3   **b.** 5   **c.** −3   **d.** −5

15. Solve: $3x - 4(x - 2) = 9$

   a. −17   **b.** 1   **c.** −1   **d.** 17

16. Translate "five increased by three times a number is twenty-six" into an equation and solve.

   a. 18   **b.** 7   **c.** $\dfrac{31}{5}$ **d.** 28

17. The depreciation on a car that originally cost \$15,400 is \$8750. Find the value of the car now. Use the formula $V = N - D$, where V is the value of the car now, N is the original value of the car, and D is the depreciation.

   a. \$24,150   **b.** \$5650   **c.** \$6650   **d.** \$6560

18. The value of a stock portfolio was \$150,000 last year. This was 80% of its value this year. What is its value this year?

   a. \$180,000   **b.** \$750,000   **c.** \$120,000   **d.** \$187,500

19. Two angles of a triangle measure $75°$ and $36°$. Find the measure of the third angle.

   a. $89°$ **b.** $39°$ **c.** $69°$ **d.** $59°$

20. In the figure, $L_1 \parallel L_2$. $\angle x = 158°$. Find $\angle y$.

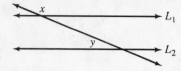

    a. 158°   **b.** 202°

    c. 32°   **d.** 22°

21. Find the perimeter of a triangle with sides measuring $2\frac{1}{2}$ in., $3\frac{3}{4}$ in., and $1\frac{7}{8}$ in.

    a. $8\frac{1}{8}$ in.   **b.** $6\frac{11}{14}$ in.   **c.** $7\frac{3}{4}$ in.   **d.** $6\frac{3}{8}$ in.

22. Find the area of the figure. Use 3.14 for π.

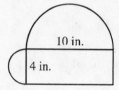

    a. 131.06 in^2 **b.** 222.12 in^2

    c. 404.24 in^2 **d.** 85.53 in^2

23. Find the volume of a cylinder with a radius of 7 cm and height of 10 cm. Use $\frac{22}{7}$ for π.

    a. 6160 cm^3 **b.** 1540 cm^3 **c.** 1740 cm^3 **d.** 6140 cm^3

24. Find the unknown leg of the right triangle. Round to the nearest tenth.

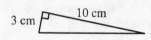

    a. 10.4 cm   **b.** 11.6 cm

    c. 10.2 cm   **d.** 11.3 cm

25. In the figure, triangles *ABC* and *DEF* are similar. Find the perimeter of triangle *DEF*.

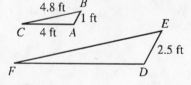

    a. 27.5 ft   **b.** 20.5 ft

    c. 24.5 ft   **d.** 23.8 ft

1. Subtract: $9304 - 876$
   a. 8518
   b. 8437
   c. 8158
   d. 8428

2. Find 35,256 divided by 26.
   a. 1365
   b. 1356
   c. 1366
   d. 2048

3. Simplify: $7^2 - 3 \cdot 2 + (7 - 4)$
   a. 95
   b. 46
   c. 11
   d. 25

4. A consumer makes a down payment of $1500 on a used car costing $10,092. The balance is to be paid in 24 monthly installments. What is the amount of each monthly payment?
   a. $358
   b. $420
   c. $483
   d. $278

5. Find the sum of $4\frac{2}{5}$ and $5\frac{1}{15}$.
   a. $10\frac{3}{15}$
   b. $9\frac{7}{15}$
   c. $9\frac{11}{15}$
   d. $9\frac{5}{15}$

6. Subtract: $10\frac{5}{36} - 7\frac{5}{9}$
   a. $2\frac{7}{12}$
   b. $3\frac{7}{12}$
   c. $3\frac{5}{12}$
   d. $2\frac{3}{4}$

7. Find the product of 5 and $2\frac{3}{10}$.
   a. $10\frac{3}{10}$
   b. $7\frac{3}{10}$
   c. $2\frac{4}{23}$
   d. $11\frac{1}{2}$

8. Divide: $18 \div 1\frac{3}{7}$
   a. $12\frac{4}{5}$
   b. $11\frac{4}{5}$
   c. $\frac{5}{63}$
   d. $12\frac{3}{5}$

9. Simplify: $\frac{2}{7} + \frac{3}{7} \cdot \frac{1}{3} + \left(\frac{1}{2} - \frac{1}{3}\right)$
   a. $\frac{17}{42}$
   b. $\frac{27}{42}$
   c. $\frac{25}{42}$
   d. $\frac{23}{42}$

10. A computer programmer worked $1\frac{3}{4}$ hours of overtime on Monday, 2 hours on Tuesday, and $2\frac{1}{2}$ hours on Wednesday. How many hours of overtime did he work in the 3 days?
    a. $6\frac{3}{8}$ hours
    b. $5\frac{3}{4}$ hours
    c. $5\frac{7}{8}$ hours
    d. $6\frac{1}{4}$ hours

11. Subtract: $7.4 - 2.536$
    a. 9.936   **b.** 4.974   **c.** 4.864   **d.** 2.918

12. Multiply: 18×0.09
    a. 16.2   **b.** 1.62   **c.** 0.005   **d.** 200

13. Find the quotient of 57 and 1.08. Round to the nearest tenth.
    a. 5.3   **b.** 0.5   **c.** 527.8   **d.** 52.8

14. Convert 0.075 to a fraction.
    a. $\dfrac{3}{40}$ **b.** $\dfrac{3}{400}$ **c.** $\dfrac{3}{200}$ **d.** $\dfrac{3}{20}$

15. Convert $\dfrac{7}{36}$ to a decimal. Round to the nearest thousandth.
    a. 0.194   **b.** 0.210   **c.** 5.1   **d.** 0.156

16. Write the comparison "95 ft to 40 ft" as a ratio in simplest form using a fraction.
    a. $\dfrac{17}{8}$ **b.** $\dfrac{8}{19}$ **c.** $\dfrac{19}{6}$ **d.** $\dfrac{19}{8}$

17. Write "876 miles on 73 gallons" as a unit rate.
    a. 14 miles/gallon   **b.** 12 miles/gallon   **c.** 8.3 miles/gallon   **d.** 16 miles/gallon

18. Solve the proportion: $\dfrac{21}{26} = \dfrac{15}{n}$ Round to the nearest hundredth.
    a. 36.40   **b.** 18.40   **c.** 18.57   **d.** 12.12

19. An automobile recall was based on engineering tests that showed 27 braking defects in 1000 cars. At this rate, how many defects will be found in 20,000 cars?
    a. 5400 defects   **b.** 54 defects   **c.** 540 defects   **d.** 54,000 defects

20. Write 0.055 as a percent.
    a. 0.55%   **b.** 5.5%   **c.** 0.055%   **d.** 0.0055%

21. What is 24% of 60?
    a. 250   **b.** 14.4   **c.** 40   **d.** 25.2

22. 6 is what percent of 16?
    a. 5%   **b.** 1.125%   **c.** 3.75%   **d.** 37.5%

23. 12 is 3% of what number?
    a. 4   **b.** 40   **c.** 4000   **d.** 400

24. A company spends $1500 of its $7500 advertising budget on newspaper advertising. What percent of its advertising budget is spent on newspaper advertising?

　　a. 20%　　　　　**b.** 2%　　　　　**c.** 5%　　　　　**d.** 50%

25. Find the unit cost of $90 for 24 boards.

　　a. $0.27/board　　　**b.** $3.75/board　　　**c.** $2.70/board　　　**d.** $37.50/board

26. A customer buys a $18,400 car with a 15% down payment. Find the amount to be financed.

　　a. $2760　　　　**b.** $8640　　　　**c.** $15,640　　　　**d.** $12,580

27. The price of a certain stock increased from $160 per share to $170 per share. Find the percent increase in the price of the stock.

　　a. 62.5%　　　　**b.** 6.25%　　　　**c.** 5.88%　　　　**d.** 94%

28. You have a bank account balance of $176.84. You write checks for $23.75 and $75.81. You deposit $97.50. Find your new account balance.

　　a. $178.90　　　**b.** $174.78　　　**c.** $175.78　　　**d.** $174.98

29. The circle graph shows the annual expense of owning and operating a car. How much money was spent on insurance if the total annual expenses were $8700?

　　a. $1305　　　　**b.** $2175
　　c. $870　　　　**d.** $900

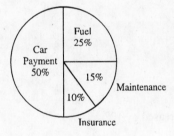

Annual Car Expenses

30. The double-bar graph shows the number of video games sold by a wholesale distributor during the last 4 months of 2000 and 2001. How many more video games did the distributor sell in 2001 than in 2000?

　　a. 3000 games　　　**b.** 2000 games
　　c. 4000 games　　　**d.** 5000 games

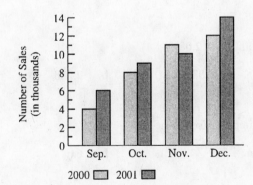

31. Convert 5000 lb to tons.

　　a. $2\frac{1}{2}$ tons　　　**b.** 5 tons　　　**c.** 50 tons　　　**d.** 25 tons

32. Convert $3\frac{1}{4}$ gal to cups.

　　a. 52 c　　　　**b.** 6 c　　　　**c.** 13 c　　　　**d.** 48 c

33. If cheddar cheese sells for 20¢ an ounce, what is the price of a wedge of cheddar cheese weighing 1 lb 6 oz?

    a. 44¢   **b.** $2.80   **c.** $3.20   **d.** $4.40

34. A piece of ribbon 1 ft long is cut from a 3-yard spool of ribbon. How much ribbon remains on the spool?

    a. 3 yd 1 ft   **b.** 3 yd 2 ft   **c.** 2 yd 2 ft   **d.** 2 yd 1 ft

35. Convert 5.32 km to meters.

    a. 532 m   **b.** 53.2 m   **c.** 0.00532 m   **d.** 5320 m

36. Convert 2560 ml to liters.

    a. 25.6 L   **b.** 256 L   **c.** 0.256 L   **d.** 2.56 L

37. A hiker can walk 5850 m in 1 hour. How many kilometers can the hiker walk in 3 hours?

    a. 175.5 km   **b.** 17.55 km   **c.** 1.755 km   **d.** 18.55 km

38. Which statement is correct?

    a. $-2 > -8$ **b.** $8 > 11$ **c.** $-8 > -4$ **d.** $0 < -5$

39. Add: $-48 + (-10)$

    a. 38   **b.** 58   **c.** -38 **d.** -58

40. What is 4 decreased by 12?

    a. -8 **b.** 8   **c.** $\dfrac{1}{3}$ **d.** $-\dfrac{1}{3}$

41. Multiply: $(2.08)(-1.1)$

    a. -2.288 **b.** 2.288   **c.** -22.88 **d.** -228.8

42. Simplify: $6xy - 3xy + 4xy - xy$

    a. $7xy$ **b.** $6xy$ **c.** $13xy$ **d.** $14xy$

43. Evaluate $a - 2b^2$ when $a = 3$ and $b = -2$.

    a. 5   **b.** -11 **c.** 11   **d.** -5

44. Solve: $y + 18 = -20$

    a. 38   **b.** -2 **c.** -38 **d.** 2

Final Exam Form H (*continued*)   Name: _____

45. Solve: $4x - 6 = 18$

    a. −6   **b.** 6   **c.** 3   **d.** −3

46. Solve: $4x - 3(x - 2) = 2(x + 3)$

    a. 1   **b.** 0   **c.** 12   **d.** −12

47. Translate "the product of five and the total of a number and ten is negative twenty" into an equation and solve.

    a. −2   **b.** −14   **c.** −6   **d.** −25

48. Find the area of the figure.

    a. 68 cm^2 **b.** 56 cm^2

    c. 72 cm^2 **d.** 64 cm^2

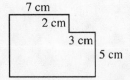

49. Find the volume of the figure.

    a. 324 ft^3 **b.** 32.4 ft^3

    c. 3240 ft^3 **d.** 344 ft^3

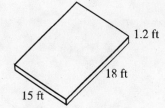

50. Triangles *ABC* and *DEF* are similar. Find the perimeter of triangle *DEF*.

    a. 8.9 m   **b.** 11.4 m

    c. 1.14 m   **d.** 12.2 m

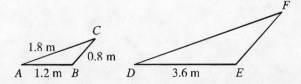

ANSWERS TO TESTS

Forms A-H

Chapter 1 Test Form A

1. $>$ (1.1A)

2. Fifty-seven thousand three (1.1B)

3. $4,007,085$ (1.1B)

4. $300,000 + 7000 + 400 + 20$ (1.1C)

5. $47,930$ (1.1D)

6. $84,995$ (1.2A)

7. $12,284$ (1.2B)

8. $859 (1.2B)

9. 1143 (1.3A)

10. $18,988$ (1.3B)

11. $638 (1.3C)

12. $211,448$ (1.4A)

13. $1,262,208$ (1.4B)

14. $11,628 (1.4C)

15. 603 (1.5A)

16. $1763\,\text{r}\,6$ (1.5B)

17. $153\,\text{r}\,42$ (1.5C)

18. 29 miles (1.5D)

19. $3^2 \cdot 5^3$ (1.6A)

20. 432 (1.6A)

21. 40 (1.6B)

22. 11 (1.6B)

23. $1, 5, 11, 55$ (1.7A)

24. $2 \cdot 2 \cdot 2 \cdot 3$ (1.7B)

25. $2 \cdot 5 \cdot 11$ (1.7B)

Chapter 2 Test Form A

1. 40 (2.1A)

2. 5 (2.1B)

3. $\dfrac{3}{2}$ (2.2A)

4. $3\dfrac{1}{3}$ (2.2B)

5. $\dfrac{55}{12}$ (2.2B)

6. 21 (2.3A)

7. $\dfrac{3}{20}$ (2.3B)

8. $1\dfrac{1}{2}$ (2.4A)

9. $\dfrac{43}{48}$ (2.4B)

10. $7\dfrac{13}{20}$ (2.4C)

11. $6\dfrac{3}{8}$ inches (2.4D)

12. $\dfrac{3}{5}$ (2.5A)

13. $\dfrac{17}{48}$ (2.5B)

14. $2\dfrac{11}{24}$ (2.5C)

15. $27\dfrac{1}{12}$ inches (2.5D)

16. $\dfrac{1}{8}$ (2.6A)

17. 9 (2.6B)

18. $539 (2.6C)

19. $1\dfrac{1}{2}$ (2.7A)

20. $1\dfrac{14}{27}$ (2.7B)

21. 12 (2.7C)

22. $<$ (2.8A)

23. $\dfrac{5}{7}$ (2.8B)

24. $\dfrac{8}{21}$ (2.8C)

25. $\dfrac{5}{21}$ (2.8C)

Answers to Chapter Tests: Form A

Chapter 3 Test Form A

1. Forty-two and eighty-five thousandths (3.1A)

2. 409.016 (3.1A)

3. 15.150 (3.1B)

4. 24.18 (3.1B)

5. 310.1282 (3.2A)

6. 4550.927 (3.2A)

7. $1670.28 (3.2B)

8. 0.749696 (3.3A)

9. 14.1124 (3.3A)

10. 1.385 inches (3.3B)

11. 26.3175 (3.4A)

12. 58.824 (3.4A)

13. $40.59 (3.4B)

14. 5.9 (3.5A)

15. 6459.4 (3.5A)

16. $247.08 (3.5B)

17. $7\frac{6}{25}$ (3.6B)

18. 0.818 (3.6A)

19. < (3.6C)

20. > (3.6C)

Cumulative Test: Chapters 1-3 Form A

1. 309 r12 (1.5C)

2. 2025 (1.6A)

3. 12 (1.6B)

4. 120 (2.1A)

5. $2\frac{1}{13}$ (2.2B)

6. $\frac{43}{9}$ (2.2B)

7. 20 (2.3A)

8. $1\frac{2}{9}$ (2.4B)

9. $7\frac{11}{35}$ (2.4C)

10. $2\frac{8}{15}$ (2.5C)

11. $\frac{55}{74}$ (2.6A)

12. $16\frac{9}{10}$ (2.6B)

13. 6 (2.7A)

14. $1\frac{13}{28}$ (2.7B)

15. $\frac{1}{24}$ (2.8B)

16. $\frac{1}{2}$ (2.8C)

17. Twenty-two and thirty-seven thousandths. (3.1A)

18. 1717.719 (3.2A)

19. 47.188 (3.3A)

20. 21.36816 (3.4A)

21. 15.058 (3.5A)

22. 0.292 (3.6A)

23. $\frac{37}{50}$ (3.6B)

24. < (3.6C)

25. $9\frac{1}{3}$ hours (2.4D)

26. $2\frac{1}{4}$ hours (2.5D)

27. 260 miles (2.6C)

28. $188.72 (3.2B)

29. $7539.52 (3.4B)

30. 27 bolts (3.5B)

Chapter 4 Test Form A

1. $\frac{1}{2}$, 1:2, 1 to 2 (4.1A)

2. $\frac{3}{4}$, 3:4, 3 to 4 (4.1A)

3. $\dfrac{3}{1}$, 3:1, 3 to 1 (4.1A)

4. $\dfrac{2}{3}$, 2:3, 2 to 3 (4.1A)

5. $\dfrac{9}{11}$ (4.1B)

6. $\dfrac{1}{7}$ (4.1B)

7. $\dfrac{10 \text{ miles}}{3 \text{ hours}}$ (4.2A)

8. $5/2 boards (4.2A)

9. $7.85/hour (4.2B)

10. $0.60/pound (4.2B)

11. $8.72 (4.2C)

12. 51.6 miles/hour (4.2C)

13. True (4.3A)

14. Not true (4.3A)

15. 7.5 (4.3B)

16. 33.33 (4.3B)

17. $28 (4.3C)

18. 3.8 gallons (4.3C)

19. 30 defects (4.3C)

20. $117 (4.3C)

Chapter 5 Test Form A

1. 275% (5.1B)

2. $\dfrac{34}{75}$ (5.1A)

3. 590% (5.1B)

4. 0.87% (5.1B)

5. 18.75% (5.1B)

6. 0.038 (5.1A)

7. 14.4 (5.2A)

8. 11.675 (5.2A)

9. 83% of 15 (5.2A)

10. 0.3% of 90 (5.2A)

11. $49.28 (5.2B)

12. $16.77/hour (5.2B)

13. 13% (5.3A)

14. 247.06% (5.3A)

15. 5% (5.3B)

16. 57.4% (5.3B)

17. 65 (5.4A)

18. 90 (5.4A)

19. 50 questions (5.4B)

20. $1900/month (5.4B)

21. 42 (5.5A)

22. 20% (5.5A)

23. $2362.50 (5.5B)

24. 7.5% (5.5B)

25. $7500 (5.5B)

Chapter 6 Test Form A

1. $0.12 per ounce (6.1A)

2. 30 grams for $1.05 (6.1B)

3. $3.35 (6.1C)

4. $10.43/hour (6.2A)

5. 7% (6.2A)

6. $3.77 (6.2B)

7. $192.50 (6.2B)

8. 32% (6.2C)

9. $62,033 (6.2C)

10. $291.85 (6.2D)

11. $21.80 (6.2D)

12. $1858 (6.4A)

13. $14,708.14 (6.3B)

14. $14,080 (6.3A)

15. $609.48 (6.4B)

16. $742.50 (6.5A)

17. $212.27 (6.5B)

18. $203.40 (6.6A)

19. $311.04 (6.7A)

20. Yes (6.7B)

Answers to Chapter Tests: Form A

Cumulative Test: Chapters 4-6 Form A

1. $\frac{4}{1}$, 4 : 1, 4 to 1 (4.1A)

2. $\frac{1}{4}$ (4.1B)

3. 203 words/page (4.2B)

4. 72 words/minute (4.2C)

5. 8.4 (4.3B)

6. 273 employees (4.3C)

7. 0.09 (5.1A)

8. $\frac{31}{50}$ (5.1A)

9. 4.2% (5.1B)

10. 44% (5.1B)

11. 24.08 (5.2A)

12. $780 (5.2B)

13. 125% (5.3A)

14. 87.5% (5.3B)

15. 150 (5.4A)

16. 68 accidents (5.4B)

17. $0.49/pound (6.1A)

18. $1.28 (6.2B)

19. $18 (6.2D)

20. $1000 (6.3A)

Chapter 7 Test Form A

1. 400 books (7.1A)

2. $\frac{8}{11}$ (7.1A)

3. 31.4% (7.1A)

4. $\frac{4}{9}$ (7.1B)

5. $\frac{25}{72}$ (7.1B)

6. 50 books (7.2A)

7. 350 books (7.2A)

8. Poor (7.4A)

9. $178,500 (7.4A)

10. $500,000 (7.2B)

11. 2nd, 3rd, 4th quarters (7.2B)

12. $1,500,000 (7.2B)

13. $\frac{1}{3}$ (7.3A)

14. 35 cars (7.3A)

15. 36% (7.3A)

16. $\frac{21}{1}$ (7.3B)

17. 6 employees (7.3B)

18. $\frac{1}{8}$ (7.5A)

19. 9.8 (7.4B)

20. 900 (7.4B)

Chapter 8 Test Form A

1. $3\frac{5}{6}$ ft (8.1A)

2. 4 ft 8 in. (8.1B)

3. 1 ft 9 in. (8.1C)

4. 4 tons 1000 lb (8.2A)

5. 52 oz (8.2A)

6. 69 ft (8.1C)

7. 14 lb 14 oz (8.2B)

8. 2 lb 12 oz (8.2B)

9. 135 lb (8.2C)

10. $9.12 (8.2C)

11. $4\frac{1}{2}$ c (8.3A)

12. 2 c (8.3A)

13. 8 gal 1 qt (8.3B)

14. 8 gal 1 qt (8.3B)

15. 8 servings (8.3C)

16. 9 qt (8.3C)

17. $600\,\frac{\text{ft} \cdot \text{lb}}{\text{s}}$ (8.4B)

18. 132,000 ft · lb (8.4A)

19. 3.5 hp (8.4B)

20. 300,000 ft · lb (8.4A)

Chapter 9 Test Form A

1. 73 cm (9.1A)
2. 34.27 m (9.1A)
3. 840,000 cm (9.1A)
4. 26.4 cm (9.1A)
5. 1.26 m (9.1B)
6. 12.96 m (9.1B)
7. 470 g (9.2A)
8. 80 cg (9.2A)
9. 0.39 kg (9.2A)
10. 2372 mg (9.2A)
11. $6.29 (9.2B)
12. 0.98 kg (9.2B)
13. 0.062 L (9.3A)
14. 9510 ml (9.3A)
15. 280 ml (9.3A)
16. 6.048 kl (9.3A)
17. 9.6 L (9.3B)
18. 6750 Calories (9.4A)
19. 45.5 m (9.5A)
20. 3280 ft (9.5B)

Cumulative Test: Chapters 7-9 Form A

1. $\frac{3}{5}$ (7.1B)
2. 2% (7.1B)
3. 600 (7.2A)
4. $\frac{5}{8}$ (7.2A)
5. 87 (7.4A)
6. 69° (7.4A)
7. 2.5 yd (8.1A)
8. 7 yd 2 ft (8.1B)
9. 88 oz (8.2A)
10. 52 oz (8.2B)
11. 56 pt (8.3A)
12. 3 c (8.3B)
13. 26 lb 6 oz (8.3B)

14. 0.00067 km (9.1A)
15. 0.071 g (9.2A)
16. 9.269 L (9.3A)
17. 8.48 qt (9.5A)
18. 109.3 mi/h (9.5B)
19. 35.2 m (9.1B)
20. 26.7 kg (9.2B)

Chapter 10 Test Form A

1. > (10.1A)
2. > (10.1A)
3. −36 (10.1B)
4. −5 (10.2A)
5. 7 (10.2A)
6. 4 (10.2B)
7. 17 (10.2B)
8. −66 (10.3A)
9. −4 (10.3B)
10. 16°C (10.3C)
11. −1°C (10.3C)
12. $-\frac{1}{4}$ (10.4B)
13. 0 (10.4A)
14. $-\frac{20}{21}$ (10.4A)
15. $\frac{17}{12}$ (10.4A)
16. $-\frac{1}{14}$ (10.4B)
17. 10 (10.4B)
18. −3.103 (10.4A)
19. −44.1 (10.4A)
20. −0.0192 (10.4B)
21. −20 (10.4B)
22. 9 (10.5B)
23. 12 (10.5B)
24. 1.02×10^{6} (10.5A)
25. 31.48°C (10.4C)

Answers to Chapter Tests: Form A

Chapter 11 Test Form A

1. -2 (11.1A)
2. -47 (11.1A)
3. $3x - 7y$ (11.1B)
4. $10x - 12$ (11.1C)
5. No (11.2A)
6. -17 (11.2B)
7. -9 (11.2C)
8. -12 (11.2C)
9. -5 (11.3A)
10. -6 (11.3A)
11. -6 (11.3A)
12. $120 (11.3B)
13. $-\dfrac{4}{3}$ (11.3A)
14. $1\dfrac{4}{5}$ (11.4A)
15. $2\dfrac{1}{2}$ (11.4B)
16. $5y^2 + x^2$ (11.5A)
17. $2n + 5$ (11.5B)
18. $n = 14$ (11.6A)
19. 8 (11.6B)
20. $2.17 (11.6B)

Chapter 12 Test Form A

1. $27°$ (12.1A)
2. $79°$ (12.1B)
3. $110°$ (12.1C)
4. $100°$ (12.1C)
5. 70 in. (12.1B)
6. 60.56 cm (12.2B)
7. $3690 (12.2C)
8. 4.55 m^2 (12.3A)
9. 975 cm^2 (12.3B)
10. 1.74 cm^2 (12.3B)
11. 7850 ft^2 (12.3C)
12. 729 cm^3 (12.4A)
13. 64 m^3 (12.4B)
14. $22\dfrac{1}{2}$ ft^3 (12.4C)
15. 12.649 (12.5A)
16. 30 in. (12.5B)
17. 15 ft (12.5C)
18. 7.5 ft (12.6A)
19. 30 ft (12.6B)
20. 4 m (12.6A)

Cumulative Test: Chapter 10-12 Form A

1. -24 (10.2A)
2. $-\dfrac{11}{12}$ (10.4A)
3. 46 (10.2B)
4. 10.3 (10.4A)
5. -105 (10.3A)
6. $\dfrac{1}{6}$ (10.4B)
7. -0.25 (10.4B)
8. 53,000 (10.5A)
9. 16 (10.5B)
10. 2 (11.1A)
11. $-14ab$ (11.1B)
12. -5 (11.2B)
13. 21 (11.2C)
14. 8 (11.3A)
15. -1 (11.4B)
16. 9 (11.6A)
17. $1860 (11.6B)
18. $95°F$ (11.6B)
19. $42°$ (12.1C)
20. $98°$ (12.1B)
21. 125.6 cm (12.2A)
22. 2464 cm^3 (12.4A)

23. 11.57 ft^2 (12.3B)

24. 11.0 in. (12.5B)

25. 3.5 in. (12.6A)

Final Exam Form A

1. 3269 (1.3B)

2. 37 (1.5C)

3. $\dfrac{1}{8}$ (2.7B)

4. $1151 (1.3C)

5. $7\dfrac{1}{12}$ (2.4C)

6. $2\dfrac{7}{8}$ (2.5C)

7. $\dfrac{1}{2}$ (2.6B)

8. 10 (1.6B)

9. $\dfrac{19}{36}$ (2.8C)

10. 1500 (3.5A)

11. 5.673 (3.3A)

12. 1.638 (3.4A)

13. $6\dfrac{3}{4}$ ft (2.5D)

14. $\dfrac{19}{20}$ (3.6B)

15. 0.778 (3.6A)

16. $\dfrac{4}{9}$ (4.1A)

17. 5¢/nail (4.2B)

18. 23.33 (4.3B)

19. $975 (4.3C)

20. 31.25% (5.1B)

21. 238.56 (5.2A)

22. 26% (5.3A)

23. 150 (5.4A)

24. 6.25% (5.3B)

25. $0.29/pen (6.1A)

26. $11.20 (6.2B)

27. 37.5% (6.2C)

28. $34,400 (6.6A)

29. $520 (7.1B)

30. $100,000 (7.2B)

31. 50 in. (8.1A)

32. 38 oz (8.2A)

33. 7 ft 10 in. (8.1C)

34. 6 mugs (8.3C)

35. 2910 g (9.2A)

36. 0.46 cm (9.1A)

37. 9.6 kg (9.2B)

38. > (10.1A)

39. −46 (10.2A)

40. 4 (10.4A)

41. $-\dfrac{5}{11}$ (10.4B)

42. 19 (10.5B)

43. 3 (11.1A)

44. 1 (11.2B)

45. −1 (11.3A)

46. −11 (11.4B)

47. 4 (11.6A)

48. 777 m^2 (12.3B)

49. 502.4 cm^3 (12.4B)

50. 45 m (12.6A)

Answers to Chapter Tests: Form B

Chapter 1 Test Form B

1. 708,020 (1.1B)
2. Three million seven thousand six hundred nine (1.1B)
3. < (1.1A)
4. $600,000 + 9000 + 5$ (1.1C)
5. 29,670 (1.1D)
6. 944,738 (1.2A)
7. 502,084 (1.2A)
8. $4316 (1.2B)
9. 2035 (1.3A)
10. 5502 (1.3B)
11. $1800 (1.3C)
12. 258,432 (1.4A)
13. 1,265,506 (1.4B)
14. 570 miles (1.4C)
15. 87 (1.5A)
16. $3561 \, r \, 2$ (1.5B)
17. $816 \, r \, 1$ (1.5C)
18. $531 (1.5D)
19. $3^3 \cdot 5^4$ (1.6A)
20. 1400 (1.6A)
21. 3 (1.6B)
22. 10 (1.6B)
23. 1, 2, 4, 7, 14, 28 (1.7A)
24. $2 \cdot 2 \cdot 5$ (1.7B)
25. $2 \cdot 3 \cdot 5 \cdot 5$ (1.7B)

Chapter 2 Test Form B

1. 120 (2.1A)
2. 9 (2.1B)
3. $1\frac{2}{3}$ (2.2A)
4. $4\frac{4}{5}$ (2.2B)
5. $\frac{32}{9}$ (2.2B)
6. 30 (2.3A)
7. $\frac{12}{23}$ (2.3B)
8. 1 (2.4A)
9. $1\frac{5}{24}$ (2.4B)
10. $6\frac{11}{35}$ (2.4C)
11. $\$48\frac{3}{8}$ (2.4D)
12. $\frac{10}{19}$ (2.5A)
13. $\frac{13}{24}$ (2.5B)
14. $7\frac{29}{36}$ (2.5C)
15. $9\frac{17}{24}$ yards (2.5D)
16. $\frac{1}{3}$ (2.6A)
17. 28 (2.6B)
18. $5\frac{1}{2}$ miles (2.6C)
19. $4\frac{4}{5}$ (2.7A)
20. $5\frac{5}{8}$ (2.7B)
21. $4875 (2.7C)
22. > (2.8A)
23. $\frac{4}{9}$ (2.8B)
24. 1 (2.8C)
25. $\frac{5}{8}$ (2.8C)

Chapter 3 Test Form B

1. Eighty-four and thirteen hundredths (3.1A)
2. 204.071 (3.1A)
3. 534.0 (3.1B)
4. 37.097 (3.1B)

5. 1799.80184 (3.2A)

6. 263.105 (3.2A)

7. $128.40 (3.2B)

8. 177.512 (3.3A)

9. 1.6782 (3.3A)

10. $11,031.37 (3.3B)

11. 233.1925 (3.4A)

12. 510.741 (3.4A)

13. $120.65 (3.4B)

14. 62.5 (3.5A)

15. 4319.2 (3.5A)

16. $2.86 (3.5B)

17. 2.556 (3.6A)

18. $\frac{5}{8}$ (3.6B)

19. > (3.6C)

20. < (3.6C)

Cumulative Test: Chapters 1-3 Form B

1. 603 r 7 (1.5C)

2. 432 (1.6A)

3. 45 (1.6B)

4. 120 (2.1A)

5. $6\frac{3}{7}$ (2.2B)

6. $\frac{51}{8}$ (2.2B)

7. 10 (2.3A)

8. $1\frac{17}{20}$ (2.4B)

9. $19\frac{4}{15}$ (2.4C)

10. $4\frac{5}{6}$ (2.5C)

11. $\frac{5}{42}$ (2.6A)

12. 4 (2.6B)

13. $\frac{2}{3}$ (2.7A)

14. $\frac{15}{32}$ (2.7B)

15. $\frac{32}{147}$ (2.8B)

16. $\frac{1}{2}$ (2.8C)

17. Nineteen and five hundred one ten-thousandths (3.1A)

18. 624.0521 (3.2A)

19. 104.442 (3.3A)

20. 0.28944 (3.4A)

21. 0.261 (3.5A)

22. 0.222 (3.6A)

23. $72\frac{3}{10}$ (3.6B)

24. < (3.6C)

25. $32\frac{1}{2}$ inches (2.4D)

26. 5 dolls (2.7C)

27. $827.15 (3.3B)

28. $304.22 (3.5B)

29. 9.4 pounds (3.2B)

30. $8673.60 (3.4B)

Chapter 4 Test Form B

1. $\frac{4}{1}$, 4:1, 4 to 1 (4.1A)

2. $\frac{8}{3}$, 8:3, 8 to 3 (4.1A)

3. $\frac{3}{7}$, 3:7, 3 to 7 (4.1A)

4. $\frac{4}{13}$, 4:13, 4 to 13 (4.1A)

5. $\frac{4}{3}$ (4.1B)

6. $\frac{21}{61}$ (4.1B)

7. $3/pound (4.2A)

Answers to Chapter Tests: Form B

8. $\dfrac{4 \text{ pounds}}{5 \text{ trees}}$ (4.2A)

9. 242 miles/day (4.2B)

10. $2.35/pound (4.2B)

11. $18.56/hour (4.2C)

12. 66 miles/hour (4.2C)

13. Not true (4.3A)

14. True (4.3A)

15. 14 (4.3B)

16. 4.22 (4.3B)

17. 12 boards (4.3C)

18. $5\dfrac{1}{4}$ teaspoons (4.3C)

19. $1306.25 (4.3C)

20. 3720 voters (4.3C)

Chapter 5 Test Form B

1. 390% (5.1B)

2. $\dfrac{4}{125}$ (5.1A)

3. 87.6% (5.1B)

4. 6.41 (5.1A)

5. 30% (5.1B)

6. 1.25% (5.1B)

7. 5.4 (5.2A)

8. 1.6 (5.2A)

9. 90% of 25,000 (5.2A)

10. 0.3% of 12 (5.2A)

11. $16,000 (5.2B)

12. $25.85 (5.2B)

13. 160% (5.3A)

14. 12.5% (5.3A)

15. 15% (5.3B)

16. 45% (5.3B)

17. 62.5 (5.4A)

18. 88 (5.4A)

19. 72,000 (5.4B)

20. 48 pages (5.4B)

21. 1600 (5.5A)

22. 16.4% (5.5A)

23. 0.4% (5.5B)

24. 136 questions (5.5B)

25. 40 students (5.5B)

Chapter 6 Test Form B

1. $6.85/pound (6.1A)

2. 12 quarts for $12.96 (6.1B)

3. $6.50 (6.1C)

4. 39% (6.2A)

5. 48 words per minute (6.2A)

6. $220.50 (6.2B)

7. $121.36 (6.2B)

8. $10,452 (6.2C)

9. 8% (6.2C)

10. $690 (6.2D)

11. $62.40 (6.2D)

12. $36,250 (6.4A)

13. $36,935.15 (6.3B)

14. $4500 (6.3A)

15. $1840.12 (6.4B)

16. $3179 (6.5A)

17. $300.86 (6.5B)

18. $2385 (6.6A)

19. $3831.09 (6.7A)

20. Yes (6.7B)

Cumulative Test: Chapters 4-6 Form B

1. $\dfrac{1}{6}$, 1:6, 1 to 6 (4.1A)

2. $\dfrac{11}{18}$ (4.1B)

3. $9.76/pound (4.2B)

4. 9.75 miles/hour (4.2C)

5. 2 (4.3B)

6. 1649 seeds (4.3C)

7. 0.59 (5.1A)

8. $\dfrac{2}{25}$ (5.1A)

9. 936% (5.1B)

10. 87.5% (5.1B)

11. 15.33 (5.2A)

12. $145,431 (5.2B)

13. 125% (5.3A)

14. 81.8% (5.3B)

15. 250 (5.4A)

16. 168 crimes (5.4B)

17. 12.4¢ / ounce (6.1A)

18. $1.30 (6.2B)

19. $24 (6.2D)

20. $9200 (6.3A)

Chapter 7 Test Form B

1. $130 (7.1A)

2. $\frac{7}{8}$ (7.1A)

3. $\frac{1}{4}$ (7.1B)

4. $\frac{24}{5}$ (7.1B)

5. $6000 (7.2A)

6. 1st quarter (7.2A)

7. $29,000 (7.2A)

8. 152.875 (7.4A)

9. 141 compact discs (7.4A)

10. March (7.2B)

11. 10,000 cars (7.2B)

12. 66,000 cars (7.2B)

13. 16 employees (7.3A)

14. 62.5% (7.3A)

15. 30 customers (7.3B)

16. 14% (7.3B)

17. $\frac{20}{37}$ (7.3B)

18. $\frac{1}{18}$ (7.5A)

19. 110 (7.4B)

20. $15,400 (7.4B)

Chapter 8 Test Form B

1. 21 yd (8.1A)

2. $\frac{7}{10}$ mi (8.1B)

3. 9 ft 8 in. (8.1C)

4. 6 pots (8.1C)

5. 3 lb 2 oz (8.2A)

6. $3\frac{4}{5}$ tons (8.2A)

7. 4 lb 13 oz (8.2B)

8. 29 lb 13 oz (8.2B)

9. 2 lb 7 oz (8.2C)

10. 3 lb 12 oz (8.2C)

11. $5\frac{1}{2}$ gal (8.3A)

12. 5 pt (8.3A)

13. 13 c 4 fl oz (8.3B)

14. 5 c 5 fl oz (8.3B)

15. 55 qt (8.3C)

16. $33\frac{3}{4}$ qt (8.3C)

17. 45,000 ft·lb (8.4A)

18. 80,000 ft·lb (8.4A)

19. 2475 $\frac{\text{ft}\cdot\text{lb}}{\text{s}}$ (8.5A)

20. 4000 $\frac{\text{ft}\cdot\text{lb}}{\text{s}}$ (8.5A)

Chapter 9 Test Form B

1. 560 mm (9.1A)

2. 76,500 m (9.1A)

3. 305 cm (9.1A)

4. 18.025 km (9.1A)

5. 2.9 m (9.1B)

6. 23.250 km (9.1B)

7. 23 mg (9.2A)

8. 3.716 kg (9.2A)

9. 7.083 kg (9.2A)

Answers to Chapter Tests: Form B

10. 5.760 kg (9.2A)

11. 1.175 kg (9.2B)

12. $35.11 (9.2B)

13. 130 ml (9.3A)

14. 0.037 L (9.3A)

15. 1.345 kl (9.3A)

16. 2.065 L (9.3A)

17. 12 L (9.3B)

18. 2.5 h (9.4A)

19. 72.73 kg (9.5A)

20. 60.06 in. (9.5B)

Cumulative Test: Chapters 7-9 Form B

1. $487.50 (7.1B)

2. $\frac{10}{7}$ (7.1B)

3. 4th quarter (7.2B)

4. $30,000 (7.2B)

5. $61.75 (7.4A)

6. 60 calls (7.4A)

7. $3\frac{1}{4}$ ft (8.1A)

8. 62 ft (8.1B)

9. 30.5 lb (8.2A)

10. 10 lb 2 oz (8.2B)

11. 20 pt (8.3A)

12. 192 servings (8.3C)

13. 18 ft (8.1C)

14. 1.96 m (9.1A)

15. 5.917 g (9.2A)

16. 0.192 L (9.3A)

17. 196.8 ft (9.5B)

18. 721.6 ft/s (9.5B)

19. 30.6 m (9.1B)

20. 14 L (9.3C)

Chapter 10 Test Form B

1. > (10.1A)

2. > (10.1A)

3. 23 (10.1B)

4. 14 (10.2A)

5. −3 (10.2A)

6. −19 (10.2B)

7. −1 (10.2B)

8. −63 (10.3A)

9. 16 (10.3B)

10. −7°C (10.3C)

11. −3° (10.3C)

12. $-\frac{1}{15}$ (10.4A)

13. $-\frac{7}{24}$ (10.4A)

14. $-\frac{7}{9}$ (10.4A)

15. $-\frac{7}{12}$ (10.4A)

16. $\frac{3}{14}$ (10.4B)

17. −2 (10.4B)

18. −9.54 (10.4A)

19. 6.4 (10.4A)

20. 13.065 (10.4B)

21. −0.2 (10.4B)

22. −1 (10.5B)

23. 15 (10.5B)

24. 6.04×10^{-5} (10.5A)

25. 4.8°C (10.4C)

Chapter 11 Test Form B

1. 14 (11.1A)

2. $-\frac{5}{18}$ (11.1A)

3. $-12x - 2y$ (11.1B)

4. $y + 12$ (11.1C)

5. Yes (11.2A)

6. −30 (11.2B)

7. 6 (11.2C)

8. −15 (11.2C)

9. 6 (11.3A)

10. 21 (11.3A)

11. 12% (11.2D)

12. $49,000 (11.3B)

13. $\frac{3}{2}$ (11.3A)

14. 1 (11.4A)

15. 4 (11.4B)

16. $m(12+m)$ (11.5A)

17. $3+(n+9)$ (11.5B)

18. 14 (11.6A)

19. 2 (11.6B)

20. $26,000 (11.6B)

Chapter 12 Test Form B

1. 165° (12.1A)

2. 53° and 90° (12.1B)

3. 105° (12.1C)

4. 45° (12.1C)

5. 50.24 cm (10.2A)

6. 30.28 ft (12.2B)

7. $169.20 (12.2C)

8. $1\frac{1}{3}$ ft^2 (12.3A)

9. 14.13 in.^{2} (12.3B)

10. 37.12 m^2 (12.3B)

11. $384 (12.3C)

12. $42\frac{7}{8}$ in.^{3} (12.4A)

13. 220.26 ft^3 (12.4B)

14. 7.0 gal (12.4C)

15. 9.055 (12.5A)

16. 8.5 in. (12.5B)

17. 10.9 ft (12.5C)

18. 7 ft (12.6A)

19. 17.5 m (12.6B)

20. 3 ft (12.6B)

Cumulative Test: Chapters 10-12 Form B

1. −20 (10.2A)

2. $-\frac{35}{36}$ (10.4A)

3. −23 (10.2B)

4. 19.66 (10.4A)

5. 140 (10.3A)

6. $\frac{15}{64}$ (10.4B)

7. −520 (10.4B)

8. −26 (10.5B)

9. 32 (10.5A)

10. $5x^2 - y$ (11.1B)

11. 28 (11.1A)

12. −3 (11.3A)

13. −30 (11.2C)

14. 12 (11.2B)

15. 8 (11.4B)

16. 6 (11.6A)

17. 4 (11.3B)

18. 77°F (11.6B)

19. 124° (12.1C)

20. 63° (12.1B)

21. $12\frac{1}{2}$ in. (12.2A)

22. 34.2 ft^2 (12.3B)

23. 8.1 mm (12.5B)

24. 373.248 cm^3 (12.4A)

25. 36 cm (12.6A)

Answers to Chapter Tests: Form B

Final Exam Form B

1. 44,808 (1.3B)
2. 34 (1.5C)
3. 6 (1.6B)
4. $890 (1.4C)
5. $2\frac{7}{9}$ (2.4C)
6. $1\frac{9}{14}$ (2.5C)
7. 2 (2.6B)
8. $\frac{11}{16}$ (2.7B)
9. $\frac{1}{2}$ (2.8C)
10. $11\frac{5}{24}$ lb (2.4D)
11. 3.018 (3.3A)
12. 0.429 (3.4A)
13. 129.03 (3.5A)
14. $\frac{18}{25}$ (3.6B)
15. 0.233 (3.6A)
16. $\frac{5}{4}$ (4.1A)
17. $0.67/tablet (4.2A)
18. 10.93 (4.3B)
19. 1.5 oz (4.3C)
20. 12.5% (5.1B)
21. 51.2 (5.2A)
22. 80% (5.3A)
23. 120 (5.4A)
24. 83.3% (5.3B)
25. $3.99/pound (6.1A)
26. $19,008 (6.5A)
27. $1290.05 (6.7A)
28. 25% (6.2A)
29. $1050 (7.1B)
30. September (7.2A)
31. 4.375 lb (8.2A)
32. 10 qt (8.3A)
33. 2 lb 8 oz (8.2C)
34. 9 bricks (8.1C)
35. 2.892 km (9.1A)
36. 2760 ml (9.3A)
37. 5 L (9.3B)
38. > (10.1A)
39. $\frac{3}{14}$ (10.4A)
40. 5 (10.2B)
41. −0.64 (10.4B)
42. 11 (10.5B)
43. 22 (11.1A)
44. 5 (11.2B)
45. 6 (11.3A)
46. 5 (11.4B)
47. 1 (11.5B)
48. 120 in.^{2} (12.3B)
49. 576 cm^3 (12.4B)
50. 13.3 cm (12.6A)

Chapter 1 Test Form C

1. < (1.1A)

2. Five hundred twelve thousand thirteen (1.1B)

3. 10,810 (1.1B)

4. $30,000 + 200 + 90$ (1.1C)

5. 13,000 (1.1D)

6. 86,899 (1.2A)

7. 592,262 (1.2A)

8. $345 (1.2B)

9. 5220 (1.3A)

10. 25,935 (1.3B)

11. $595 (1.3C)

12. 5778 (1.4A)

13. 1,542,794 (1.4B)

14. $480 (1.4C)

15. 294 (1.5A)

16. $2310\,r\,6$ (1.5B)

17. $13\,r\,190$ (1.5C)

18. 1,440,000 (1.5D)

19. $2^3 \cdot 3^2 \cdot 5^2$ (1.6A)

20. 1568 (1.6A)

21. 8 (1.6B)

22. 14 (1.6B)

23. 1, 2, 4, 8, 16, 32 (1.7A)

24. $3 \cdot 5 \cdot 7$ (1.7B)

25. $2 \cdot 2 \cdot 2 \cdot 2 \cdot 2 \cdot 2$ (1.7B)

Chapter 2 Test Form C

1. 98 (2.1A)

2. 7 (2.1B)

3. $\frac{17}{6}$ (2.2A)

4. $4\frac{1}{2}$ (2.2B)

5. $\frac{39}{5}$ (2.2B)

6. 8 (2.3A)

7. $\frac{11}{15}$ (2.3B)

8. $1\frac{1}{2}$ (2.4A)

9. $\frac{23}{24}$ (2.4B)

10. $9\frac{19}{24}$ (2.4C)

11. 11 (2.4D)

12. $\frac{3}{8}$ (2.5A)

13. $\frac{19}{40}$ (2.5B)

14. $11\frac{77}{100}$ (2.5C)

15. $\$66\frac{3}{4}$ (2.5D)

16. $\frac{9}{14}$ (2.6A)

17. $3\frac{41}{60}$ (2.6B)

18. 425 miles (2.6C)

19. $1\frac{5}{7}$ (2.7A)

20. $2\frac{3}{10}$ (2.7B)

21. $960 (2.7C)

22. < (2.8A)

23. $\frac{3}{5}$ (2.8B)

24. $\frac{19}{24}$ (2.8C)

25. $\frac{17}{45}$ (2.8C)

Answers to Chapter Tests: Form C

Chapter 3 Test Form C

1. One hundred twenty-nine and four hundredths (3.1A)

2. 7.0205 (3.1A)

3. 47.28 (3.1B)

4. 3792.70 (3.1B)

5. 219.839 (3.2A)

6. 1921.333 (3.2A)

7. $954.97 (3.2B)

8. 2.1657 (3.3A)

9. 83.073 (3.3A)

10. $2275.32 (3.3B)

11. 0.19872 (3.4A)

12. 0.02511 (3.4A)

13. 381.1 miles (3.4B)

14. 548 (3.5A)

15. 0.149 (3.5A)

16. $7.55/hour (3.5B)

17. 0.389 (3.6A)

18. $\dfrac{9}{40}$ (3.6B)

19. < (3.6C)

20. < (3.6C)

Cumulative Test: Chapters 1-3 Form C

1. 217 r 4 (1.5C)

2. 441 (1.6A)

3. 44 (1.6B)

4. 120 (2.1A)

5. $6\dfrac{1}{6}$ (2.2B)

6. $\dfrac{59}{9}$ (2.2B)

7. 42 (2.3A)

8. $1\dfrac{17}{36}$ (2.4B)

9. $11\dfrac{31}{35}$ (2.4C)

10. $2\dfrac{19}{24}$ (2.5C)

11. $\dfrac{2}{25}$ (2.6A)

12. 70 (2.6B)

13. $1\dfrac{1}{6}$ (2.7A)

14. 16 (2.7B)

15. $\dfrac{1}{18}$ (2.8B)

16. $\dfrac{25}{28}$ (2.8C)

17. Fifty-eight and twenty-three thousandths (3.1A)

18. 226.939 (3.2A)

19. 159.254 (3.3A)

20. 1.56716 (3.4A)

21. 23.911 (3.5A)

22. 0.308 (3.6A)

23. $\dfrac{3}{200}$ (3.6B)

24. > (3.6C)

25. $9\dfrac{1}{8}$ miles (2.5D)

26. $473 (2.6C)

27. 13 hours (2.4D)

28. $1082 (3.2B)

29. 11,975.80 (3.4B)

30. 22,000 gallons (3.5B)

Chapter 4 Test Form C

1. $\dfrac{1}{9}$, 1:9, 1 to 9 (4.1A)

2. $\dfrac{4}{9}$, 4:9, 4 to 9 (4.1A)

3. $\dfrac{3}{7}$, 3:7, 3 to 7 (4.1A)

4. $\dfrac{1}{4}$, 1:4, 1 to 4 (4.1A)

5. $\frac{1}{3}$ (4.1B)

6. $\frac{1}{5}$ (4.1B)

7. $\frac{40 \text{ miles}}{3 \text{ gallons}}$ (4.2A)

8. $\frac{28 \text{ ounces}}{5 \text{ vials}}$ (4.2A)

9. 27.2 miles/gallon (4.2B)

10. 65.8 meters/second (4.2B)

11. $1.84 (4.2C)

12. $2.40/pound (4.2C)

13. Not true (4.3A)

14. True (4.3A)

15. 36 (4.3B)

16. 30.5 (4.3B)

17. 400 pounds (4.3C)

18. 20 miles (4.3C)

19. 6900 voters (4.3C)

20. $21.60 (4.3C)

Chapter 5 Test Form C

1. 0.05 (5.1A)

2. 0.068 (5.1A)

3. 7.2% (5.1B)

4. 360% (5.1B)

5. 60% (5.1B)

6. 162.5% (5.1B)

7. 18.24 (5.2A)

8. 20.8 (5.2A)

9. 115% of 8 (5.2A)

10. 0.6% of 1110 (5.2A)

11. $504 (5.2B)

12. 69 (5.2B)

13. 28% (5.3A)

14. 66.67% (5.3A)

15. 85% (5.3B)

16. 6% (5.3B)

17. 120 (5.4A)

18. 205 (5.4A)

19. $12,400 (5.4B)

20. 6500 students (5.4B)

21. 12,000 (5.5A)

22. 30% (5.5A)

23. $600 (5.5B)

24. 7.5% (5.5B)

25. 22,152 people (5.5B)

Chapter 6 Test Form C

1. $3.79/pound (6.1A)

2. 250 tablets for $10.50 (6.1B)

3. $4.45 (6.1C)

4. $455.40/week (6.2A)

5. 12% (6.2A)

6. $406 (6.2B)

7. $0.17 (6.2B)

8. 160 people (6.2C)

9. 4% (6.2C)

10. $285 (6.2D)

11. $220 (6.2D)

12. $31,875 (6.3A)

13. $3131.36 (6.3B)

14. $2700 (6.4A)

15. $719.78 (6.4B)

16. $835 (6.5A)

17. $176.79 (6.5B)

18. $18.63/hour (6.6A)

19. $1470.81 (6.7A)

20. Yes (6.7B)

Cumulative Test: Chapters 4-6 Form C

1. $\frac{1}{4}$, 1:4, 1 to 4 (4.1A)

2. $\frac{8}{7}$ (4.1B)

3. 24 miles/hour (4.2B)

Answers to Chapter Tests: Form C

4. 340 words/minute (4.2C)

5. 57 (4.3B)

6. 1000 students (4.3C)

7. 1.07 (5.1A)

8. $\frac{16}{25}$ (5.1A)

9. 380% (5.1B)

10. 45.8% (5.1B)

11. 11.5 (5.2A)

12. 180 fewer units (5.2B)

13. 20% (5.3A)

14. 71.4% (5.3B)

15. 500 (5.4A)

16. 260 cars (5.4B)

17. $0.09/ounce (6.1A)

18. $10.80 (6.2B)

19. $26.25 (6.2D)

20. $12,948 (6.3A)

Chapter 7 Test Form C

1. 2800 students (7.1A)

2. $\frac{7}{2}$ (7.1A)

3. 57.9% (7.1A)

4. $480 (7.1B)

5. $704 (7.1B)

6. $320 (7.1B)

7. 27,000 cars (7.2A)

8. 1000 cars (7.2A)

9. Good (7.4A)

10. $\frac{3}{7}$ (7.5A)

11. 20,000 (7.2B)

12. 2nd week (7.2B)

13. 135,000 (7.2B)

14. $\frac{5}{4}$ (7.3A)

15. 17 (7.3A)

16. 34.2% (7.3A)

17. 25 (7.3B)

18. 30.8% (7.3B)

19. 19 points (7.4A)

20. 72 points (7.4B)

Chapter 8 Test Form C

1. 8 ft (8.1A)

2. 16 ft 8 in. (8.1B)

3. $3\frac{1}{24}$ in. (8.1C)

4. 45 in. (8.1C)

5. $2\frac{1}{2}$ lb (8.2A)

6. 4500 lb (8.2A)

7. 5 tons 700 lb (8.2B)

8. 1 ton 800 lb (8.2B)

9. 27 lb (8.2C)

10. 4 lb 14 oz (8.2C)

11. 8 qt (8.3A)

12. $4\frac{1}{2}$ gal (8.3A)

13. 1 gal 3 qt (8.3B)

14. 9 qt (8.3B)

15. 16 mugs (8.3C)

16. 1 gallon (8.3C)

17. 1,750,000 ft·lb (8.4A)

18. 405,000 ft·lb (8.4A)

19. $2475 \frac{\text{ft} \cdot \text{lb}}{\text{s}}$ (8.4B)

20. $120 \frac{\text{ft} \cdot \text{lb}}{\text{s}}$ (8.4B)

Chapter 9 Test Form C

1. 23,200 m (9.1A)

2. 43.2 cm (9.1A)

3. 7.89 m (9.1A)

4. 2.035 km (9.1A)

5. 32 m (9.1B)

6. 1.25 m (9.1B)

7. 0.027 g (9.2A)

8. 46 g (9.2A)

9. 2.470 kg (9.2A)

10. 35.004 g (9.2A)

11. 2300 g (9.2B)

12. 197 kg (9.2B)

13. 36 cm³ (9.3A)

14. 2050 ml (9.3A)

15. 5.294 L (9.3A)

16. 6.050 kl (9.3A)

17. 12 L (9.3B)

18. 7800 Calories (9.4A)

19. 39.62 L (9.5A)

20. 14.64 oz (9.5B)

Cumulative Test: Chapters 7-9 Form C

1. $\frac{7}{11}$ (7.1B)

2. $\frac{3}{145}$ (7.1B)

3. 30 (7.3A)

4. 22.2% (7.3A)

5. $128.67 (7.4A)

6. 6.5 alarms (7.4A)

7. 14 ft (8.1A)

8. 6 ft 6 in. (8.1B)

9. 112 oz (8.2A)

10. 16 tons 100 lb (8.2B)

11. 6 c (8.3A)

12. 24 fl oz (8.3C)

13. $21\frac{1}{3}$ ft (8.1A)

14. 7.539 km (9.1A)

15. 1,347,000 mg (9.2A)

16. 1340 ml (9.2A)

17. $26\frac{2}{5}$ lb (9.5A)

18. $8.04/kg (9.5A)

19. 625 people (9.3B)

20. 115.75 kg (9.2B)

Chapter 10 Test Form C

1. < (10.1A)

2. > (10.1A)

3. $-\frac{1}{2}$ (10.1B)

4. −55 (10.2A)

5. −7 (10.2A)

6. −12 (10.2B)

7. 0 (10.2B)

8. −480 (10.3A)

9. 23 (10.3B)

10. 31° (10.3B)

11. 5° (10.3B)

12. $\frac{1}{4}$ (10.4A)

13. $\frac{11}{24}$ (10.4A)

14. $-\frac{1}{3}$ (10.4A)

15. $-8\frac{1}{24}$ (10.4A)

16. $\frac{2}{7}$ (10.4B)

17. −36 (10.4B)

18. −2.15 (10.4A)

19. −6.19 (10.4A)

20. 0.1203 (10.4B)

21. −180 (10.4B)

22. 2 (10.5B)

23. −3 (10.5B)

24. 1.07×10^{-4} (10.5A)

25. 66.38°C (10.4C)

Answers to Chapter Tests: Form C

Chapter 11 Test Form C

1. -21 (11.1A)

2. $-\dfrac{1}{12}$ (11.1A)

3. $7x - 13y$ (11.1B)

4. $2n + 7$ (11.1C)

5. No (11.2A)

6. -11 (11.2B)

7. -9 (11.2C)

8. 24 (11.2C)

9. -6 (11.2D)

10. -15 (11.3A)

11. $188 (11.3A)

12. 20% (11.3B)

13. $\dfrac{13}{3}$ (11.3A)

14. 5 (11.4A)

15. 10 (11.4B)

16. $\dfrac{z}{3+z}$ (11.5A)

17. $\dfrac{2n}{n-2}$ (11.5B)

18. -50 (11.6A)

19. 9 (11.6B)

20. $24,250 (11.6B)

Chapter 12 Test Form C

1. $14°$ (12.1A)

2. $80°$ (12.1B)

3. $125°$ (12.1C)

4. $140°$ (12.1C)

5. 5 ft 4 in. (12.2A)

6. 64 cm (12.2B)

7. $11\dfrac{2}{3}$ ft (12.2C)

8. 9.61 m^2 (12.3A)

9. 121.12 in.^{2} (12.3B)

10. $629 (12.3C)

11. 69.3 yd^2 (12.3C)

12. 904.32 cm^3 (12.4A)

13. 45.42 ft^3 (12.4B)

14. $10,597.5$ ft^3 (12.4C)

15. 11.402 (12.5A)

16. 6.6 m (12.5B)

17. 50 mi (12.5C)

18. 25 m (12.6A)

19. 21.3 ft (12.6B)

20. $85°$ (12.6B)

Cumulative Test: Chapters 10-12 Form C

1. -14 (10.2A)

2. $-\dfrac{7}{8}$ (10.4A)

3. 2 (10.2B)

4. 7.47 (10.4A)

5. 600 (10.3A)

6. $-\dfrac{6}{13}$ (10.4B)

7. 42 (10.3B)

8. -20 (10.5B)

9. -12 (10.5B)

10. -13 (11.1A)

11. 25 (11.2C)

12. $6y^2 - 3$ (11.1B)

13. 5 (11.3A)

14. $-\dfrac{5}{6}$ (11.2B)

15. 2 (11.4B)

16. -8 (11.5B)

17. $48 (11.6B)

18. $70,400 (11.6B)

19. $132°$ (12.1A)

20. $73°$ (12.1C)

21. $8\frac{1}{2}$ in. (12.2A)

22. 98 cm² (12.3B)

23. 310.18 m³ (12.4A)

24. 29.2 cm (12.6A)

25. 6.3 m (12.5B)

Final Exam Form C

1. 3429 (1.3B)

2. 63 (1.5C)

3. 8 (1.6B)

4. $342.44/month (1.5D)

5. $2\frac{13}{20}$ (2.4C)

6. $5\frac{7}{9}$ (2.5B)

7. $9\frac{1}{2}$ (2.6B)

8. $1\frac{5}{9}$ (2.7B)

9. $\frac{7}{18}$ (2.8C)

10. 40 questions (2.6C)

11. 22.87 (3.3A)

12. 5.705 (3.4A)

13. 63.16 (3.5A)

14. $\frac{3}{5}$ (3.6B)

15. 0.471 (3.6A)

16. $\frac{6}{5}$ (4.1A)

17. 12 tiles/ft (4.2A)

18. 12.8 (4.3B)

19. $5.88 (4.3C)

20. 95% (5.1B)

21. 24.22 (5.2A)

22. 20% (5.3A)

23. 148 (5.4A)

24. 2100 students (5.2B)

25. $0.89/lb (6.1A)

26. 28 oz for $0.65 (6.1B)

27. $700 (6.2D)

28. $2231.25 (6.3A)

29. $412.50 (7.1B)

30. 8 (7.3A)

31. $4\frac{1}{3}$ ft (8.1A)

32. 40 c (8.3A)

33. 3 qt (8.3C)

34. 7 yd 1 ft (8.1C)

35. 25.6 cm (9.1A)

36. 800 cm (9.1A)

37. 5.25 m (9.1B)

38. < (10.1A)

39. $-1\frac{1}{12}$ (10.4A)

40. 19 (10.2B)

41. 7.44 (10.4B)

42. −5 (10.5B)

43. −5 (11.1A)

44. 11 (11.2B)

45. 6 (11.3A)

46. 2 (11.4B)

47. 2 (11.6A)

48. 146.24 cm² (12.3B)

49. 80 cm³ (12.4B)

50. 3.6 mm (12.6A)

Answers to Chapter Tests: Form D

Chapter 1 Test Form D

1. < (1.1A)

2. One hundred ten thousand three hundred forty-seven (1.1B)

3. 22,022 (1.1B)

4. $60,000 + 7000 + 20$ (1.1C)

5. 325,700 (1.1D)

6. 241,000 (1.2A)

7. 43,402 (1.2B)

8. 1474 (1.2C)

9. 5231 (1.3A)

10. 2758 (1.3B)

11. 20,400 miles (1.3C)

12. 4842 (1.4A)

13. 10,764 (1.4B)

14. $5028 (1.4C)

15. 420 (1.5A)

16. 1250 r 3 (1.5B)

17. 420 r 36 (1.5C)

18. $175 (1.5D)

19. $2^2 \cdot 7^3 \cdot 9$ (1.6A)

20. 432 (1.6A)

21. 0 (1.6B)

22. 6 (1.6B)

23. 1, 2, 4, 23, 46, 92 (1.7A)

24. $2 \cdot 2 \cdot 2 \cdot 11$ (1.7B)

25. $2 \cdot 3 \cdot 3 \cdot 5$ (1.7B)

Chapter 2 Test Form D

1. 90 (2.1A)

2. 9 (2.1B)

3. $3\frac{1}{4}$ (2.2A)

4. $4\frac{1}{3}$ (2.2B)

5. $\frac{37}{8}$ (2.2B)

6. 56 (2.3A)

7. $\frac{3}{8}$ (2.3B)

8. $\frac{1}{2}$ (2.4A)

9. $\frac{2}{3}$ (2.4B)

10. $6\frac{5}{24}$ (2.4C)

11. 12 (2.4D)

12. $\frac{3}{10}$ (2.5A)

13. $\frac{5}{48}$ (2.5B)

14. $5\frac{19}{36}$ (2.5C)

15. $8\frac{3}{4}$ pounds (2.5D)

16. $\frac{6}{35}$ (2.6A)

17. $17\frac{17}{18}$ (2.6B)

18. 350 miles (2.6C)

19. $\frac{25}{64}$ (2.7A)

20. 4 (2.7B)

21. 600 people (2.7C)

22. < (2.8A)

23. 36 (2.8B)

24. 1 (2.8C)

25. $7\frac{3}{4}$ (2.8C)

Chapter 3 Test Form D

1. Four and six hundred thirty-two thousandths (3.1A)

2. 12.06 (3.1A)

3. 12.14 (3.1B)

4.   43.1 (3.1B)

5.   1169.48 (3.2A)

6.   194.637 (3.2A)

7. $138.44 (3.2B)

8.   27.91 (3.3A)

9.   74.6373 (3.3A)

10. $4.84 (3.3B)

11. 0.00602 (3.4A)

12. 3.96 (3.4A)

13. 197.4 miles (3.4B)

14. 0.003 (3.5A)

15. 0.382 (3.5A)

16. $25.76/month (3.5B)

17. 0.225 (3.6A)

18. $\frac{1}{6}$ (3.6B)

19. > (3.6C)

20. > (3.6C)

Cumulative Test: Chapters 1-3 Form D

1.   261 r 7 (1.5C)

2.   4800 (1.6A)

3.   16 (1.6B)

4.   140 (2.1A)

5. $7\frac{3}{7}$ (2.2B)

6. $\frac{65}{7}$ (2.2B)

7.   68 (2.3A)

8. $1\frac{7}{18}$ (2.4B)

9. $10\frac{3}{70}$ (2.4C)

10. $4\frac{3}{8}$ (2.5C)

11. $\frac{5}{12}$ (2.6A)

12. 30 (2.6B)

13. $1\frac{2}{9}$ (2.7A)

14. $1\frac{1}{2}$ (2.7B)

15. $\frac{2}{225}$ (2.8B)

16. $\frac{37}{56}$ (2.8C)

17. Sixty-seven and thirteen thousandths (3.1A)

18. 422.439 (3.2A)

19. 2.27 (3.3A)

20. 0.48472 (3.4A)

21. 0.636 (3.5A)

22. 0.132 (3.6A)

23. $\frac{3}{25}$ (3.6B)

24. < (3.6C)

25. 60\frac{3}{4}$ (2.4D)

26. 110 problems (2.6C)

27. $696.57 (3.3B)

28. $9,328.40 (3.4B)

29. $90.56 (3.5B)

30. $5987.60 (3.5B)

Chapter 4 Test Form D

1. $\frac{3}{10}$, 3:10, 3 to 10 (4.1A)

2. $\frac{1}{3}$, 1:3, 1 to 3 (4.1A)

3. $\frac{9}{19}$, 9:19, 9 to 19 (4.1A)

4. $\frac{8}{5}$, 8:5, 8 to 5 (4.1A)

5. $\frac{1}{15}$ (4.1B)

6. $\frac{11}{17}$ (4.1B)

Answers to Chapter Tests: Form D

7. $\dfrac{\$25}{3 \text{ hours}}$ (4.2A)

8. $\dfrac{105 \text{ trees}}{1 \text{ acre}}$ (4.2A)

9. 55.4 miles/hour (4.2B)

10. 105 trees/acre (4.2B)

11. $42.56 (4.2C)

12. $36.00 (4.2C)

13. True (4.3A)

14. Not true (4.3A)

15. 57.6 (4.3B)

16. 18.5 (4.3B)

17. $\dfrac{9}{10}$ ounce (4.3C)

18. 280 faculty (4.3C)

19. $225 (4.3C)

20. 480 errors (4.3C)

Chapter 5 Test Form D

1. 0.0425 (5.1A)

2. $\dfrac{1}{6}$ (5.1A)

3. 9.2% (5.1B)

4. 275% (5.1B)

5. 37.5% (5.1B)

6. 240% (5.1B)

7. 286 (5.2A)

8. 0.99 (5.2A)

9. 0.6% of 8 (5.2A)

10. 28% of 2000 (5.2A)

11. 178,560 votes (5.2B)

12. $912 (5.2B)

13. 12% (5.3A)

14. 33.33% (5.3A)

15. 43.75% (5.3B)

16. 280% (5.3B)

17. 700 (5.4A)

18. 65.6 (5.4A)

19. $10.20/hour (5.4B)

20. 4.6 minutes (5.4B)

21. 350 (5.5A)

22. 180% (5.5A)

23. 50 questions (5.5B)

24. 1.6% (5.5B)

25. $478.80 (5.5B)

Chapter 6 Test Form D

1. $0.29/pound (6.1A)

2. 40 feet for $46.00 (6.1B)

3. $28.00 (6.1C)

4. 5% (6.2A)

5. $44.37 (6.2A)

6. $110.20 (6.2B)

7. $170.40 (6.2B)

8. 640 employees (6.2C)

9. $12,300 (6.2C)

10. $21 (6.2D)

11. $75.04 (6.2D)

12. $45.50 (6.3A)

13. $49,268.03 (6.3B)

14. $32,400 (6.4A)

15. $1071.45 (6.4B)

16. $269.10 (6.5A)

17. $0.11/mile (6.5B)

18. $14.49/hour (6.6A)

19. $1395.48 (6.7A)

20. Yes (6.7B)

Cumulative Test: Chapters 4-6 Form D

1. $\dfrac{3}{5}$, 3 : 5, 3 to 5 (4.1A)

2. $\dfrac{1}{6}$ (4.1B)

3. $1.60/foot (4.2B)

4. 29.2 miles/gallon (4.2C)

5. 0.5 (4.3B)

330

6. 2400 students (4.3C)

7. 1.45 (5.1A)

8. $\dfrac{21}{25}$ (5.1A)

9. 0.3% (5.1B)

10. 137.5% (5.1B)

11. 37.8 (5.2A)

12. $33,750 (5.2B)

13. 20% (5.3A)

14. 550% (5.3B)

15. 66 (5.4A)

16. $25,000 (5.4B)

17. $0.32 (6.1A)

18. $48.64 (6.2B)

19. $19.21 (6.2D)

20. $12 (6.3A)

Chapter 7 Test Form D

1. 3800 students (7.1A)

2. 26.3% (7.1A)

3. $\dfrac{3}{5}$ (7.1B)

4. $\dfrac{9}{8}$ (7.1B)

5. $\dfrac{8}{35}$ (7.1B)

6. $\dfrac{5}{7}$ (7.2A)

7. 1600 units (7.2A)

8. 150 units (7.2A)

9. Those who owed more than $150 (7.4A)

10. 33.4 cellular phones (7.4A)

11. 30,000 disks (7.2B)

12. November (7.2B)

13. 140,000 disks (7.2B)

14. 7 years (7.3A)

15. 57.5% (7.3A)

16. 21.9% (7.3B)

17. 8 cars (7.3B)

18. $\{(HH),(HT),(TH),(TT)\}$ (7.5A)

19. 69.5 words per minute (7.4A)

20. 89 points (7.4B)

Chapter 8 Test Form D

1. $6\dfrac{2}{3}$ yd (8.1A)

2. 2 ft 5 in. (8.1B)

3. 1 ft 3 in. (8.1C)

4. 26 ft (8.1C)

5. 50 oz (8.2A)

6. $3\dfrac{1}{4}$ tons (8.2A)

7. 1 ton 1800 lb (8.2B)

8. 6 lb 5 oz (8.2B)

9. 5 lb 10 oz (8.2C)

10. 5 lb 9 oz (8.2C)

11. 3 gal (8.3A)

12. $\dfrac{5}{8}$ gal (8.3A)

13. 1 gal 1 qt (8.3B)

14. 3 qt (8.3B)

15. $9\dfrac{3}{8}$ gal (8.3C)

16. 9 qt (8.3C)

17. 384,000 ft·lb (8.4A)

18. 216,000 ft·lb (8.4A)

19. 9.6 hp (8.4B)

20. $240\,\dfrac{\text{ft}\cdot\text{lb}}{\text{s}}$ (8.4B)

Chapter 9 Test Form D

1. 3.792 km (9.1A)

2. 6800 m (9.1A)

3. 52 mm (9.1A)

4. 72.4 cm (9.1A)

5. 120.96 m (9.1B)

6. 18.8 m (9.1B)

Answers to Chapter Tests: Form D

7. 60 g (9.2A)

8. 4.237 g (9.2A)

9. 2467 g (9.2A)

10. 6.084 g (9.2A)

11. 99 kg (9.2B)

12. $14.24 (9.2B)

13. 40 ml (9.3A)

14. 9.2 ml (9.3A)

15. 7.1 kl (9.3A)

16. 3.412 L (9.3A)

17. 74 servings (9.3B)

18. 9000 Calories (9.3B)

19. 1.75 m (9.4A)

20. 8.69 gal (9.4B)

Cumulative Test: Chapters 7-9 Form D

1. $450 (7.1B)

2. $90 (7.1B)

3. $\frac{5}{22}$ (7.3B)

4. 31.8% (7.3B)

5. 6.1 in. (7.4A)

6. 6.5 boxes (7.4A)

7. $2\frac{2}{3}$ ft (8.1A)

8. 19 ft 1 in. (8.1B)

9. 5.625 lb (8.2A)

10. 5 tons 1500 lb (8.2B)

11. 18 qt (8.3A)

12. 9 yd (8.1C)

13. 64 servings (8.3C)

14. 560 mm (9.1A)

15. 123 g (9.2A)

16. 1028 cm^3 (9.3A)

17. 3632 g (9.5B)

18. $2.07/qt (9.5B)

19. 31 m (9.1B)

20. 40 (9.2B)

Chapter 10 Test Form D

1. > (10.1A)

2. > (10.1A)

3. −2 (10.1B)

4. 18 (10.2A)

5. 2 (10.2A)

6. −20 (10.2B)

7. 1 (10.2B)

8. −400 (10.3A)

9. −3 (10.3B)

10. 19°C (10.3C)

11. 7° (10.3C)

12. $-\frac{1}{2}$ (10.4A)

13. $-3\frac{11}{12}$ (10.4A)

14. $-4\frac{2}{3}$ (10.4A)

15. $\frac{17}{30}$ (10.4A)

16. $-\frac{7}{24}$ (10.4B)

17. $2\frac{3}{5}$ (10.4B)

18. −2.9 (10.4A)

19. −1.97 (10.4A)

20. 4.32 (10.4B)

21. −3.52 (10.4B)

22. 1 (10.5B)

23. 2 (10.5B)

24. 1.476×10^7 (10.5A)

25. 6.27°C (10.4C)

Chapter 11 Test Form D

1. 14 (11.1A)

2. $\frac{3}{2}$ (11.1A)

3. $8x^2 - x$ (11.1B)

4. $-4y$ (11.1C)

5. No (11.2A)

6. -6 (11.2B)

7. 7 (11.2C)

8. 36 (11.2C)

9. 2 (11.3A)

10. -4 (11.3A)

11. $780 (11.2D)

12. 3.63 s (11.3B)

13. $\frac{4}{3}$ (11.3A)

14. -3 (11.4A)

15. -2 (11.4B)

16. $x+15x$ (11.5A)

17. $15(n+6)$ (11.5B)

18. -8 (11.6A)

19. -4 (11.6B)

20. $240 (11.6B)

Chapter 12 Test Form D

1. 155° (12.1A)

2. 67° (12.1B)

3. 160° (12.1C)

4. 70° (12.1C)

5. 140 cm (12.2A)

6. $13\frac{3}{4}$ in. (12.2B)

7. $14\frac{2}{3}$ ft (12.2C)

8. $18\frac{7}{9}$ ft^2 (12.3A)

9. 936 ft^2 (12.3B)

10. 78.50 ft^2 (12.3C)

11. 79.625 m^2 (12.3B)

12. 62.8 ft^3 (12.4A)

13. 504 m^3 (12.4B)

14. 5595.48 ft^3 (12.4C)

15. 9.899 (12.5A)

16. 6.9 cm (12.5A)

17. 22.4 ft (12.5A)

18. 13.5 cm (12.6A)

19. 15 m (12.6B)

20. 8 in. (12.6B)

Cumulative Test: Chapters 10-12 Form D

1. $-\frac{11}{18}$ (10.4A)

2. -14 (10.2A)

3. -40 (10.2B)

4. 13.3 (10.4A)

5. -3200 (10.3A)

6. $\frac{10}{21}$ (10.4B)

7. 42 (10.4B)

8. -18 (10.5A)

9. -8 (10.5A)

10. -24 (11.1A)

11. -15 (11.2B)

12. $-4w+5v$ (11.1B)

13. -24 (11.2C)

14. $-\frac{9}{5}$ (11.4B)

15. -3 (11.3A)

16. $4\frac{4}{5}$ (11.6A)

17. $3000/month (11.6B)

18. $217.50 (11.6B)

19. 136° (12.1C)

20. 7° (12.1B)

21. 50.24 cm (12.2A)

22. 153.12 in.^{2} (12.3B)

23. 46.92 m^3 (12.4A)

24. 4.7 in. (12.6B)

25. 16.4 ft (12.5B)

Answers to Chapter Tests: Form D

Final Exam Form D

1. 7833 (1.3B)
2. 32 (1.5C)
3. 21 (1.6B)
4. $1123 (1.3C)
5. $1\frac{11}{14}$ (2.4C)
6. $1\frac{11}{14}$ (2.5C)
7. $\frac{2}{3}$ (2.6B)
8. 5 (2.7B)
9. $\frac{13}{24}$ (2.8C)
10. $48\frac{7}{8}$ (2.4D)
11. 4.52 (3.3A)
12. 0.3 (3.4A)
13. 13.1 (3.5A)
14. $\frac{9}{20}$ (3.6B)
15. 0.76 (3.6A)
16. $\frac{3}{7}$ (4.1A)
17. $52.25/day (4.2B)
18. 31.2 (4.3B)
19. 7875 people (4.3C)
20. 140% (5.1B)
21. 128 (5.2A)
22. 5% (5.3A)
23. 550 (5.4A)
24. 84 days (5.2B)
25. $0.28/lb (6.1A)
26. 25% (6.2A)
27. $17.40 (6.2B)
28. $912.94 (6.7A)
29. $468 (7.1B)
30. November (7.2A)
31. 60 oz (8.2A)
32. $11\frac{1}{3}$ yd (8.1A)
33. 6 ft (8.1C)
34. 300 lb (8.2C)
35. 1.4 m (9.1A)
36. 2.5 kg (9.2A)
37. 2.775 kg (9.2B)
38. > (10.1A)
39. $1\frac{3}{4}$ (10.4A)
40. 3 (10.2B)
41. $-1\frac{1}{5}$ (10.4B)
42. 20 (10.5B)
43. −3 (11.1A)
44. −1 (11.4B)
45. −18 (11.2B)
46. 2 (11.3A)
47. −5 (11.6A)
48. 96 in.^{2} (12.3B)
49. 2310 cm^3 (12.4B)
50. 10 in.^{2} (12.6B)

Answers to Chapter Tests: Form E

Chapter 1 Test Form E

1. b (1.1A)
2. c (1.1B)
3. d (1.1B)
4. b (1.1C)
5. a (1.1D)
6. c (1.2A)
7. a (1.2A)
8. d (1.2B)
9. a (1.3A)
10. b (1.3B)
11. d (1.3C)
12. c (1.4A)
13. d (1.4B)
14. a (1.4C)
15. c (1.5A)
16. a (1.5B)
17. b (1.5C)
18. d (1.5D)
19. b (1.6A)
20. b (1.6A)
21. a (1.6B)
22. b (1.6B)
23. b (1.7A)
24. a (1.7B)
25. a (1.7B)

Chapter 2 Test Form E

1. c (2.1A)
2. b (2.1B)
3. a (2.2A)
4. b (2.2B)
5. d (2.2B)
6. a (2.3A)
7. c (2.3B)
8. a (2.4A)
9. d (2.4B)
10. a (2.4C)

11. c (2.4D)
12. d (2.5A)
13. b (2.5B)
14. a (2.5C)
15. a (2.5D)
16. c (2.6A)
17. b (2.6B)
18. a (2.6C)
19. c (2.7A)
20. d (2.7B)
21. c (2.7C)
22. b (2.8A)
23. a (2.8B)
24. d (2.8C)
25. b (2.8C)

Chapter 3 Test Form E

1. b (3.1A)
2. d (3.1A)
3. c (3.1B)
4. b (3.1B)
5. d (3.2A)
6. c (3.2A)
7. a (3.2B)
8. d (3.3A)
9. b (3.3A)
10. b (3.3B)
11. a (3.4A)
12. c (3.4A)
13. a (3.4B)
14. d (3.5A)
15. a (3.5A)
16. d (3.5B)
17. d (3.6A)
18. b (3.6B)
19. b (3.6C)
20. a (3.6C)

Cumulative Test: Chapters 1–3 Form E

1. c (1.5C)
2. a (1.6A)
3. b (1.6B)
4. c (2.1B)
5. d (2.2B)
6. b (2.2B)
7. b (2.3A)
8. a (2.4B)
9. c (2.4C)
10. b (2.5C)
11. c (2.6A)
12. b (2.6B)
13. d (2.7A)
14. c (2.7B)
15. b (2.8B)
16. a (2.8C)
17. b (3.1A)
18. d (3.2A)
19. b (3.3A)
20. c (3.4A)
21. b (3.5A)
22. a (3.6A)
23. d (3.6B)
24. b (3.6C)
25. c (2.4D)
26. b (2.7C)
27. a (2.6C)
28. d (3.3B)
29. d (3.3B)
30. c (3.4B)

Chapter 4 Test Form E

1. c (4.1A)
2. a (4.1A)
3. d (4.1A)
4. a (4.1A)

Answers to Chapter Tests: Form E

5. b (4.1B)

6. b (4.1B)

7. d (4.2A)

8. d (4.2A)

9. b (4.2B)

10. a (4.2B)

11. a (4.2C)

12. d (4.2C)

13. b (4.3A)

14. d (4.3A)

15. a (4.3B)

16. b (4.3B)

17. b (4.3C)

18. c (4.3C)

19. c (4.3C)

20. d (4.3C)

Chapter 5 Test Form E

1. c (5.1A)

2. a (5.1A)

3. a (5.1B)

4. d (5.1B)

5. c (5.1B)

6. c (5.1B)

7. b (5.2A)

8. a (5.2A)

9. c (5.2A)

10. b (5.2A)

11. d (5.2B)

12. b (5.2B)

13. a (5.3A)

14. b (5.3A)

15. d (5.3B)

16. d (5.3B)

17. a (5.4A)

18. c (5.4A)

19. b (5.4B)

20. a (5.4B)

21. b (5.5A)

22. d (5.5A)

23. b (5.5B)

24. a (5.5B)

25. c (5.5B)

Chapter 6 Test Form E

1. a (6.1A)

2. c (6.1B)

3. d (6.1C)

4. b (6.2A)

5. d (6.2A)

6. a (6.2B)

7. a (6.2B)

8. c (6.2C)

9. a (6.2C)

10. d (6.2D)

11. d (6.2D)

12. c (6.3A)

13. b (6.3B)

14. a (6.4A)

15. c (6.4B)

16. d (6.5A)

17. c (6.5B)

18. d (6.6A)

19. c (6.7A)

20. a (6.7B)

Cumulative Test:
Chapters 4–6 Form E

1. b (4.1A)

2. c (4.1B)

3. a (4.2B)

4. d (4.2C)

5. d (4.3B)

6. c (4.3C)

7. b (5.1A)

8. d (5.1A)

9. c (5.1B)

10. a (5.1B)

11. b (5.2A)

12. b (5.2B)

13. a (5.3A)

14. d (5.3B)

15. c (5.4A)

16. a (5.4B)

17. b (6.1A)

18. d (6.2B)

19. b (6.2D)

20. d (6.3A)

Chapter 7 Test Form E

1. b (7.1A)

2. d (7.1A)

3. c (7.1B)

4. a (7.1B)

5. b (7.1B)

6. d (7.2A)

7. c (7.2A)

8. c (7.2A)

9. b (7.4A)

10. c (7.4A)

11. a (7.2B)

12. d (7.2B)

13. a (7.2B)

14. c (7.3A)

15. d (7.3A)

16. d (7.3B)

17. d (7.3B)

18. c (7.3B)

19. b (7.5A)

20. c (7.4B)

Chapter 8 Test Form E

1. d (8.1A)
2. a (8.1B)
3. d (8.1C)
4. c (8.1C)
5. b (8.2A)
6. c (8.2A)
7. c (8.2B)
8. d (8.2B)
9. d (8.2C)
10. b (8.2C)
11. a (8.3A)
12. c (8.3A)
13. d (8.3B)
14. c (8.3B)
15. a (8.3C)
16. b (8.3C)
17. c (8.4A)
18. b (8.4A)
19. a (8.4B)
20. d (8.4B)

Chapter 9 Test Form E

1. c (9.1A)
2. c (9.1A)
3. b (9.1A)
4. c (9.1A)
5. d (9.1B)
6. b (9.1B)
7. b (9.2A)
8. b (9.2A)
9. d (9.2A)
10. c (9.2A)
11. b (9.2B)
12. b (9.2B)
13. a (9.3A)
14. d (9.3A)

15. c (9.3A)
16. b (9.3A)
17. d (9.3B)
18. a (9.4A)
19. a (9.5A)
20. c (9.5B)

**Cumulative Test:
Chapters 7–9 Form E**

1. a (7.1B)
2. c (7.1B)
3. b (7.2A)
4. a (7.2A)
5. d (7.4A)
6. c (7.4A)
7. b (8.1A)
8. c (8.1B)
9. a (8.2A)
10. c (8.2B)
11. d (8.3A)
12. d (8.1C)
13. d (8.3C)
14. b (9.1A)
15. c (9.2A)
16. c (9.3A)
17. a (9.5A)
18. c (9.5A)
19. b (9.2B)
20. a (9.2B)

Chapter 10 Test Form E

1. b (10.1A)
2. b (10.1A)
3. a (10.1B)
4. b (10.2A)
5. d (10.2A)
6. a (10.2B)
7. a (10.2B)

8. a (10.3A)
9. b (10.3A)
10. a (10.3C)
11. d (10.3C)
12. a (10.4A)
13. d (10.4A)
14. c (10.4A)
15. c (10.4A)
16. b (10.4B)
17. a (10.4B)
18. a (10.4A)
19. c (10.4B)
20. c (10.4B)
21. b (10.4B)
22. c (10.5B)
23. b (10.5B)
24. d (10.5A)
25. a (10.4C)

Chapter 11 Test Form E

1. b (11.1A)
2. d (11.1A)
3. a (11.1B)
4. d (11.1C)
5. c (11.2A)
6. b (11.2B)
7. a (11.2C)
8. a (11.2C)
9. b (11.2D)
10. b (11.3A)
11. d (11.3A)
12. c (11.3A)
13. d (11.3B)
14. c (11.4A)
15. b (11.4B)
16. a (11.5A)
17. b (11.5B)
18. d (11.6A)

Answers to Chapter Tests: Form E

19. c (11.6B)

20. d (11.6B)

Chapter 12 Test Form E

1. d (12.1A)
2. c (12.1B)
3. c (12.1C)
4. b (12.1C)
5. c (12.2A)
6. d (12.2B)
7. a (12.2C)
8. a (12.3A)
9. c (12.3B)
10. b (12.3B)
11. d (12.3C)
12. a (12.4A)
13. c (12.4B)
14. c (12.4C)
15. b (12.5A)
16. d (12.5B)
17. d (12.5C)
18. c (12.6A)
19. a (12.6B)
20. b (12.6B)

Cumulative Test: Chapters 10–12 Form E

1. b (10.2A)
2. a (10.4A)
3. a (10.2B)
4. c (10.4A)
5. c (10.3A)
6. a (10.4B)
7. b (10.4B)
8. b (10.5B)
9. d (10.5B)
10. a (11.1A)
11. d (11.1B)

12. d (11.2B)
13. c (11.2C)
14. a (11.3A)
15. b (11.4A)
16. c (11.6A)
17. d (11.3B)
18. b (11.6B)
19. c (12.1B)
20. a (12.1C)
21. b (12.2A)
22. a (12.3B)
23. a (12.4A)
24. d (12.5B)
25. d (12.6A)

Final Exam Form E

1. a (1.3B)
2. b (1.5C)
3. c (1.6B)
4. b (1.3C)
5. d (2.4C)
6. b (2.5C)
7. a (2.6B)
8. a (2.7B)
9. a (2.8C)
10. c (2.5D)
11. d (3.3A)
12. c (3.4A)
13. a (3.5A)
14. c (3.6B)
15. d (3.6A)
16. a (4.1A)
17. c (4.2B)
18. d (4.3B)
19. d (4.3C)
20. b (5.1B)
21. c (5.2A)
22. a (5.3A)

23. a (5.4A)
24. b (5.3B)
25. a (6.1A)
26. b (6.6A)
27. c (6.2A)
28. c (6.2B)
29. a (7.1B)
30. c (7.2B)
31. b (8.1A)
32. b (8.3A)
33. a (8.2C)
34. d (8.1C)
35. d (9.2A)
36. a (9.3A)
37. c (9.2B)
38. b (10.1A)
39. a (10.4A)
40. d (10.2B)
41. b (10.4B)
42. c (10.5B)
43. a (11.1A)
44. d (11.2B)
45. a (11.3A)
46. c (11.4B)
47. c (11.6A)
48. a (12.3B)
49. b (12.4B)
50. c (12.6B)

Chapter 1 Test Form F

1. b (1.1A)
2. d (1.1B)
3. b (1.1B)
4. d (1.1C)
5. a (1.1D)
6. b (1.2A)
7. c (1.2A)
8. c (1.2B)
9. b (1.3A)
10. d (1.3B)
11. a (1.3C)
12. b (1.4A)
13. b (1.4B)
14. a (1.4C)
15. c (1.5A)
16. d (1.5B)
17. b (1.5C)
18. d (1.5D)
19. d (1.6A)
20. b (1.6A)
21. b (1.6B)
22. a (1.6B)
23. a (1.7A)
24. b (1.7B)
25. d (1.7B)

Chapter 2 Test Form F

1. d (2.1A)
2. d (2.1B)
3. c (2.2A)
4. a (2.2B)
5. c (2.2B)
6. a (2.3A)
7. a (2.3B)
8. c (2.4A)
9. b (2.4B)
10. a (2.4C)

11. d (2.4D)
12. b (2.5A)
13. c (2.5B)
14. d (2.5C)
15. a (2.5D)
16. b (2.6A)
17. d (2.6B)
18. a (2.6C)
19. c (2.7A)
20. b (2.7B)
21. a (2.7C)
22. d (2.8A)
23. c (2.8B)
24. a (2.8C)
25. c (2.8C)

Chapter 3 Test Form F

1. c (3.1A)
2. a (3.1A)
3. c (3.1B)
4. a (3.1B)
5. d (3.2A)
6. c (3.2A)
7. b (3.2B)
8. d (3.3A)
9. a (3.3A)
10. b (3.3B)
11. a (3.4A)
12. b (3.4A)
13. d (3.4B)
14. b (3.5A)
15. b (3.5A)
16. c (3.5B)
17. a (3.6A)
18. a (3.6B)
19. a (3.6C)
20. b (3.6C)

Cumulative Test: Chapters 1–3 Form F

1. b (1.5C)
2. a (1.6A)
3. d (1.6B)
4. a (2.1A)
5. c (2.2B)
6. d (2.2B)
7. c (2.3A)
8. a (2.4B)
9. c (2.4C)
10. b (2.5C)
11. d (2.6A)
12. c (2.6B)
13. a (2.7A)
14. a (2.7B)
15. b (2.8B)
16. d (2.8C)
17. a (3.1A)
18. a (3.2A)
19. b (3.3A)
20. d (3.4A)
21. a (3.5A)
22. c (3.6A)
23. b (3.6B)
24. a (3.6C)
25. d (2.4D)
26. d (2.7C)
27. c (2.6C)
28. a (3.3B)
29. d (3.3B)
30. c (3.5B)

Chapter 4 Test Form F

1. c (4.1A)
2. a (4.1A)
3. c (4.1A)
4. b (4.1A)

Answers to Chapter Tests: Form F

5. c (4.1B)

6. b (4.1B)

7. c (4.2A)

8. b (4.2A)

9. b (4.2B)

10. d (4.2B)

11. c (4.2C)

12. c (4.2C)

13. b (4.3A)

14. b (4.3A)

15. a (4.3B)

16. a (4.3B)

17. c (4.3C)

18. c (4.3C)

19. d (4.3C)

20. b (4.3C)

Chapter 5 Test Form F

1. a (5.1A)

2. b (5.1A)

3. b (5.1B)

4. c (5.1B)

5. a (5.1B)

6. b (5.1B)

7. d (5.2A)

8. d (5.2A)

9. b (5.2A)

10. c (5.2A)

11. a (5.2B)

12. a (5.2B)

13. c (5.3A)

14. b (5.3A)

15. a (5.3B)

16. b (5.3B)

17. d (5.4A)

18. c (5.4A)

19. a (5.4B)

20. a (5.4B)

21. d (5.5A)

22. a (5.5A)

23. b (5.5B)

24. b (5.5B)

25. d (5.5B)

Chapter 6 Test Form F

1. b (6.1A)

2. d (6.1B)

3. c (6.1C)

4. d (6.2A)

5. c (6.2A)

6. b (6.2B)

7. c (6.2B)

8. d (6.2C)

9. a (6.2C)

10. b (6.2D)

11. a (6.2D)

12. c (6.3A)

13. a (6.3B)

14. b (6.4A)

15. a (6.4B)

16. d (6.5A)

17. c (6.5B)

18. a (6.6A)

19. b (6.7A)

20. a (6.7B)

Cumulative Test: Chapters 4–6 Form F

1. d (4.1A)

2. a (4.1B)

3. c (4.2B)

4. b (4.2C)

5. b (4.3B)

6. b (4.3C)

7. c (5.1A)

8. a (5.1A)

9. b (5.1B)

10. c (5.1B)

11. b (5.2A)

12. d (5.2B)

13. a (5.3A)

14. b (5.3B)

15. c (5.4A)

16. a (5.4B)

17. b (6.1A)

18. d (6.2B)

19. a (6.2D)

20. c (6.3A)

Chapter 7 Test Form F

1. c (7.1A)

2. b (7.1A)

3. c (7.1B)

4. c (7.1B)

5. d (7.1B)

6. a (7.2A)

7. c (7.2A)

8. d (7.2A)

9. c (7.5A)

10. d (7.4A)

11. d (7.4B)

12. c (7.2B)

13. a (7.2B)

14. a (7.2B)

15. c (7.3A)

16. d (7.3A)

17. b (7.3A)

18. c (7.3B)

19. a (7.3B)

20. a (7.4A)

Chapter 8 Test Form F

1. c (8.1A)

2. b (8.1B)

3. d (8.1C)

4. d (8.1C)

5. a (8.2A)

6. a (8.2A)

7. d (8.2B)

8. a (8.2B)

9. c (8.2C)

10. c (8.2C)

11. b (8.3A)

12. d (8.3A)

13. a (8.3B)

14. d (8.3B)

15. b (8.3C)

16. c (8.3C)

17. d (8.4A)

18. c (8.4A)

19. b (8.4B)

20. a (8.4B)

Chapter 9 Test Form F

1. c (9.1A)

2. b (9.1A)

3. c (9.1A)

4. d (9.1A)

5. d (9.1B)

6. b (9.1B)

7. c (9.2A)

8. c (9.2A)

9. a (9.2A)

10. d (9.2A)

11. d (9.2B)

12. c (9.2B)

13. b (9.3A)

14. a (9.3A)

15. d (9.3A)

16. c (9.3A)

17. a (9.3B)

18. b (9.3B)

19. b (9.4A)

20. c (9.4B)

Cumulative Test: Chapters 7-9 Form F

1. b (7.1B)

2. d (7.1B)

3. c (7.2B)

4. b (7.2B)

5. c (7.4A)

6. d (7.4A)

7. a (8.1A)

8. c (8.1B)

9. b (8.2A)

10. d (8.2B)

11. a (8.3A)

12. a (8.3C)

13. b (8.2C)

14. c (9.1A)

15. d (9.2A)

16. d (9.3A)

17. b (9.5A)

18. b (9.5A)

19. a (9.2B)

20. a (9.5A)

Chapter 10 Test Form F

1. a (10.1A)

2. c (10.1A)

3. b (10.1B)

4. c (10.2A)

5. a (10.2A)

6. c (10.2B)

7. b (10.2B)

8. b (10.3A)

9. d (10.3B)

10. a (10.3C)

11. a (10.3C)

12. b (10.4A)

13. a (10.4A)

14. d (10.4A)

15. b (10.4A)

16. c (10.4B)

17. b (10.4B)

18. b (10.4A)

19. d (10.4B)

20. d (10.4B)

21. c (10.4B)

22. d (10.5B)

23. c (10.5B)

24. a (10.5A)

25. b (10.4C)

Chapter 11 Test Form F

1. c (11.1A)

2. b (11.1A)

3. b (11.1B)

4. a (11.1C)

5. d (11.2A)

6. c (11.2B)

7. a (11.2C)

8. b (11.2C)

9. c (11.2D)

10. d (11.3A)

11. a (11.3A)

12. c (11.3A)

13. a (11.3B)

14. d (11.4A)

15. c (11.4B)

16. b (11.5A)

17. d (11.5B)

18. a (11.6A)

19. d (11.6B)

20. a (11.6B)

Answers to Chapter Tests: Form F

Chapter 12 Test Form F

1. a (12.1A)
2. c (12.1B)
3. a (12.1C)
4. c (12.1C)
5. d (12.2A)
6. a (12.2B)
7. b (12.2C)
8. a (12.3A)
9. d (12.3B)
10. c (12.3C)
11. a (12.3B)
12. b (12.4A)
13. d (12.4B)
14. d (12.4C)
15. c (12.5A)
16. a (12.5B)
17. a (12.5C)
18. c (12.6A)
19. b (12.6B)
20. c (12.6B)

Cumulative Test: Chapters 10–12 Form F

1. a (10.2A)
2. b (10.4A)
3. d (10.2B)
4. c (10.4A)
5. d (10.3A)
6. b (10.4B)
7. c (10.4B)
8. c (10.5B)
9. c (10.5B)
10. b (11.1A)
11. a (11.1B)
12. a (11.2B)
13. c (11.2C)
14. a (11.3A)
15. c (11.4A)
16. d (11.6A)
17. a (11.3B)
18. b (11.6B)
19. a (12.1B)
20. b (12.1C)
21. c (12.2A)
22. b (12.3B)
23. d (12.4A)
24. c (12.5B)
25. a (12.6A)

Final Exam Form F

1. b (1.3B)
2. d (1.5C)
3. d (1.6B)
4. c (1.3C)
5. a (2.4C)
6. c (2.5C)
7. b (2.6B)
8. b (2.7B)
9. a (2.8C)
10. c (2.7C)
11. a (3.3A)
12. d (3.4A)
13. b (3.5A)
14. d (3.6B)
15. a (3.6A)
16. b (4.1A)
17. d (4.2B)
18. a (4.3B)
19. b (4.3C)
20. d (5.1B)
21. d (5.2A)
22. b (5.3A)
23. b (5.4A)
24. c (5.4B)
25. b (6.1A)

26. c (6.6A)
27. d (6.3A)
28. d (6.2D)
29. b (7.2A)
30. d (7.1B)
31. c (8.2A)
32. c (8.3A)
33. b (8.1C)
34. a (8.3C)
35. a (9.1A)
36. b (9.3A)
37. d (9.3B)
38. c (10.1A)
39. a (10.4A)
40. a (10.2B)
41. c (10.4B)
42. d (10.5B)
43. b (11.1A)
44. a (11.2B)
45. b (11.3A)
46. a (11.4B)
47. d (11.6A)
48. b (12.3B)
49. c (12.4B)
50. c (12.6B)

Chapter 1 Test Form G

1. c (1.1A)
2. a (1.1B)
3. c (1.1B)
4. b (1.1C)
5. b (1.1D)
6. c (1.2A)
7. a (1.2A)
8. d (1.2B)
9. c (1.3A)
10. a (1.3B)
11. d (1.3C)
12. c (1.4A)
13. d (1.4B)
14. b (1.4C)
15. c (1.5A)
16. c (1.5B)
17. a (1.5C)
18. a (1.5D)
19. a (1.6A)
20. b (1.6A)
21. b (1.6B)
22. a (1.6B)
23. c (1.7A)
24. a (1.7B)
25. a (1.7B)

Chapter 2 Test Form G

1. d (2.1A)
2. d (2.1B)
3. a (2.2A)
4. b (2.2B)
5. b (2.2B)
6. d (2.3A)
7. a (2.3B)
8. c (2.4A)
9. b (2.4B)
10. d (2.4C)
11. b (2.4D)
12. a (2.5A)
13. d (2.5B)
14. c (2.5C)
15. a (2.5D)
16. d (2.6A)
17. d (2.6B)
18. b (2.6C)
19. a (2.7A)
20. c (2.7B)
21. c (2.7C)
22. c (2.8A)
23. d (2.8B)
24. b (2.8C)
25. a (2.8C)

Chapter 3 Test Form G

1. d (3.1A)
2. b (3.1A)
3. a (3.1B)
4. d (3.1B)
5. c (3.2A)
6. d (3.2A)
7. c (3.2B)
8. b (3.3A)
9. b (3.3A)
10. c (3.3B)
11. a (3.4A)
12. b (3.4A)
13. c (3.4B)
14. c (3.5A)
15. b (3.5A)
16. b (3.5B)
17. c (3.6A)
18. a (3.6B)
19. a (3.6C)
20. b (3.6C)

Cumulative Test: Chapters 1-3 Form G

1. c (1.5C)
2. a (1.6A)
3. b (1.6B)
4. c (2.1A)
5. a (2.2B)
6. b (2.2B)
7. a (2.3A)
8. d (2.4B)
9. b (2.4C)
10. b (2.5C)
11. b (2.6A)
12. a (2.6B)
13. d (2.7A)
14. d (2.7B)
15. c (2.8B)
16. b (2.8C)
17. a (3.1A)
18. a (3.2A)
19. b (3.3A)
20. d (3.4A)
21. a (3.5A)
22. d (3.6A)
23. d (3.6B)
24. b (3.6C)
25. c (2.4D)
26. a (2.6C)
27. d (2.7C)
28. b (3.4B)
29. b (3.2B)
30. d (3.5B)

Chapter 4 Test Form G

1. d (4.1A)
2. b (4.1A)
3. a (4.1A)
4. d (4.1A)

Answers to Chapter Tests: Form G

5. a (4.1B)

6. b (4.1B)

7. a (4.2A)

8. a (4.2A)

9. c (4.2B)

10. d (4.2B)

11. b (4.2C)

12. c (4.2C)

13. a (4.3A)

14. d (4.3A)

15. c (4.3B)

16. b (4.3B)

17. b (4.3C)

18. a (4.3C)

19. d (4.3C)

20. c (4.3C)

Chapter 5 Test Form G

1. c (5.1A)

2. c (5.1A)

3. a (5.1B)

4. b (5.1B)

5. d (5.1B)

6. c (5.1B)

7. a (5.2A)

8. b (5.2A)

9. c (5.2A)

10. b (5.2A)

11. b (5.2B)

12. d (5.2B)

13. c (5.3A)

14. c (5.3A)

15. a (5.3B)

16. a (5.3B)

17. d (5.4A)

18. d (5.4A)

19. c (5.4B)

20. a (5.4B)

21. b (5.5A)

22. a (5.5A)

23. b (5.5B)

24. b (5.5B)

25. b (5.5B)

Chapter 6 Test Form G

1. c (6.1A)

2. d (6.1B)

3. d (6.1C)

4. a (6.2A)

5. b (6.2A)

6. c (6.2B)

7. c (6.2B)

8. d (6.2C)

9. a (6.2C)

10. c (6.2D)

11. c (6.2D)

12. a (6.3A)

13. a (6.3B)

14. c (6.4A)

15. c (6.4B)

16. d (6.5A)

17. a (6.5B)

18. d (6.6A)

19. d (6.7A)

20. a (6.7B)

Cumulative Test: Chapters 4–6 Form G

1. a (4.1A)

2. c (4.1B)

3. c (4.2B)

4. d (4.2C)

5. b (4.3B)

6. a (4.3C)

7. b (5.1A)

8. a (5.1A)

9. d (5.1B)

10. b (5.1B)

11. a (5.2A)

12. d (5.2B)

13. a (5.3A)

14. d (5.3B)

15. b (5.4A)

16. a (5.4B)

17. b (6.1A)

18. d (6.2B)

19. b (6.2D)

20. c (6.3A)

Chapter 7 Test Form G

1. b (7.1A)

2. b (7.1A)

3. a (7.1B)

4. c (7.1B)

5. d (7.1B)

6. d (7.2A)

7. a (7.2A)

8. c (7.2A)

9. c (7.4A)

10. d (7.4A)

11. c (7.2B)

12. b (7.2B)

13. a (7.2B)

14. d (7.3A)

15. a (7.3A)

16. b (7.3B)

17. b (7.3B)

18. b (7.5A)

19. d (7.4A)

20. b (7.4B)

Chapter 8 Test Form G

1. b (8.1A)
2. c (8.1B)
3. b (8.1C)
4. b (8.1C)
5. d (8.2A)
6. d (8.2A)
7. a (8.2B)
8. b (8.2B)
9. d (8.2C)
10. d (8.2C)
11. c (8.3A)
12. a (8.3A)
13. b (8.3B)
14. a (8.3B)
15. c (8.3C)
16. b (8.3C)
17. a (8.4A)
18. d (8.4A)
19. c (8.4B)
20. b (8.4B)

Chapter 9 Test Form G

1. b (9.1A)
2. a (9.1A)
3. d (9.1A)
4. a (9.1A)
5. b (9.1B)
6. b (9.1B)
7. c (9.2A)
8. d (9.2A)
9. b (9.2A)
10. a (9.2A)
11. a (9.2B)
12. d (9.2B)
13. c (9.3A)
14. b (9.3A)
15. a (9.3A)
16. a (9.3A)
17. b (9.3B)
18. c (9.3B)
19. c (9.4A)
20. b (9.4B)

Cumulative Test: Chapters 7-9 Form G

1. d (7.1B)
2. a (7.1B)
3. b (7.3A)
4. c (7.3A)
5. b (7.4A)
6. a (7.4B)
7. c (8.1A)
8. d (8.1B)
9. c (8.2A)
10. a (8.2B)
11. b (8.3A)
12. b (8.1C)
13. a (8.2C)
14. d (9.1A)
15. a (9.2A)
16. a (9.3A)
17. c (9.5B)
18. d (9.5A)
19. b (9.1B)
20. c (9.3B)

Chapter 10 Test Form G

1. c (10.1A)
2. d (10.1A)
3. c (10.1B)
4. d (10.2A)
5. b (10.2A)
6. b (10.2B)
7. c (10.2B)

8. c (10.3A)
9. a (10.3B)
10. c (10.3C)
11. b (10.3C)
12. c (10.4A)
13. b (10.4A)
14. a (10.4A)
15. b (10.4A)
16. d (10.4B)
17. c (10.4B)
18. c (10.4A)
19. d (10.4B)
20. a (10.4B)
21. d (10.4B)
22. a (10.5B)
23. d (10.5B)
24. c (10.5A)
25. d (10.4C)

Chapter 11 Test Form G

1. d (11.1A)
2. b (11.1A)
3. c (11.1B)
4. b (11.1C)
5. a (11.2A)
6. d (11.2B)
7. b (11.2C)
8. c (11.2C)
9. d (11.2D)
10. d (11.3A)
11. b (11.3A)
12. d (11.3A)
13. b (11.3B)
14. a (11.4A)
15. d (11.4B)
16. c (11.5A)
17. c (11.5B)
18. b (11.6A)

Answers to Chapter Tests: Form G

19. a (11.6B)

20. b (11.6B)

Chapter 12 Test Form G

1. b (12.1A)
2. a (12.1B)
3. b (12.1C)
4. d (12.1C)
5. a (12.2A)
6. b (12.2B)
7. c (12.2C)
8. b (12.3A)
9. a (12.3B)
10. d (12.3B)
11. b (12.3C)
12. c (12.4A)
13. d (12.4B)
14. a (12.4C)
15. d (12.5A)
16. b (12.5B)
17. b (12.5C)
18. b (12.6A)
19. c (12.6B)
20. d (12.6B)

Cumulative Test: Chapters 10–12 Form G

1. d (10.2A)
2. c (10.4A)
3. a (10.2B)
4. c (10.4A)
5. a (10.3A)
6. c (10.4B)
7. d (10.4B)
8. d (10.5B)
9. c (10.5B)
10. b (11.1B)
11. c (11.1A)

12. b (11.3A)
13. c (11.3A)
14. a (11.4B)
15. d (11.4B)
16. b (11.2D)
17. a (11.6A)
18. c (11.6B)
19. b (12.1C)
20. a (12.1B)
21. d (12.2A)
22. d (12.3B)
23. a (12.4A)
24. d (12.5B)
25. b (12.6B)

Final Exam Form G

1. c (1.3B)
2. a (1.5C)
3. a (1.6B)
4. d (1.3C)
5. c (2.4C)
6. d (2.5C)
7. c (2.6B)
8. c (2.7B)
9. b (2.8C)
10. a (2.7C)
11. b (3.3A)
12. a (3.4A)
13. c (3.5A)
14. b (3.6B)
15. b (3.6A)
16. c (4.1A)
17. a (4.2B)
18. b (4.3B)
19. b (4.3C)
20. c (5.1B)
21. a (5.2A)
22. c (5.3A)

23. c (5.4A)
24. d (5.2B)
25. c (6.1A)
26. d (6.2B)
27. a (6.6A)
28. a (6.3A)
29. c (7.1B)
30. b (7.3A)
31. a (8.3A)
32. d (8.2A)
33. c (8.1C)
34. b (8.2C)
35. c (9.2A)
36. c (9.1A)
37. a (9.3C)
38. d (10.1A)
39. c (10.4A)
40. b (10.2B)
41. d (10.4B)
42. a (10.5A)
43. c (11.1A)
44. b (11.2B)
45. b (11.3A)
46. a (11.4B)
47. a (11.6A)
48. c (12.3B)
49. d (12.4B)
50. c (12.6A)

Chapter 1 Test Form H

1. d (1.1A)
2. d (1.1B)
3. d (1.1B)
4. a (1.1C)
5. c (1.1D)
6. b (1.2A)
7. a (1.2A)
8. c (1.2B)
9. b (1.3A)
10. c (1.3B)
11. d (1.3C)
12. b (1.4A)
13. c (1.4B)
14. a (1.4C)
15. d (1.5A)
16. d (1.5B)
17. c (1.5C)
18. a (1.5D)
19. b (1.6A)
20. d (1.6A)
21. d (1.6B)
22. a (1.6B)
23. b (1.7A)
24. c (1.7B)
25. c (1.7B)

Chapter 2 Test Form H

1. a (2.1A)
2. c (2.1B)
3. b (2.2A)
4. d (2.2B)
5. d (2.2B)
6. a (2.3A)
7. b (2.3B)
8. a (2.4A)
9. c (2.4B)
10. d (2.4C)
11. d (2.4D)
12. b (2.5A)
13. a (2.5B)
14. c (2.5C)
15. c (2.5D)
16. a (2.6A)
17. b (2.6B)
18. a (2.6C)
19. d (2.7A)
20. c (2.7B)
21. b (2.7C)
22. a (2.8A)
23. b (2.8B)
24. d (2.8C)
25. d (2.8C)

Chapter 3 Test Form H

1. a (3.1A)
2. a (3.1A)
3. b (3.1B)
4. a (3.1B)
5. d (3.2A)
6. c (3.2A)
7. b (3.2B)
8. a (3.3A)
9. d (3.3A)
10. b (3.3B)
11. a (3.4A)
12. b (3.4A)
13. a (3.4B)
14. b (3.5A)
15. a (3.5A)
16. d (3.5B)
17. a (3.6A)
18. c (3.6B)
19. b (3.6C)
20. a (3.6C)

Cumulative Test: Chapters 1-3 Form H

1. c (1.5C)
2. b (1.6A)
3. b (1.6B)
4. c (2.1A)
5. d (2.2B)
6. b (2.2B)
7. a (2.3A)
8. c (2.4B)
9. c (2.4C)
10. a (2.5C)
11. a (2.6A)
12. d (2.6B)
13. c (2.7A)
14. b (2.7B)
15. c (2.8B)
16. b (2.8C)
17. d (3.1A)
18. a (3.2A)
19. d (3.3A)
20. d (3.4A)
21. b (3.5A)
22. a (3.6A)
23. c (3.6B)
24. c (3.6C)
25. d (2.4D)
26. a (2.6C)
27. c (2.6C)
28. d (3.4B)
29. b (3.2B)
30. a (3.5B)

Chapter 4 Test Form H

1. c (4.1A)
2. a (4.1A)
3. b (4.1A)
4. b (4.1A)

Answers to Chapter Tests: Form H

5. d (4.1B)
6. a (4.1B)
7. c (4.2A)
8. b (4.2A)
9. a (4.2B)
10. b (4.2B)
11. a (4.2C)
12. c (4.2C)
13. b (4.3A)
14. b (4.3A)
15. d (4.3B)
16. d (4.3B)
17. a (4.3C)
18. b (4.3C)
19. d (4.3C)
20. b (4.3C)

Chapter 5 Test Form H

1. d (5.1A)
2. b (5.1A)
3. a (5.1B)
4. b (5.1B)
5. c (5.1B)
6. a (5.1B)
7. d (5.2A)
8. b (5.2A)
9. b (5.2A)
10. b (5.2A)
11. c (5.2B)
12. c (5.2B)
13. a (5.3A)
14. c (5.3A)
15. d (5.3B)
16. a (5.3B)
17. d (5.4A)
18. b (5.4A)
19. c (5.4B)
20. b (5.4B)

21. d (5.5A)
22. a (5.5A)
23. b (5.5B)
24. b (5.5B)
25. d (5.5B)

Chapter 6 Test Form H

1. a (6.1A)
2. b (6.1B)
3. c (6.1C)
4. b (6.2A)
5. a (6.2A)
6. d (6.2B)
7. c (6.2B)
8. b (6.2C)
9. c (6.2C)
10. a (6.2D)
11. d (6.2D)
12. c (6.3A)
13. a (6.3B)
14. c (6.4A)
15. b (6.4B)
16. d (6.5A)
17. d (6.5B)
18. a (6.6A)
19. b (6.7A)
20. a (6.7B)

Cumulative Test: Chapters 4–6 Form H

1. a (4.1A)
2. c (4.1B)
3. c (4.2B)
4. b (4.2C)
5. a (4.3B)
6. d (4.3C)
7. a (5.1A)
8. c (5.1A)

9. b (5.1B)
10. c (5.1B)
11. d (5.2A)
12. d (5.2B)
13. b (5.3A)
14. c (5.3B)
15. a (5.4A)
16. a (5.4B)
17. c (6.1A)
18. d (6.2B)
19. b (6.2D)
20. c (6.3A)

Chapter 7 Test Form H

1. a (7.1A)
2. c (7.1A)
3. d (7.1B)
4. d (7.1B)
5. a (7.1B)
6. c (7.2A)
7. a (7.2A)
8. b (7.2A)
9. a (7.4A)
10. b (7.4A)
11. d (7.2B)
12. d (7.2B)
13. c (7.2B)
14. a (7.3B)
15. c (7.3B)
16. a (7.3A)
17. b (7.3A)
18. b (7.3A)
19. a (7.5A)
20. d (7.4B)

Chapter 8 Test Form H

1. b (8.1A)
2. d (8.1B)
3. c (8.1C)
4. b (8.1C)
5. b (8.2A)
6. d (8.2A)
7. b (8.2B)
8. a (8.2B)
9. a (8.2C)
10. a (8.2C)
11. d (8.3A)
12. b (8.3A)
13. c (8.3B)
14. b (8.3B)
15. d (8.3C)
16. a (8.3C)
17. a (8.4A)
18. a (8.4A)
19. d (8.4B)
20. b (8.4B)

Chapter 9 Test Form H

1. b (9.1A)
2. b (9.1A)
3. a (9.1A)
4. c (9.1A)
5. c (9.1B)
6. d (9.1B)
7. a (9.2A)
8. d (9.2A)
9. a (9.2A)
10. a (9.2A)
11. b (9.2B)
12. b (9.2B)
13. d (9.3A)
14. c (9.3A)

15. d (9.3A)
16. c (9.3A)
17. c (9.3B)
18. d (9.3B)
19. a (9.4A)
20. d (9.4B)

Cumulative Test: Chapters 7-9 Form H

1. b (7.1B)
2. b (7.1B)
3. a (7.3B)
4. a (7.3B)
5. d (7.4A)
6. b (7.4B)
7. d (8.1A)
8. a (8.1B)
9. d (8.2A)
10. b (8.2B)
11. c (8.3A)
12. c (8.1C)
13. d (8.2C)
14. a (9.1A)
15. b (9.2A)
16. a (9.3A)
17. d (9.5B)
18. a (9.5B)
19. c (9.2C)
20. d (9.1C)

Chapter 10 Test Form H

1. d (10.1A)
2. a (10.1A)
3. d (10.1B)
4. a (10.2A)
5. c (10.2A)
6. a (10.2B)
7. d (10.2B)

8. d (10.3A)
9. b (10.3B)
10. c (10.3C)
11. c (10.3C)
12. d (10.4A)
13. c (10.4A)
14. b (10.4A)
15. d (10.4A)
16. a (10.4B)
17. d (10.4B)
18. d (10.4A)
19. c (10.4B)
20. c (10.4B)
21. a (10.4B)
22. b (10.5B)
23. a (10.5B)
24. b (10.5A)
25. a (10.4C)

Chapter 11 Test Form H

1. a (11.1A)
2. c (11.1A)
3. d (11.1B)
4. c (11.1C)
5. b (11.2A)
6. a (11.2B)
7. c (11.2C)
8. d (11.2C)
9. a (11.2D)
10. a (11.3A)
11. a (11.4B)
12. c (11.3A)
13. c (11.3B)
14. b (11.4A)
15. a (11.4B)
16. d (11.5A)
17. a (11.5B)
18. c (11.6A)

Answers to Chapter Tests: Form H

19. b (11.6B)

20. c (11.6B)

Chapter 12 Test Form H

1. c (12.1A)
2. b (12.1B)
3. c (12.1C)
4. a (12.1C)
5. b (12.2A)
6. c (12.2B)
7. d (12.2C)
8. c (12.3A)
9. b (12.3B)
10. a (12.3B)
11. d (12.4A)
12. c (12.3C)
13. b (12.4B)
14. b (12.4C)
15. a (12.5A)
16. c (12.5B)
17. c (12.5C)
18. d (12.6A)
19. d (12.6B)
20. b (12.6B)

Cumulative Test: Chapters 10–12 Form H

1. a (10.2A)
2. d (10.4A)
3. b (10.2B)
4. b (10.4A)
5. b (10.3A)
6. d (10.4B)
7. a (10.4B)
8. a (10.5B)
9. d (10.5A)
10. d (11.1A)
11. c (11.1C)

12. c (11.2B)
13. a (11.4B)
14. c (11.3A)
15. c (11.4B)
16. b (11.6A)
17. c (11.2B)
18. d (11.6B)
19. c (12.1B)
20. d (12.1C)
21. a (12.2A)
22. d (12.3B)
23. b (12.4A)
24. a (12.5B)
25. c (12.6B)

Final Exam Form H

1. d (1.3B)
2. b (1.5C)
3. b (1.6B)
4. a (1.5D)
5. b (2.4C)
6. a (2.5C)
7. d (2.6B)
8. d (2.7B)
9. c (2.8C)
10. d (2.4D)
11. c (3.3A)
12. b (3.4A)
13. d (3.5A)
14. a (3.6B)
15. a (3.6A)
16. d (4.1A)
17. b (4.2B)
18. c (4.3B)
19. c (4.3C)
20. b (5.1B)
21. b (5.2A)
22. d (5.3A)

23. d (5.4A)
24. a (5.3B)
25. b (6.1A)
26. c (6.5A)
27. b (6.2A)
28. b (6.7A)
29. c (7.1B)
30. c (7.2A)
31. a (8.2A)
32. a (8.3A)
33. d (8.2C)
34. c (8.1C)
35. d (9.1A)
36. d (9.3A)
37. b (9.1B)
38. a (10.1A)
39. d (10.2A)
40. a (10.2B)
41. a (10.4B)
42. b (10.5B)
43. d (11.1A)
44. c (11.2B)
45. b (11.3A)
46. b (11.4B)
47. b (11.6A)
48. d (12.3B)
49. a (12.4B)
50. b (12.6B)

AIM For Success Slide Show printouts

AIM for Success

Motivation

- Prepare to succeed
  - Be motivated!
  - Actively pursue success!
- List two reasons you are taking this course
- Are the reasons you listed sufficient motivation for you to succeed?

Commitment

- List one or two current activities (sports, hobbies, music, dance, art, etc.) in which you would like to improve

- Next to each activity, put the number of hours per week you spend doing that activity

- You must commit at least the same amount of time to math

Develop a "Can Do" Attitude

- Be an active learner
- Take responsibility for studying
- Attend class
- Participate in class discussions.
- Math is not a spectator sport
- Do the homework—**regularly!**
- Create good study habits

Strategies for Success

- Know the course requirements
- Time management
- Take complete notes in class
- Ask a question when you are confused

Study Strategies

- Use flash cards for important definitions and formulas
- Set aside time for study and homework
- Form a study group
- Keep up to date

Text Features
that Promote Success

- Prep Tests
- Annotated examples
- "You Try It" problems
- Chapter Reviews
- Chapter Tests
- Cumulative Reviews

Word Problems

- Read the problem
- Make a list of known and unknown quantities
- Develop a strategy
- Solve the problem
- Check your answer

Preparing for a Test

- Start at least three days before the test
- Read the Chapter Summary
- Review every section
- Do the Chapter Review Exercises
- Do the Chapter Test

Stay Focused!

- Do not fall behind
- Remind yourself why you are taking this course
- Success demands effort

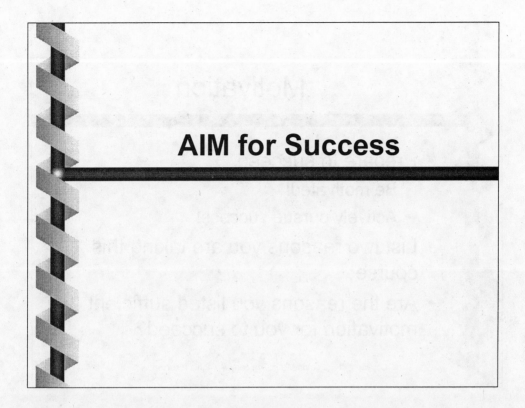

AIM for Success

Explain to students that the purpose of this lesson is to suggest to them successful strategies that will help them succeed in your class. The most important aspect of success is consistent practice.

Instructor Notes

Motivation

- Prepare to succeed
  - Be motivated!
  - Actively pursue success!
- List two reasons you are taking this course
- Are the reasons you listed sufficient motivation for you to succeed?

It is easy for students to be motivated during the first week of class. An important key to success is to revitalize that motivation throughout the term. Have students list reasons they are taking this class. A reason does not have to be, "to learn math." Whatever reasons students mention, suggest they reflect on those reasons when their enthusiasm wanes.

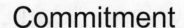

Commitment

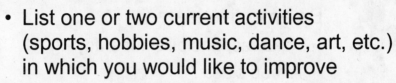

- List one or two current activities (sports, hobbies, music, dance, art, etc.) in which you would like to improve
- Next to each activity, put the number of hours per week you spend doing that activity
- You must commit at least the same amount of time to math

Having students list activities they currently pursue and the amount of time they spend doing those activities will help them understand that success in math requires devoting a lot of time to studying it.

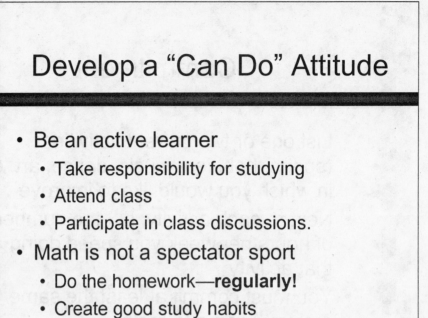

Develop a "Can Do" Attitude

- Be an active learner
  - Take responsibility for studying
  - Attend class
  - Participate in class discussions.
- Math is not a spectator sport
  - Do the homework—**regularly!**
  - Create good study habits

People who feel part of a community are generally active in the community. This activity is rewarding to the participant and it benefits the community. The same is true for the community of the classroom. Students who participate in class become active learners who take responsibility for learning.

Encourage students to consistently study math. Studying a half-hour every day (which is probably not enough for most students) is better than spending three and one-half hours once a week.

Learning math is much like learning to play the guitar, piano, or any other musical instrument. It cannot be achieved by watching. The student must practice.

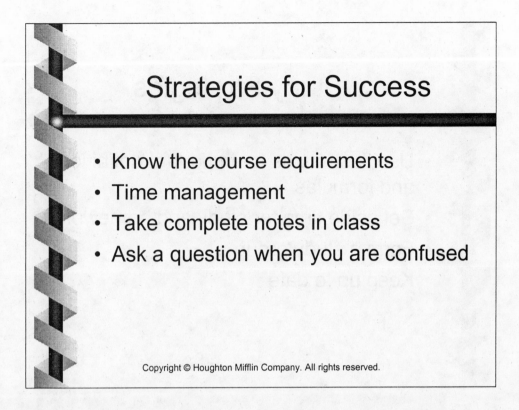

Give students a course syllabus and go over it with them. Besides the course requirements, let students know where they can go for help. Encourage them to seek help immediately upon having difficulty.

There is a sample time management form in the AIM for Success portion of the text. Many people have unrealistic expectations of how much time is available to meet personal, work, and educational demands. Encourage students to complete the form. It may help them in becoming more realistic about how much time they have available to study.

Students should take complete notes that include all steps to the solution of a problem. These notes can then be used as additional models for doing homework.

Encourage students to ask questions but to stay away from "I don't understand anything." First, it is not true, and second, it does not help in finding the root of the confusion.

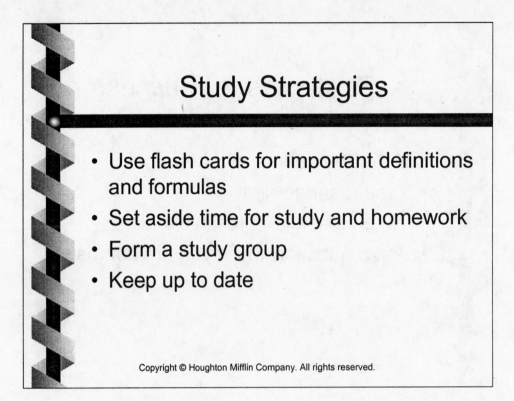

Study Strategies

- Use flash cards for important definitions and formulas
- Set aside time for study and homework
- Form a study group
- Keep up to date

Encourage students to keep flash cards with them. Any time they have a few minutes (waiting for a friend, on the subway) they should take them out and review them.

It is an advantage for students to arrange their schedules so they have a free hour right after class. This is the perfect time to review the class material. Also suggest that they rework the examples in their notes before starting on the homework.

Urge students to form a study group. These groups should meet at the same time each week.

To be a successful math student requires constant practice. The best time to start homework is right after class when the topic is fresh. This will help solidify new knowledge. Another learning aid is to review the homework before class.

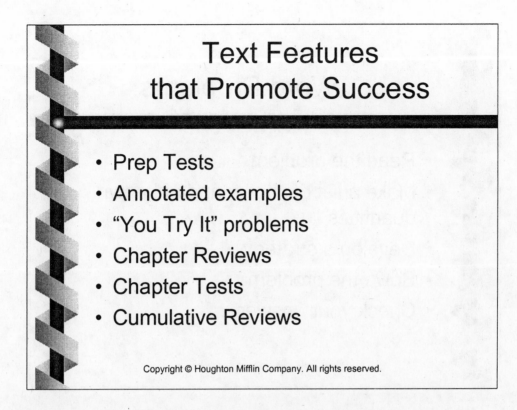

Text Features
that Promote Success

- Prep Tests
- Annotated examples
- "You Try It" problems
- Chapter Reviews
- Chapter Tests
- Cumulative Reviews

Guide students through the features of the text that will help them succeed. Students should turn to the pages mentioned below.

•Prep Tests – These tests (see page 196) focus on skills that are required for the upcoming chapter. The answers to the Prep Test are in the Answer Section (see page A10). Next to each answer, there is a reference (except in Chapter 1) to the objective from which that question was taken. Students should review the lesson material corresponding to any question that was missed.

•Annotated examples are designated by an orange arrow (see page 83). After reading through an annotated example, the student should cover up the solution and try to solve the problem without looking at it.

•You Try It – Next to each Example (see page 84), there is a corresponding You Try It. Students should study the solution to the Example and then attempt the You Try It. A complete solution to the You Try It can be found in the Appendix (see page S5).

•Chapter Reviews (see page 115) and Chapter Tests (see page 117) help students prepare for a test. As with the Prep Tests, the Chapter Review and Chapter Test have objective references so that students can focus on the objectives associated with questions they missed.

•The Cumulative Reviews (see page 225) allow students to refresh skills learned in earlier chapters. The answers to all Cumulative Review exercises are in the Answer Section along with an objective reference.

Word Problems

- Read the problem
- Make a list of known and unknown quantities
- Develop a strategy
- Solve the problem
- Check your answer

Urge students to take a disciplined approach to solving word problems. The most fundamental part of solving word problems is to identify what must be found. Have students turn to page 86 and look at Exercise 6. Without asking students to solve the problem, have them write a <u>sentence</u> that states what must be found.

Each of the word problem examples in the text shows both a strategy and the solution for solving the problem. For the You Try It problems, students are given a place to write their own strategies (see page 86).

Encourage students to check their answers.

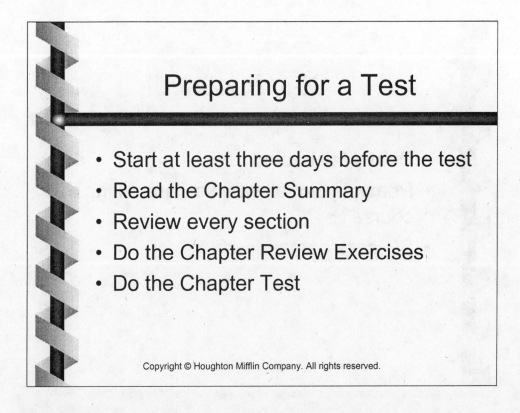

Preparing for a Test

- Start at least three days before the test
- Read the Chapter Summary
- Review every section
- Do the Chapter Review Exercises
- Do the Chapter Test

Preparing for a test should start well before the actual date. Remind students that if they keep up with class assignments, preparing for a test will be much easier.

At least 3 days before the test, students should:

•Read the Chapter Summary.

•Review every section, paying close attention to items mentioned in the Chapter Summary. Attempt about five problems from about the middle third of the exercise set.

•Do the Chapter Review exercises. Remind students that the objective reference next to each answer indicates the objective from which the exercise was taken.

•Do the Chapter Test. Set aside the amount of time allotted for the actual test, making sure there are no interruptions.

Stay Focused!

- Do not fall behind
- Remind yourself why you are taking this course
- Success demands effort

Remind students that the most important factor that leads to success in math is to keep up—they must not fall behind.

Encourage students to review the reasons why they are taking this course. Even if it is to complete a degree requirement and they hate math, completing this course is a necessary prerequisite to reaching that goal. Urge them to complete the class so that math is not an obstacle to success.

Remind students that all successful endeavors require effort.

Transparency Masters

TRANSPARENCY LIST

#	Text Source	#	Text Source	#	Text Source
1	Section 1.1, p. 3	49	Section 6.2, p. 242, Ex. 40	96	Section 7.5, p. 320, Ex. 20
2	Section 1.2, p. 4	50	Section 6.6, p. 266, Ex. 22-25	97	Section 8.1, p. 338, Ex. 33
3	Section 1.2, p. 15, Ex. 71-73	51	Section 6.7, p. 269	98	Section 8.1, p. 338, Ex. 34
4	Section 1.2, p. 16, Ex. 76-79	52	Section 6.7, p. 270	99	Section 8.1, p. 338, Ex. 35
5	Section 1.3, p. 20	53	Section 6.7, p. 271, Example 2	100	Section 8.1, p. 338, Ex. 36
6	Section 1.3, p. 24, Ex. 113-114	54	Section 6.7, p. 272, You Try It, 2	101	Section 9.1, p. 366, Ex. 29
7	Section 1.3, p. 24, Ex. 115	55	Section 6.7, p. 274, Ex. 13	102	Section 9.1, p. 366, Ex. 32
8	Section 1.3, p. 24, Ex. 116-117	56	Section 6.7, p. 275, Ex. 14	103	Section 9.2, p. 370, Ex. 29
9	Section 1.4, p. 31, Ex. 101-102	57	Section 6.7, p. 276, Ex. 15	104	Section 9.4, p. 377, Ex. 3
10	Section 1.4, p. 32, Ex. 103-105	58	Section 7.1, p. 289	105	Section 9.5, p. 379
11	Section 1.5, p. 39	59	Section 7.1, p. 189	106	Section 9.5, p. 385
12	Section 1.5, p. 43, Ex. 104-106	60	Section 7.1, p. 190	107	Section 10.1, p. 398, Ex. 73
13	Section 1.5, p. 44, Ex. 107-108	61	Section 7.l, p. 291	108	Section 10.2, p. 399
14	Section 1.5, p. 44, Ex. 109-110	62	Section 7.1, p. 291	109	Section 10.2, p. 405, Ex. 89
15	Section 2.4, p. 82, Ex. 97	63	Section 7.1, p. 292	110	Section 10.2, p. 406, Ex. 92-94
16	Section 2.5, p. 89, Ex. 68	64	Section 7.1, p. 292	111	Section 10.2, p. 406, Ex. 95-97
17	Section 2.5, p. 89, Ex. 69	65	Section 7.1, p. 293, Ex. 1-3	112	Section 10.3, p. 414, Ex. 116
18	Section 2.5, p. 90, Ex. 76	66	Section 7.1, p. 293, Ex. 4-6	113	Section 10.4, p. 424, Ex. 90-91
19	Section 2.6, p. 93	67	Section 7.1, p. 293, Ex. 7-9	114	Section 10.5, p. 429, Ex. 27
20	Section 2.8, p. 110, Ex. 48	68	Section 7.1, p. 294, Ex. 10-13	115	Section 11.6, p. 488, Ex. 48-49
21	Section 3.1, p. 123	69	Section 7.1, p. 294, Ex. 14-17	116	Section 11.6, p. 491
22	Section 3.2, p. 130, Ex. 28-30	70	Section 7.1, p. 295, ex. 18-21	117	Section 11.6, p. 491
23	Section 3.2, p. 130, Ex. 31-32	71	Section 7.1, p. 295, Ex. 22-25	118	Section 12.1, p. 508
24	Section 3.3, p. 134, Ex. 33	72	Section 7.1, p. 296, Ex. 26-29	119	Section 12.1, p. 512, Ex. 57
25	Section 3.3, p. 134, Ex. 34	73	Section 7.1, p. 296, Ex. 30-33	120	Section 12.1, p. 512, Ex. 58
26	Section 3.3, p. 134, Ex. 39-40	74	Section 7.2, p. 297	121	Section 12.1, p. 512, Ex. 59
27	Section 3.4, p. 137	75	Section 7.2, p. 297	122	Section 12.1, p. 512, Ex. 60
28	Section 3.4, p. 142, Ex. 129	76	Section 7.2, p. 298	123	Section 12.1, p. 512, Ex. 61
29	Section 3.4, p. 143, Ex. 131	77	Section 7.2, p. 298	124	Section 12.1, p. 512, Ex. 62
30	Section 3.4, p. 143, Ex. 132	78	Section 7.2, p. 299	125	Section 12.1, p. 512, Ex. 63
31	Section 3.4, p. 143, Ex. 133	79	Section 7.2, p. 299, Ex. 4-6	126	Section 12.1, p. 512, Ex. 64
32	Section 3.4, p. 144, Ex. 134	80	Section 7.2, p. 299, Ex. 7-10	127	Section 12.2, p. 513
33	Section 3.5, p. 148	81	Section 7.2, p. 300, Ex. 11-14	128	Section 12.2, p. 513
34	Section 3.5, p. 152, Ex. 104	82	Section 7.2, p. 300, Ex. 15-17	129	Section 12.2, p. 513
35	Section 3.6, p. 156, Ex. 70-71	83	Section 7.2, p. 300, Ex. 18-19	130	Section 12,2, p. 514
36	Section 4.3, p. 184, Ex. 72	84	Section 7.3, p. 301	131	Section 12.2, p. 514
37	Section 4.3, p. 185	85	Section 7.3, p. 301	132	Section 12.2, p. 514
38	Section 5.2, p. 204, Ex. 37-38	86	Section 7.3, p. 302	133	Section 12.2, p. 514
39	Section 5.3, p. 208, Ex. 35-36	87	Section 7.3, p. 302	134	Section 12.4, p. 538, Ex. 17
40	Section 5.4, p. 212, Ex. 34-35	88	Section 7.3, p. 303, Ex. 1-4	135	Section 12.4, p. 538, Ex. 18
41	Section 5.5, p. 216, Ex. 27	89	Section 7.3, p. 303, Ex.5-8	136	Section 12.4, p. 538, Ex. 19
42	Section 5.5, p. 216, Ex. 30	90	Section 7.3, p. 303, Ex. 9-12	137	Section 12.4, p. 538, Ex. 20
43	Section 5.5, p. 216, Ex. 31	91	Section 7.3, p. 304, Ex. 13-15	138	Section 12.4, p. 539, Ex. 21
44	Section 5.5, p. 218	92	Section 7.3, p. 304, Ex. 16-19	139	Section 12.4, p. 539, Ex. 22
45	Section 5.5, p. 219	93	Section 7.3, p. 304, Ex. 20-23	140	Appendix, p. 568
46	Section 6.2, p. 239, Ex. 1	94	Section 7.4, p. 308	141	Appendix, p. 569
47	Section 6.2, p. 239, Ex. 4	95	Section 7.5, p. 317	142	Appendix, p. 570
48	Section 6.2, p. 239, Ex. 6				

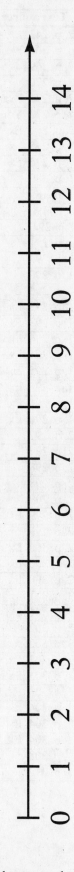

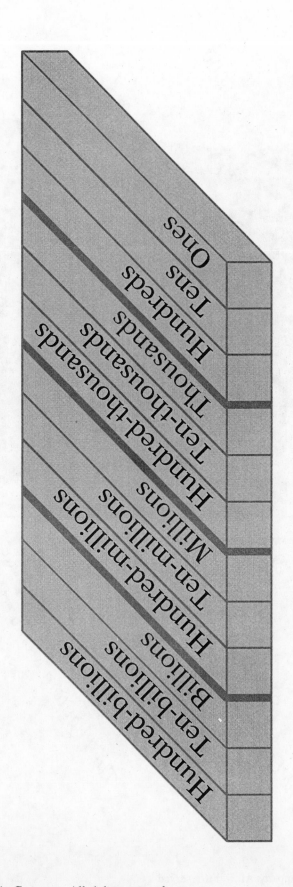

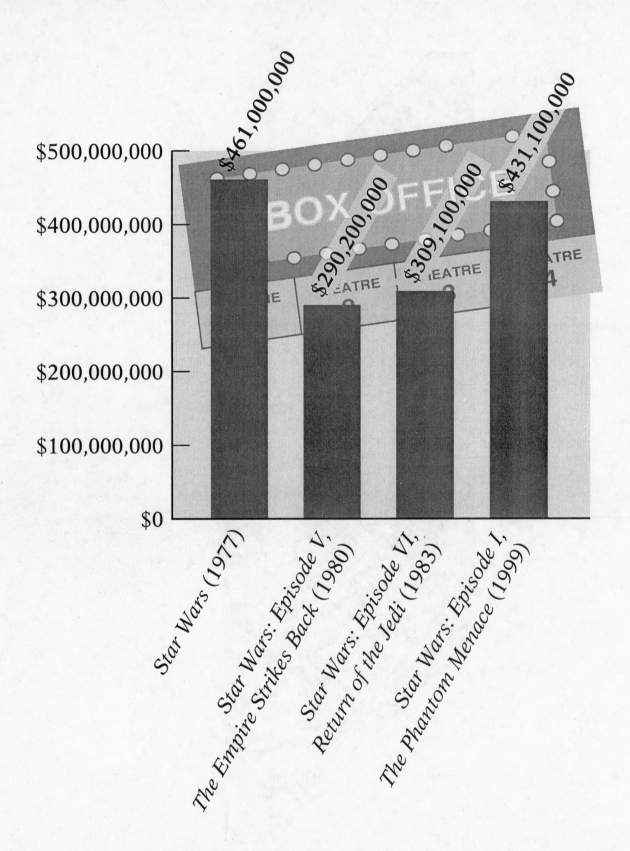

	All Americans	Ages 16 to 34
Checking accounts	$487	$375
Savings accounts	$3,494	$1,155
U.S. Savings Bonds	$546	$266
Money market	$10,911	$4,427
Stock/mutual funds	$4,510	$1,615
Home equity	$43,070	$17,184
Retirement	$9,016	$4,298

Branch	1940	1945
U.S. Army	267,767	8,266,373
U.S. Navy	160,997	3,380,817
U.S. Air Force	51,165	2,282,259
U.S. Marine Corps	28,345	474,680

Source: Dept. of the Army, Dept. of the Navy, Air Force Dept., Dept. of the Marines, U.S. Dept. of Defense

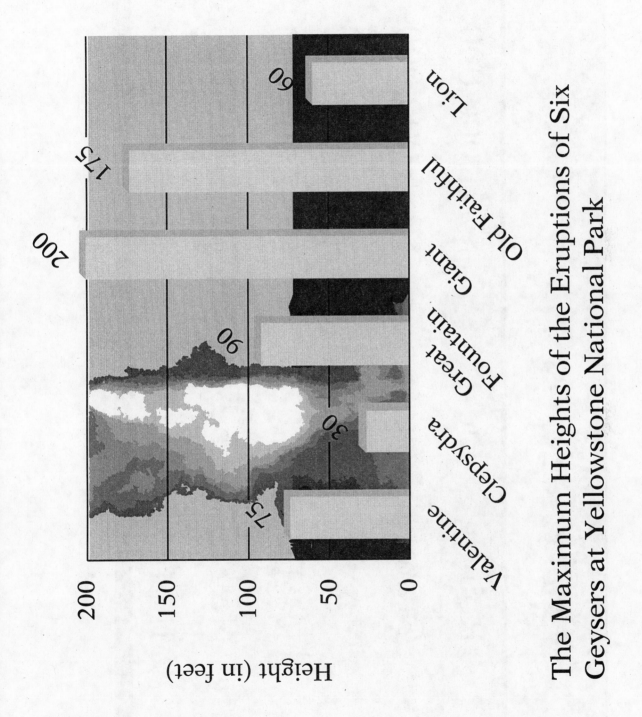

The Maximum Heights of the Eruptions of Six
Geysers at Yellowstone National Park

Live Acts	Gross
Rolling Stones	$751,000,000
Grateful Dead	$285,000,000
U2	$283,000,000
Eagles	$197,000,000
Neil Diamond	$183,000,000
Jimmy Buffett	$167,000,000

Source: Amusement Business BOXSCORE

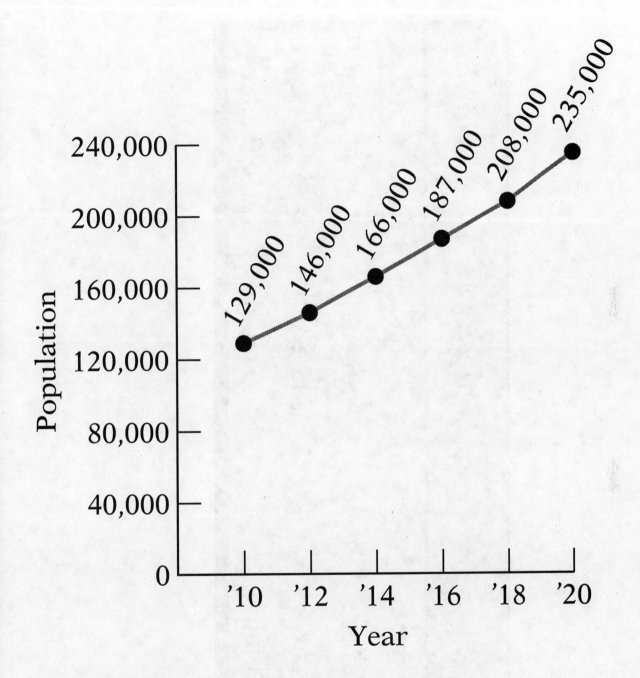

Expected U.S. Population Aged 100 and Over

Source: Census Bureau

	Company A	Company B
Can lights	$2 each	$3 each
High-intensity	$6 each	$4 each
Fire safety	$12 each	$11 each
Chandelier	$998 each	$1089 each

Type of Work	Wage per Hour
Electrician	$34
Plumber	$30
Clerk	$16
Bookkeeper	$20

Stadium	Seating Capacity
Columbus Crew Stadium	30,000
Giants Stadium	79,649
Mile High Stadium	76,098
Raymond James Stadium	66,321
Ericsson Stadium	73,250
Legion Field	83,000
Peoria Stadium	10,123
The Rose Bowl	92,542

Source: www.stadianet.com

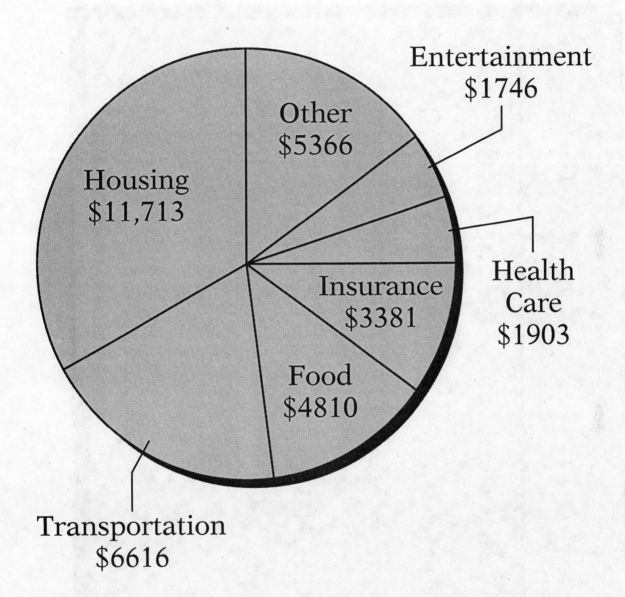

Entertainment $1746

Other $5366

Housing $11,713

Health Care $1903

Insurance $3381

Food $4810

Transportation $6616

Average Annual Household Expenses

Source: Bureau of Labor Statistics Consumer Expenditure Survey

Source	Claims
Accidents	$560,000
Theft	$300,000
Power surge	$80,000
Lightning	$50,000
Transit	$20,000
Water/flood	$20,000
Other	$110,000

Source: Safeware, The Insurance Company

Country	Annual Number of Hours Worked
Britain	1731
France	1656
Japan	1889
Norway	1399
United States	1966

Source: International Labor Organization

Aufmann/Barker/Lockwood *Basic College Mathematics: An Applied Approach* Seventh Edition
Transparency #15: Section 2.4, p. 82, Ex. 97

Where Americans Moved

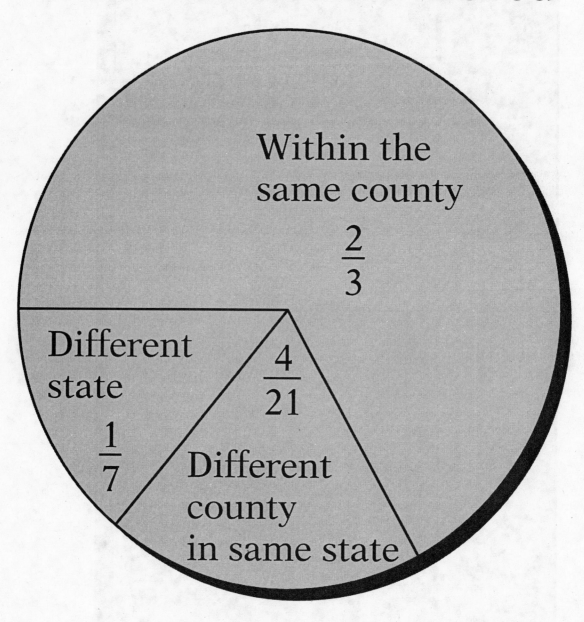

Within the same county $\dfrac{2}{3}$

Different state $\dfrac{1}{7}$

$\dfrac{4}{21}$

Different county in same state

Source: Census Bureau; *Geographical Mobility*

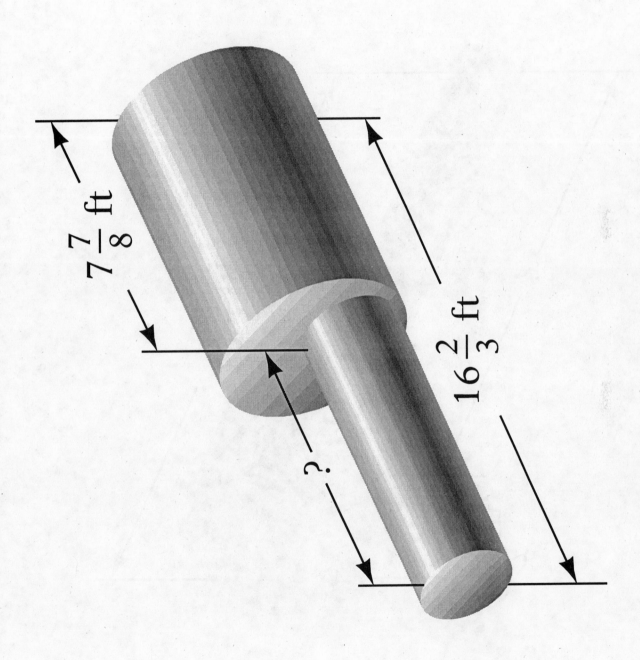

$7\frac{7}{8}$ ft

$16\frac{2}{3}$ ft

?

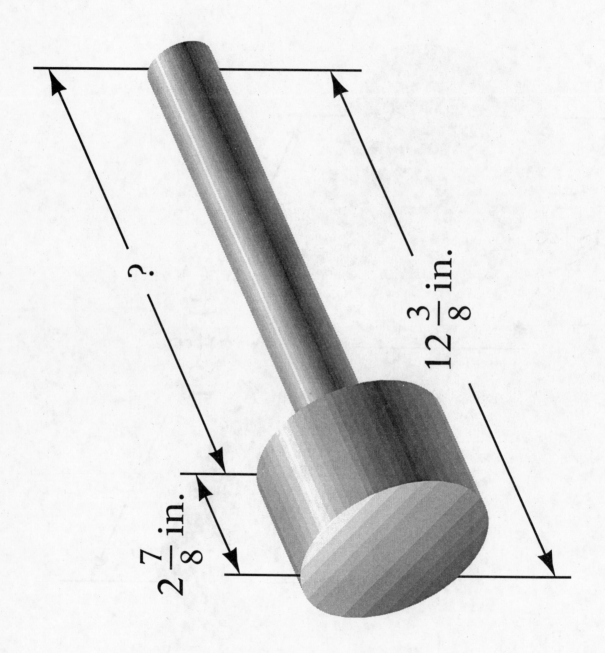

Aufmann/Barker/Lockwood *Basic College Mathematics: An Applied Approach* Seventh Edition
Transparency #18: Section 2.5, p. 90, Ex. 76

Sources of Federal Income

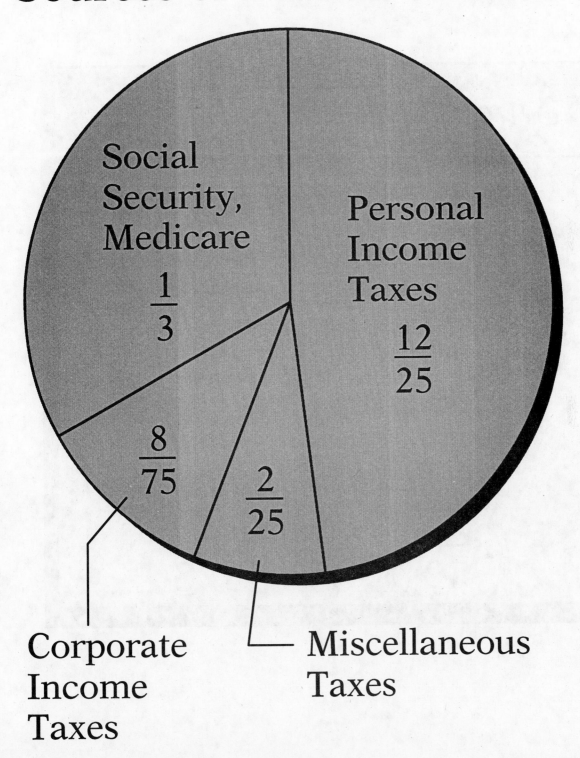

Length (ft)	Weight (lb/ft)
$6\frac{1}{2}$	$\frac{3}{8}$
$8\frac{5}{8}$	$1\frac{1}{4}$
$10\frac{3}{4}$	$2\frac{1}{2}$
$12\frac{7}{12}$	$4\frac{1}{3}$

Aufmann/Barker/Lockwood *Basic College Mathematics: An Applied Approach* Seventh Edition
Transparency #20: Section 2.8, p. 110, Ex. 48

Fast-Food Patrons' Top Criteria for Fast-Food Restaurants

Food Quality	$\dfrac{1}{4}$
Location	$\dfrac{13}{50}$
Menu	$\dfrac{4}{25}$
Price	$\dfrac{2}{25}$
Speed	$\dfrac{3}{25}$
Other	$\dfrac{3}{100}$

Source: Maritz Marketing Research, Inc.

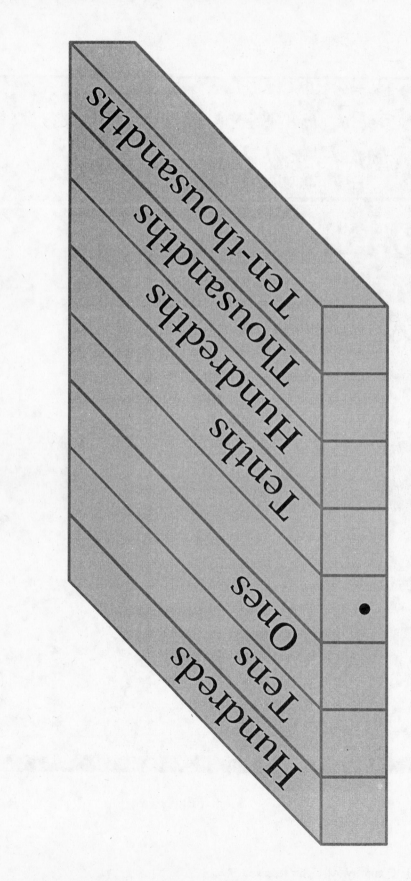

Annual Earnings	Number of Self-Employed (in millions)
Less than $5000	5.1
$5000 – $24,999	3.9
$25,000 – $49,999	1.6
$50,000 or more	1.0

Source: U.S. Small Business Administration

Product	Cost
Raisin bran	$3.29
Butter	$2.79
Bread	$1.49
Popcorn	$1.19
Potatoes	$2.49
Cola (6-pack)	$1.99
Mayonnaise	$2.99
Lunch meat	$3.39
Milk	$2.59
Toothpaste	$2.69

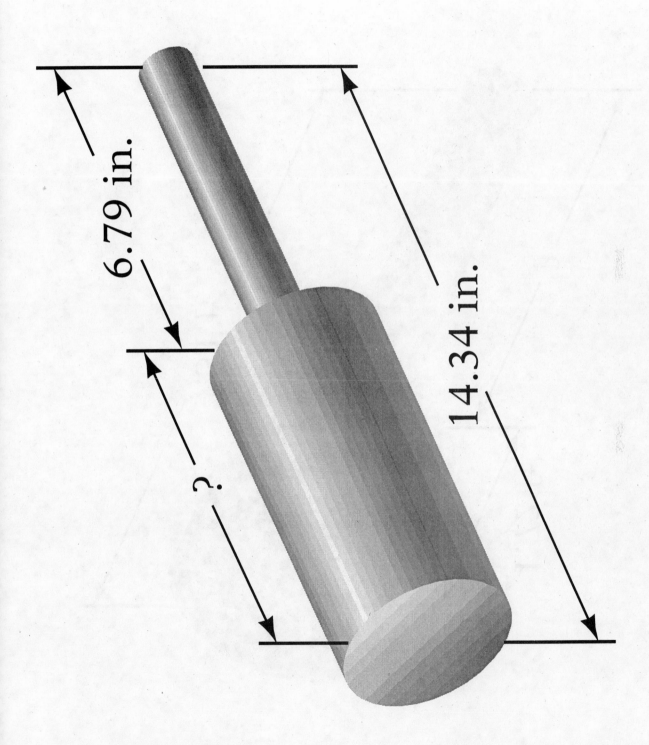

6.79 in.

14.34 in.

?

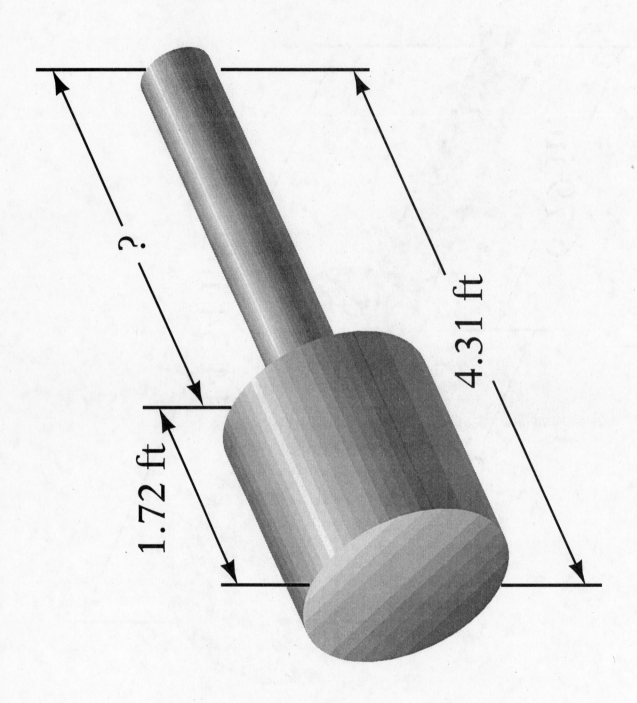

Year	Number of Households Shopping Online (in millions)
1998	8.7
1999	13.1
2000	17.7
2001	23.1
2002	30.3
2003	40.3

Source: Forrester Research Inc.

Meter Charges

Meter	Meter Fee
5/8" & 3/4"	$13.50
1"	$21.80
1-1/2"	$42.50
2"	$67.20
3"	$133.70
4"	$208.20
6"	$415.10
8"	$663.70

Water Charges

Commercial	$1.39/1000 gal
Comm Restaurant	$1.39/1000 gal
Industrial	$1.39/1000 gal
Institutional	$1.39/1000 gal
Res—No Sewer	
Residential—SF	
>0 <200 gal per day	$1.15/1000 gal
>200 <1500 gal per day	$1.39/1000 gal
>1500 gal per day	$1.54/1000 gal

Aufmann/Barker/Lockwood *Basic College Mathematics: An Applied Approach* Seventh Edition
Transparency #28: Section 3.4, p. 142, Ex. 129

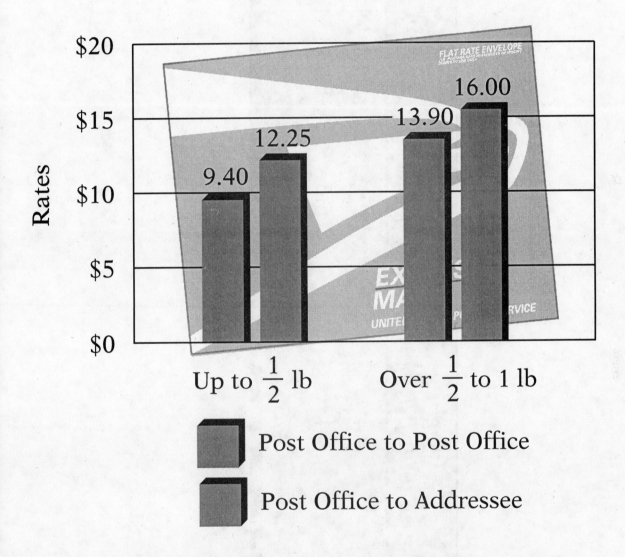

U.S. Postal Service Rates for Express Mail

Grade of Steel	Weight (pounds per foot)	Required Number of Feet	Cost per Pound
1	2.2	8	$1.20
2	3.4	6.5	$1.35
3	6.75	15.4	$1.94

Pounds	Zone 1	Zone 2	Zone 3	Zone 4
1–3	$6.55	$6.85	$7.25	$7.75
4–6	$7.10	$7.40	$7.80	$8.30
7–9	$7.50	$7.80	$8.20	$8.70
10–12	$7.90	$8.20	$8.60	$9.10

Code	Description	Price
112	Almonds 16 oz	$4.75
116	Cashews 8 oz	$2.90
117	Cashews 16 oz	$5.50
130	Macadamias 7 oz	$5.25
131	Macadamias 16 oz	$9.95
149	Pecan halves 8 oz	$6.25
155	Mixed nuts 8 oz	$4.80
160	Cashew brittle 8 oz	$1.95
182	Pecan roll 8 oz	$3.70
199	Chocolate peanuts 8 oz	$1.90

a. Code	Quantity	b. Code	Quantity	c. Code	Quantity
116	2	112	1	117	3
130	1	117	4	131	1
149	3	131	2	155	2
182	4	160	3	160	4
Mail to zone 4.		182	5	182	1
		Mail to zone 3.		199	3
				Mail to zone 2.	

Car	Total Engine Exhaust	Hydrocarbon Emission
1	367,921	36
2	401,346	42
3	298,773	21
4	330,045	32
5	432,989	45

Price List

Item Number	Description	Unit Price
27345	Valve spring	$1.85
41257	Main bearing	$3.40
54678	Valve	$4.79
29753	Ring set	$33.98
45837	Gasket set	$48.99
23751	Timing chain	$42.95
23765	Fuel pump	$77.59
28632	Wrist pin	$2.71
34922	Rod bearing	$2.67
2871	Valve seal	$0.42

Parts Used

Item	Quantity
Gasket set	1
Ring set	1
Valves	8
Wrist pins	8
Valve springs	16
Rod bearings	8
Main bearings	5
Valve seals	16
Timing chain	1

Time Spent

Day	Hours
Monday	7.0
Tuesday	7.5
Wednesday	6.5
Thursday	8.5
Friday	9.0

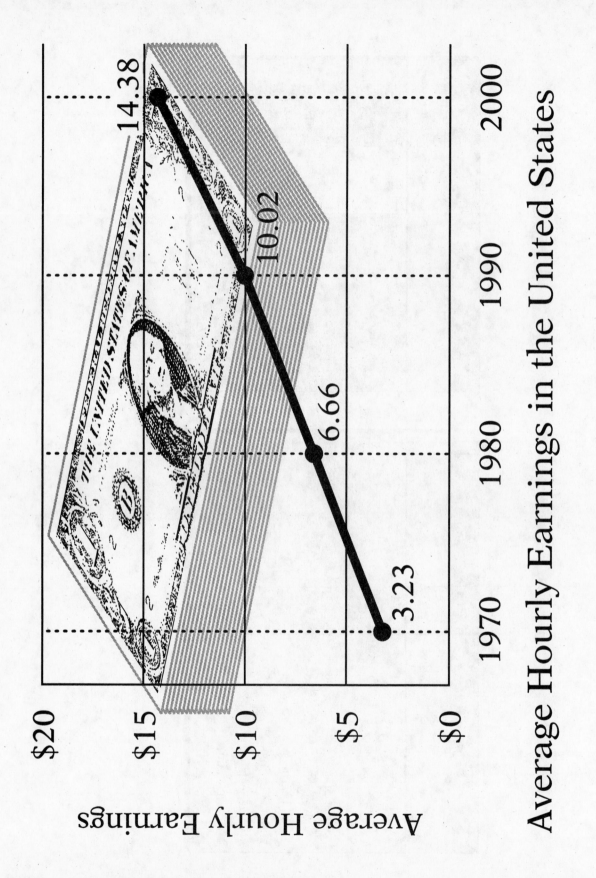

Average Hourly Earnings in the United States

Average Hourly Earnings

Source: Statistical Abstract of the United States; Bureau of Labor Statistics

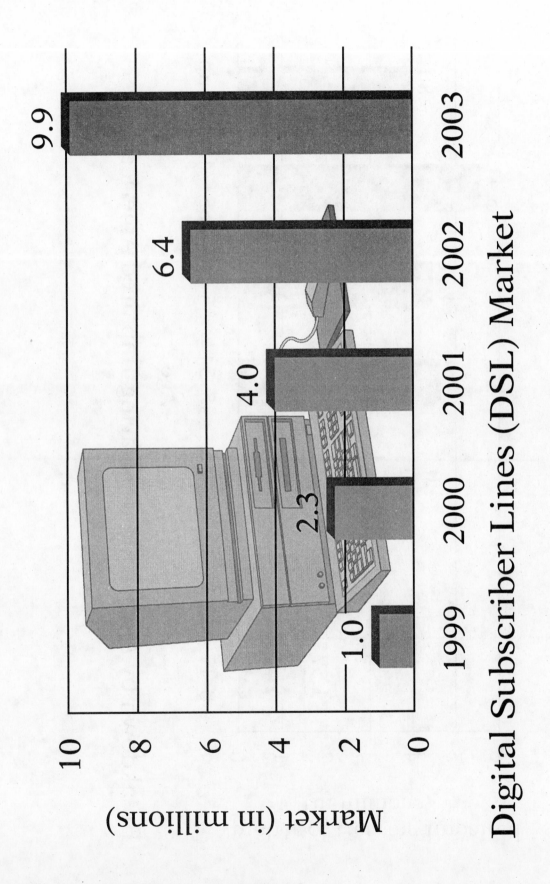

Digital Subscriber Lines (DSL) Market

Market (in millions)

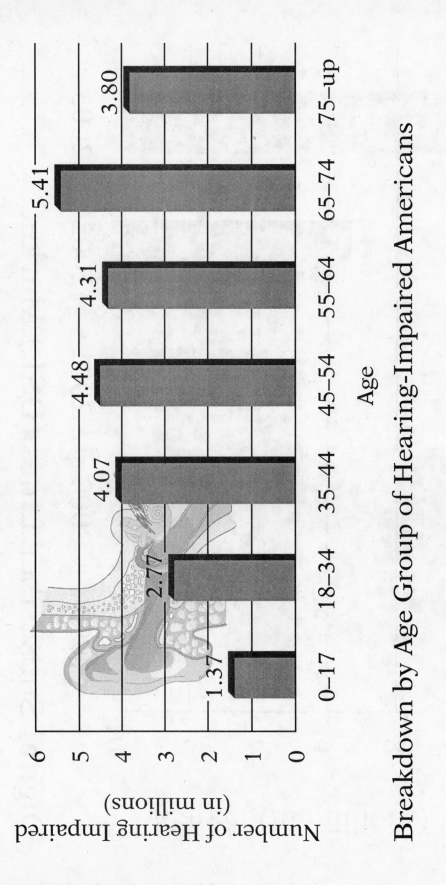

Breakdown by Age Group of Hearing-Impaired Americans

Age

Number of Hearing Impaired (in millions)

Source: American Speech-Language-Hearing Association

How Your Federal Tax Dollar Is Spent

Social Security	23 cents
Health	21 cents
Income security	14 cents
Net interest	11 cents
Edu., Vets, Transp.	10 cents
Defense	16 cents
Other	5 cents

Source: Tax Foundation, Office of Management and Budget

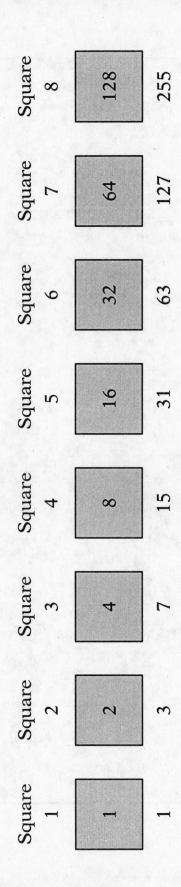

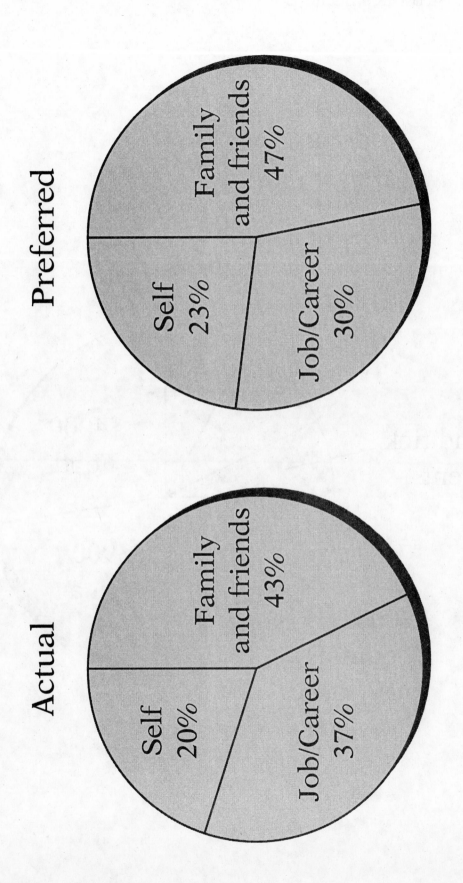

Source: WSJ Supplement, Work & Family; from *Families and Work Institute*

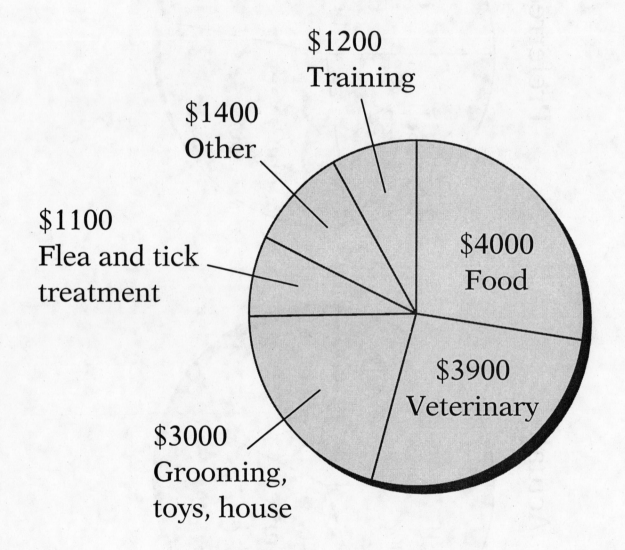

NUTRITION INFORMATION

SERVING SIZE: 1.4 OZ WHEAT FLAKES WITH
0.4 OZ. RAISINS: 39.4 g. ABOUT 1/2 CUP
SERVINGS PER PACKAGE: 14

	CEREAL & RAISINS	WITH 1/2 CUP VITAMINS A & D SKIM MILK

PERCENTAGE OF U.S. RECOMMENDED DAILY ALLOWANCES (U.S. RDA)

	CEREAL & RAISINS	WITH SKIM MILK
PROTEIN	4	15
VITAMIN A	15	20
VITAMIN C	**	2
THIAMIN	25	30
RIBOFLAVIN	25	35
NIACIN	25	35
CALCIUM	**	15
IRON	100	100
VITAMIN D	10	25
VITAMIN B_6	25	25
FOLIC ACID	25	25
VITAMIN B_{12}	25	30
PHOSPHOROUS	10	15
MAGNESIUM	10	20
ZINC	25	30
COPPER	2	4

* 2% MILK SUPPLIES AN ADDITIONAL 20 CALORIES.
  2 g FAT, AND 10 mg CHOLESTEROL.
** CONTAINS LESS THAN 2% OF THE U.S. RDA OF
   THIS NUTRIENT

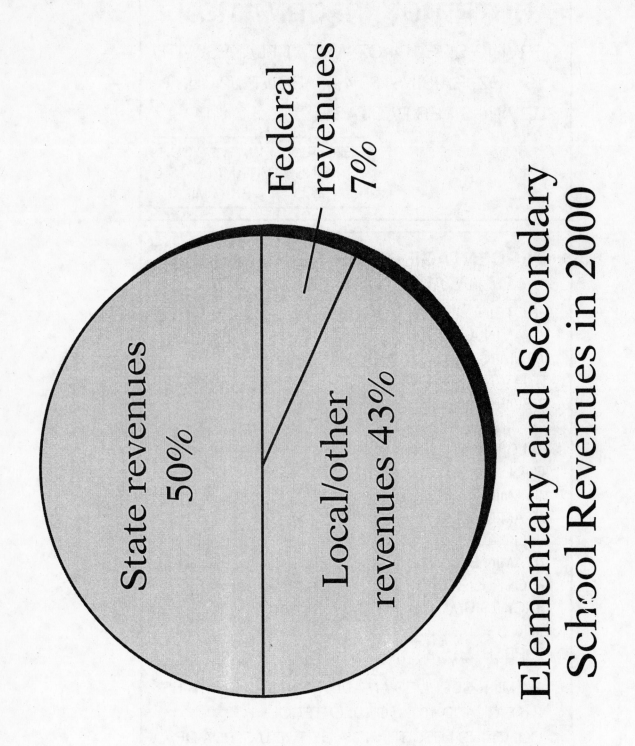

Federal revenues 7%

Elementary and Secondary School Revenues in 2000

State revenues 50%

Local/other revenues 43%

Source: U.S. Census Bureau

County	2000 Population	Projected Increase
Sacramento	1,200,000	900,000
Kern	651,700	948,300
Fresno	794,200	705,800
San Joaquin	562,000	737,400

Source: California Department of Finance

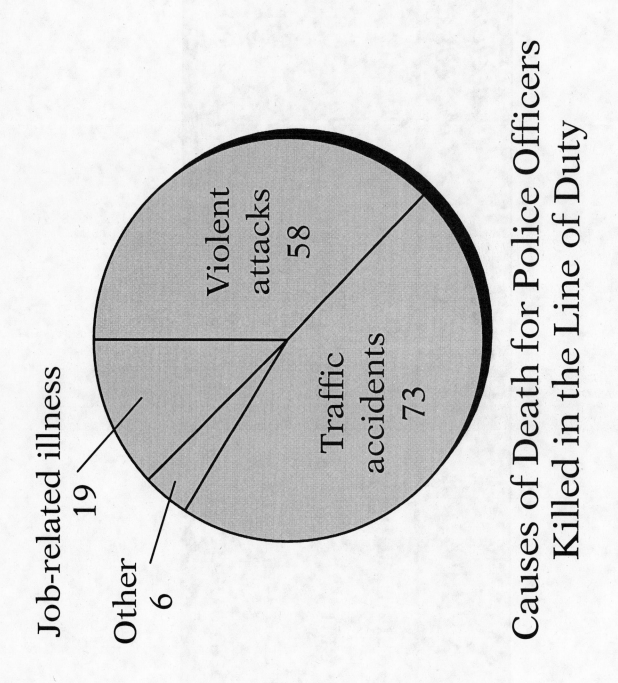

Causes of Death for Police Officers Killed in the Line of Duty

Violent attacks 58

Traffic accidents 73

Job-related illness 19

Other 6

Product	CPI
All items	172.3
Food and beverages	167.9
Housing	169.4
Clothes	128.3
Transportation	155.7
Medical care	260.5
Entertainment	103.4
Education	101.5

Source: Bureau of Labor Statistics

Age:		Under 5	5–17	18–24	25–34	35–44	45–54	55–64	65 and Older
2010	Male	10,272	26,639	15,388	19,286	19,449	21,706	16,973	16,966
	Female	9,827	25,363	14,774	19,565	19,993	22,455	18,457	22,749
2050	Male	13,748	35,227	18,734	25,034	24,550	22,340	21,127	36,289
	Female	13,165	33,608	18,069	25,425	25,039	23,106	22,517	45,710

Population Projections for the United States, by Age and Sex (in thousands)

Source: www.census.gov

Aufmann/Barker/Lockwood *Basic College Mathematics: An Applied Approach* Seventh Edition
Transparency #46: Section 6.2, p. 239, Ex. 1

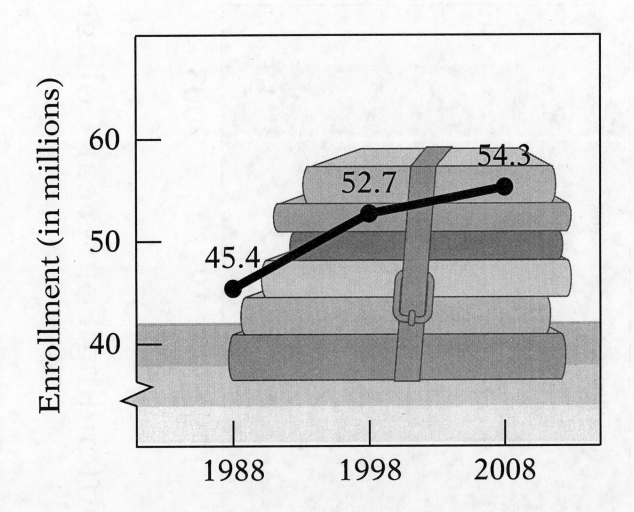

Elementary and Secondary School Enrollments

Source: National Center for Education

Aufmann/Barker/Lockwood *Basic College Mathematics: An Applied Approach* Seventh Edition
Transparency #47: Section 6.2, p. 239, Ex. 4

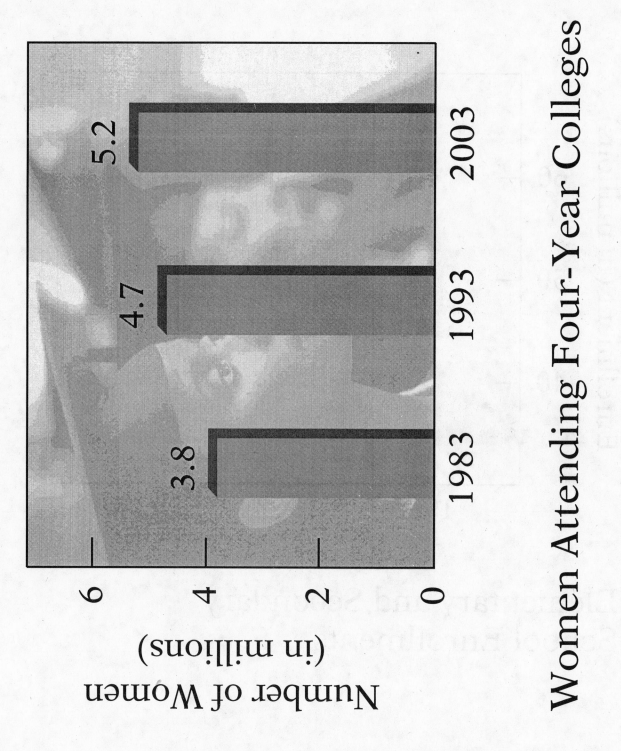

Women Attending Four-Year Colleges

Number of Women (in millions)

5.2

4.7

3.8

2003

1993

1983

6

4

2

0

Year	Number of Households Containing Millionaires
1975	350,000
1997	3,500,000
2005	5,600,000

Source: Affluent Market Institute

Number of Active-Duty U.S. Military Personnel

Source: Fiscal 2000 Annual Report to the President and Congress by the Secretary of Defense

Estimated Starting Salaries

Bachelor's Degree	Estimated Starting Salary	% Change from Previous Year
Top 5		
Chemical engineering	$42,758	4.3%
Mechanical engineering	$39,852	4.5%
Electrical engineering	$38,811	4.0%
Industrial engineering	$37,732	4.0%
Computer science	$36,964	4.5%
Bottom 5		
Liberal arts	$24,102	3.5%
Natural resources	$22,950	3.5%
Home economics	$22,916	3.5%
Telecommunications	$22,447	4.0%
Journalism	$22,102	4.0%

Source: Michigan State University

RECORD ALL CHARGES OR CREDITS THAT AFFECT YOUR ACCOUNT

NUMBER	DATE	DESCRIPTION OF TRANSACTION	PAYMENT/DEBIT (−)		√ T	FEE (IF ANY) (−)	DEPOSIT/CREDIT (+)		BALANCE $	
									840	27
263	5/20	Dentist	$ 75	00	√	$	$		765	27
264	5/22	Post Office	33	61	√				731	66
265	5/22	Gas Company	67	14					664	52
	5/29	Deposit			√		192	00	856	52
266	5/29	Pharmacy	38	95	√				817	57
267	5/30	Telephone	63	85					753	72
268	6/2	Groceries	73	19	√				680	53
	6/3	Deposit			√		215	00	895	53
269	6/7	Insurance	103	00	√				792	53
	6/10	Deposit					225	00	1017	53
270	6/15	Photo Shop	16	63	√				1000	90
271	6/18	Newspaper	27	00					973	90

CHECKING ACCOUNT Monthly Statement   Account Number: 924-297-8

Date	Transaction	Amount	Balance
5/20	OPENING BALANCE		840.27
5/21	CHECK	75.00	765.27
5/23	CHECK	33.61	731.66
5/29	DEPOSIT	192.00	923.66
6/1	CHECK	38.95	884.71
6/1	INTEREST	4.47	889.18
6/3	CHECK	73.19	815.99
6/3	DEPOSIT	215.00	1030.99
6/9	CHECK	103.00	927.99
6/16	CHECK	16.63	911.36
6/20	SERVICE CHARGE	3.00	908.36
6/20	CLOSING BALANCE		908.36

RECORD ALL CHARGES OR CREDITS THAT AFFECT YOUR ACCOUNT

NUMBER	DATE	DESCRIPTION OF TRANSACTION	PAYMENT/DEBIT (−)		√ T	FEE (IF ANY) (−)	DEPOSIT/CREDIT (+)		BALANCE $	1620	42
413	3/2	Car Payment	$ 232	15	√	$	$			1388	27
414	3/2	Utility	67	14	√					1321	13
415	3/5	Restaurant	78	14						1242	99
	3/8	Deposit			√		1842	66		3085	65
416	3/10	House Payment	672	14	√					2413	51
417	3/14	Insurance	177	10						2236	41

CHECKING ACCOUNT Monthly Statement   Account Number: 924-297-8

Date	Transaction	Amount	Balance
3/1	OPENING BALANCE		1620.42
3/4	CHECK	232.15	1388.27
3/5	CHECK	67.14	1321.13
3/8	DEPOSIT	1842.66	3163.79
3/10	INTEREST	6.77	3170.56
3/12	CHECK	672.14	2498.42
3/25	SERVICE CHARGE	2.00	2496.42
3/30	CLOSING BALANCE		2496.42

RECORD ALL CHARGES OR CREDITS THAT AFFECT YOUR ACCOUNT

NUMBER	DATE	DESCRIPTION OF TRANSACTION	PAYMENT/DEBIT (–)		√ T	FEE (IF ANY) (–)	DEPOSIT/CREDIT (+)		BALANCE $ 412	64
345	1/14	Phone Bill	$ 54	75	√	$	$		357	89
346	1/19	News Shop	18	98	√				338	91
347	1/23	Theatre Tickets	95	00					243	91
	1/31	Deposit			√		947	00	1190	91
348	2/5	Cash	250	00	√				940	91
349	2/12	Rent	840	00					100	91

CHECKING ACCOUNT Monthly Statement		Account Number: 924-297-8	
Date	Transaction	Amount	Balance
1/10	OPENING BALANCE		412.64
1/18	CHECK	54.75	357.89
1/23	CHECK	18.98	338.91
1/31	DEPOSIT	947.00	1285.91
2/1	INTEREST	4.52	1290.43
2/10	CHECK	250.00	1040.43
2/10	CLOSING BALANCE		1040.43

RECORD ALL CHARGES OR CREDITS THAT AFFECT YOUR ACCOUNT

NUMBER	DATE	DESCRIPTION OF TRANSACTION	PAYMENT/DEBIT (−)		√ T	FEE (IF ANY) (−)	DEPOSIT/CREDIT (+)		BALANCE $	
									903	17
	2/15	Deposit	$			$	$ 523	84	1427	01
234	2/20	Mortgage	773	21					653	80
235	2/27	Cash	200	00					453	80
	3/1	Deposit					523	84	977	64
236	3/12	Insurance	275	50					702	14
237	3/12	Telephone	78	73					623	41

CHECKING ACCOUNT Monthly Statement   Account Number: 314-271-4

Date	Transaction	Amount	Balance
2/14	OPENING BALANCE		903.17
2/15	DEPOSIT	523.84	1427.01
2/21	CHECK	773.21	653.80
2/28	CHECK	200.00	453.80
3/1	INTEREST	2.11	455.91
3/14	CHECK	275.50	180.41
3/14	CLOSING BALANCE		180.41

RECORD ALL CHARGES OR CREDITS THAT AFFECT YOUR ACCOUNT

NUMBER	DATE	DESCRIPTION OF TRANSACTION	PAYMENT/DEBIT (–)		√ T	FEE (IF ANY) (–)	DEPOSIT/CREDIT (+)		BALANCE $	
									2466	79
223	3/2	Groceries	$ 167	32		$	$		2299	47
	3/5	Deposit					960	70	3260	17
224	3/5	Rent	860	00					2400	17
225	3/7	Gas & Electric	142	35					2257	82
226	3/7	Cash	300	00					1957	82
227	3/7	Insurance	218	44					1739	38
228	3/7	Credit Card	419	32					1320	06
229	3/12	Dentist	92	00					1228	06
230	3/13	Drug Store	47	03					1181	03
	3/19	Deposit					960	70	2141	73
231	3/22	Car Payment	241	35					1900	38
232	3/25	Cash	300	00					1600	38
233	3/25	Oil Company	166	40					1433	98
234	3/28	Plumber	155	73					1278	25
235	3/29	Department Store	288	39					989	86

CHECKING ACCOUNT Monthly Statement   Account Number: 122-345-1

Date	Transaction	Amount	Balance
3/1	OPENING BALANCE		2466.79
3/5	DEPOSIT	960.70	3427.49
3/7	CHECK	167.32	3260.17
3/8	CHECK	860.00	2400.17
3/8	CHECK	300.00	2100.17
3/9	CHECK	142.35	1957.82
3/12	CHECK	218.44	1739.38
3/14	CHECK	92.00	1647.38
3/18	CHECK	47.03	1600.35
3/19	DEPOSIT	960.70	2561.05
3/25	CHECK	241.35	2319.70
3/27	CHECK	300.00	2019.70
3/29	CHECK	155.73	1863.97
3/30	INTEREST	13.22	1877.19
4/1	CLOSING BALANCE		1877.19

RECORD ALL CHARGES OR CREDITS THAT AFFECT YOUR ACCOUNT

NUMBER	DATE	DESCRIPTION OF TRANSACTION	PAYMENT/DEBIT (–)		√T	FEE (IF ANY) (–)	DEPOSIT/CREDIT (+)		BALANCE $ 1219 43	
	5/1	Deposit	$			$	$ 619	14	1838	57
515	5/2	Electric Bill	42	35					1796	22
516	5/2	Groceries	95	14					1701	08
517	5/4	Insurance	122	17					1578	91
518	5/5	Theatre Tickets	84	50					1494	41
	5/8	Deposit					619	14	2113	55
519	5/10	Telephone	37	39					2076	16
520	5/12	Newspaper	22	50					2053	66
	5/15	Interest					7	82	2061	48
	5/15	Deposit					619	14	2680	62
521	5/20	Computer Store	172	90					2507	72
522	5/21	Credit Card	313	44					2194	28
523	5/22	Eye Exam	82	00					2112	28
524	5/24	Groceries	107	14					2005	14
525	5/24	Deposit					619	14	2624	28
526	5/25	Oil Company	144	16					2480	12
527	5/30	Car Payment	288	62					2191	50
528	5/30	Mortgage Payment	877	42					1314	08

CHECKING ACCOUNT Monthly Statement   Account Number: 122-345-1

Date	Transaction	Amount	Balance
5/1	OPENING BALANCE		1219.43
5/1	DEPOSIT	619.14	1838.57
5/3	CHECK	95.14	1743.43
5/4	CHECK	42.35	1701.08
5/6	CHECK	84.50	1616.58
5/8	CHECK	122.17	1494.41
5/8	DEPOSIT	619.14	2113.55
5/15	INTEREST	7.82	2121.37
5/15	CHECK	37.39	2083.98
5/15	DEPOSIT	619.14	2703.12
5/23	CHECK	82.00	2621.12
5/23	CHECK	172.90	2448.22
5/24	CHECK	107.14	2341.08
5/24	DEPOSIT	619.14	2960.22
5/30	CHECK	288.62	2671.60
6/1	CLOSING BALANCE		2671.60

Aufmann/Barker/Lockwood *Basic College Mathematics: An Applied Approach* Seventh Edition
Transparency #57: Section 6.7, p. 276, Ex. 15

RECORD ALL CHARGES OR CREDITS THAT AFFECT YOUR ACCOUNT

NUMBER	DATE	DESCRIPTION OF TRANSACTION	PAYMENT/DEBIT (–)	√T	FEE (IF ANY) (–)	DEPOSIT/CREDIT (+)	BALANCE $ 2035 18
218	7/2	Mortgage	$ 984 60		$	$	1050 58
219	7/4	Telephone	63 36				987 22
220	7/7	Cash	200 00				787 22
	7/12	Deposit				792 60	1579 82
221	7/15	Insurance	292 30				1287 52
222	7/18	Investment	500 00				787 52
223	7/20	Credit Card	414 83				372 69
	7/26	Deposit				792 60	1165 29
224	7/27	Department Store	113 37				1051 92

CHECKING ACCOUNT Monthly Statement   Account Number: 122-345-1

Date	Transaction	Amount	Balance
7/1	OPENING BALANCE		2035.18
7/1	INTEREST	5.15	2040.33
7/4	CHECK	984.60	1055.73
7/6	CHECK	63.36	992.37
7/12	DEPOSIT	792.60	1784.97
7/20	CHECK	292.30	1492.67
7/24	CHECK	500.00	992.67
7/26	DEPOSIT	792.60	1785.27
7/28	CHECK	200.00	1585.27
7/30	CLOSING BALANCE		1585.27

Figure 1 Net worth of America's richest billionaires

Source: *Forbes*

Aufmann/Barker/Lockwood *Basic College Mathematics: An Applied Approach* Seventh Edition
Transparency #59: Section 7.1, p. 289

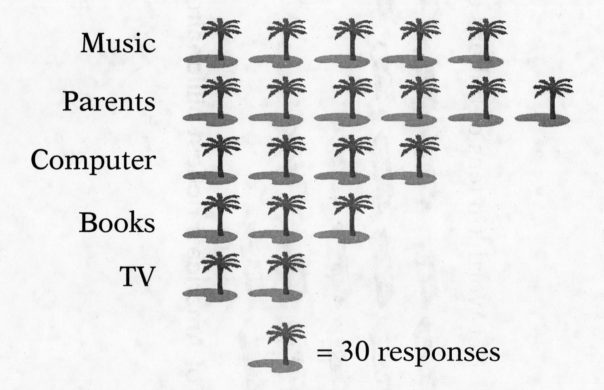

Music
Parents
Computer
Books
TV

= 30 responses

Figure 2 What 600 young Americans want on a desert island

Source: *Time*, June 30, 1997

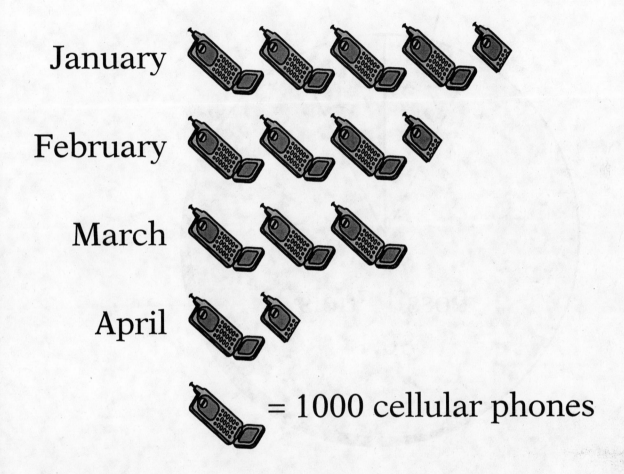

January

February

March

April

= 1000 cellular phones

Figure 3 Monthly cellular phone
purchases

Aufmann/Barker/Lockwood *Basic College Mathematics: An Applied Approach* Seventh Edition
Transparency #61: Section 7.1, p. 291

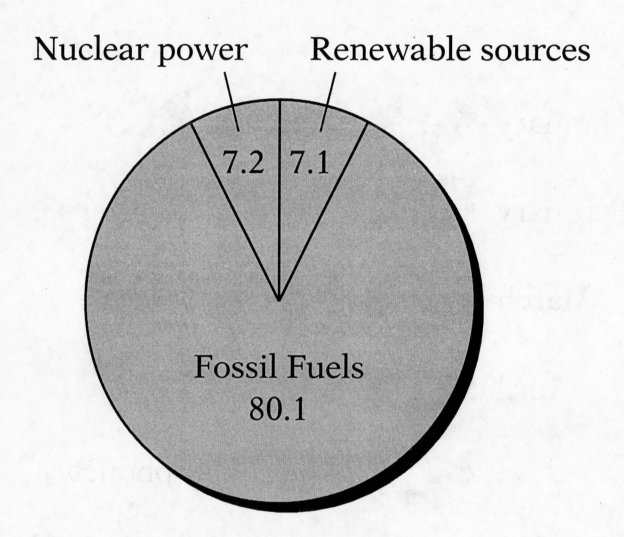

Nuclear power   **Renewable sources**

7.2 7.1

Fossil Fuels
80.1

Figure 4 Annual energy
consumption in quadrillion Btu in
the United States

Source: *The World Almanac and Book of Facts 2000*

Aufmann/Barker/Lockwood *Basic College Mathematics: An Applied Approach* Seventh Edition
Transparency #62: Section 7.1, p. 291

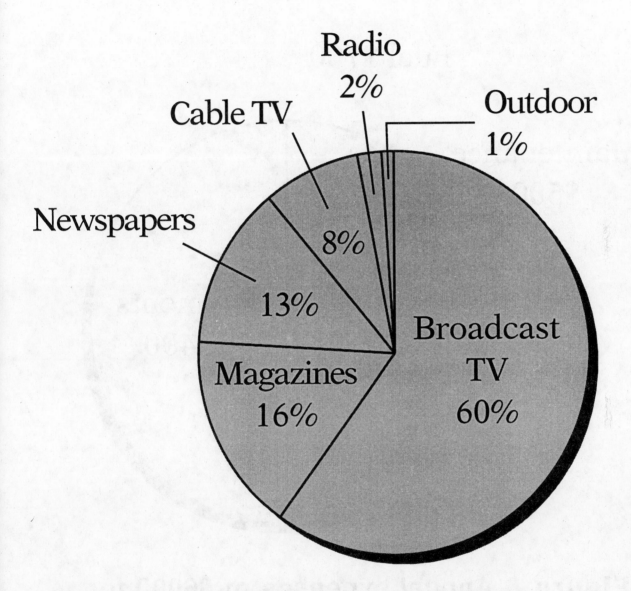

Figure 5 Distribution of advertising dollars for 25 companies

Source: Interep research

Aufmann/Barker/Lockwood *Basic College Mathematics: An Applied Approach* Seventh Edition
Transparency #63: Section 7.1, p. 292

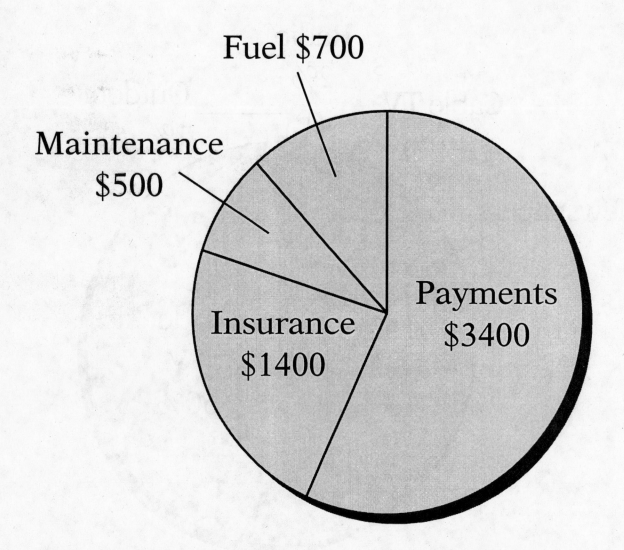

Figure 6 Annual expenses of $6000 for owning, operating, and financing a car

Source: Based on data from IntelliChoice

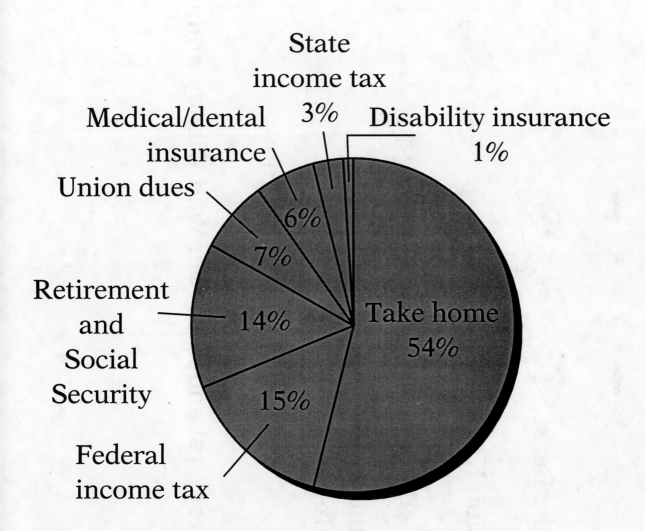

Figure 7 Distribution of gross monthly income of $2900

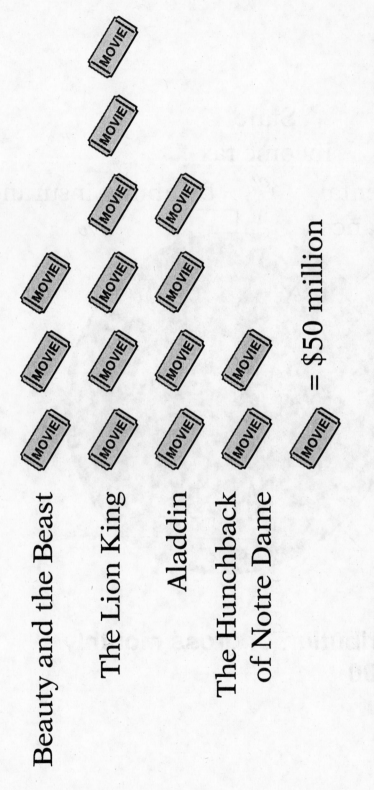

Figure 8 Gross revenues of four Walt Disney animated movies

Source: www.worldboxoffice.com

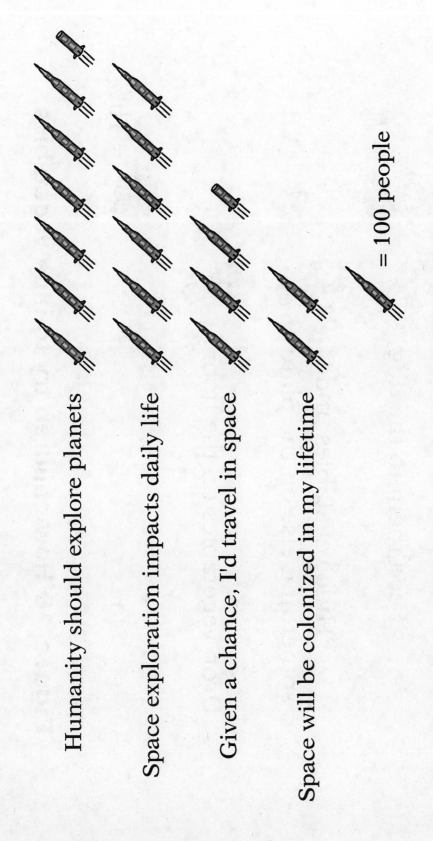

= 100 people

Figure 9 Number of adults who agree with the statement

Source: Opinion Research for Space Day Partners

Aufmann/Barker/Lockwood *Basic College Mathematics: An Applied Approach* Seventh Edition
Transparency #67: Section 7.1, p. 293, Ex. 7-9

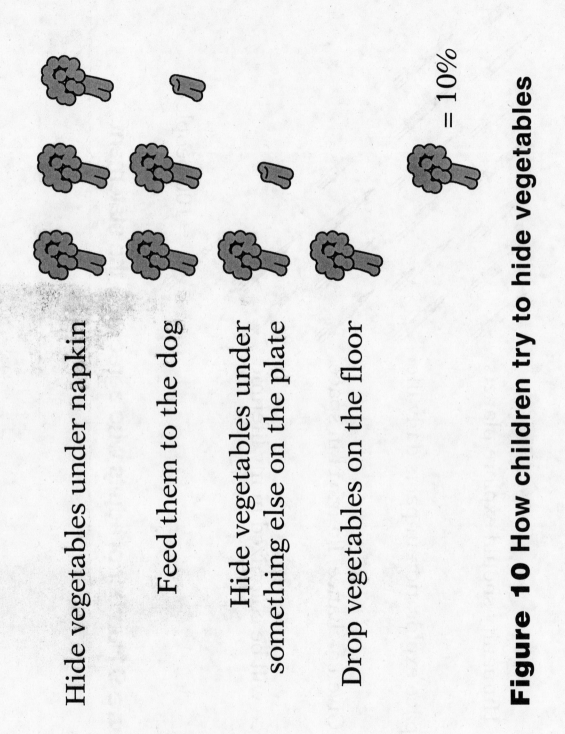

Figure 10 How children try to hide vegetables

= 10%

Hide vegetables under napkin

Feed them to the dog

Hide vegetables under something else on the plate

Drop vegetables on the floor

Source: Strategic Consulting and Research for Del Monte

Aufmann/Barker/Lockwood *Basic College Mathematics: An Applied Approach* Seventh Edition
Transparency #68: Section 7.1, p. 294, Ex. 10-13

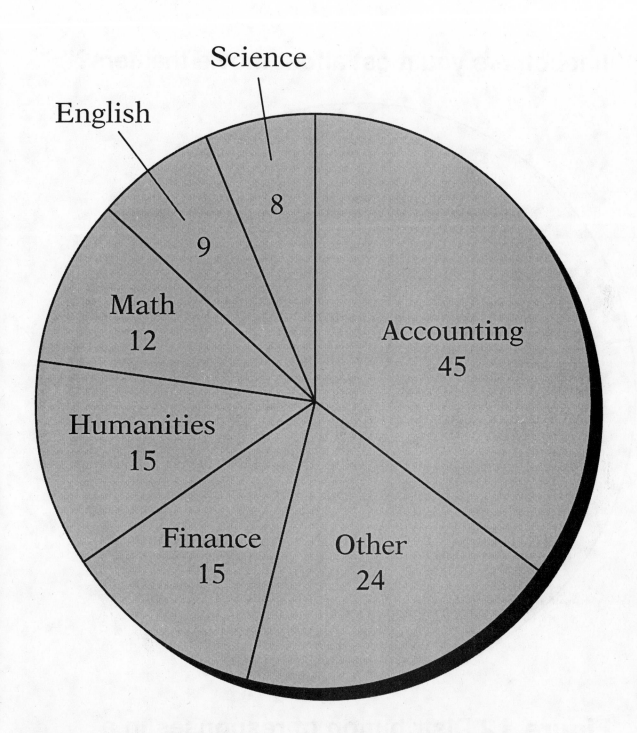

Figure 11 Number of units required to graduate with an accounting degree

Aufmann/Barker/Lockwood *Basic College Mathematics: An Applied Approach* Seventh Edition
Transparency #69: Section 7.1, p. 294, Ex. 14-17

"What bothers you most about movie theaters?"

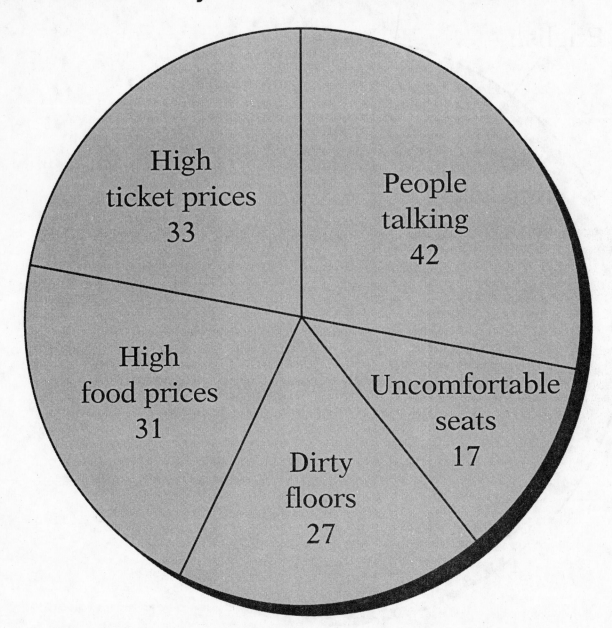

Figure 12 Distribution of responses in a survey

Aufmann/Barker/Lockwood *Basic College Mathematics: An Applied Approach* Seventh Edition
Transparency #70: Section 7.1, p. 295, Ex. 18-21

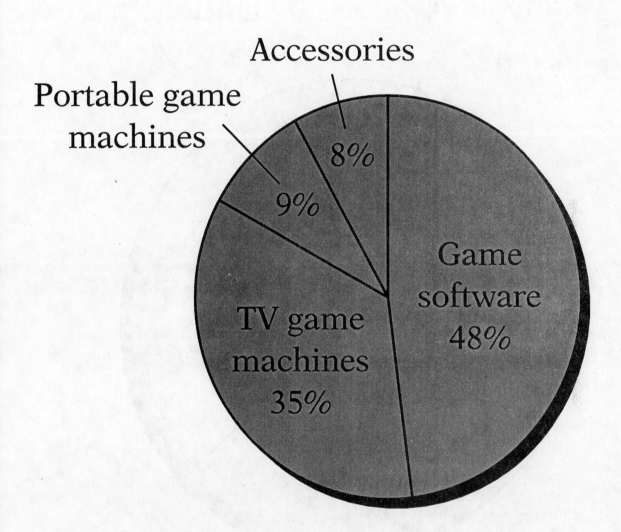

Figure 13 Percents of $3,100,000,000
spent annually on home video games

Source: The NPD Group, Toy Manufacturers of America

Aufmann/Barker/Lockwood *Basic College Mathematics: An Applied Approach* Seventh Edition
Transparency #71: Section 7.1, p. 295, Ex. 22-25

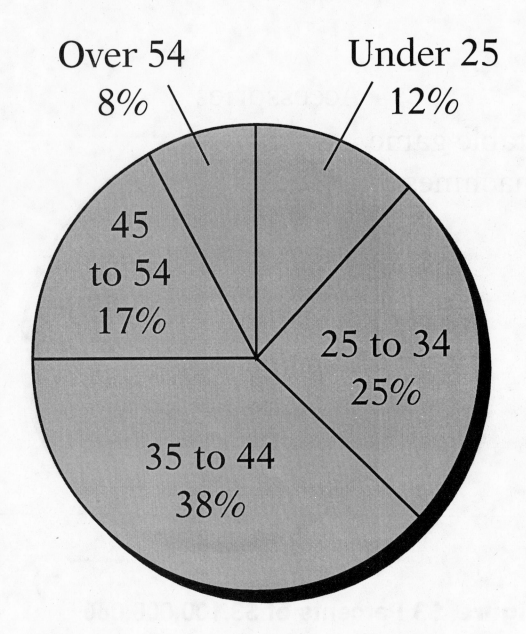

Figure 14 Ages of the homeless in America

Source: The Department of Housing and Urban Development

Aufmann/Barker/Lockwood *Basic College Mathematics: An Applied Approach* Seventh Edition
Transparency #72: Section 7.1, p. 296, Ex. 26-29

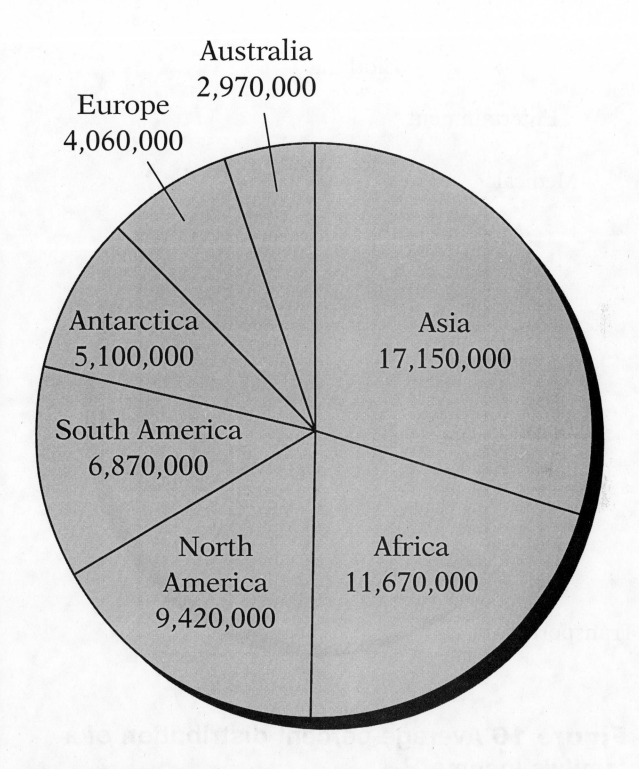

Figure 15 Land area of the seven continents (in square miles)

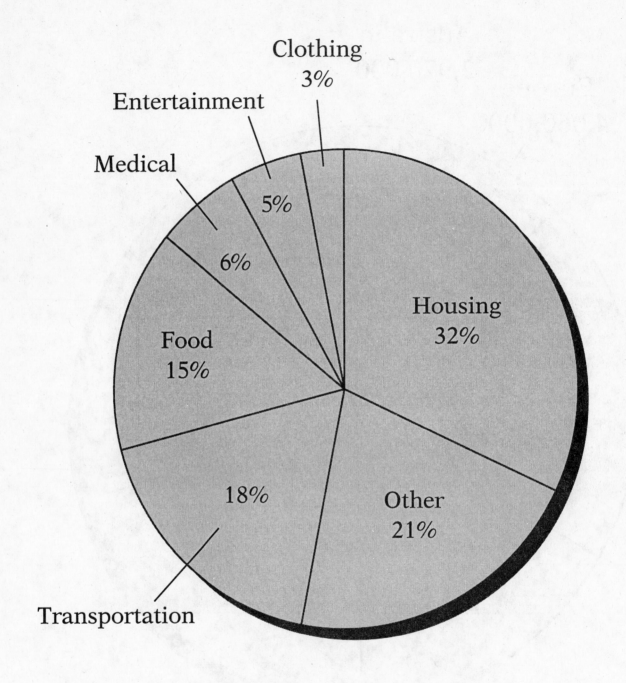

Figure 16 Average percent distribution of a family's income

Source: Consumer Expenditure Survey for the Bureau of Labor Statistics

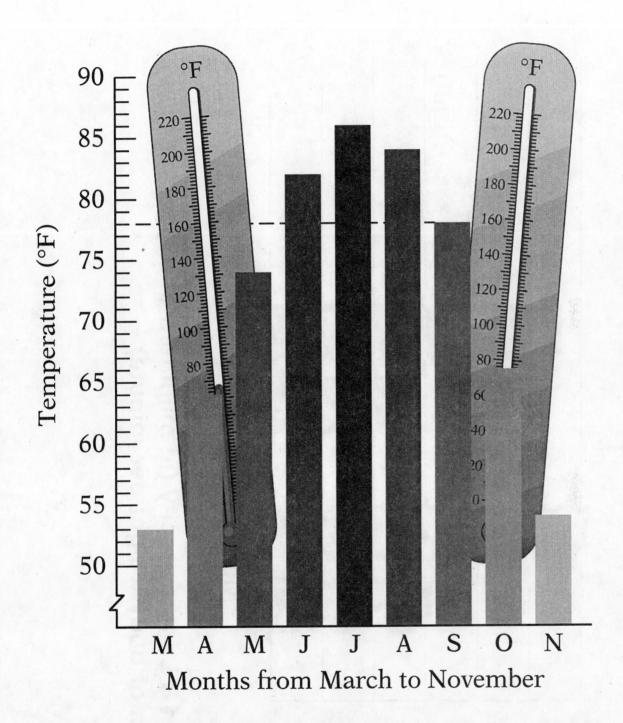

Figure 17 Daily high temperatures in Cincinnati, Ohio

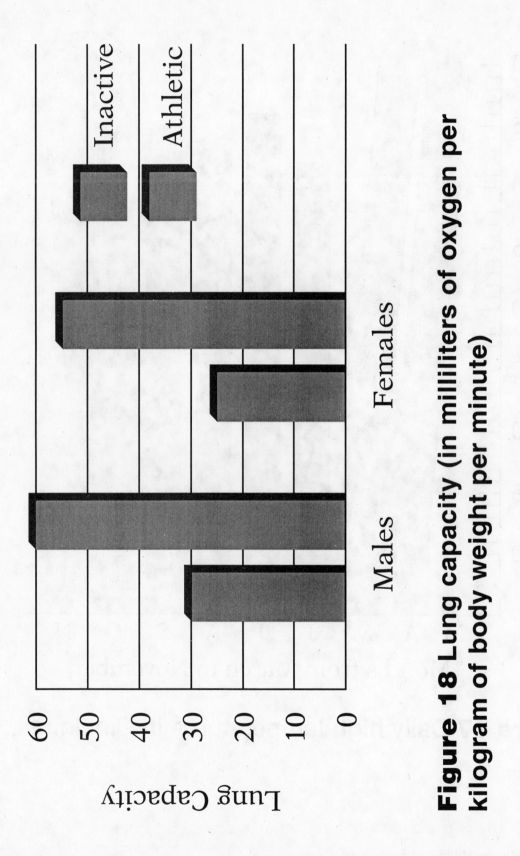

Figure 18 Lung capacity (in milliliters of oxygen per kilogram of body weight per minute)

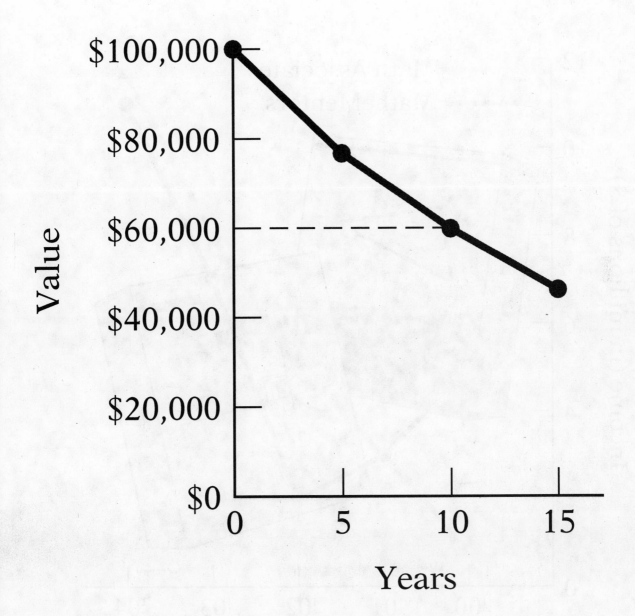

Figure 19 **Effect of inflation on the value of a $100,000 life insurance policy**

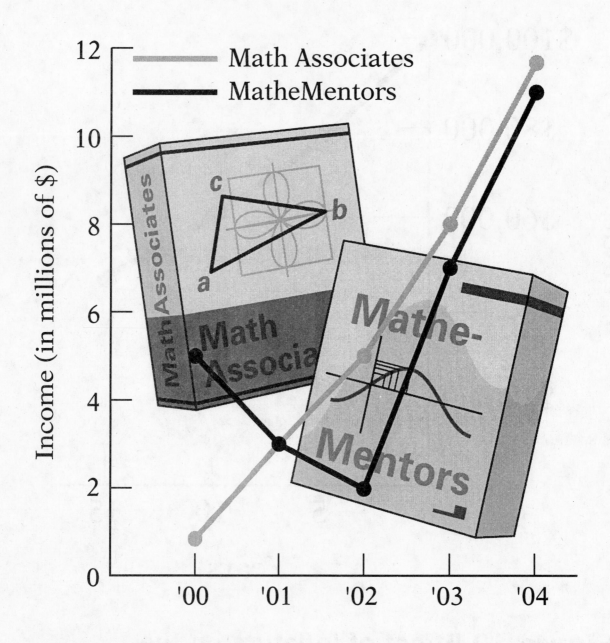

Figure 20 Net incomes of Math Associates
and MatheMentors

Aufmann/Barker/Lockwood *Basic College Mathematics: An Applied Approach* Seventh Edition
Transparency #78: Section 7.2, p. 299

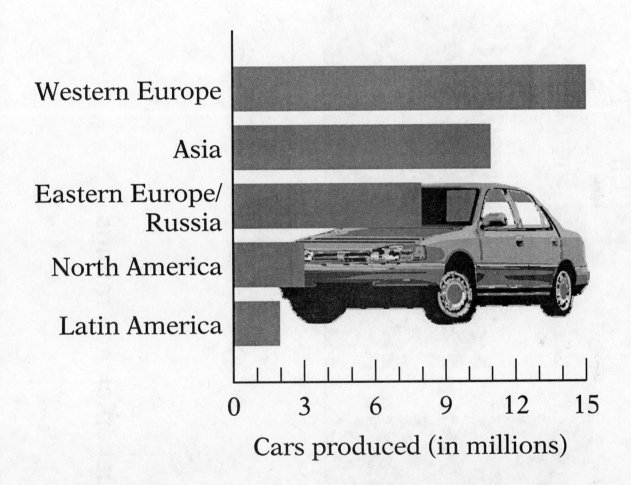

Figure 21 Number of passenger cars produced
(in a recent year)

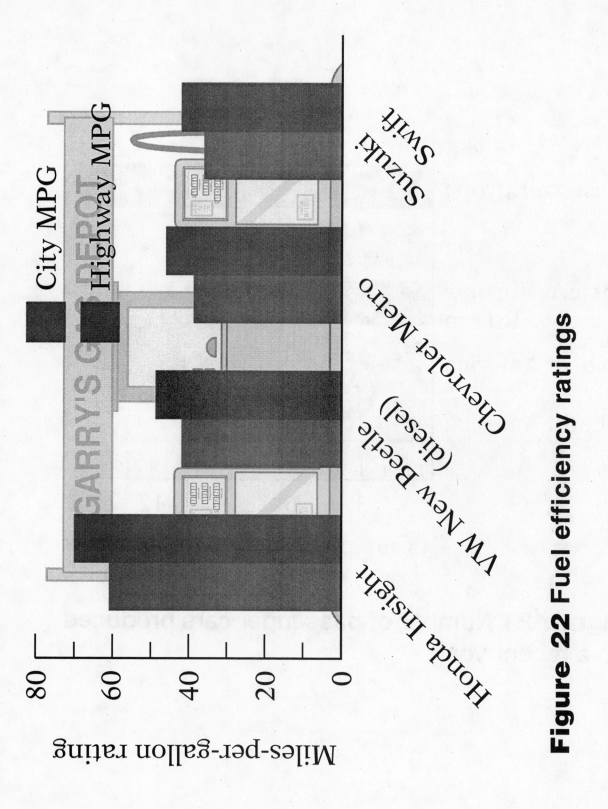

Figure 22 Fuel efficiency ratings

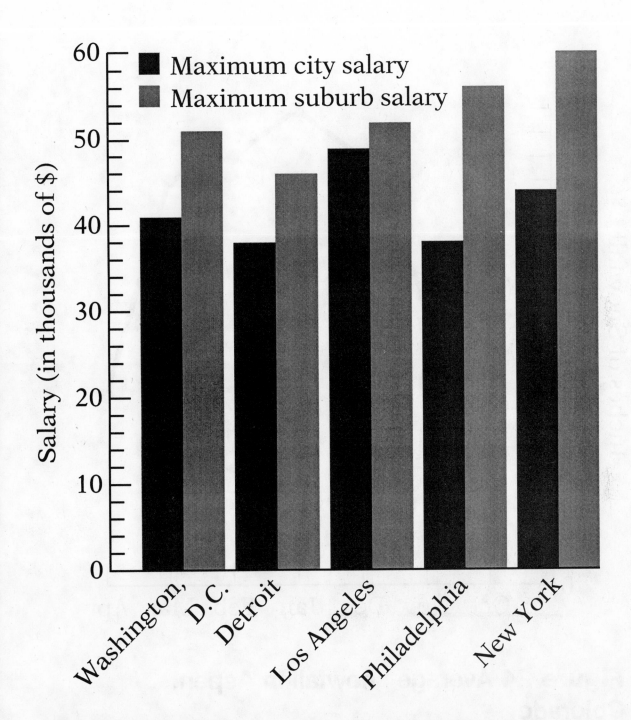

Figure 23 Maximum salaries of police officers in the city and suburbs

Source: *USA Today*

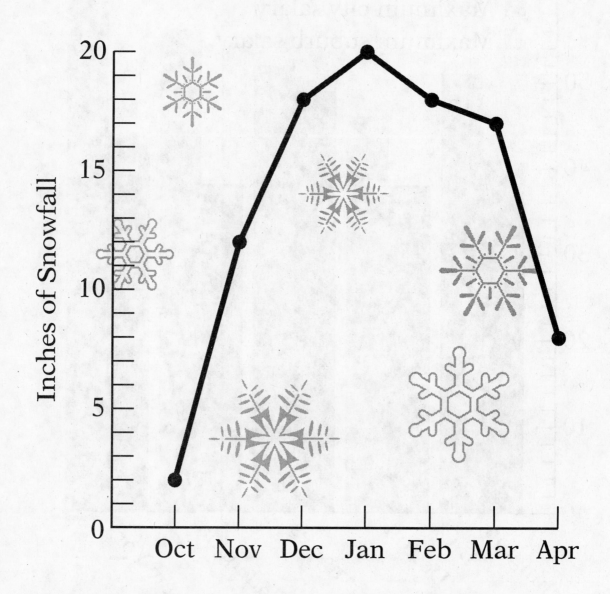

Figure 24 Average snowfall in Aspen, Colorado

Source: *Weather America,* by Alfred Garwood

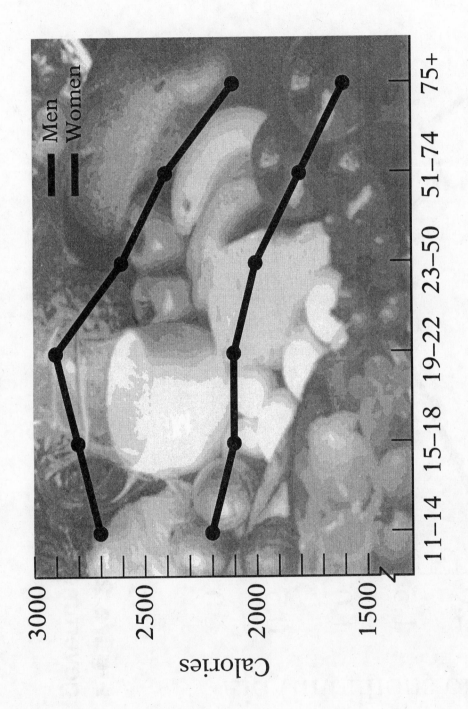

Figure 25 Recommended number of calories per day for women and men

Source: *Numbers,* by Andrea Sutcliffe (HarperCollins)

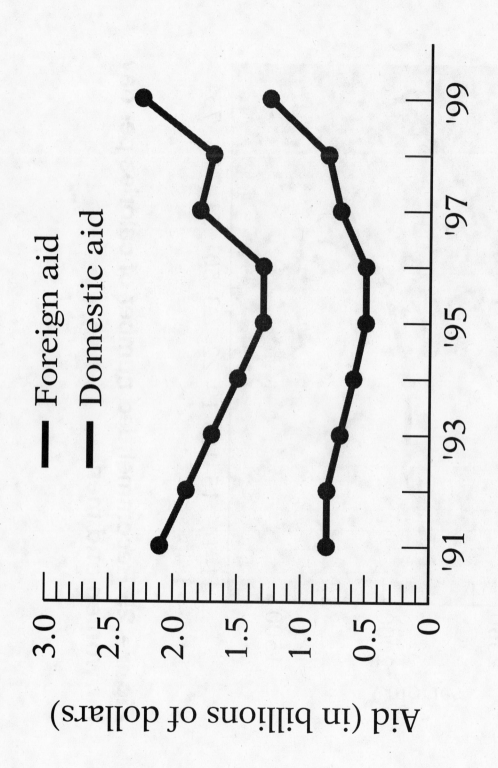

Figure 26 Aid provided by the U.S. government for drug prevention

Class Intervals (miles per gallon)	Class Frequencies (number of cars)
18–20	12
20–22	19
22–24	24
24–26	17
26–28	15
28–30	5

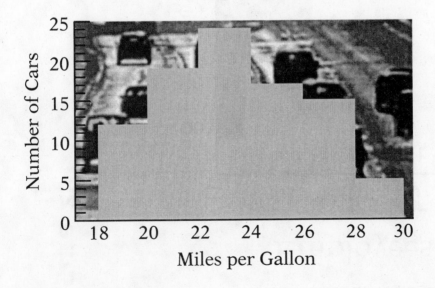

Figure 27

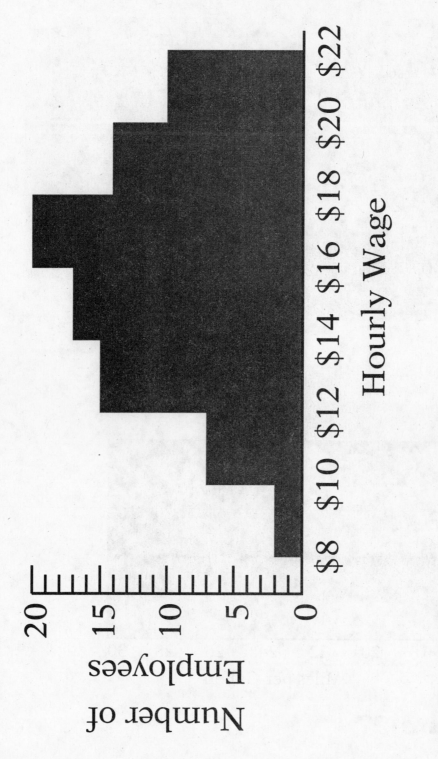

Figure 28

Class Inteval (miles per hour)	Class Midpoint	Class Frequency
30–40	35	7
40–50	45	13
50–60	55	25
60–70	65	21
70–80	75	4

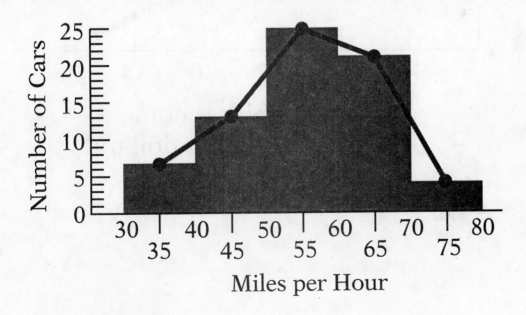

Figure 29

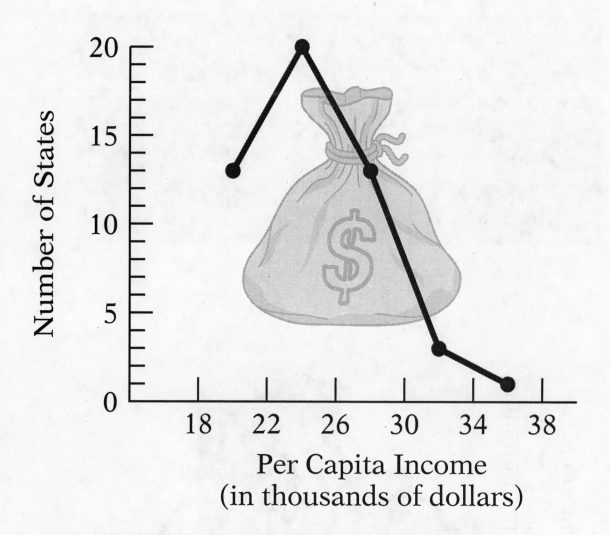

Figure 30

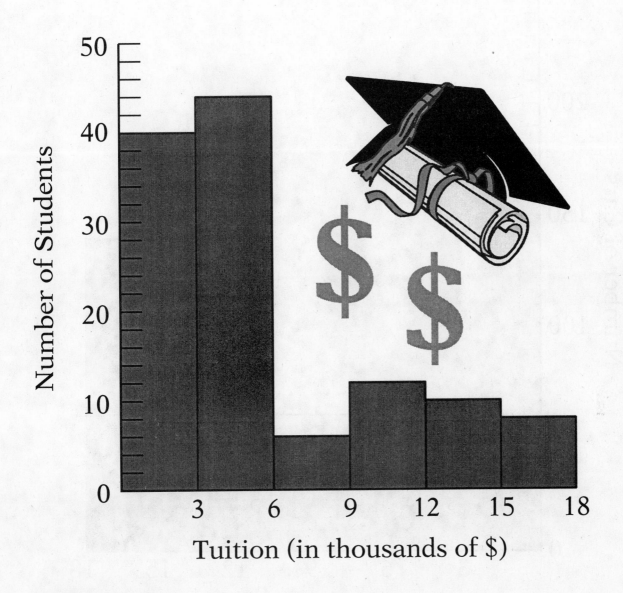

Figure 31

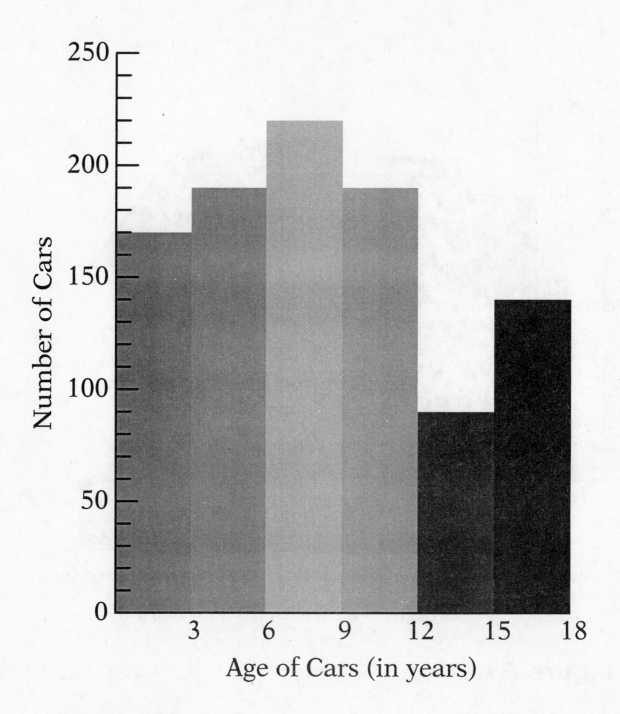

Figure 32

Source: American Automobile Manufacturers Association

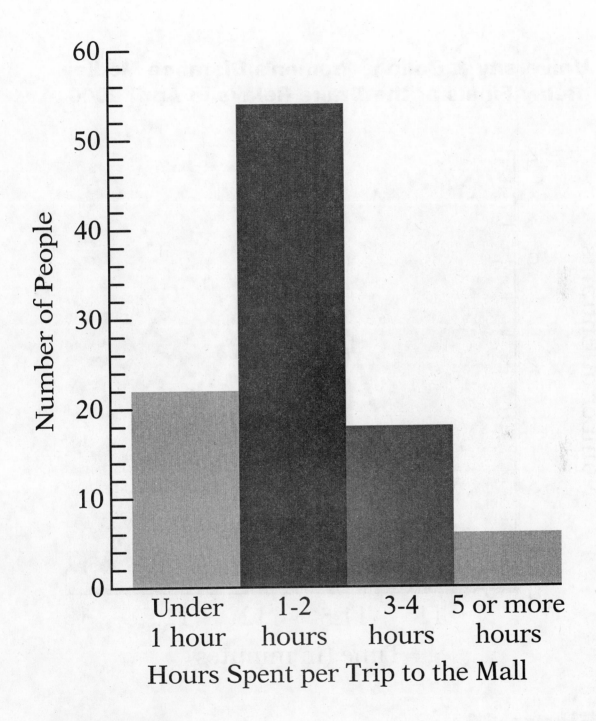

Figure 33

Source: Maritz AmeriPoll

Aufmann/Barker/Lockwood *Basic College Mathematics: An Applied Approach* Seventh Edition
Transparency #91: Section 7.3, p. 304, Ex. 13-15

University & College Women's Distance Medley Relay Finals at the Drake Relays in April 2000

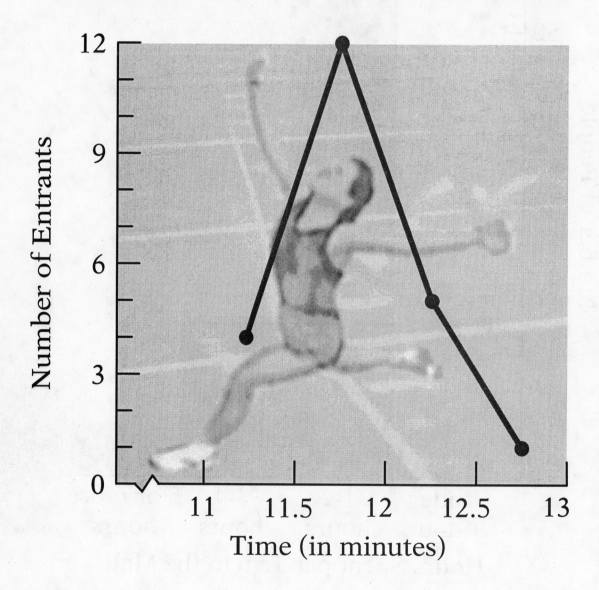

Figure 34

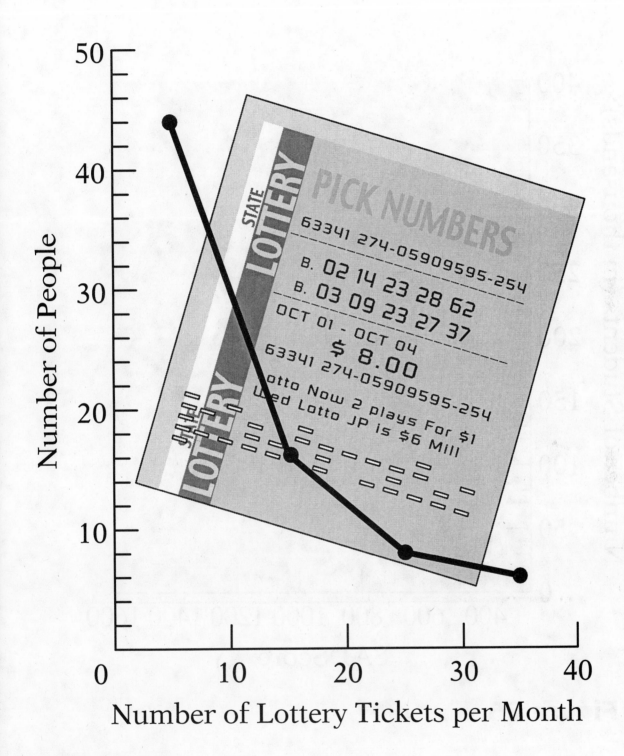

Figure 35

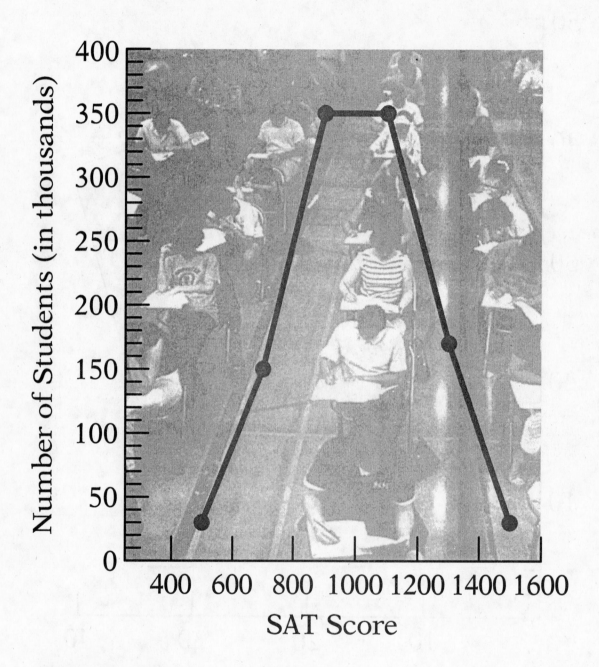

Figure 36

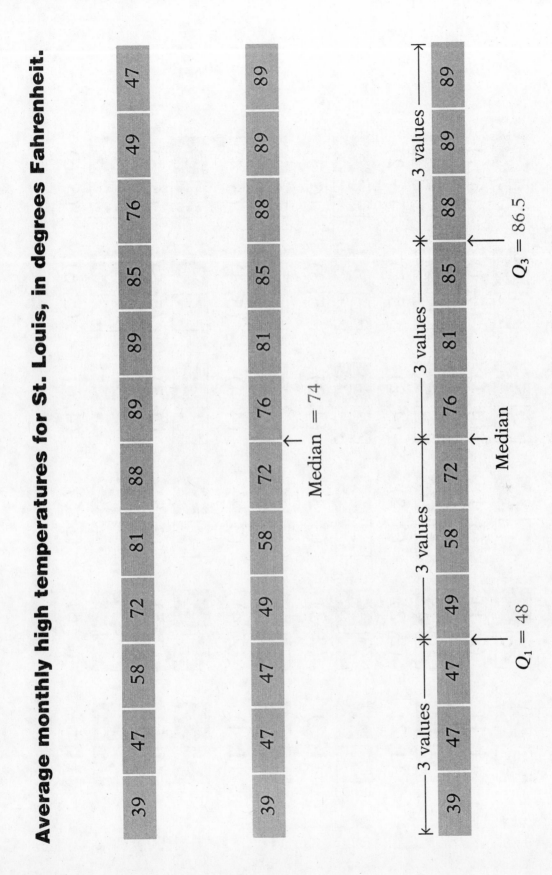

Average monthly high temperatures for St. Louis, in degrees Fahrenheit.

Possible Outcomes from Rolling Two Dice

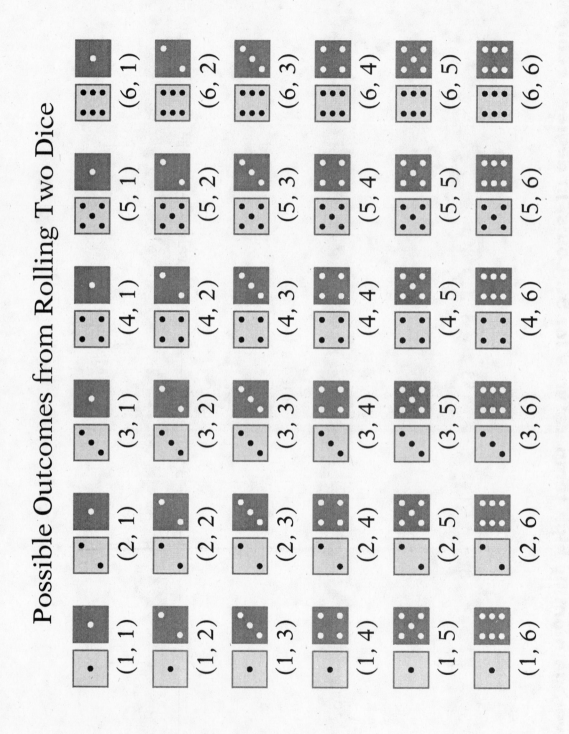

Quality of Service	Number Who Voted
Excellent	98
Satisfactory	87
Average	129
Unsatisfactory	42
Poor	21

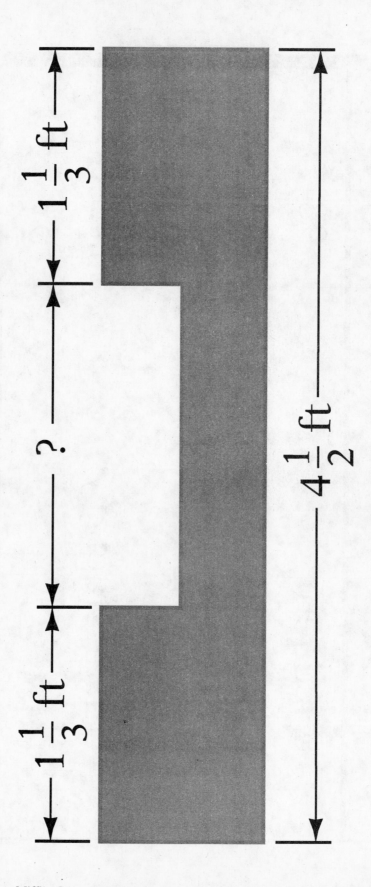

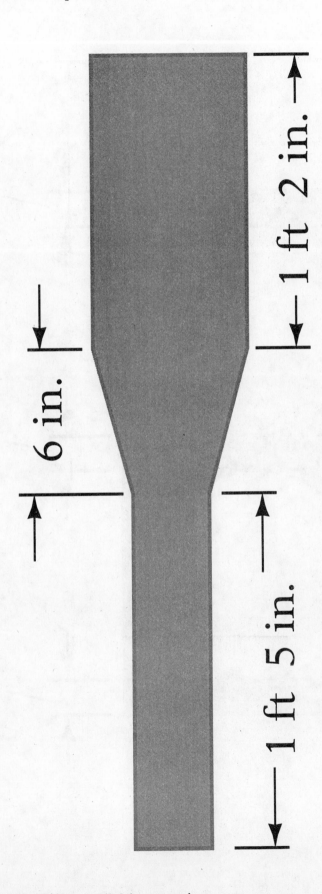

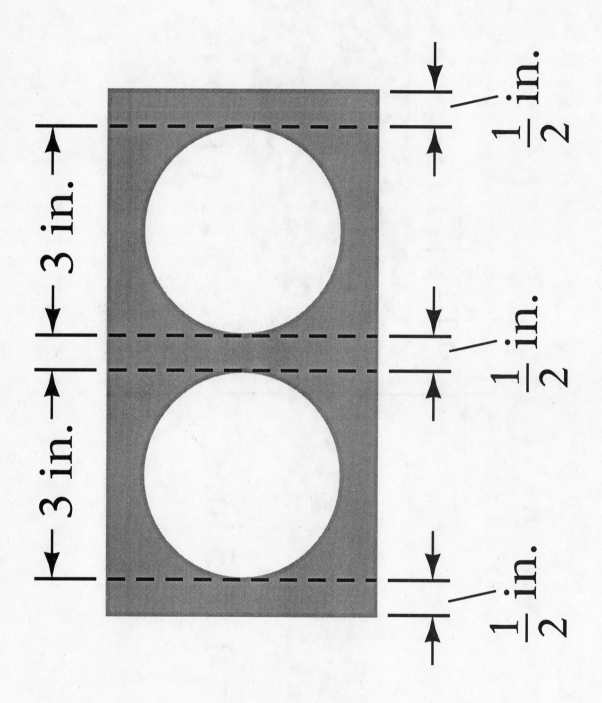

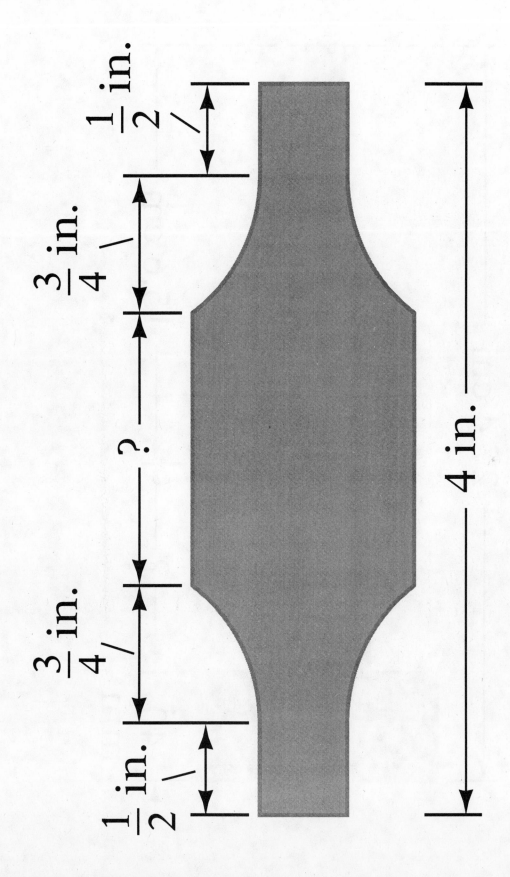

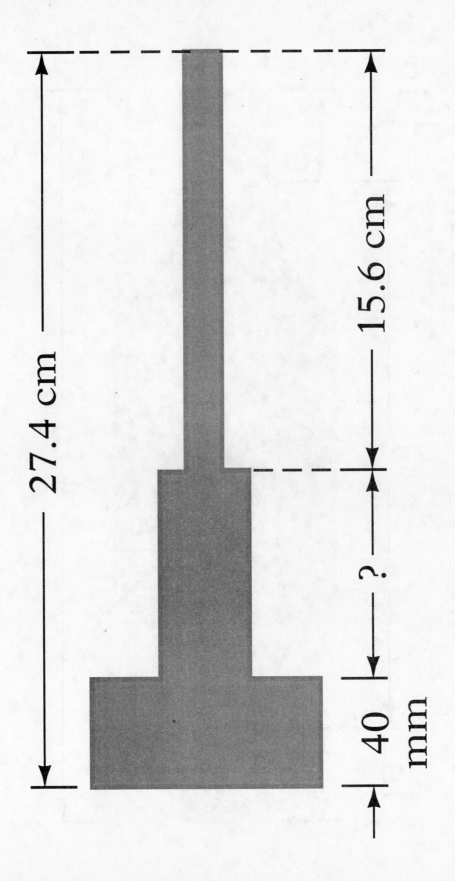

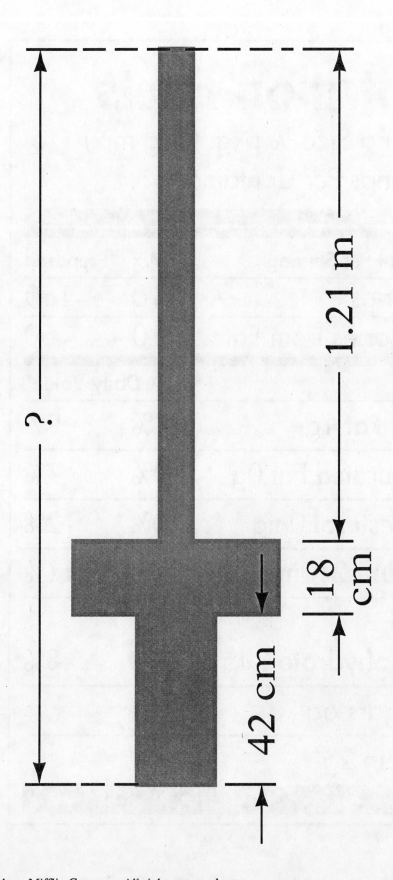

Nutrition Facts

Serving Size ⅙ pkg. (31g mix)

Servings Per Container 6

Amount Per Serving	Mix	Prepared
Calories	110	160
Calories from Fat	10	50
	% Daily Value*	
Total Fat 1g	1%	9%
Saturated Fat 0g	0%	7%
Cholesterol 0mg	0%	12%
Sodium 210mg	9%	11%
Total Carbohydrate 24g	8%	8%
Sugars 6g		
Protein 2g		

Nutrition Facts

Serving Size 2 Slices (18g)
Servings Per Container about 15

Amount Per Serving

Calories 60   Calories from Fat 10

% Daily Value*

Total Fat 1g	**2%**
Saturated Fat 0g	**0%**
Polyunsaturated Fat 0.5g	
Monounsaturated Fat 0.5g	
Cholesterol 0mg	**0%**
Sodium 60mg	**3%**
Total Carbohydrate 10g	**3%**
Dietary Fiber 3g	**10%**
Sugars 1g	
Protein 2g	

Vitamin A 0%	•	Vitamin C 0%	
Calcium 0%	•	Iron	4%

* Percent Daily Values are based on a 2,000
calorie diet. Your daily values may be higher
or lower depending on your calorie needs.

	Calories:	2,000	2,500
Total Fat	Less than	65g	80g
Saturated Fat	Less than	20g	25g
Cholesterol	Less than	300mg	300mg
Sodium	Less than	2,400mg	2,400mg
Total Carbohydrate		300g	375g
Dietary Fiber		25g	30g

Calories per gram:
Fat 9 • Carbohydrate 4 • Protein 4

Units of Length	Units of Weight	Units of Capacity
1 in. = 2.54 cm	1 oz $\approx$ 28.35 g	1 L $\approx$ 1.06 qt
1 m $\approx$ 3.28 ft	1 lb $\approx$ 454 g	1 gal $\approx$ 3.79 L
1 m $\approx$ 1.09 yd	1 kg $\approx$ 2.2 lb	
1 mi $\approx$ 1.61 km		

	Compact	Sedan	Sports Car	Wagon
Chris				
Dana				
Leslie				
Pat				

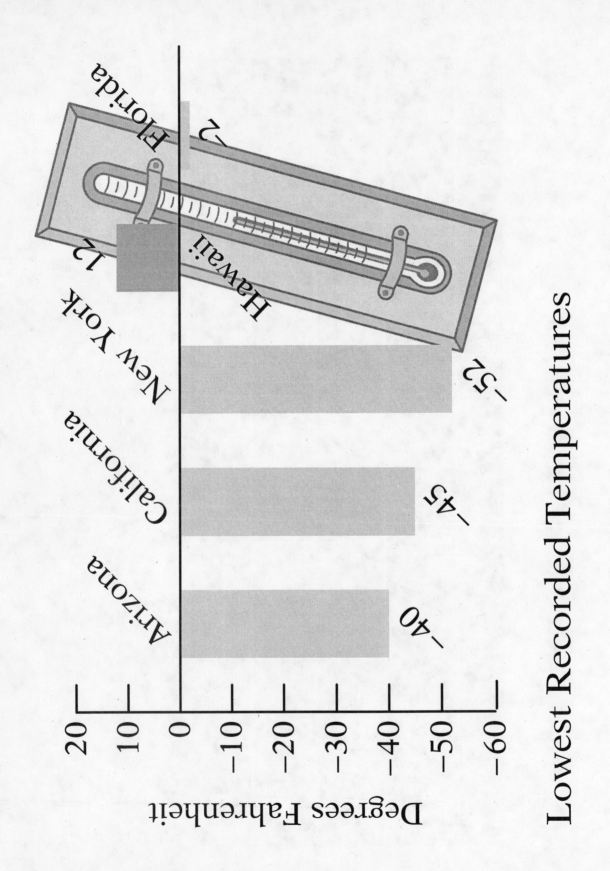

Lowest Recorded Temperatures

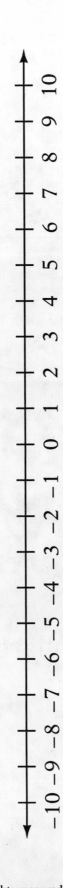

Aufmann/Barker/Lockwood *Basic College Mathematics: An Applied Approach* Seventh Edition
Transparency #109: Section 10.2, p. 405, Ex. 89

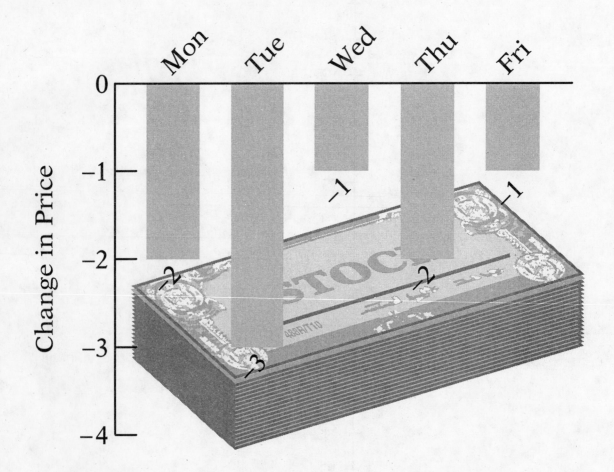

Change in Price, in Dollars,
of Byplex Corporation

Continent	Highest Elevation (in feet)		Lowest Elevation (in feet)	
Africa	Mt. Kilimanjaro	19,340	Lake Assal	−512
Asia	Mt. Everest	29,028	Dead Sea	−1312
North America	Mt. McKinley	20,320	Death Valley	−282
South America	Mt. Aconcagua	22,834	Valdes Peninsula	−131

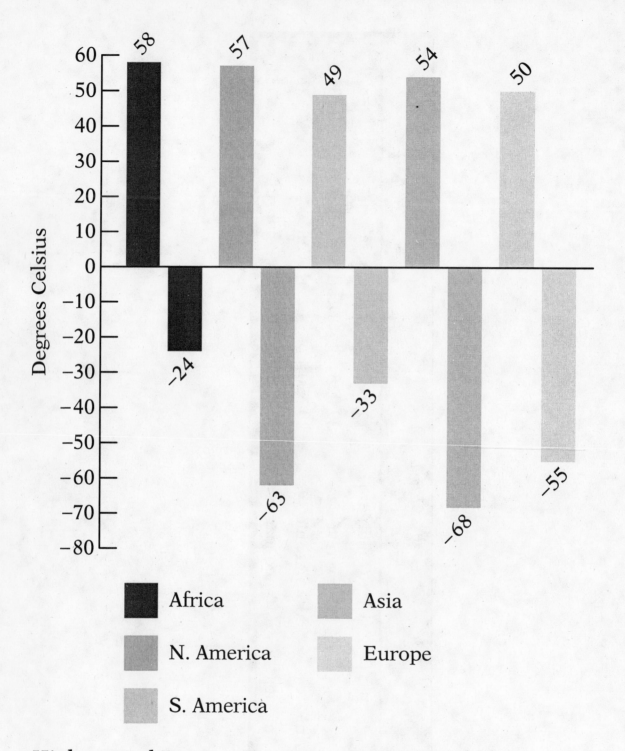

Highest and Lowest Temperatures Recorded (in degrees Celsius)

Source: National Climatic Data Center

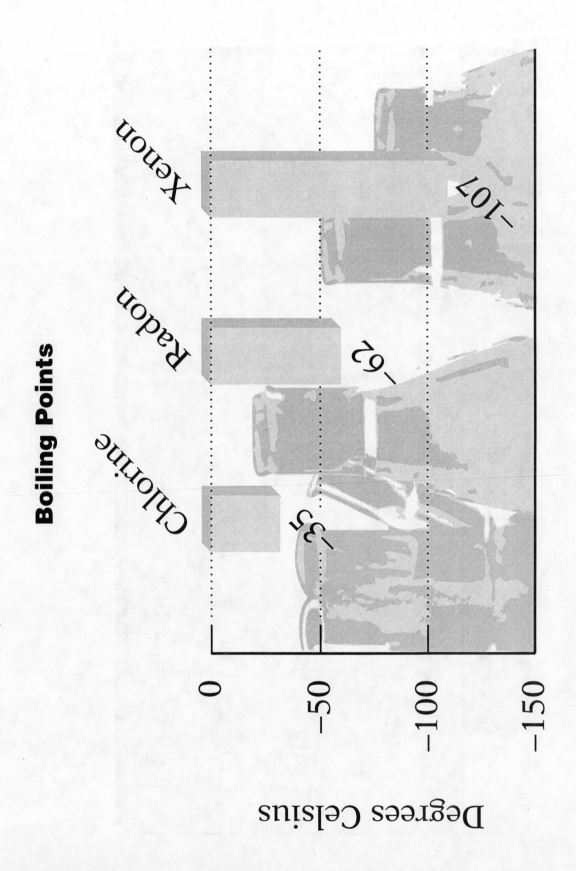

Boiling Points

Xenon

Radon

Chlorine

−107

−62

−35

Degrees Celsius

0

−50

−100

−150

Company	Closing Price	Change in Price
Campbell Soup	$25\frac{7}{8}$	$-\frac{5}{8}$
Coca Cola Co.	$58\frac{5}{16}$	$-\frac{13}{16}$
Kellogg Co.	$24\frac{13}{16}$	$-\frac{1}{2}$
Unilever PLC	$27\frac{1}{4}$	$+\frac{5}{8}$
Wm. Wrigley Jr.	$75\frac{3}{8}$	$-1\frac{5}{16}$

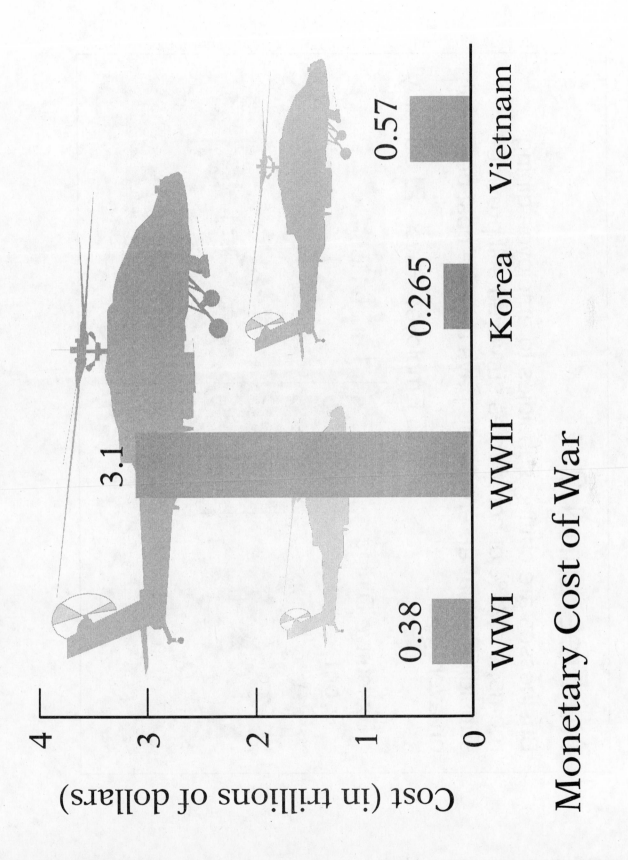

Source: Congressional Research Service, using numbers from the *Statistical Abstract of the United States*

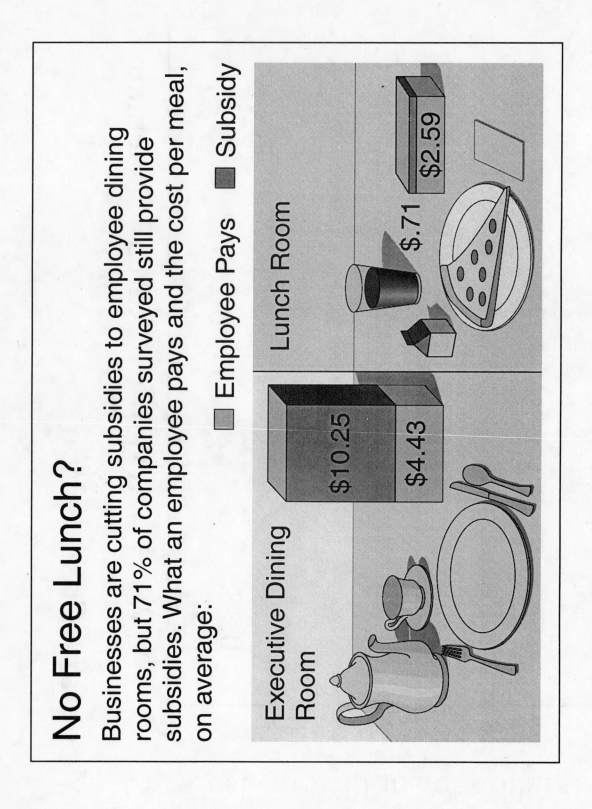

No Free Lunch?

Businesses are cutting subsidies to employee dining rooms, but 71% of companies surveyed still provide subsidies. What an employee pays and the cost per meal, on average:

■ Employee Pays ■ Subsidy

Lunch Room

$2.59

$.71

Executive Dining Room

$10.25

$4.43

×	£	¿	&
£	£	¿	&
¿	¿	¿	¿
&	&	¿	*

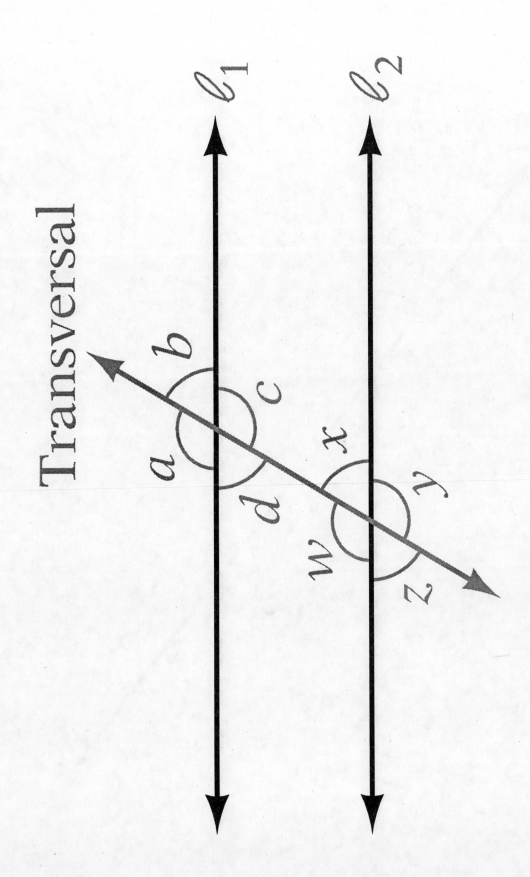

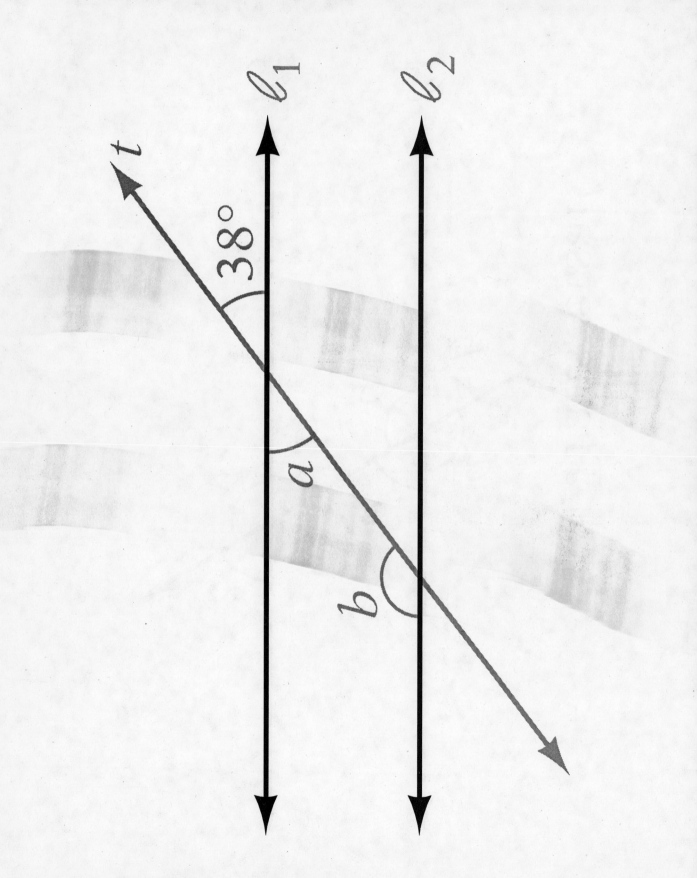

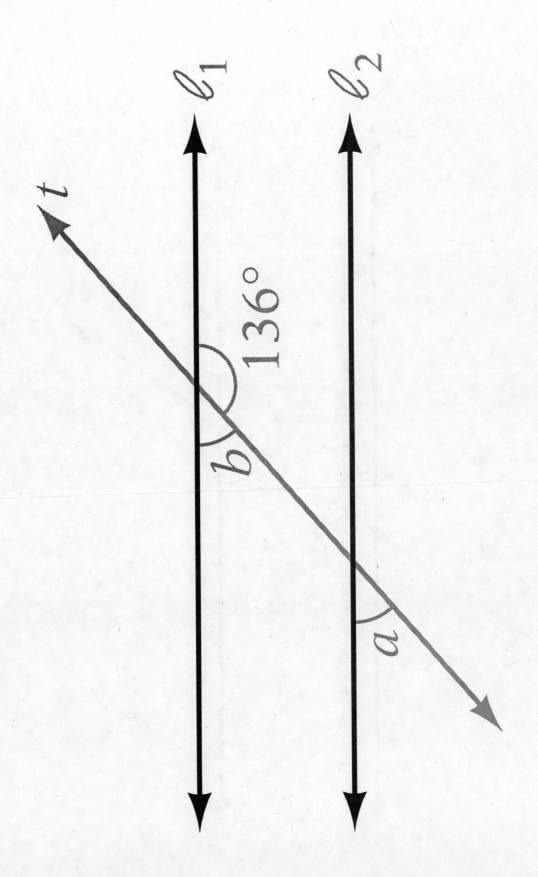

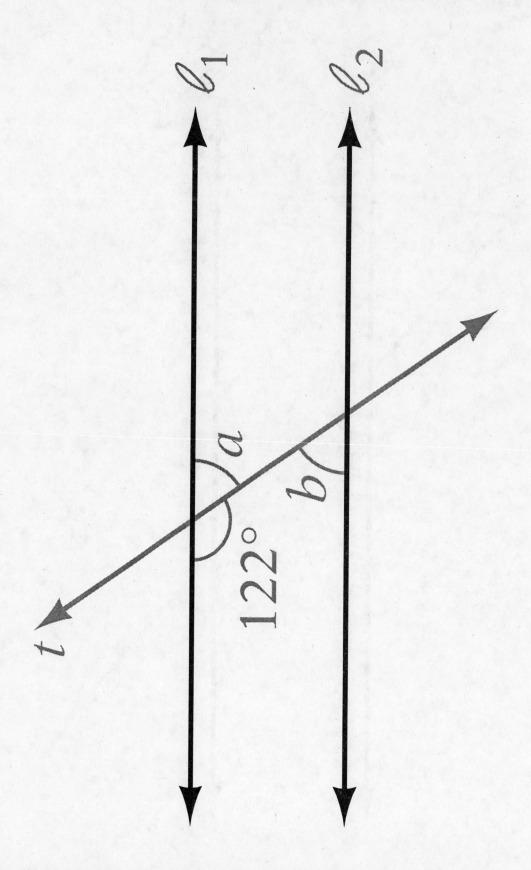

Aufmann/Barker/Lockwood *Basic College Mathematics: An Applied Approach* Seventh Edition
Transparency #122: Section 12.1, p. 512, Ex. 60

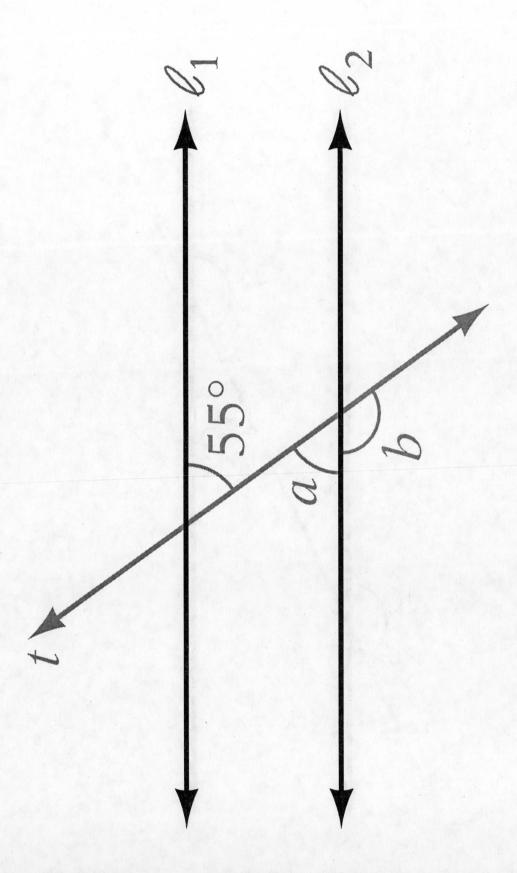

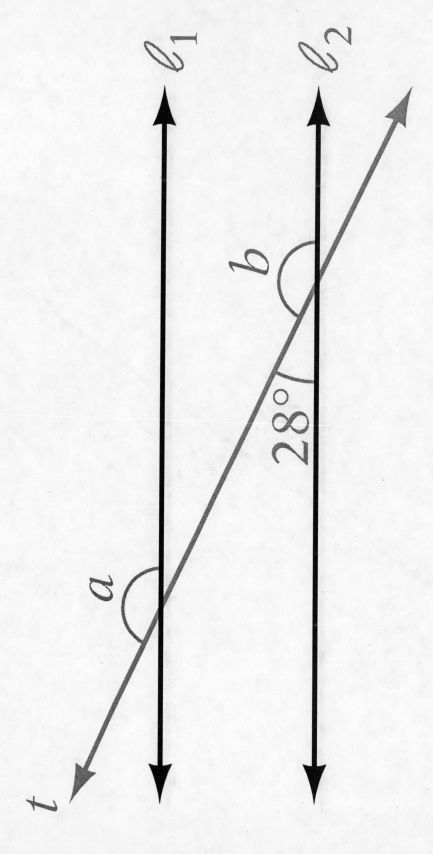

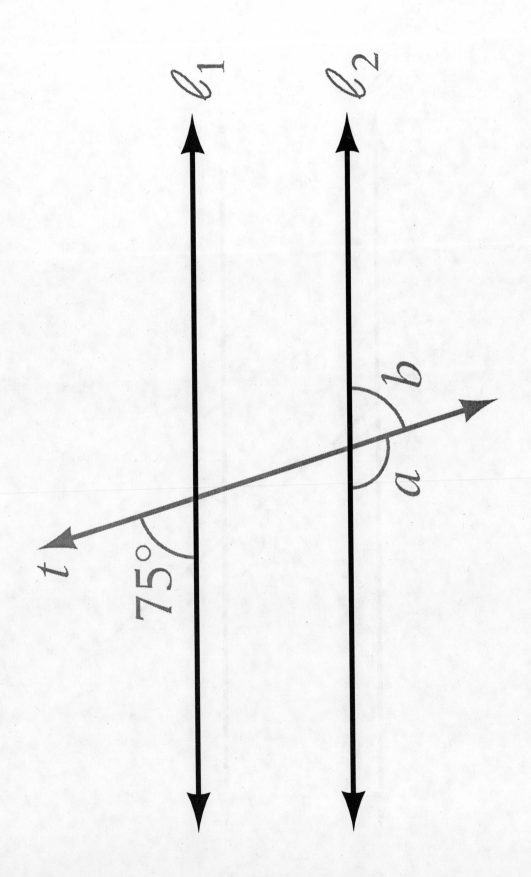

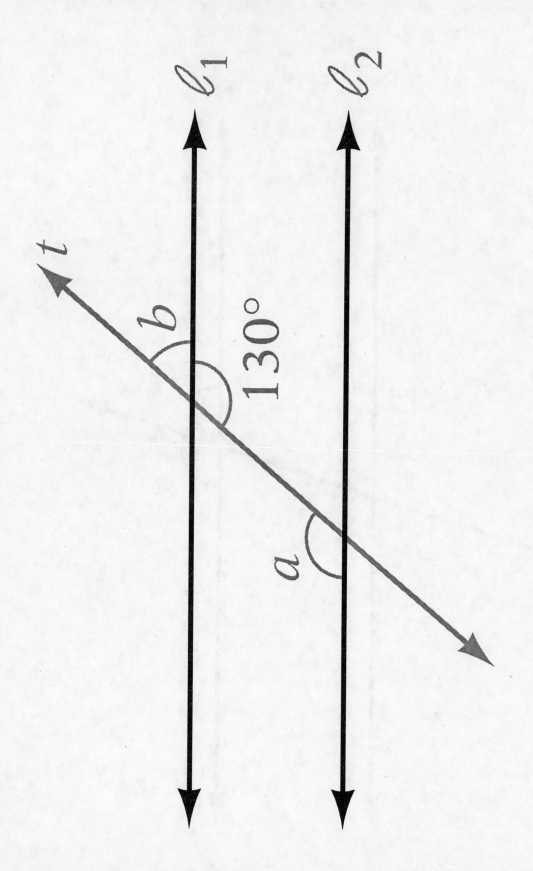

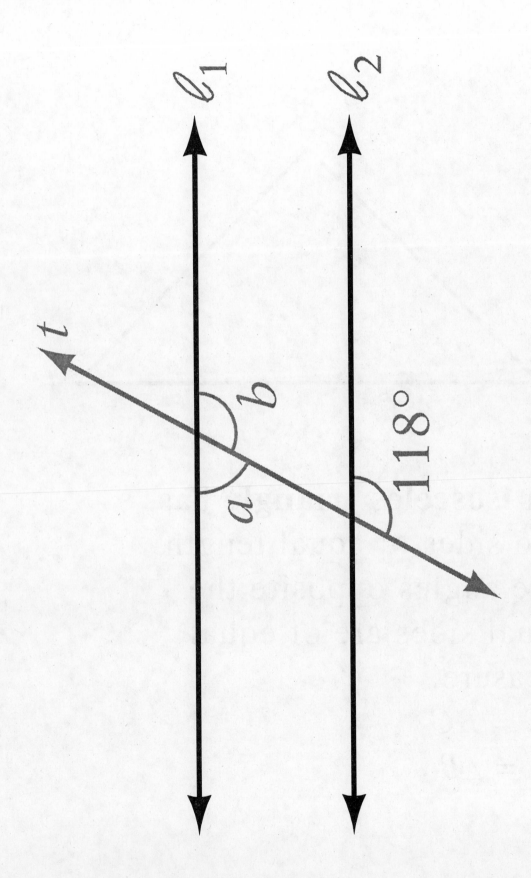

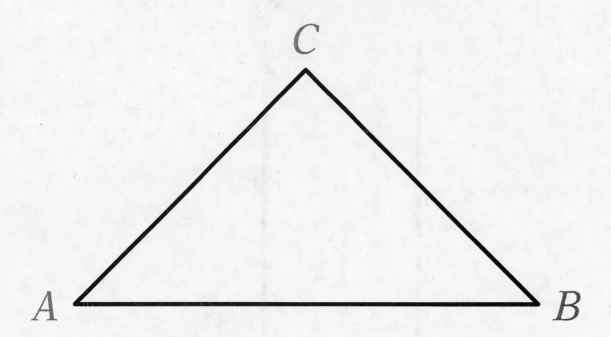

An **isosceles triangle** has two sides of equal length. The angles opposite the equal sides are of equal measure.

$AC = BC$

$\angle A = \angle B$

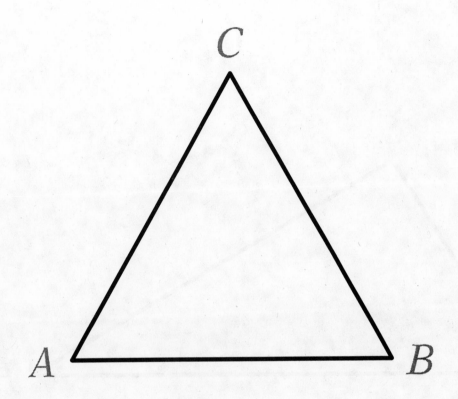

The three sides of an
equilateral triangle
are of equal length.
The three angles are
of equal measure.

$AB = BC = AC$

$\angle A = \angle B = \angle C$

Aufmann/Barker/Lockwood *Basic College Mathematics: An Applied Approach* Seventh Edition
Transparency #129: Section 12.2, p. 513

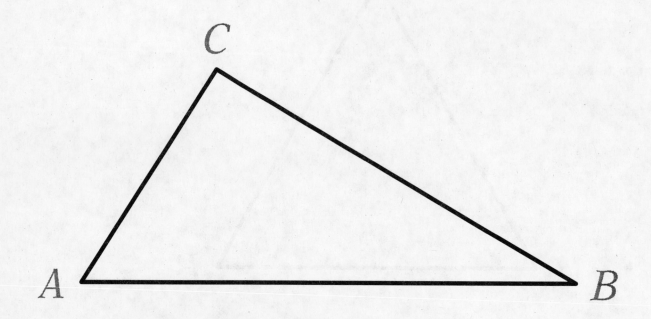

A **scalene triangle** has
no two sides of equal
length. No two angles
are of equal measure.

Aufmann/Barker/Lockwood *Basic College Mathematics: An Applied Approach* Seventh Edition
Transparency #130: Section 12.2, p. 514

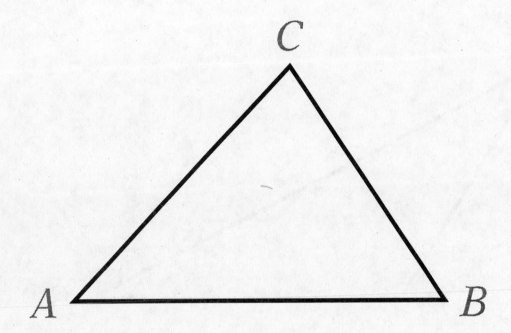

An **acute triangle** has three acute angles.

Aufmann/Barker/Lockwood *Basic College Mathematics: An Applied Approach* Seventh Edition
Transparency #131: Section 12.2, p. 514

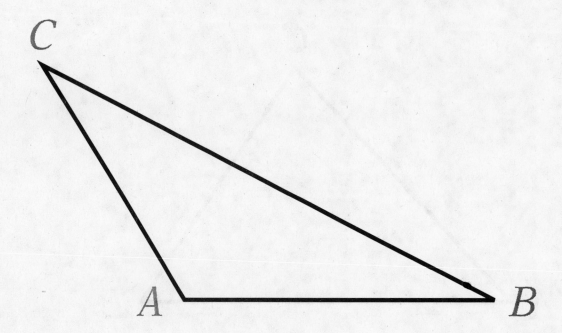

An **obtuse triangle** has
one obtuse angle.

Aufmann/Barker/Lockwood *Basic College Mathematics: An Applied Approach* Seventh Edition
Transparency #132: Section 12.2, p. 514

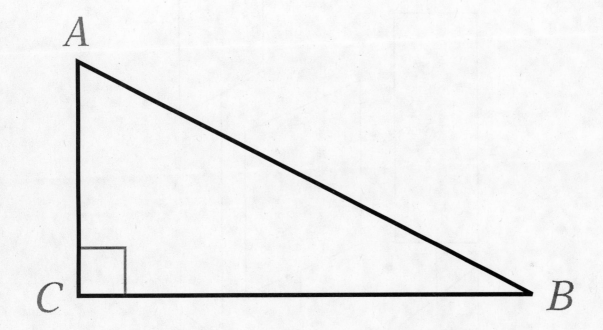

A **right triangle** has
a right angle.

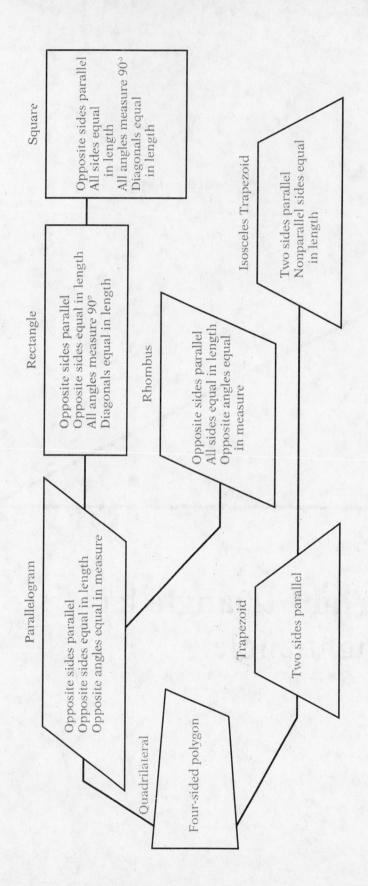

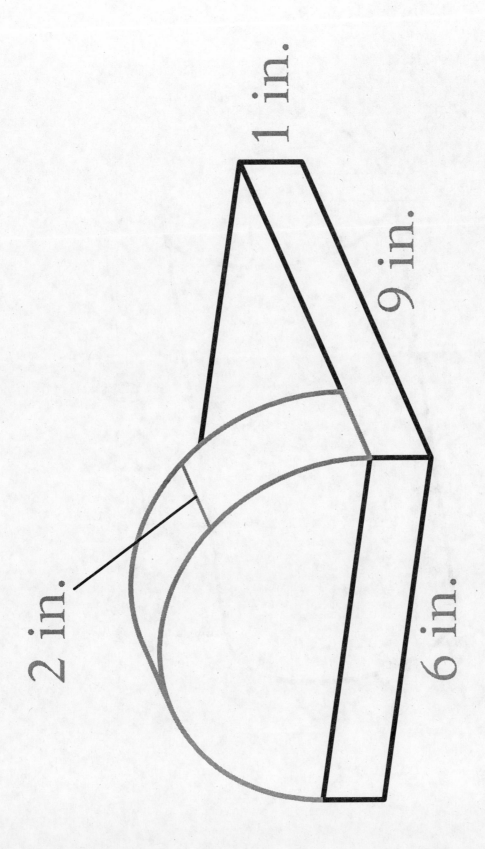

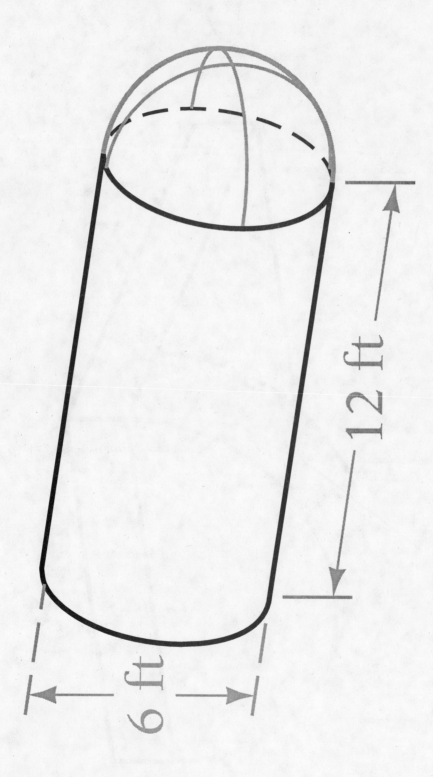

12 ft

6 ft

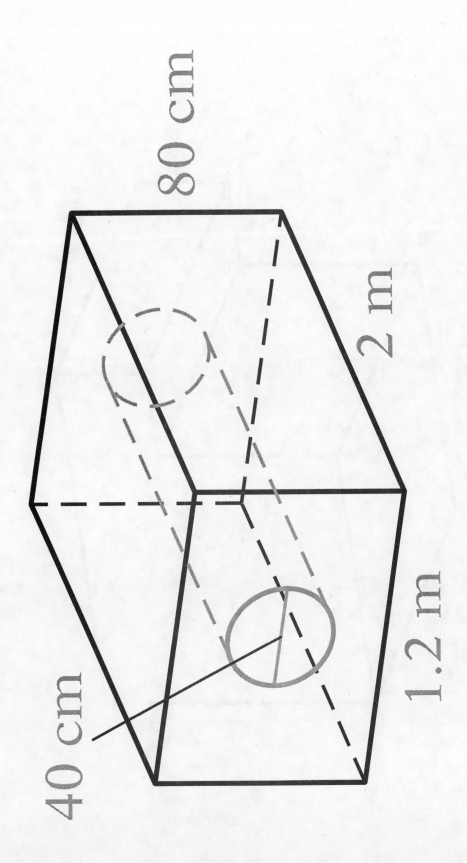

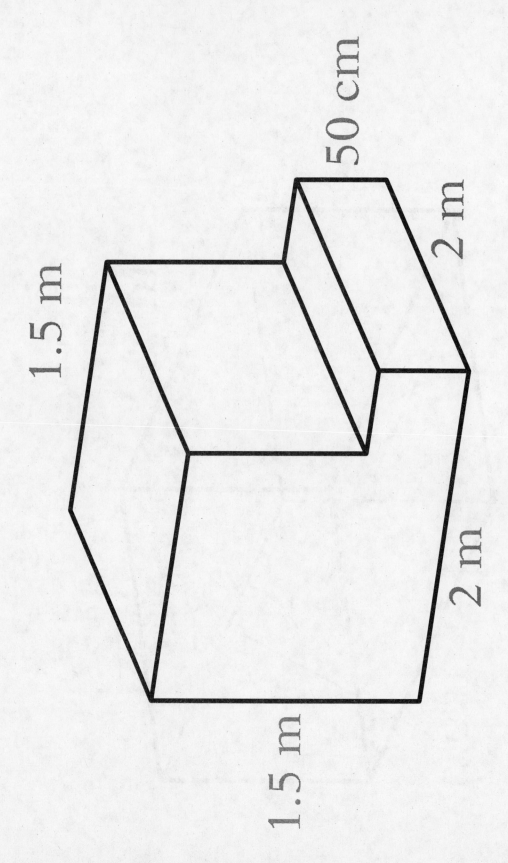

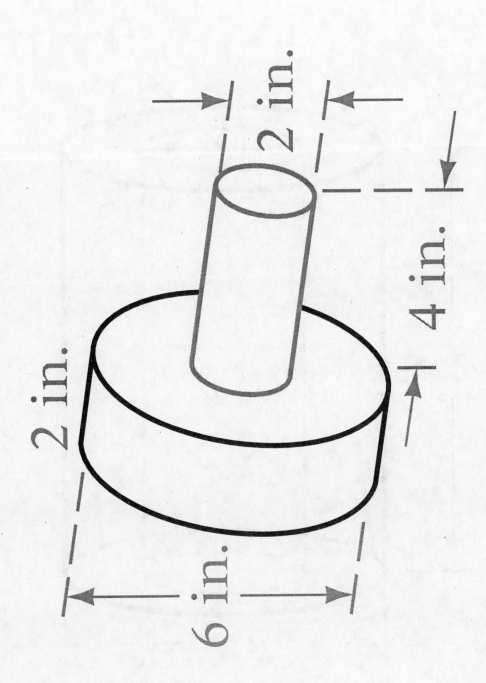

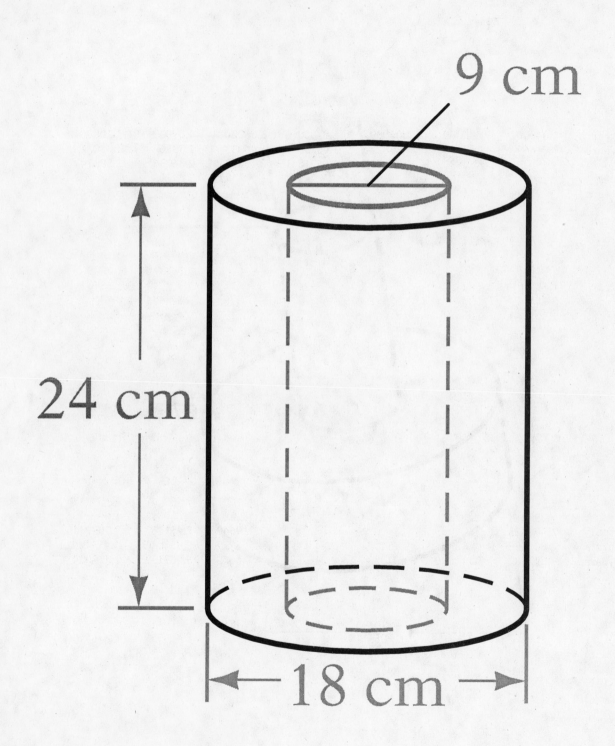

9 cm

24 cm

18 cm

Compound Interest Table

Compounded Annually

	4%	5%	6%	7%	8%	9%	10%
1 year	1.04000	1.05000	1.06000	1.07000	1.08000	1.09000	1.10000
5 years	1.21665	1.27628	1.33823	1.40255	1.46933	1.53862	1.61051
10 years	1.48024	1.62890	1.79085	1.96715	2.15893	2.36736	2.59374
15 years	1.80094	2.07893	2.39656	2.75903	3.17217	3.64248	4.17725
20 years	2.19112	2.65330	3.20714	3.86968	4.66095	5.60441	6.72750

Compounded Semiannually

	4%	5%	6%	7%	8%	9%	10%
1 year	1.04040	1.05062	1.06090	1.07123	1.08160	1.09203	1.10250
5 years	1.21899	1.28008	1.34392	1.41060	1.48024	1.55297	1.62890
10 years	1.48595	1.63862	1.80611	1.98979	2.19112	2.41171	2.65330
15 years	1.81136	2.09757	2.42726	2.80679	3.24340	3.74531	4.32194
20 years	2.20804	2.68506	3.26204	3.95926	4.80102	5.81634	7.03999

Compounded Quarterly

	4%	5%	6%	7%	8%	9%	10%
1 year	1.04060	1.05094	1.06136	1.07186	1.08243	1.09308	1.10381
5 years	1.22019	1.28204	1.34686	1.41478	1.48595	1.56051	1.63862
10 years	1.48886	1.64362	1.81402	2.00160	2.20804	2.43519	2.68506
15 years	1.81670	2.10718	2.44322	2.83182	3.28103	3.80013	4.39979
20 years	2.21672	2.70148	3.29066	4.00639	4.87544	5.93015	7.20957

Compounded Monthly

	4%	5%	6%	7%	8%	9%	10%
1 year	1.04074	1.051162	1.061678	1.072290	1.083000	1.093807	1.104713
5 years	1.220997	1.283359	1.348850	1.417625	1.489846	1.565681	1.645309
10 years	1.490833	1.647009	1.819397	2.009661	2.219640	2.451357	2.707041
15 years	1.820302	2.113704	2.454094	2.848947	3.306921	3.838043	4.453920
20 years	2.222582	2.712640	3.310204	4.038739	4.926803	6.009152	7.328074

Compounded Daily

	4%	5%	6%	7%	8%	9%	10%
1 year	1.04080	1.05127	1.06183	1.07250	1.08328	1.09416	1.10516
5 years	1.22139	1.28400	1.34983	1.41902	1.49176	1.56823	1.64861
10 years	1.49179	1.64866	1.82203	2.01362	2.22535	2.45933	2.71791
15 years	1.82206	2.11689	2.45942	2.85736	3.31968	3.85678	4.48077
20 years	2.22544	2.71810	3.31979	4.05466	4.95217	6.04830	7.38703

Compound Interest Table

Compounded Annually

	11%	12%	13%	14%	15%	16%	17%
1 year	1.11000	1.12000	1.13000	1.14000	1.15000	1.16000	1.17000
5 years	1.68506	1.76234	1.84244	1.92542	2.01136	2.10034	2.19245
10 years	2.83942	3.10585	3.39457	3.70722	4.04556	4.41144	4.80683
15 years	4.78459	5.47357	6.25427	7.13794	8.13706	9.26552	10.53872
20 years	8.06239	9.64629	11.52309	13.74349	16.36654	19.46076	23.10560

Compounded Semiannually

	11%	12%	13%	14%	15%	16%	17%
1 year	1.11303	1.12360	1.13423	1.14490	1.15563	1.16640	1.17723
5 years	1.70814	1.79085	1.87714	1.96715	2.06103	2.15893	2.26098
10 years	2.91776	3.20714	3.52365	3.86968	4.24785	4.66096	5.11205
15 years	4.98395	5.74349	6.61437	7.61226	8.75496	10.06266	11.55825
20 years	8.51331	10.28572	12.41607	14.97446	18.04424	21.72452	26.13302

Compounded Quarterly

	11%	12%	13%	14%	15%	16%	17%
1 year	1.11462	1.12551	1.13648	1.14752	1.15865	1.16986	1.18115
5 years	1.72043	1.80611	1.89584	1.98979	2.08815	2.19112	2.29891
10 years	2.95987	3.26204	3.59420	3.95926	4.36038	4.80102	5.28497
15 years	5.09225	5.89160	6.81402	7.87809	9.10513	10.51963	12.14965
20 years	8.76085	10.64089	12.91828	15.67574	19.01290	23.04980	27.93091

Compounded Monthly

	11%	12%	13%	14%	15%	16%	17%
1 year	1.115719	1.126825	1.138032	1.149342	1.160755	1.172271	1.183892
5 years	1.728916	1.816697	1.908857	2.005610	2.107181	2.213807	2.325733
10 years	2.989150	3.300387	3.643733	4.022471	4.440213	4.900941	5.409036
15 years	5.167988	5.995802	6.955364	8.067507	9.356334	10.849737	12.579975
20 years	8.935015	10.892554	13.276792	16.180270	19.715494	24.019222	29.257669

Compounded Daily

	11%	12%	13%	14%	15%	16%	17%
1 year	1.11626	1.12747	1.13880	1.15024	1.16180	1.17347	1.18526
5 years	1.73311	1.82194	1.91532	2.01348	2.11667	2.22515	2.33918
10 years	3.00367	3.31946	3.66845	4.05411	4.48031	4.95130	5.47178
15 years	5.20569	6.04786	7.02625	8.16288	9.48335	11.01738	12.79950
20 years	9.02203	11.01883	13.45751	16.43582	20.07316	24.51534	29.94039

Monthly Payment Table

	4%	5%	6%	7%	8%	9%
1 year	0.0851499	0.0856075	0.0860664	0.0865267	0.0869884	0.0874515
2 years	0.0434249	0.0438714	0.0443206	0.0447726	0.0452273	0.0456847
3 years	0.0295240	0.0299709	0.0304219	0.0308771	0.0313364	0.0317997
4 years	0.0225791	0.0230293	0.0234850	0.0239462	0.0244129	0.0248850
5 years	0.0184165	0.0188712	0.0193328	0.0198012	0.0202764	0.0207584
15 years	0.0073969	0.0079079	0.0084386	0.0089883	0.0095565	0.0101427
20 years	0.0060598	0.0065996	0.0071643	0.0077530	0.0083644	0.0089973
25 years	0.0052784	0.0058459	0.0064430	0.0070678	0.0077182	0.0083920
30 years	0.0047742	0.0053682	0.0059955	0.0066530	0.0073376	0.0080462

	10%	11%	12%	13%
1 year	0.0879159	0.0883817	0.0888488	0.0893173
2 years	0.0461449	0.0466078	0.0470735	0.0475418
3 years	0.0322672	0.0327387	0.0332143	0.0336940
4 years	0.0253626	0.0258455	0.0263338	0.0268275
5 years	0.0212470	0.0217424	0.0222445	0.0227531
15 years	0.0107461	0.0113660	0.0120017	0.0126524
20 years	0.0096502	0.0103219	0.0110109	0.0117158
25 years	0.0090870	0.0098011	0.0105322	0.0112784
30 years	0.0087757	0.0095232	0.0102861	0.0110620